OBERLIN,
Hotbed of Abolitionism

OBERLIN,
Hotbed of Abolitionism

College, Community, and the Fight for Freedom and Equality in Antebellum America

J. Brent Morris

The University of North Carolina Press   Chapel Hill

© 2014 The University of North Carolina Press

All rights reserved. Manufactured in the United States of America. Designed by Sally Scruggs and set in Quadraat by codeMantra. The paper in this book meets the guidelines for permanence and durability of the Committee on Production Guidelines for Book Longevity of the Council on Library Resources.

The University of North Carolina Press has been a member of the Green Press Initiative since 2003.

Library of Congress Cataloging-in-Publication Data
Morris, J. Brent.
Oberlin, hotbed of abolitionism : college, community, and the fight for freedom and equality in antebellum America / J. Brent Morris.
pages cm
Includes bibliographical references and index.
ISBN 978-1-4696-1827-2 (cloth : alk. paper)
ISBN 978-1-4696-4559-9 (pbk. : alk. paper)
ISBN 978-1-4696-1828-9 (ebook)
1. Antislavery movements—Ohio—Oberlin—History—19th century.
2. Abolitionists—Ohio—Oberlin—History—19th century.
3. Oberlin (Ohio)—History—19th century. I. Title.
F499.O2M67 2014
326'.80977123—dc23
2014002680

An earlier version of chapter 5 appeared as J. Brent Morris, "'All the Truly Wise or Truly Pious Have One and the Same End in View': Oberlin, the West, and Abolitionist Schism," *Civil War History* 57, no. 3 (September 2011). Copyright © 2011 by The Kent State University Press. Reprinted with permission.

To John DeCarrico and Louise Sites, our first historians

Freemen! Are ye idle yet?
Are your hearts on evil set?
Do ye still intend to let
The slave remain in chains?
Do ye not hear his groans,
Bursting forth in sorrow's tones,
Caused by Southern vagabonds!
Wipe away the stains
Which debase your country's pride,
Open all your bosoms wide—
Let the land from side to side,
Cry "justice for the slave."
Let each gurgling mountain rill—
Let each valley, plain, and hill,
With the love of freedom thrill
In honor to the brave.
Let each galling chain be broke—
Take away each grievous yoke—
Banish at a single stroke
Your heaven-daring sin—
Lest the God of Truth and right,
All your future prospects blight—
He's your strength and he's your might,
If you once begin
To pull the Devil's kingdom down,
Tho' the world with fiendish power
Look upon you, there's a crown
Of glory in the skies,
Which he'll give to those who stand
Firm for truth and raise the hand
Against this demon of the land—
Press onward for the prize.

EDWARD HENRY, "Lines Written After Hearing an A.S. Address by Jas. Monroe," *Anti-Slavery Bugle*, December 18, 1846

Contents

Acknowledgments xi

Abbreviations xv

INTRODUCTION Facts Are Sometimes Stranger Than Fiction 1

ONE To Save the Godless West
Revivalism, Abolition, and the Founding of Oberlin 12

TWO The Worthies of Oberlin
Antislavery Expansion in the Late 1830s 40

THREE A City upon a Hill *Utopian Oberlin* 61

FOUR A Hotbed of Abolitionism 81

FIVE All the Truly Wise or Truly Pious Have the Same End in View
Oberlin and Abolitionist Schism 108

SIX The Tyrant's Grapple by Our Vote, We'll Loosen from Our Brother's Throat *Oberlin, Free Soil, and the Fight for Equal Rights* 132

SEVEN We Must Watch and Improve This Tide
Oberlin Confronts the Slave Power, 1850–1858 161

EIGHT That Railroad Center at Which All Branches Converged
Oberlin and the Underground Railroad 187

NINE This Drama of Genuine Manhood and Courage
Oberlin and the Fight for Freedom 212

EPILOGUE Be Not Conformed to This World 239

Notes 249

Works Cited 303

Index 323

Illustrations

Charles Grandison Finney in the early 1830s 20

The Oberlin Big Tent on Tappan Square 37

Slab Hall or Cincinnati Hall 38

"Partial View Oberlin" 42

Theodore Dwight Weld 44

William Lloyd Garrison 52

A class photo from the 1855 preparatory department 66

Fanny Jackson (Coppin) 70

Sarah Margru Kinson 74

Lucy Stone 76

Charles Grandison Finney in the 1850s 98

Henry Cowles 105

"Father" John Keep 112

Abby Kelley Foster 121

Asa Mahan 129

Charles Langston 147

William Howard Day 149

Betsey Mix Cowles 153

John Mercer Langston 167

Professors James Fairchild, John Morgan, and James Monroe 182

Calvin Fairbank 191

Lewis Clarke 193

Samuel Adair in the Kansas cabin 195

Lee Howard Dobbins grave marker 199

"The Confidence Game" 204

The Oberlin-Wellington Rescuers at the Cleveland jail 218

Lewis Sheridan Leary 227

John Copeland 229

John Mercer Langston presenting the colors to the 5th
Ohio United States Colored Troops 237

A bird's-eye view of Oberlin, 1868 241

Acknowledgments

On my first research trip to Oberlin many years ago, I arrived at the college library about an hour before the archives opened. Sitting down to a cup of coffee in the café, I pulled out an old and tattered biography of abolitionist Arthur Tappan (written by his brother Lewis) to look over before heading upstairs to begin my real work. The Tappans had given tens of thousands of dollars to Oberlin in the 1830s, saving the colony and the college from financial ruin and earning the reward of having Oberlin's central square named in their honor. I had just scurried across Tappan Square and past John Mercer Langston Hall, Keep Cottage, First Church, and the Underground Railroad monument on my way to the library. I was beyond excited to be starting my archival work on Oberlin—I had read almost everything there was to be read on the subject in the secondary scholarship, and I couldn't wait to begin my own project.

But there, toward the end of the Tappan biography, I came across a challenge that brought me back to earth. Charles Grandison Finney, America's most famous revivalist of the nineteenth century, Oberlin professor of theology, and its second president, seemed to have some words for me before I dug into the archives myself. In a letter to Lewis Tappan reprinted in an appendix, Finney wrote of Oberlin and the antislavery movement, "The fact is that Oberlin turned the scale in all of the Northwest. No man can tell the story right unless he knows this." I knew that, of course. The purpose of my whole project was to illuminate and emphasize that fact. But what else might Finney have thought necessary to "tell the story right"? I had yet to turn over a page in the archives, and Charles Finney was already looking over my shoulder.

I hope that this book would earn his approval. Besides the rich records that Finney and his colleagues left for me, I could not have possibly completed this task without the help and inspiration of many, many people. In Oberlin, I was made to feel like an honorary Oberlinite (as they were called in the nineteenth century) by archivists Roland Baumann, Ken Grossi, and their incredible staff. They more than anyone else will be able to evaluate my use of the Oberlin archives. Also, I am indebted to Gary Kornblith and Carol Lasser for sharing with me their own work on Oberlin, their unique insight as Obies (as they are now called), an insider's tour of the town, and well needed midday cups of coffee. Other scholars, including Richard Newman, Fergus Bordewich, James Horton, Marlene Merrill, William McFeely, Stanley Harrold, Maggi Morehouse, and Peter Wood, also helped me interpret what I discovered in Oberlin and pointed me to new sources as well. My undergraduate mentor and friend at the University of South Carolina, Walter Edgar, drew me from the clutches of law school into the graduate study of history and a career I love, and offered invaluable and continuous moral support and guidance through some tough times.

The only way that I can repay my Cornell graduate advisers is by striving to be as much like them as possible in my own academic career. Jon Parmenter, Richard Bensel, and my chair, Ed Baptist, kept their standards high, helped me whenever I asked for it, and stood firmly behind me when I most needed it. They are responsible for making sure my graduate experience was more of a "celebration" than the "ordeal" it could have been. Margaret Washington was also involved in the early development of this work, and it is better for her efforts. Paul E. Johnson was a close adviser on early drafts of the manuscript, and he was just as valuable in that capacity as he was as my professor years ago at the University of South Carolina. In addition, I want to thank the participants in Cornell's Americas Colloquium who helped me work through several of these chapters around seminar tables in McGraw Hall and then at the table under our picture at the Chapter House. My Ithaca family made everything not just bearable but a joy. I hope I did the same for them. Daegan Miller (who helped me give my final draft a twenty-five-page haircut), Mike Schmidli, Daniel Sledge, Julian Lim, Chris Cantwell, Mari Crabtree, Rebecca Tally, Vernon Mitchell, Heather Furnas, Candace Katungi, and others all read parts of my manuscript, shared their thoughts, and, most importantly, shared their lives. I wish that Ann Wilde, a great friend and constant cheerleader for me and my project, could have seen the end results, since she in particular would have appreciated the abolitionists' burning urgency to change the world for the better.

David Perry, Brandon Proia, Lucas Church, Mary Caviness, and the other staff at the University of North Carolina Press have been generous with their enthusiasm, assistance, and patience throughout the publication process. The two anonymous readers, unmistakably giants in the field of abolition studies, offered critiques and suggestions that were both keen and insightful, each clearly demonstrating a commitment to and desire for the success of this project.

To my colleagues and students at the University of South Carolina at Aiken and Beaufort, thank you for your support and encouragement. And to my Volkswagen Research Bus, thank you for not killing me in the mountains, not leaving me to die there in the desert, and keeping me safe from skunks, drunks, and unicyclists on the streets of Oberlin.

I am indebted to the staffs of the Oberlin College Archives, the Oberlin College Special Collections, the Kent State University Special Collections, the Western Reserve Historical Society, the Ohio Historical Society, the South Caroliniana Library, and the Cornell University Carl A. Kroch Division of Rare Books and Manuscripts. The interlibrary loan departments at Cornell and the Columbia, Aiken, and Beaufort campuses of the University of South Carolina were lifesavers.

I was supported financially by numerous grants from the History and American Studies departments and the Society for the Humanities at Cornell University as well as by Cornell Sage and Daughters of the American Revolution fellowships. Oberlin College awarded me a Frederick B. Artz research grant, and the University of South Carolina Institute for Southern Studies named me a visiting research fellow, and gave me library privileges and generous funds to pursue my research while in Columbia. I have also benefited from the generous faculty development funds made available at the University of South Carolina, Beaufort.

Most importantly, my family has been the bedrock of support that most people only experience in the best of dreams. I can never thank my parents enough for the curiosity they fostered in my childhood and the opportunities they have made possible in my life. My wife, Kim, has been there at every step along the way, from high school to Ph.D., from ramen noodles and adjunct gigs to slightly better noodles and the tenure track, and from the first page to the last. And my boy, Daegan—you light up my world, arrange a hundred post-it notes exactly as they should be, add just the right amount of crayon underlining and commentary in my books, and close my computer when it's time to stop working and "hold-joo." I love you all; thank you.

JBM, Beaufort, S.C.
October 4, 2013

Abbreviations

AANO   Kansas Emigrant Aid Association of Northern Ohio
AASS   American Anti-Slavery Society
ACS   American Colonization Society
AFASS American and Foreign Anti-Slavery Society
AMA   American Missionary Association
OAASS Ohio American Anti-Slavery Society
OASS   Ohio Anti-Slavery Society
WASS   Western Anti-Slavery Society
YYLS   Young Ladies' Literary Society

OBERLIN,
Hotbed of Abolitionism

INTRODUCTION

Facts Are Sometimes Stranger Than Fiction

When the Ohio legislature gathered in Columbus to convene its 1842–43 session, the first pressing order of business was debate over a proposal to revoke the charter of the Oberlin Collegiate Institute. One critic of the school from southern Ohio described the largely abolitionist faculty and students there as a "great maelstrom of seditious faction . . . exerting a more potent influence in exciting sectional animosities . . . than any, I may say all, all other malcontent institutions in the U.S."[1] Other lawmakers seeking revocation called Oberlinites in general a "banditti of lawbreakers," "negro stealers supported by enemies of this country abroad, and emissaries at home," and a "thoroughfare for slaves en route to Canada."[2]

Still, as anti-abolitionist lawmakers heaped abuse upon the name "Oberlin" and sought to crush its spirit through legislation, a small handful of more-sympathetic politicians sought to get beyond the prejudicial cant and vague anecdotes offered up by the school's detractors. On what specific events or facts, they asked, did critics base their censure? Just what did the conservatives mean by such imprecise terms as "infamous"?[3] "Why Sir," Oberlin's harshest critic bellowed matter-of-factly from the floor, "the evidence of the iniquitous character of that institution is as broad as the light of day; and those who control it, glory in their villainy." He believed it sufficient and damning evidence that "rumor, with her thousand tongues, has published the enormities of that institution all over the State and the Union." "Such being the fact," he argued, "it was folly to waste time debating details."[4]

Despite the abuse, the Oberlin Collegiate Institute did not lose its educational charter that legislative term, nor would it in years to come, and its safety may have been partially shielded by critics' vague accusations regarding just what "Oberlin" stood for and what the town and organically connected school of the same name had done and were doing for the abolition of slavery. However, exactly what was assumed regarding Oberlin in the nineteenth century has been largely lost to American historical memory. The result has been regular but brief appearances in historical narratives of a place and institution of apparently tremendous importance yet very few indicators of why and how it earned that lofty reputation. Historians have largely taken their cues regarding Oberlin from the vague and loose characterizations that the school and the town attracted during the antebellum years. The radical reputation the community earned in its first three decades has allowed scholars to confidently use its name as a shorthand to denote zealous abolitionism, religiosity, and social reform before hurriedly moving on to other topics. At the other extreme in this regard are histories of Oberlin College mostly written from the 1880s to 1940s that simply take Oberlin notables at their word and produce an overly romantic picture of the town and school that has been uncritically perpetuated. This book gives substance to the symbolic idea of "the Oberlin," as British abolitionist and community booster Harriet Martineau referred to the town and school together in 1840, and fully examines the vital significance of the Oberlin community in the fight to end slavery, a story neglected for too long.[5]

Oberlin was, beyond question, one of the most important communities in the abolitionist movement. In its symbolic and practical importance, it rivaled larger and more well-known eastern reform centers. It quietly achieved this distinction because of the unique circumstances in its early years that gathered an unprecedented multiracial and cohesive abolitionist population in the Ohio wilderness that maintained a fever pitch of reform agitation throughout the antebellum period. Yet rivalry was never Oberlin's intention. Rather than considering the "perfection" of Oberlin an end in itself, the community would have rightfully considered itself, in the words of sociologist Aldon Morris (though in the context of a different civil rights struggle), a "movement center" where reformers "developed an interrelated set of protest leaders, organizations, and followers who collectively define the common ends of the group, devise necessary tactics and strategies . . . and engage in actions designed to attain the goals of the group."[6]

Oberlin was founded as a utopian community whose sole mission was to save souls and prepare the world for the coming millennium of Christ.[7] Within two years, the community of only a few hundred residents had begun sending abolitionist missionaries out across the West in numbers unmatched by even the largest eastern cities, and its college had become the most progressive academic environment in the nation, perhaps the world. The Oberlin Collegiate Institute was the first institution of higher education in the United States to admit men and women of all races, and as more conservative schools persecuted or expelled outspoken student-abolitionists, Oberlin welcomed the outcasts with open arms. The school became a beacon for the nation's most progressive students, and together with a thoroughly abolitionist faculty and community, they set about the mission of ridding America of its greatest and most pressing sin—slavery. The unanimity of spirit within the community allowed unparalleled free discussion of abolitionism and the development of independent ideology and practical plans of action.

In the mid-1830s campaign of the American Anti-Slavery Society (AASS) to send a host of antislavery agents across the nation, national leaders appreciated the unrivaled importance, caliber, and potential of the Oberlin abolitionists. The organization's eastern-based leadership made special efforts to recruit, train, and equip Oberlinites as traveling lecturers, and they sent out representatives of the community as the first significant group into the field. At the height of the agency system in the late 1830s, Oberlinites were also the most numerous. These reformers played a significant role in swelling the number of antislavery societies across the nation by nearly 900 percent in just two years, 1835–37.

Back in Oberlin, the nearly unanimous community offered its town as a forum to develop an abolitionist ideology that both promised results and appealed to large numbers of otherwise skeptical Northerners turned off both by ultraradicals' shock tactics and conservatives' reactionary assaults on citizens' rights. Even as eastern abolitionists feuded among themselves and proslavery forces stepped up their attacks in the late 1830s and 1840s, the Oberlin approach continued to stand out as a more practical alternative, one with emancipation and equal rights as its twin goals and unencumbered by narrow ideological constraints. As the practical influence of the eastern abolitionists waned in the 1840s–1850s, Oberlinites and those they influenced filled the void and kept antislavery at the front of American discourse. By the 1850s, some of the strongest and most insistent demands for an end to slavery were coming from Oberlin and the West.

The Oberlin community remained a constant "Gibraltar of Freedom," as Frederick Douglass, himself the father of an Oberlin student, called it. Abolitionist-missionaries who went out from the town not only established countless churches and antislavery societies on the Oberlin model, but also helped found towns and colleges across the nation meant to replicate the Oberlin mission. These included at least twelve sister towns named "Oberlin" (plus the "Oberlin Complex" missionary station in Jamaica), and at least fifteen institutions of higher education in six states. Though Oberlin's critics (and even its allies in other proud antislavery strongholds) may have questioned the claim that the true Tree of Liberty grew within the town's boundaries, no one could deny that the scattered fruits of the community put down strong and sprawling roots. Wherever an Oberlinite settled, abolitionism spread.[8]

The recovery of this dynamic story also brings into accord the romantic reputation of the Oberlin community as a homogenous radical base with the wide range of ideological influences and allegiances actually present and peacefully coexisting within the town and institution. Oberlin's history has led to a nearly unanimous portrayal of Oberlin as a consistent bastion of radicalism in an inconstant antebellum period. This view is not altogether wrong, but it is incomplete. Over the antebellum years the degree of the community's radicalism (relative to the overall abolitionist movement) waxed and waned, and the Oberlin community's place within the antebellum antislavery movement was not static. Moreover, leadership did not always rest in the hands of a few white leaders. The torch of leadership changed hands several times in the years before the Civil War. Which portion of the community actually led the others often determined whether Oberlin could be counted as a radical force among reformers or a voice of relative moderation.

Most often, especially from the late 1840s on, Oberlin's progressive stance followed the example of the group arguably the most important to the development of their antislavery agenda and remarkable antebellum reputation: its African American constituency.[9] Although Oberlin's historical significance has most often been acknowledged for its distinction as the first institution of higher learning in America to admit men and women "irrespective of color," the absolute number of black Oberlinites was never more than 5 percent of its antebellum student body, and African Americans represented approximately 20 percent of the town's overall population. These numbers may initially seem insignificant, but both figures were unheard of in the antebellum North. Oberlin educated more black students before the Civil War than all other American colleges *combined*, and the community's proportion of black residents was truly extraordinary. By comparison, according to the 1860 census, the African American populations of New York City, Philadelphia, Cincinnati, Boston, and Pittsburgh represented 2, 4, 2, and

1 percent of their overall totals, respectively.[10] Moreover, black alumni and nonstudent members of the community were also vital parts of the town's antislavery ethos and abolitionist leaders nationally. These men and women were most often the steadfast and radical conscience for the rest of the community as it sometimes threatened to drift off course, zealously guarding their core principles and keeping the radical edge of antislavery from being dulled to the point of irrelevance for expediency's sake. Despite their status as a small (though significant) contingent, this group of African American reformers exerted an influence far beyond what their absolute numbers might suggest. They, more than anyone else, provided the essence of the "Oberlin mystique" that permeates the American historical mythology.

Properly understood, the "real" history of Oberlin encourages a shift in attention to the West as a critical region in the abolition and antislavery movement. The influence of this region (and the Oberlin community in particular) has been greatly underestimated. Concentrating exclusively on the activities of historical actors in the East who left the heaviest paper trail misses a vital part of the antislavery story.[11] Secular as well as religious leaders of the early decades of the nineteenth century held up the West as the salvation of a growing nation. There, many believed, all things were to be made anew, improving and progressing toward ultimate perfection. However, the rapid expansion west was also a source of anxiety for the most religious-minded of them, and they shuddered at the sinfulness of the frontier. The Reverend John Jay Shipherd, founder of Oberlin, called Ohio of the early nineteenth century the "valley of moral death," and men like him saw the conquest of the "godless West" for Christianity as the first essential step toward converting the world. Going west to ensure the continuation of god-fearing virtues became for many a patriotic and religious duty.

Oberlin was founded to be the very standard-bearer of the movement to "save" the West (and by extension, America and the world) for Christianity. As the slavery issue fermented, antislavery agitation became the most important means within the Oberlin crusade to shape America's identity. The Oberlin academics whose primary purpose was to train evangelical missionaries operated on the premise that the conversion of sinners would open the way to other reforms, abolitionism chief among them. Oberlinites spread across the Northwest in the late 1830s and injected themselves into public roles, and their influence in the antislavery movement grew enormously.

By the mid-1840s, developments and divisions within the national movement had thrust the West to the forefront of abolitionism in America. In its midst, Oberlinites continued to be key players in the development of a workable, practical abolitionist ideology. In the late 1840s and 1850s, the community's influential body of African American reformers was instrumental in keeping pressure on the antislavery movement when reformers were tempted by compromise for popularity's sake. Representatives of this, by far the largest body of college-educated African Americans, filled many of the most important leadership positions in western and national black convention movements, and they extended the Oberlin antislavery agenda to all corners of the free states and into the margins of the South.

It was also in the West where the supposed divisions within the national abolitionist movement seem most blurred. Strict attention on the East has too often forced historians to feel the need to draw distinct lines between groups of antislavery activists. Though some scholars have begun to criticize the view that the abolitionist movement was "thoroughly afflicted with hopeless factionalism and infighting,"[12] too many others seem to share a belief with the scholar Andrew Delbanco that the antislavery movement was so divided that "it can seem a distortion to call it a movement at all."[13] The most common view in the scholarship is that three wholly separate abolitionist factions emerged out of the late 1830s and 1840s: radical Garrisonians, moderate evangelicals, and political abolitionists.[14] However, such assumptions are not borne out, especially where the Oberlin influence was the strongest, the West. In the final analysis, more abolitionists more closely followed the diverse Oberlin example than stood aloof from fellow reformers because of disagreements over issues of antislavery doctrines. Opposition to slavery, the most powerful political and cultural interest in antebellum America, placed all abolitionists so far from the mainstream of public opinion, even into the midst of the Civil War, that their similarities far overshadowed their differences. Most abolitionists did not follow one or another exceptional leader or set ideology to the full exclusion of all others.

To be sure, the national abolitionist "split" in 1840 occurred because of significant ideological differences among eastern abolitionists, and there was indeed a bitter fraternal feud among a handful of highly visible reformers. However, the accounts of the schism of 1840 and the usual explanations offered by many contemporaries and historians are misleading.[15] Divisions existed, but they were not unbridgeable, and they were far from uniform. An analysis of abolitionism and antislavery in the West provides an alternate interpretation of the "schism." By 1840, control of the antislavery movement was already shifting to local societies, especially some of those that Oberlin missionary-abolitionists had helped form in the western states. If the moral heart of abolitionism remained in New England, and the political heart was in upstate New York, the Ohio abolitionists united these two and became their counterpart in the West. At the time of the national division in 1840, Ohio contained nearly 20 percent of all antislavery societies in the nation, more than any other state besides New York.[16] Increasingly, the West became the most dynamic and vital center of abolitionist ideological expansion.

Moreover, an investigation of western antislavery and Oberlin's influence therein makes it even clearer that the issues dividing the eastern movement were not representative. There was simply not a comparable schism among abolitionists away from the East Coast. Western antislavery crusaders were often far from consistent in their doctrines and allegiances, and their meetings were less ideologically charged. Ohio abolitionists of all persuasions coexisted more peacefully and with more civility after 1840 than their eastern counterparts. Even after a nominal division did occur, Ohio "Garrisonians" selected an antislavery politician as head of their state organization, and members of one group saw little inconsistency in retaining their membership in the other.[17]

By moving away from the ideological rifts among eastern leaders, one encounters significant numbers of abolitionists who selectively picked and chose various elements of their antislavery ethos from multiple and diverse examples. This was the Oberlin tradition of "practical abolitionism," a pragmatic philosophy that approved of whatever tactics promised the highest likelihood of success or progress. If the particular measures promised progress, then the means to that end were generally accepted wholeheartedly and in due course recommended to the various antislavery organizations in which Oberlinites claimed membership and positions of leadership. A more appropriate focus must be on what antislavery men and women had in common and what factors brought them all together.

Thus, there is no need to suggest that one or another group of reformers were "better" abolitionists, or that there was any "true" standard of abolitionism to which one either did or did not measure up. Rather, the term "abolitionist" should apply generally to those who demanded immediate emancipation. An abolitionist was willing to take a public stand in support of that principle and to perform positive acts toward that end. Such activists also at least espoused commitment to the creation of a society where all races coexisted as equals. However, racism, racialism, and condescension sometimes lingered within the white-dominated movement. White abolitionists were people of their times, fully human, and fully fallible, an awareness often unappreciated by some abolitionists themselves. However, one must credit the genuineness of abolitionists' expressions in support of equality unless other evidence clearly discredits them. Abolitionists cherished an ideal of racial equality, though that ideal always proved an elusive reality, even in Oberlin. Rather than attempting to judge the propriety and genuineness of abolitionist means and tactics, this work more closely examines the motivations behind them and resulting progress toward the desired end. Naïveté or excessive optimism or pessimism (even relative among abolitionists), rather than suggesting a somehow "flawed" abolitionism, simply marks different paths toward the same goal.

Moreover, as the example of many abolitionists from the Oberlin community makes clear, one could be an abolitionist and seek "perfect," immediatist ends but still work to extinguish slavery through "imperfect" or moderate means. Some of these men and women used radical, strictly moral abolitionist meetings and spiritual means to encourage a speedy end to slavery while also speaking out against racism and inequality. Some simultaneously cast their lot with organizations that they admitted were deeply flawed, such as the Free-Soil or Republican Parties, thinking they offered the most realistic hope for positive steps toward emancipation. Abolitionists could and often did adopt expediency without abandoning principle, and there is much to be learned in that regard from the Oberlin example. Strict ideological consistency may have been morally admirable to some reformers, but without a practical plan, it would not free a single slave.

Oberlin—the town, the college, the idea—has been remembered, if not fully understood, as one of the most powerful symbols of the American abolitionist movement. The actual substance behind that symbol, however, was even greater, and its history contributes to a fuller understanding of the movement Oberlin helped lead. It is more than the story of a progressive college town in the antebellum era. Rather, it is a tale of antislavery development and its remarkable potency in local, regional, and national affairs. As Charles Grandison Finney remembered in 1874, Oberlin's history had truly been quite "romantic." He vividly recalled the obstacles overcome in the community's early years, and Oberlin's role of David to the Slave Power's Goliath reminded him of the saying, "A little one shall chase a thousand." At eighty-two years old, the man who had played such a fundamental role in that drama had decided to leave the chronicling of that past to others. He anticipated, though, that if Oberlin's future historian could cut through the layers of exaggeration, slander, encomium, myth, and sweeping generalities, the real story of those early decades "would prove that 'facts are sometimes stranger than fiction.'"[18]

The beginnings of that account lie in the inspiration of the Reverend John J. Shipherd and the founding of the Oberlin community. A product of the Great Western Revival of the late 1820s and early 1830s, Shipherd went to Ohio as a missionary to "the Godless West." He and colleague Philo Stewart founded a utopian community in the northern Ohio wilderness in 1833 and named it Oberlin, after the famous French minister. As a part of their enterprise, they also founded a school, the Oberlin Institute, and opened its doors to both men and women. They recruited pious families from New England to emigrate there, sign a religious covenant, and consecrate their lives to God and the Oberlin missionary enterprise. However, the initial going was rough, and financial hardship nearly crippled the embryonic settlement and school before they could have any noticeable impact upon the region.

As Shipherd and Stewart busied themselves establishing their colony, simultaneous developments nearby and in the East had a significant impact on the development of both the school and community. There were numerous and important connections between Oberlin's founding generation and the developing modern abolitionist movement in the 1830s, particularly the Lane Seminary rebellion and the early career of Finney, the man who would eventually figure as the most important individual in Oberlin's first half century. When the revivalist left his New York City pastorate to join the Oberlin Institute, it was on the condition that African American students be admitted alongside white scholars and that freedom of discussion be categorically encouraged on all issues, abolitionism included.

The Oberlin trustees' decision to endorse their founding covenant of equality and accept African American students of both sexes injected a powerful dose of egalitarianism and abolitionism into their midst. This more than anything helped Oberlin quickly develop into a multiracial and genuinely democratic utopian community, and a beacon for the most progressive students across the North. While some of its favorite sons were traveling across the region seeking antislavery converts, the Oberlin community continued to transform itself into one great antislavery society, in the words of contemporaries, a "hot-bed of abolitionism." The community used its isolation in the Ohio wilderness to freely discuss antislavery reform and all related issues with an openness that was rare in the often hostile outside world. With free speech prevailing, the community developed an independent antislavery ideology that placed them beyond more narrow definitions of what it meant to be a "true" abolitionist. As its representatives canvassed the region, the "Oberlin school" of abolitionism took strong hold among legions of western reformers.

As dissent grew within the eastern wing of the movement, abolitionists in Ohio and Oberlin in particular were able to remain above the fray. Though not always completely consistent in their antislavery ideology, reformers from Oberlin pursued whatever means they thought would best advance their foremost goal, total emancipation. Accordingly, Oberlinites were among the most vocal supporters of independent antislavery politics, and played leading roles in its development in the late 1830s and early 1840s. Even as antislavery became more popular in America and the radical edge of abolitionism was dulled to appeal to a larger constituency, abolitionists from Oberlin freely offered their collaboration in the rise of the Free-Soil coalition in the late 1840s. Unlike the majority of Free-Soilers, however, most Oberlinites remained immediatists. Though politics offered no real hope of immediate emancipation in the foreseeable future, Oberlin abolitionists hoped to secure incremental victories through the electoral process while keeping up a simultaneous moral appeal that expanded the boundaries of what was possible. Moreover, Free-Soil politics was a potent weapon that helped Oberlin representatives pursue the other important aspect of their abolitionism: equal rights for free African Americans.

The antislavery struggles of the 1830s and 1840s well prepared the Oberlin community to meet the sectional crises of the 1850s. Oberlinites played crucial roles in shaping abolitionist responses to the transgressions of the Slave Power, from the Fugitive Slave Law of 1850 to the *Dred Scott* decision seven years later. Importantly, it was also during the 1850s that Oberlin's black leaders, a group that had always played a vital role in the town's reform agenda, assumed the leadership of the community's abolitionists. Led by such men as John Mercer Langston and William Howard Day, Oberlinites were instrumental in shepherding Northern outrage over the usurpations of the Slave Power into a national movement in opposition to slavery.

Nothing any individual Oberlinite could do, however, could equal the abolitionist reputation the community earned through its participation in a busy Underground Railroad. Friends and foes alike acknowledged Oberlin as a hub of underground activity from its founding years through the Oberlin-Wellington Rescue of 1858, an episode that involved hundreds of Oberlinites in the rescue of one of the community's residents from Kentucky slave catchers. Though dozens of Oberlin residents, students, and professors were subsequently arrested for their open flouting of the authority of the Slave Power, abolitionists skillfully manipulated the incident into a propaganda triumph that reenergized the lagging Republican Party in Ohio and the nation. The rescue also hardened sectional animosities and moved the nation another step closer to the war that many Oberlinites feared, though they knew it must bring the final emancipation of four million slaves. In the aftermath of the rescue, Oberlinites braced for violent sectional conflict. Several men from the community heeded John Brown's call to arms later that year, and when their country made its own appeal, Oberlinites, white and black, enlisted and gave their lives in the final fight for freedom.

CHAPTER ONE

To Save the Godless West

Revivalism, Abolition, and the Founding of Oberlin

The story of Oberlin in the antislavery movement does not begin in Ohio, or even the Old Northwest for that matter. Its origins lay, in varying degrees, in Connecticut farmhouses, New York City parlors, Virginia plantation fields, Mohawk Valley revival tents, West African villages, and other locales to the east. Slavery was not a new phenomenon when the Oberlin colony and school of the same name were founded in 1833, and neither was the abolitionist movement. For years, great revivals had been occurring, missionaries had been preaching on the frontier, and abolitionists had been speaking out against slavery, long before Oberlin, Ohio, became a central hub of those activities.

"Oberlin" was an idea before it was a place. The story of Oberlin in the antislavery movement, therefore, begins largely in the less tangible realm of revelation and dreams: the motivation of Yankees to emigrate west, a desire to follow the biblical injunction to be perfect in God's eyes, plans to educate a missionary army of Christian soldiers to save the world and inaugurate God's government on earth, and the radical notion that slavery was America's most horrendous sin that should be instantly repented of and immediately brought to an end.

* * *

THE GREAT EVANGELICAL REVIVALIST Charles Grandison Finney called the Upstate New York region of the late 1820s and early 1830s a "burnt district," an area where sinners had been touched by "a wasting fire in the fullness of its strength," flames that consumed everything in their paths, leaving no unconverted souls left to bring to God.[1] His extended revival in Rochester from the fall of 1830 to the summer of 1831 would be remembered as one of the most extraordinary religious events in American history.[2] At the height of the revival, the town's streets, alleyways, sidewalks, and nearly every building overflowed with men and women fervently praying and discussing all matters religious, and at all hours of the clock.[3] Families opened their homes for prayer meetings that could not find room in the overcrowded churches, and troops of devout women went door to door praying by name for those souls about which they felt the least bit anxious.

The Reverend John Jay Shipherd had read vivid accounts of Finney's revival in the eastern press, and he decided to stop over in Rochester with his family for the weekend as they traveled west pursuing God's call in late October. They had followed the Erie Canal for a time on their voyage from Shipherd's former ministry in Vermont, and were headed to the Western Reserve of northern Ohio to begin new lives as missionaries. A man of deep faith, Shipherd did not wish to risk profaning the Sabbath by traveling on Sunday, and neither did he wish to miss the chance to renew his friendship with Finney. However, when the young New Englander stepped off of his barge into the bustling street, the most remarkable thing he initially observed were full suits of wet wool clothing drip drying on sagging clotheslines. He later found out that the night before his arrival, the old First Presbyterian Church had begun to implode, partially collapsing upon itself and those inside it, unable to support the weight of the crowds that had been packing its sanctuary day in and day out. Some of the more frightened worshippers who did not join the stampede out the church's doors had leapt from the windows into the cold and dirty waters of the adjacent canal.[4] It was at once a baptism of fire and immersion.

The temporary closing of the First Church for repairs only slightly lessened Finney's preaching load, and he welcomed the arrival of any clergyman with time to spare for a sermon or two. Shipherd did not disappoint, and he preached the Sunday morning service at Rochester's Second Church before listening to Finney exhort from the same pulpit that evening. However, despite compelling private conversations and Finney's desperate assurances that he had never needed his help more, Shipherd could not be talked into remaining as an assistant in the revival. He fully appreciated the magnitude of what was happening in Rochester but felt that he had his own important part to play in bringing on the millennium, God's triumphant reign on Earth.[5] Finney's desires were one thing, but Shipherd believed that the Lord's work for him lay farther west. For his part, Shipherd tried to convince Finney to travel on with him, but with no more success. Still, the great revivalist's parting prayer for Shipherd that day as the friends bade each other farewell was for him to go as his "pioneer" to prepare his way for an eventual mission into the "valley of death."[6]

Finney would remain in Rochester for several more months and eventually move his revival labors east to New York City. The Shipherds returned to their barge that next Monday and girded themselves for the trials they knew awaited them to the west, the Valley of the Mississippi, which John noted was "fast filling up with bones which are dry" and where "the Sprit that giveth life is not wont to breathe upon them, till the prophet's voice be uttered." He admitted that the more cultivated regions of New England and the mid-Atlantic were more inviting than the western frontier, but these places also had more Christian laborers for the Lord's work. Though others hesitated, and though the way was rough, Shipherd simply answered his missionary call, "Here am I send me."[7]

The Valley of Dry Bones

For generations, many Americans had looked upon the newly opened West as an area of profound importance. Thomas Jefferson and his republican followers had always viewed the trans-Appalachian West as the place where a "pure" America could flourish and remain virtuous. Increasing numbers of small farmers moving west would ensure agrarian supremacy as well as delay the Malthusian catastrophe that Jefferson and others envisioned as the result of an overpopulated industrial East.[8] Just as many secular Americans viewed the West as the future of the nation, sponsors of its religious missions there viewed it as the potential salvation of the country and perhaps the world. Many of these people also believed that the era in which they were living was what theologian Paul Tillich calls a "kairos," a moment in history where the kingdom of God enters into human affairs. Historian David Brion Davis, in applying this concept to antebellum reform, describes it as a period in which "an eschatological leap" becomes possible, one that overcomes a "demonic power" and transcends the limits of previous eras.[9] Lyman Beecher, a powerful Boston divine before his own removal to Ohio in 1832, recalled that Jonathan Edwards had predicted that the millennium would commence in America, and it was plain to Beecher that the spiritual destiny of the nation was to be decided in the West.[10]

Like Beecher, Shipherd was an example of one who followed God's call into the interior. By the time Beecher had published his book *Plea for the West*, Shipherd was already en route to Ohio. He had long since crossed paths with Finney in Rochester and was busily engaged in developing his own plan to redeem the "valley of moral death." Shipherd had lived a life dedicated to God and the ministry since a brush with death in 1819.[11] After considering the appeals for missionaries he read in the religious press, he decided to lend his arm to the breaking of the "unplowed spiritual fields" of the Mississippi Valley.[12] By May 1831, he was well on his way down "the stream of God's mercy," the Erie Canal, toward the Great Lakes and Ohio.[13] He settled into a vacant pulpit in the sparsely populated frontier outpost of Elyria, Ohio, in the Western Reserve county of Lorain.[14] Though green, he impressed those who heard him preach, and he inspired one listener enough to write to Finney to tell him that Shipherd was "of the right Stamp." His outspoken abolitionism also earned the approbation of antislavery champion Beriah Green, who preached the sermon at Shipherd's Elyria induction ceremony.[15] Still, he felt overwhelmed, and at least once desperately appealed to Finney for help. "I remember your parting prayer," he wrote of Finney's Rochester benediction, and reported, "As a pioneer I have opened the way." If Finney himself could not come west, Shipherd begged him for advice on how to produce better results.[16]

Finney's reply has been lost, but by the end of May, Shipherd was piloting a revival that even the great evangelist would have been proud of. One observer wrote to the *New York Evangelist* that the Elyria revival "already seems like the scenes exhibited in Rochester."[17] Shipherd reported to his family in New York that "God is truly doing great things for us in the valley. Oh that we had help to gather the rich harvest already whitened around us!"[18] He had helped bring the Holy Spirit to Ohio, and the dry and barren souls of Ohioans, "with many tears & sorrows, [had] begun to live."[19] Moreover, Shipherd began to train other young men for western ministries, including a young man from Connecticut whom he had befriended years earlier, Philo Penfield Stewart.[20]

The Oberlin Colony

As his thoughts shifted to something of an even grander scale, Shipherd nurtured his relationship with his boyhood friend.[21] Stewart, or "Steadfast," as Shipherd called him, had first acted on his own western calling as a missionary among the Choctaws, and he continued to crave a role in the great western battle for the soul of the nation.[22] Both men were on the cusp of new lives of "usefulness." Shipherd was preparing to vacate his pastorate; Stewart believed that he could be more useful as a layman but did not know how or where to best employ his talents. Together, they developed a plan that would redirect both of their lives toward a potentially productive goal.[23] They would found a colony that would be "divorced from Mammon, & wedded to simplicity & true wisdom," one whose pious community would "make our churches ashamed of their unholy alliances with earth."[24] They would name the settlement "Oberlin" after the French clergyman John Frederic Oberlin (1740–1826), whose compassionate social work in an isolated area of Alsace for sixty years had earned him worldwide recognition.[25]

The plan was simple yet perspicacious. The two would find a favorable location for their colony, then gather their community to live under a covenant, the main terms of which would be that "each member of the colony shall consider himself a steward of the Lord, & hold only so much property as he can advantageously manage for the Lord. Every one, regardless of worldly maxims, shall return to Gospel simplicity of dress, diet, houses, and furniture, all appertaining to him, & be industrious & economical with the view of earning & saving as much as possible, not to hoard up for old age, & for children, but to glorify God in the salvation of men: And that no one need to be tempted to hoard up, the colonists (as members of one body, of which Christ is the head), mutually pledge that they will provide in all respects for the widowed, orphan, & all the needy as well as for themselves & households."[26]

"Oberlin" would also include a school in the colony for students of all ages, and importantly, for both sexes, in hopes of becoming "an institution which will afford the best education for the Ministry." Students would work several hours a day at an affiliated farm or workshop in order to finance their education. In addition to the youth of the colony, the founders planned to educate teachers and ministers drawn "from the four winds" to serve in the West.[27] Indeed, the Oberlin Institute would be the centerpiece of the enterprise. All colonists would be committed to the school's success, since it was to be the most obvious embodiment of their evangelical and revivalist impulse.

Shipherd and Stewart obtained a tract of land in a still-unsettled corner of Russia Township and then began the task of recruiting two dozen pious families to form the core settlement.[28] No one was actually living in

Oberlin until the spring of 1833. The first true colonist of Oberlin, Peter Pindar Pease, moved into the first rough house in April and assumed the job of resident supervisor of land clearing. With axe and fire, he had cleared nearly ten acres by the end of May, erected another log house, and cut the first road in the forest.[29] By mid-June, at least ten families were on the ground in Oberlin, religious meetings were taking place, cleared land was under cultivation, roadwork was under way, and a boardinghouse and steam mill for the use of the school were being raised.[30] Oberlinites officially organized their church in August with a membership of sixty-one people (232 by year's end).[31] "Does not this look like a good beginning?" Stewart asked Shipherd.[32]

It did indeed, and in the early fall of 1833, Shipherd published the prospectus for the Oberlin Collegiate Institute in journals from Ohio to the East Coast. "The growing millions of the Mississippi Valley are perishing through want of well qualified ministers and teachers," Shipherd explained to the nation, and "in view of these facts the founders of the Oberlin institute, having waited on God for counsel, and being encouraged by the wise and good, resolved to rise and build." Attendance would be inexpensive, students' education would be first-rate, and manual labor and acclimation to the West would well prepare them for their challenging missions to come. The founders aimed at the education of the *"whole man,"* yet women would be welcome as well when the school's doors opened to students December 3, 1833, making Oberlin the nation's first coeducational collegiate institution.[33]

However, finances were tight. Though individuals sent donations, the sums were often small. Others sent gifts of goods that, though generous, could not pay professors' salaries.[34] By the summer of 1834, Shipherd was lamenting his inability to admit all the students who sought to study at the Oberlin Institute. Some, after being informed that the school was filled to capacity, made the trek to Oberlin anyway, often over hundreds of miles, to beg for admission in person. However, necessity forbade it. "I am under the distressing necessity," Shipherd remarked, "of rejecting such for want of a few thousand dollars by which I could place them in such circumstances as would through the Lord's blessing, in a few years send them forth to 'endure hardness as good soldiers of Jesus Christ.'"[35] Oberlin needed a new boardinghouse, several other buildings for students' use, more professors, and a president, yet it lacked the funds necessary to expand.[36] It was clear that unless something was done soon to put Oberlin in the black, "the design must fail."[37] The trustees, in a desperate effort to stay afloat, sent Shipherd out as general agent on a last-ditch fund-raising mission.[38] And so, the man whom Finney had once called his pioneer to the Valley of Death headed back east toward New York on a lame horse, seeking the deep pockets of reform-minded businessmen and the guidance and counsel of the great revivalist.

The Subject of the Slavery Question

Finney was already busy in New York City. The success of his revivals earlier in the decade had convinced wealthy New York admirers that his services were desperately needed in their "Perishing City."[39] Merchant Lewis Tappan told Finney that he believed the metropolis was "the headquarters of Satan," and he did not think the necessary revival would take place unless he came to lead it.[40] To Tappan and his brother Arthur, New York *was* America, and they tried to appeal to Finney's keen sense of utility to draw him there. Lewis Tappan described to Finney the "mighty influence" New York had upon the rest of the country. "A blow struck here," he assured Finney, "reverberates to the extremities of the republic."[41]

Finney was convinced, and he soon moved his base of operations to the newly christened Chatham Street Chapel (formerly Chatham Street Theater) in New York City. By this time, Finney said that he had "made up [his] mind on the subject of the slavery question" and "was exceedingly anxious to arouse public attention to the subject."[42] Although he did not wish to divert the attention of his congregants from the worthy work of converting souls, antislavery was an important aspect of his ministry.[43] Finney declared in an 1834 sermon that "he could not *recognize* men as [Christians] who trafficked in the bodies and souls of fellow men."[44] Even more powerful was his refusal as early as 1833 to allow slaveholders to commune in his church.[45] "I do not baptize slavery by some soft and Christian name, if I call it a SIN," he explained, and "its perpetrators cannot be fit subjects for Christian communion and fellowship."[46]

As Finney waged an all-out war against sin in its myriad forms and insisted on immediate and total repentance on the part of his parishioners, so too did he join other friends of the slave in New York in castigating half-hearted and limited schemes for emancipation, especially those of the American Colonization Society (ACS). He realized that many Americans mistakenly viewed the colonization movement as a "benevolent" organization devoted to the cause of the slave. The defining feature of the colonization movement was the expulsion, or "colonization," of free African Americans from the United States to Africa. Many Northern philanthropists supported the movement because, through the early 1830s, it was the only national secular organization that encouraged emancipation, though only on the condition that the freed people emigrate, and that had any meaningful influence that was available for their patronage. To most of them at the time, slavery was primarily an economic evil. Though many Americans did believe that moral and material progress were twinned, they hardly ever demonstrated empathy with the enslaved. Southerners also supported colonization for its proposals to rid their society of its unwanted (and, they believed, dangerous) free black population. At its base, however, colonization rested on racism, strengthened slavery, and provided an ideological cover for its expansion. As James G. Birney realized, colonization only allowed slave owners "an opiate to the conscience," and allowed racist Northerners to congratulate themselves on rescuing "degraded" African Americans from the supposedly "irremediable" prejudice and hatred of American whites.[47]

Yet the most dedicated opponents of colonization were the free African Americans themselves, the very heart and soul of the early radical abolitionist movement. For most of them, America was their native land, no less so than for their white neighbors. They felt that they had more than earned the right to stay there. From the organization of the ACS in 1817, many free black men and women spoke out in thunder tones on the iniquity of colonization schemes, declaring them to be "in direct violation of those principles, which have been the boast of this republic." They further resolved to never voluntarily abandon the enslaved population of their country, since they were "our brethren by the ties of consanguinity, of suffering, and of wrong."[48] They realized that in an emigration scheme like the one proposed by the ACS, those still enslaved who were left behind would be "assured perpetual slavery and augmented sufferings."[49] Rather than lessening the strong spirit of racism that pervaded American society, an 1831 New York African American gathering noted with disgust, colonization schemes assumed it to be unyielding and unchangeable.[50]

Their most significant convert to the cause of anticolonization was the young journalist William Lloyd Garrison. By the end of 1830, the counsel of free African Americans had convinced Garrison that any organization that, even for a minute, upheld the institution of slavery was a corrupt one; gradualist schemes for ending slavery were morally and politically appalling.[51] Encouraged and principally supported financially by free African Americans, Garrison hoped to shock Americans out of their complacency on January 1, 1831, with the publication of the first issue of his abolitionist newspaper, the *Liberator*. He intended to unceasingly cry the alarm until

Charles Grandison Finney in the early 1830s (from Finney, *Sermons on Important Subjects* [1836])

slavery had been abolished, declaring to his readers, "I am in earnest—I will not equivocate—I will not excuse—I will not retreat a single inch—AND I WILL BE HEARD."[52] As Garrison's friend Samuel J. May put it, the great abolitionist was "all on fire."[53]

Garrison's clarion call fit well with the evangelical call for immediate repentance that was simultaneously echoing across America. Both were centered on the idea of "perfectionism," the notion that individuals could choose to live without sin.[54] As these men and women followed the scriptural command to "be ye therefore perfect, even as your Father which is in heaven is perfect" and converted others to their path, they could potentially form a truly perfect society and commence the kingdom of God on earth, a world without sin or slavery. As both Finney and Garrison believed, there could be no middle road—no accommodation with sin. Slavery was the most conspicuous sin before America in the early 1830s, and it had to be swept away completely and immediately.

Many of Finney's followers soon proved to be some of the most enthusiastic supporters of immediate emancipation, and in New York, Finney was in the center of one of the dual capitals of the budding antislavery movement in America. Garrison's efforts were striking bright sparks in Boston, and Finney's New York benefactors held the purse strings to the "benevolent empire." As the New Yorkers began informal discussions among themselves about immediatism, they also came to Garrison's conclusion that colonization was an insufficient and unprincipled solution to the blight of American slavery.[55] The *New York Evangelist* reported as early as September 1831 that "men of wealth and influence" were about organizing an "American National Anti-Slavery Society," and it soon became clear in the paper's pages that there was considerable opposition to colonization among the philanthropic New York elite.[56] Through the *New York Evangelist*, reformers stressed that "colonizationists and abolitionists cannot walk together."[57] Finney reminded his Chatham Street congregation that the notion of gradual repentance or "partial repentance" was "nonsense."[58] Since slavery was clearly a sin *at that very moment*, there was no excuse for letting it survive another day or hour or minute.

In March of 1833, Finney, along with the Tappans, Theodore Dwight Weld, *Evangelist* editor Joshua Leavitt, and others, directly confronted the ACS over its duplicity. In an attempt to embarrass the ACS and expose its shortcomings, they demanded in a public letter that the society explain its position on the "complete extinction of Slavery" in the United States and whether expatriation was the absolute necessity that must follow the emancipation. The reply they received from the ACS was, as they expected, evasive, imprecise, and unsatisfactory. Its spokesman stumbled over questions of semantics before denying that the society sought to effect emancipation at all by any influence it could or would exert.[59]

New York philanthropists met in Finney's church in October 2, 1833, to found the New York Anti-Slavery Society. Their goal was to inspire men and women to immediately repent of the sin of slavery as well as immediately commence efforts to remedy the wrong. Their program implied that the process of ending slavery once and for all must begin "now" rather than "someday," and though their plans were not specific, they demanded at the very least an immediate declaration of emancipation followed by a series of steps to prepare freed slaves for full citizenship. Though their meeting was supposed to have been secret, they barely avoided a raucous mob that had gathered at their planned convention location, and could only observe in horror from a distance as the gang later wreaked havoc on the city and black New Yorkers.[60]

The fallout in New York City from the abolitionist agitation troubled Finney. He approved of the basic motives of the New York abolitionists— his own perfectionism demanded it—but he discouraged reformers from making antislavery their single concern at the expense of what he saw as the most important work of saving souls.[61] Slaveholding was a heinous sin, and he clearly considered it one of the most grave. However, to Finney, the smallest sin was no less a sin than the greatest. An evil proslavery mind-set was but one of many that would fall away whenever a man or woman was fully and genuinely saved. What Finney desired was to make abolition an "appendage" of revivalism.

However, Finney believed that the sin of slavery did not always extend to racial prejudice. He considered it more a matter of personal "constitutional taste" and understood the issue to be one of the fundamental obstacles to emancipation in the United States.[62] This led Lewis Tappan, some of his associates, and many historians to suggest that Finney more resembled a racist than an abolitionist. However, this merely highlights the messiness of race in antebellum America, even among committed reformers.[63] To Finney's credit, in his many denouncements of Ohio's Black Laws after he arrived in Oberlin in 1835, he invoked the "equalizing" notion of the Golden Rule and loving one's neighbor as one's self.[64] Yet Finney believed that the sin of slavery could not be exposed as powerfully as it could be if the populace was thrown into a frenzy over what he called a "collateral point." It "distracted the public attention with two questions at the same time instead of one," and just like a successful revival, the only way to "consummate[e] an excitement & public action upon any subject" was to "confine the publick mind to a point." Finney never expressed a personal dislike for those of another race, yet his commands to his followers to "love thy neighbor as thyself" are legion, and he criticized colleagues who had "not wholly renounced the hateful prejudice against the people of color that so generally prevailed in the country and in the churches." He explained in a letter to Arthur Tappan that he was "unwilling to see the indignation & rage of the lawless mob excited against" the free African Americans of New York and elsewhere. Lewis Tappan refused to read this letter.[65] A distressed Theodore Weld was forced to come to Finney's aid. "I believe," he wrote of Finney, "that he is an abolitionist in full . . . *as he conscientiously believed was his duty.*" It was no sin for Finney to stress revivals as his absorbing passion. Indeed, Weld cautioned Tappan that Finney could justifiably criticize the two of them for not praying enough, lacking sufficient faith, and not encouraging revivals to a proper degree. That, in Weld's mind, gave Finney "far more reason for the upbraiding than you have for upbraiding him" for what Tappan had called "his coldness and unfaithfulness to the cause of antislavery."[66]

Even though Finney was a revivalist, however, a primary question before him remained, "How can we save our country and affect the speedy abolition of slavery?" His solution was to instruct his followers to first make things right with God, then "every new convert will be an abolitionist of course." Though overly optimistic, Finney thought that conversion to immediatism would be the visible proof of a new life in Christ, not a substitute for it. His own methods for ending slavery would produce the same result, yet reach it without the "wave of blood" that he saw as threatening to undo in a minute what God built up over months and years.⁶⁷

As Southern intransigence became more offensive in the mid-1830s, Finney seemed to come around to the more radical position of the Tappans and others on abolition's privileged place in reform. He admonished his followers, "God forbid that we should be silent" rather than constantly rebuke slaveholders, never mind the consequences. Abolition required *constant agitation*, and so long as it was not done *to the detriment* of revivalism, all was well. "Are we to hold our peace," he asked, "and be partakers in the sin of slavery, by connivance, as we have been? God Forbid." Instead, Finney commanded his followers to constantly speak of it, bear testimony against it, pray about it, "and complain of it to God and man.—Heaven shall know, and the world shall know, and Hell shall know, that we protest against the sin, and will continue to rebuke it, till it is broken up."⁶⁸

Still, Finney remained troubled by the anarchy that conservative New Yorkers had unleashed upon their city in response to abolitionist agitation. His anxiety was compounded by physical weakness from a bout with cholera. It had been nearly three years since his undeniable successes at Rochester, and he feared he did not have the physical strength to save his New York congregation from the destruction that seemed imminent at the hands of the anti-abolitionist mobs. He considered taking an extended vacation to England or South America, but on January 20, 1834, Finney boarded the Mediterranean-bound brig *Padang*.⁶⁹ He hoped that by the time he returned, both his health and calm in the city would have returned.⁷⁰

God Has Finally Opened a Door to Our Infant Seminary

John J. Shipherd was not aware of the progress of eastern immediatists or of Finney's departure when he set out from Oberlin in search of the revivalist's guidance on the mission that many Oberlinites thought could be the final lifesaving measure for the college. When Shipherd and his horse limped away from northwestern Ohio, the school's debts were in arrears, it was in desperate need of more sufficient facilities, its board of trustees was deserting, and its first annual report reflected the dismal state of college administration—conspicuous blanks stood beside the office of president and the professorships of mathematics and natural philosophy.⁷¹

Shipherd headed first to Cincinnati. On the way, he encountered in Columbus the son of Oberlin Institute trustee John Keep, who was able to confirm fascinating rumors that Shipherd had heard echoing across the Ohio countryside. It seemed that a large group of theological students at Cincinnati's Lane Seminary had been expelled for their insistence on debating the merits of immediate emancipation, for the formation of their own antislavery society, and for integrating themselves into Cincinnati's black community. Shipherd's friend Theodore Weld had gone from New York to Lane to study theology, and he had become the leader of the Lane Rebels (as they were called). Some prominent Lane professors and trustees had also resigned their posts in support of these students. The younger Keep had intended to enroll at Lane but was returning home to Oberlin after discovering the disappointing and unacceptable state of affairs in Cincinnati. Shipherd, alert to the potential of administrators, professors, theological students, and monetary support without a home base, hurried south to suggest Oberlin as an ideal solution to the problem.[72]

Shipherd was welcomed into the home of his old friend Asa Mahan. Formerly a member of Finney's western New York "Holy Band," Mahan now occupied a pulpit in Cincinnati and was until his recent resignation a trustee of Lane Seminary. As Shipherd relaxed from his trek, a group of the former Lane students arrived. After being introduced to Shipherd and being apprised of his Oberlin mission, the young theologians filled in the details of the "Lane Rebellion."[73] Under Weld's leadership, many Lane students had formed themselves into an antislavery society. Weld had shared Finney's prioritization of the West as the stage for the battle for America's soul, and he made Lane the headquarters for his "revival in benevolence."[74] So convinced was he that Lane was the best place to strike a blow at slavery, he turned down an appointment as an agent of the newly formed American Anti-Slavery Society to pursue his antislavery agenda in Cincinnati.[75] Hoping to prepare a "line of attack for a general pitched battle with the colonizationists," who were the majority among the Lane students, Weld and the other abolitionist students organized, against the admonitions of the Lane administrators, a series of debates on two questions: "Ought the people of the Slave holding States to abolish Slavery immediately?" and "Are the doctrines, tendencies, and measures of the American Colonization Society, and the influence of its principle supporters, such as render it worthy of the patronage of the Christian public?" Each topic was debated for nine evenings, and over the protracted course of the three weeks of debate, nearly all of the Lane students and many of the faculty were able to witness at least some part of the proceedings.[76]

The debates went on like a revival. In fact, many of the Rebels had themselves been converted by Finney only a few years earlier and were well-versed in the workings of revivalism.[77] Scions of slaveholders and sons of the South became their first targets. Once converted, those formerly entangled with slavery gave their own testimony of the barbarity of the system from personal experience and became some of the most effective speakers. They presented their firsthand observations for all to consider: visions of the bloody whips, cries of agony, and red-hot brands moved the impressionable students with great effect. "The facts developed in the debate have almost curdled my blood," one student wrote, and he noted that "facts are the great instruments of conviction on this question."[78]

After the conclusion of the first "annihilative onset upon slavery," there was a unanimous vote by the students in favor of immediate emancipation. Without delay, the second nine-day debate commenced on the colonization question. The Lane students agreed with James Bradley, a black seminarian who had been kidnapped into slavery directly from Africa, that the scheme was patently outrageous and offensive. If slaves could take care of themselves *as slaves*, with the weight of supporting themselves and their masters on their shoulders, Bradley reasoned, "strange if they couldn't do it when it tumbled off."[79] Despite the fact that "even Liberty" was bitter to him while anyone remained in bondage, he articulated his refusal to submit to any emigration scheme and leave his "brethren under the yoke."[80] Thanks in no small part to the skill of Bradley, who at least one observer grouped with the most skilled black abolitionists and who could "not be equaled by the more logical and polished of our Birney and Weld," the colonization debate ended with a similar result as the first.[81] Another vote was eagerly called for to form a student antislavery society. Among the officers and managers were Weld, Henry Stanton, and George Whipple of New York, James Thome of Kentucky, and James Bradley, listed as hailing from Guinea.[82]

The Lane Rebels also fervently believed that "faith without *works* is dead"—and the "works" were just as important as the faith that sustained them.[83] Even as the abolition debates were taking place on the Lane campus, student abolitionists were integrating themselves into the Cincinnati black community, giving testimony to their abolitionist declarations.[84] In the lyceum they founded for Cincinnati's blacks, Lane students lectured three or four evenings a week on grammar, geography, arithmetic, natural philosophy, and other subjects. Since most Cincinnati African Americans were former slaves who had just recently become free, Lane tutors founded another school to teach basic reading and writing skills. This was especially important because Ohio law barred African Americans from being educated in any school that was supported in any way by the tax dollars of white citizens.[85]

But the racism of Cincinnati loomed large. Residents could easily recall the scenes of carnage from race riots just a few years earlier. Lane itself was dependent to a large degree on the financial support of slaveholding Southerners. News of the debates, not to mention the students' extracurricular interracial social work, was not received sympathetically by the school's patrons, many of them Southerners.[86] Supportive trustee Asa Mahan was accused of promoting "the principle of amalgamation" and was "practically disfellowshipped and treated as an alien and outcast by the churches, and mass of the community." An anti-abolitionist mob even attacked Mahan's children in front of his Cincinnati house and attempted to stone them.[87]

The combination of Lane students interacting socially with Cincinnati's African American population and their insistence on debating abolitionism on campus was more than most school officials could stomach.[88] In response, the board resolved that public meetings among students should not be held without official sanction, and that all antislavery societies in the school should be immediately abolished. Even antislavery discussion around college dining tables was prohibited. A committee of trustees and faculty were vested with the power of dismissal for violators.[89] The Rebels remained defiant, refusing to submit to what they considered the board's tyranny, and even compared the crackdown on abolitionists to the Spanish Inquisition.[90]

Most of the Rebels remained near Cincinnati. Asa Mahan, who had severed all connections with Lane, continued to give them his support and wisdom, while John Morgan, their former Lane professor, joined him in continuing as best they could the students' education. Thus Shipherd's appearance at Mahan's home and his unfolding of the Oberlin plan to them seemed a fortuitous development. The students saw in Shipherd a man of strong convictions, an avowed advocate of immediate emancipation, and one who could provide them with an institution in which to complete their theological studies in a progressive atmosphere. Shipherd, for his part, was equally thrilled. He rejoiced to John Keep that "God has kindly opened a door to our infant seminary, wide & effectual, thro' which I sanguinely hope, it will send forth a multitude of well qualified laborers into the plenteous harvest of our Lord."[91] To Shipherd's further delight, the students insisted that Mahan and Morgan accompany them to Oberlin as the president and professor of mathematics Shipherd so desperately sought.

The Monday morning after Shipherd met with the Rebels, he and Mahan boarded the first steamer that was heading up the Ohio River in search of Weld, who had set out on a series of antislavery lectures after cutting his ties with Lane. Upon locating their man, they discussed their plans and relayed to Weld that he was the choice of the Rebels to fill the professorship of theology. Weld demurred, however, and argued that there was but one man worthy of filling such an important position—their mutual friend and mentor, Charles Grandison Finney.[92]

Before Shipherd started east with Mahan to sound out Finney, he posted an important letter to the trustees back in Oberlin, already making arrangements for the accession. Mahan, Morgan, and the students demanded that absolute freedom of speech be granted as a condition of their moving to Oberlin. Most importantly, they required that African Americans be admitted to Oberlin together with and on the same terms as white students. To satisfy the Rebels, Shipherd wholeheartedly agreed with their demands and instructed trustee Nathan Fletcher to introduce a resolution at the next board meeting that students be received at the institute "*irrespective of color.*" Only by doing so, he wrote, would they gain God's favor, the services of two first-rate intellectuals, and the confidence of "benevolent & able men."[93] He added, "If our Board would violate right so as to reject youth of talent and piety because they were *black*, I should have *no heart* to labor for the upholding of our Seminary." He believed that if Oberlin fell short, God's curse would fall upon them just as it had upon Lane, "for its unchristian abuse of the poor slave."[94] After all, even Lane had admitted African Americans into its ranks, including former slave James Bradley, who was also ready to enroll in the Oberlin Institute if they would have him.

Race and Abolitionism in Early Ohio

Still, despite the Oberlin community's professed idealism, its initial reaction proved that it had a ways to go before it would catch up with that of its founder. Upon the receipt of Shipherd's news, the community fell into a frenzied panic. Notwithstanding the practice of Lane and other schools to admit black students, many Oberlinites seemed convinced of its novelty. Others feared that the town and school were to be "overwhelmed with colored students, and the mischiefs that would follow were frightful in the extreme."[95] Some young ladies declared that if black students were admitted of equal privileges, they would return to their homes, "if they had to 'wade Lake Erie' to accomplish it."[96] Philo Stewart publicly pronounced Shipherd "mad."[97] On December 31, 1834, a group of students circulated a petition among themselves to ascertain their position on the issue of "admitting persons of color, to this Institution, under existing circumstances." The final tally stood thirty-two "Against," twenty-six "In favour."[98]

The decision in Oberlin, though disappointing to some parties involved, still proved the community more progressive on racial issues than much of the rest of Ohio. The state was far from a commitment to antislavery and much further from any true sense of racial egalitarianism. Its history as a state began with delegates to its constitutional convention of 1802 seriously considering legalized slavery within its borders, despite the antislavery clauses of the Northwest Ordinance.[99] Notwithstanding the ultimate decision to retain the ban on slavery and involuntary servitude, it was no humanitarian triumph. Those lawmakers who opposed slavery for racist reasons set the policy tone in early Ohio and did everything in their power to keep free African Americans out as well. The first state constitution recognized the rights of white men only, and the first of the state's infamous Black Laws were passed by the legislature in 1804 and 1807. These required two white sponsors and a prohibitive bond of $500 for African Americans to enter the state, barred them from militia service, and denied them the right to testify against whites in court or to vote. Legislation in the 1820s also barred African Americans from attending public schools created for whites or paid for by taxes collected from white citizens.[100] Those African Americans who did settle within Ohio's borders were to be made as uncomfortable as possible and to acutely feel their supposed degradation. As black activist John Malvin remembered of Ohio in the 1820s, he was not only "personally despised" but not even under the protection of the laws themselves. "I found every door closed against the colored man," he noted, "excepting the jails and penitentiaries."[101] Still, to many black families, living under restrictions in a free state was preferable to the limbo of living in the South. One historian estimates that in the town of Oberlin, nearly two-thirds of the antebellum African American population was born in the slave states of Virginia, North Carolina, and Kentucky. A sizeable number of the other third hailed from Tennessee, Washington, D.C., South Carolina, Maryland, Alabama, and Mississippi.[102] Farther south in Cincinnati, over one three-year period in the late 1820s, the African American population ballooned from just 690 to nearly 2,300, most of whom came from slave states.[103]

Alarmed whites retrenched, and their reaction to the black influx into Ohio was often swift and severe. In 1829, Cincinnati officials gave local African Americans sixty days to comply with the security bond required of them by the Black Laws or to leave the city. Few did, and when authorities hesitated to act, mobs of angry white men ruled the city for three days and nights, killing or seriously injuring many unfortunate African Americans in the process. In January of 1830 in Portsmouth, Ohio, the entire African

American population, about eighty in number, was forcibly driven out of the community.[104]

Colonization was a wildly popular cause in Ohio. The "negro problem" struck many as so grave an issue that a special legislative committee convened in 1827 to investigate its causes and potential solutions. Prefacing his remarks by declaring Ohio's African Americans "a serious political and moral evil," the committee's chairman spoke for "the white laboring classes of the state" when he expressed his hope that the "excrescence on the body politic" would be not just prevented from entering the state but removed altogether through colonizationist efforts.[105] By the time the committee's report was made public, there were numerous branches of the ACS across Ohio, including four in the Western Reserve, where the African American population was still relatively miniscule.[106] In 1834, Ohio governor Robert Lucas was selected as the state society's president, and even ladies' and youth auxiliaries were operating in various parts of the state.[107]

Conservative leaders in the Western Reserve won a striking victory over budding abolitionist agitation in the fall of 1832 when they accomplished the removal of three radical faculty members of Western Reserve College in Hudson. After having led heated discussion on immediatism, professors Beriah Green, Elizur Wright Jr., and President Charles Storrs resigned their posts under pressure. A local paper celebrated the removal of "the malign influence" of the abolitionists in its ranks and looked forward to the school's potential "usefulness" now that it would not be bothered by "the negro question."[108]

However, the seed of abolitionism that had been planted decades earlier continued to germinate. As conservatives dug in, abolitionists consolidated their forces. In September of 1833, immediately following commencement at Western Reserve College, area antislavery men gathered to form the Western Reserve Anti-Slavery and Colonization Society. After hours of strenuous debate over the society's goals, the colonizationists withdrew. The remainder of the delegates drafted a constitution based upon the principle of "total and immediate emancipation," struck "colonization" from its name, and elected officers, including Elizur Wright Sr., Austinburg's Henry Cowles, and Hudson's Owen Brown. Cowles was a minister who would be appointed professor of languages at Oberlin in 1835. Brown, father of the then-unknown John Brown, was a former Western Reserve College trustee who had resigned after the faculty antislavery controversy. He would serve as Oberlin Institute trustee from 1835 to 1844.[109] In August of 1833, the annual meeting of the society added another staunch immediatist, John J. Shipherd, to its list of "counselors."[110] On February 26, 1835, reformers founded the Lorain County Anti-Slavery Society, and among its officers were Levi Burnell, a Finney convert from Rochester currently living in Elyria, who served as the society's secretary (the same position he would soon fill at the Oberlin Institute); and current Oberlin Institute trustee Nathan Fletcher.[111]

An Institution Where Abolition Is Concentrated

As the West developed the American identity anew, the question of whether there would be a place for African Americans remained open. Shipherd's ambitious plan for American regeneration was inclusive. Indeed, the Oberlin Institute had not excluded anyone from its fellowship until its board of trustees first declared African American admissions inexpedient in response to Shipherd's request. To him, the glaring sins standing in the way of the America millennium were slavery and racism, and it would fall to Shipherd once again to make a Herculean effort to clear the way. He had gathered the forces he hoped would bring down sin and slavery in one fell swoop, and he would have the commission for their deployment or exhaust himself in the attempt.

Shipherd did not immediately receive news of the failure of the board to pass his resolution. It was not in his constitution, however, to hesitate. He hired Mahan as Oberlin's president without first consulting the trustees, unilaterally guaranteed all the Lane Rebels' demands, hired Morgan as professor, and went to New York to obtain the blessing and financial support of some of the nation's wealthiest merchants and the services of America's most famous and celebrated preacher without first receiving any reply to his request that the Oberlin Institute admit African American students. When he finally did receive word of the resolution's failure, it was through but one of a flurry of letters circulating among the interested parties. He was sure that in addition to Mahan and Morgan, most of the Lane Rebels would soon be calling Oberlin their new home and the Tappans their enduring benefactors. It seemed to Shipherd, who was brimming with confidence that Finney would join them all in Ohio, as if God had put his hand upon "a golden chain which [he would] be able to link to Oberlin & thro' it bind many souls in holy allegiance to our Blessed King."[112]

William Allan, Lane Rebel and reformed Alabama slaveholder, wrote to Weld that if he and Finney went to Oberlin, he would join them. Never one for understatement, Allan estimated the effect his enrollment at Oberlin would have on his family and Southern acquaintances. "That, with me," he predicted, "will be putting on the capstone—I shall have passed the rubicon if I should go to an institution where abolition is concentrated—at the head of which is that arch-heretic Finney."[113] James Thome, a Lane Rebel from a slaveholding Kentucky family, believed that "the Lord has been gracious to me in throwing me into such circumstances." He was eager to continue his studies and abolitionism and welcomed any adversity that he may encounter toward those ends. "I don't care about beginning my work with ever so great opposition," he wrote, "if that opposition is incurred by doing duty. I will surely not meet with more than our Saviour faced."[114]

In mid-January 1835, all interested parties converged on New York City to determine the fate of the Oberlin Institute and the exiled Lane students. The Rebels set the tone for the negotiations that were to follow in a direct appeal to Finney. Henry Stanton and George Whipple, writing on the unanimous behalf of their classmates, shared their deep valuation of "the cause of theological education in the West." It appeared to them that "the impenitent West is rushing to death, unresisted & almost unwarned." The only preventative, in their opinion, was a strong revival presence, maintained by "a new race of ministers" trained and sent out by the ablest revivalist America had ever seen: Finney. "Our eyes have for a long time been turned toward you," they told him, and they could not avoid the conviction that God himself was calling Finney to the professorship of theology at the Oberlin Institute.[115]

When Shipherd and Mahan arrived in the city, they arranged a meeting with Finney and his closest New York associates to hear their plans.[116] Arthur and Lewis Tappan had previously suggested to the indecisive Finney that he relocate to Cincinnati in the immediate wake of the Lane debates.[117] This time, their entreaties that Finney go to Oberlin were seconded by those of Shipherd, Mahan, and the students themselves. Shipherd laid out his plans for Oberlin and the West, and Mahan relayed the demands and conditions of the Lane contingent. Arthur Tappan pledged $10,000 to the Oberlin venture; Lewis Tappan and other New York philanthropists agreed to fund the salaries of eight professors. These pledges all came with two conditions, however: the Lane Rebels' demands must be met, and Finney must go to Oberlin as professor of theology.[118]

With little hesitation, Finney agreed to accept the Oberlin call, and he reiterated his insistence on the list of conditions that he shared with the Rebels.[119] He wrote the same to the anxious former Lane students.[120] However, the agreements struck in New York City would amount to nothing unless Oberlin proved to its potential benefactors that it was more worthy of their support than Lane had been. Oberlin needed to be right on the question of the admission of students "irregardless of color." The former Lane students themselves were first and most vocal in their insistence that Oberlin live up to its Christian charter and potential by establishing a color-blind admissions policy. If the Rebels did not matriculate, there would be no need for their support. It was an essential point with potentially ruinous consequences if Oberlin did not comply. The school and community were seamlessly intertwined, and the fate of a bankrupt and rudderless Oberlin College could also mean the dissolution of the Oberlin community and the end of its utopian experiment almost before it got off the ground.

Some Oberlin trustees feared that black admissions would so enrage outsiders that they might converge on the town and destroy the school, a fate that had recently befallen integrated preparatory schools elsewhere. Yet Finney pointed out that Shipherd's resolution did not ask a novel or unreasonable concession on the part of the trustees that might expose it to the same dangers that destroyed other schools that admitted black students.[121] What also made Oberlin's short-sightedness so patently absurd was the fact that even Lane itself had admitted African American students for years, and Western Reserve College, less than fifty miles distant, had passed resolutions opening its doors to African Americans.[122] Finney criticized the Oberlin community for not having "wholly renounced" the antiblack prejudice so common outside Oberlin's town limits.[123] John Morgan also took a turn critiquing the trustees. To Finney he wrote, "I do not see how consistent abolitionists can give either money or their personal labors & influence to Oberlin till the trustees are 'prepared' to rescind this enactment & do justice to their colored brethren whether other institutions do so or not." Mahan wondered what it would take for the trustees "to quit themselves like men . . . and give the public manifestation of the fact."[124]

It was clear to Shipherd that the entire enterprise depended on the resolution of the single question of race-blind admission. The institution was certainly no better off financially than it had been when he left, and the ideological support for its continued existence seemed to be crumbling before his eyes. Oberlin had been established as a gathered community, supposedly of like mind with regard to its mission and egalitarian evangelicalism. Now, a majority of the institute's trustees had exposed their individual shortcomings on a principle that a significant minority felt was absolutely essential to the continuance of the Oberlin experiment.

From New York, Shipherd wrote what are perhaps the two most important letters in Oberlin's early history as a last-ditch effort to salvage his utopian dream. His disappointment was tempered by his ultimate faith in the community members he had gathered, and the love he felt for them all was evident in his words. He wrote similar notes to the Oberlin Church, of which he was the pastor, and the board of trustees in which he desperately appealed to their shared sense of mission and urged them to remain faithful to the promises that they had made when they took up the cause of Oberlin.

Shipherd urged his colonists to continue to seek the Lord's favor, something they could only do by altering their earlier decisions regarding black students. He urged them to recall their covenant to live their lives for God unencumbered by worldly influences. Emphasizing the importance of their decision, he reminded them that the choice at hand was vital to "peace, your usefulness, and the glory of God our Heavenly Father." If they would do their duty, Shipherd predicted, Oberlin would be "a living fountain whose waters will refresh the far-off, thirsty, dying Gentiles and wretched Jews." He pleaded with his flock "as the Lord's peculiar people" to be zealous in pursuing those means by which the world would be converted and to banish their fear "to lead in doing right."[125]

To be sure, Oberlin had been founded two years earlier without any reference to racial issues or American slavery. Shipherd frankly admitted that fact while also regretting his decision to leave such significant details unstated. Although he realized that some of his colonists were not necessarily in favor of the idea of immediate emancipation, he supposed that they at least thought it expedient and their Christian duty to see to the elevation and education of African Americans as quickly as possible. However, the community had proven him wrong, and Shipherd offered members a comprehensive list of twenty points at which the admission and education of black students coincided with their pledges to each other and God at the community's founding.[126] In a sense, Shipherd was presenting them with the first exegesis of their colonial charter.

As a practical matter, African Americans were needed to spread God's gospel, especially to "their untaught, injured, perishing brethren." "Their education," he surmised, was "highly essential if not indispensable" to the emancipation and salvation of their race, and it must not be limited to racially segregated institutions. If they were to remain faithful to their ideals, Oberlinites had to recognize that God made all people of one blood, and that, as their Christian neighbors, "whatsoever we would they should do unto us, we must do unto them, or become guilty before God." He urged his flock, in an appeal to the empathy that would become an Oberlin hallmark, to imagine themselves in the shoes of their oppressed brethren. What then, he asked, should "be your due as a neighbor?"[127]

On a more basic level, Shipherd reminded Oberlinites that the very survival of their community depended on their changed hearts. Simply put, the men and money Oberlin Institute needed for its continued existence would vanish if they rejected black students.[128] Eight paid professorships, $10,000, and the services of Finney, Mahan, and Morgan could not be had upon compromised principles. He wrote that these men of "anti-slavery sentiments" were just the stalwarts Oberlin needed, and he worried that if the trustees "suffer[ed] expediency or prejudice to pervert justice" in this case, others would as well.[129] All other potential donors, Shipherd wrote in another note to Finney, seemed to have been turned off by "their fear of Abolitionism [which] unstrung their *benevolent* nerves."[130] Shipherd even professed his own inability to remain the leader of a half-hearted utopia and told his congregation that he would consider the rejection of black students at Oberlin as a rejection of him as well.

The colonists and trustees thus had before them a clear choice: either remain ensnared by the prevailing prejudices of the day, deny their fundamental principles, and lose their visionary leader, or recommit themselves to the utopian vision of the founders and concentrate their efforts into a millennial work the likes of which America had never seen. To decide the matter once and for all, the trustees called a special meeting for February 9, 1835.[131] Though Shipherd remained absent, they met at his house, and the crucible that followed was intense. One participant wrote that the assembly was not only "riotous" and "turbulent" but "filled with detraction" and "slander." Shipherd's letter was read again, but the board remained unable to reach a decision on the matter. After much prayer, "especially by a band of godly women," they adjourned to meet again the next morning.[132]

The factions were almost evenly matched. Nathan Fletcher and the three other abolitionists on the board stood on the side of admission of black students, while Philo Stewart and three others opposed the measure. It fell to John Keep, the newly appointed president of the board, to cast the deciding vote.[133] As a religious convert of Finney and an abolitionist convert of Weld, Keep could only consistently vote one way.[134] On February 10, "Father" John Keep's vote in favor of admission "irregardless of color" decided the matter.[135] The board resolved: "That the education of the people of color is a matter of great interest and should be encouraged & sustained in this institution" and that all admissions decisions be entirely the responsibility of the faculty.[136]

In fact, the resolution passed by the board was almost exactly as Finney would have drafted it himself. In a January letter to some of the Rebels, Finney had laid out his main condition for coming to Oberlin: "that the question of receiving students without distinction of color *be left with the faculty*."[137] Following this decision, a common complaint of critics was that the school's race-blind policy would "congregate such a mass of negroes at Oberlin as to darken the whole atmosphere," eventually turning it into an all-black "Dyed in the Wool" school.[138] In the racist atmosphere of Ohio, a policy explicitly committed to this end, however admirable in purists' eyes, could be fatal to Oberlin's survival. Finney realized that by demanding faculty control of the admissions process, it would be placed it in the hands of avowed antislavery men like himself, Mahan, Morgan, and others who would soon be recruited in no small part because of their commitment to abolitionism. The effect, as Finney and the majority of the board saw it, would be no different than an explicit commitment to equality, yet it would do so in a way that protected the institution from racist assaults and accusations of unmerited affirmative action in behalf of abolitionism.

Thus satisfied, the Lane Rebels left Cincinnati in April 1835 to begin the trek north to Oberlin.[139] On their way, they were joined at Putnam by several of their new Oberlin colleagues, including Timothy Hudson and Henry Cowles, at the inaugural state convention of Ohio abolitionists. The Western Reserve Anti-Slavery Society, including several men with Oberlin connections such as Shipherd, Owen Brown, Cowles, and Hudson, had issued a call for the state convention in the fall of 1834. With the new students from Lane included among the delegates, it was clear that Oberlinites would make up the core of the new society. Cowles and Hudson were primarily responsible for writing the society's constitution, and though still en route to Oberlin, Finney was appointed as one of the society's vice presidents and Mahan to the board of managers (which also included Cowles and Hudson). Mahan made his apologies in a letter to the convention, but its tone reflected the mood for the entire three-day assembly, as well as the society's years of agitation to come. Boldly, he announced, "Sir, I am an abolitionist. In every station and relation in life, I would be known as such, while a single slave groans beneath the oppressor's yoke, or bleeds beneath the oppressor's scourge."[140]

Weld headed up the committee responsible for drafting a declaration of sentiments. When he presented the document to the convention, the Oberlin throng "fearlessly" subscribed their names to it. The ideas expressed in the declaration were not new, but they were yet another fresh vindication of the perfectionist bases of abolitionism. They rejected slavery because it was a sin, "always, every where, and only sin. . . . All the incidental effects of the system flow spontaneously from this fountain-head." It was wrapped up in every aspect of American life; its victims were not only the slaves but the slaveholders, the church, the nation, and all its citizens. It contradicted God's law that the slave was a man distinct from a thing, a moral agent rather than an extension of another's will. The only solution, the only chance of salvation, was immediate emancipation, "the sacred duty of the slaves and the imperative duty of their masters."[141]

The Oberlin community quickly became the darling of abolitionists and the scourge of anti-abolitionists across the country. Oberlinites' wholesale adoption of the Lane castoffs and assumption of the leadership of the antislavery movement in Ohio thrust them into the realm of antislavery celebrity. In April of 1835, Shipherd was the special guest at a meeting of abolitionists in Boston including Samuel May and George Thompson, who resolved to cordially recommend Oberlin "to the *confidence* & support of the Christian public." In addition, the Boston convention appointed a committee to solicit donations, and many, including May, Thompson, and Amasa Walker made generous subscriptions.[142] Arthur Tappan, president of the AASS, made good his word to Oberlin by advertising the college whenever he could as well as making available more than $17,000 to Oberlin by October of 1835.[143] Other eastern abolitionists repented of their earlier financial support of Lane, now generally viewed in antislavery circles as an "anti abolition school," and offered penance by making even more generous donations to the Oberlin Institute and publicly chronicling their turnabout in the antislavery press.[144]

Agents of the school went out in the fall of 1835 specifically to recruit committed abolitionists into the faculty. Shipherd wrote from Utica, New York, that he hoped his visit to an antislavery convention there would result in the securing of a general agent for foreign service and also several professors. Ultimately, distinguished abolitionists Cowles, Hudson, James Thome, Horace Taylor, Alvan Stewart, James G. Birney, and others were appointed to faculty positions (though Birney and Stewart would be unable to make the move to Oberlin). Passionate abolitionist Owen Brown was named a member of the board of trustees.[145] Moreover, opponents of the admission of African American students, including founder Philo Stewart, left Oberlin or resigned their positions on the board. Nathan Fletcher remarked that these men, "unholy in principles," should have resigned long before they did.[146] Finneyite abolitionists soon dominated the administration, a fact that was reflected in the excuses of many of those critics who now

The Oberlin Big Tent on Tappan Square, a gift from Finney's New York benefactors in 1835 (courtesy Oberlin College Archives)

refused to aid the Oberlin enterprise; "Finneyism, Abolitionism, etc." were damnable offenses in many people's eyes.[147]

On July 1, a new age in American reform commenced in Oberlin when Finney, Mahan, and Morgan were officially inaugurated at the school's first-anniversary meeting. There, the community and college renewed their binding vows to one another and clarified certain latent points of their founding ideals. Shipherd's letter and their response to it had recommitted the Oberlin community to unqualified Christian brotherhood, now explicitly embodied in racial inclusiveness and pledged to the abolition of slavery. Under the "Great Tent," a huge canvas construction purchased for the Oberlin Institute by their New York benefactors and called the "Tabernacle of the Most High God," John Keep presented the three men with copies of the charter of the Oberlin Collegiate Institute. Keep, the champion and protector of Shipherd's ideals, was symbolically entrusting the new heads of the school with the responsibility for carrying out Oberlin's sacred mission from that point forward.[148]

In his sermon that afternoon, Finney laid out Oberlin's future for all to behold. He announced his intention to adhere to Shipherd's dream, namely, to train up multitudes of ministers and influence laymen who would then go out from Oberlin to do God's bidding and hasten the millennium. With his new flock, Finney designed to "pitch [the Great Tent] in the enemies' camp."[149] Shipherd wholeheartedly approved of Finney's direction and prayed that God would guide this course "by the pillar of cloud and fire; and through this new mode of warfare conquer multitudes of his enemies."[150]

Slab Hall or Cincinnati Hall, the first Oberlin residence of the
Lane Rebels (from Fairchild, *Oberlin: The Colony and the College* [1883])

Luckily for Oberlin, student-soldiers were never in short supply since the school was one of the few educational opportunities still open to them in the mid to late 1830s. Indeed, conservatives in academia had made it nearly impossible for progressive young students to pursue their education unencumbered.[151] The contagion of anti-abolitionism was not limited to Lane or Western Reserve College. Also in 1835, fifty students left Phillips-Andover Academy because they were forbidden to form antislavery societies.[152] Amherst president Heman Humphrey demanded the dissolution of his school's antislavery society, and similar demands and circumstances embroiled Hamilton College, Hanover College, Marietta College, and Miami College in the battle over the right to discuss abolitionism.[153] After recounting the events that had "reformed" nearly all other schools of any abolitionist tendencies, the conservative editor of the *Western Monthly Magazine* remarked that "it is believed that there now remains but one school in which murder and robbery are inculcated as christian [sic] virtues": it was "the Oberlin Institute in Ohio."[154]

Thus by 1835, many of America's more progressive students had enrolled at Oberlin. From its opening in 1833 to the 1835 academic year, the student population grew by nearly 700 percent, and once again, the school was strapped for space.[155] One colonist assured a correspondent that they did not quite have to "live in 'hollow trees,'" but still, most were considerably cramped in their quarters.[156] Even its new president felt the squeeze. When Mahan and his family arrived in Oberlin, they were initially crammed into the old Pease cabin, and even after they moved into their own house, the Mahans had as many as eighteen people living under their roof at one time.[157]

A makeshift and too-obviously temporary barracks was raised to house the Rebels and their followers. Originally called Slab Hall after the material of its construction, the 20-by-144-foot building would come to be better known as Cincinnati Hall or Rebel Hall after its primary occupants.[158]

Even while the residence halls were under construction, they were often occupied by students who had nowhere else to bunk. Eager students filled Ladies Hall and Tappan Hall long before either building was completed, despite considerable danger to their safety.[159] Yet they continued to come, despite hardship and overcrowding, all hoping to be a part of what everybody agreed would be something important and special.[160] The vision of Finney praying and Mahan singing hymns while the buildings were being raised could only confirm them in their convictions.[161] A capable and pious group of people had joined together in the West to become, as one Oberlin trustee boasted, "*the decided opponent* of SLAVERY as it is practiced upon the colored people of the country."[162] From that point onward, the Oberlin community would self-consciously stand as an example to the rest of the nation in that fight.

CHAPTER TWO

The Worthies of Oberlin

Antislavery Expansion in the Late 1830s

Before their classes began in the fall, many of the Lane Rebels and their new professors joined the ranks of traveling lecturers for the American Anti-Slavery Society. Their exploits in Cincinnati and acceptance at Oberlin had made them antislavery celebrities, and their skills in converting people to abolitionism were immediately put to use. They were some of the first into the field, constituting half of the AASS lecturing force in 1835–36, and eventually representing a third of all society agents at the height of its agency system late in the decade. These Oberlin abolitionists were fundamental leaders in the greatest period of growth of American abolitionism, and they helped make antislavery palatable to a burgeoning constituency.

The efforts of these Oberlinites enhanced the community's development into an antislavery hub of the West. However, its distance (both spatially and ideologically) from the arguments that were dividing the eastern wing of the movement from within placed the Oberlin community in a privileged spot nationally. The Oberlin Collegiate Institute increasingly became a symbol around which all abolitionists could rally despite their differences. Even as their own financial stability was threatened by the Panic of 1837, antislavery leaders of all backgrounds lifted up Oberlin, that "nursery for Abolitionists," as a vital institution that could not be permitted to fail.[1]

★ ★ ★

ALTHOUGH MANY OF THE MEN AND WOMEN now at Oberlin had not known each other very long, their gathering together on the ground that would eventually be designated as Tappan Square was a great spiritual reunion. John J. Shipherd, many of the Lane Rebels, and other Oberlin officials and students had been converted in one of Charles Grandison Finney's revivals. Some, like Shipherd and Asa Mahan, had been among those who assisted the evangelist in his revival efforts. Many of those gathered on that spot looked back to the revivals of the 1820s and 1830s as a formative motivating force in their lives.[2] Almost immediately, Finney initiated a revival that refreshed the souls of the students, and then he commended them back to their education and crusade to save the world.[3]

Unlike at Lane, however, at Oberlin there would be no separation between moral endeavors and the students' formal scholarship. The Oberlin system was designed to enrich "the whole man" (and woman), and classes were seldom so narrow as to preclude the discussion of American slavery and abolitionism, since aspects of those topics could easily be brought to bear on subjects as wide-ranging as political economy to moral philosophy.[4] Moreover, especially with abolitionists leading class discussions, it would have been difficult if not unrealistic to expect academics and abolition to remain separate. As Edward Fairchild reasoned, slavery was the foremost intellectual topic of the age, and to exclude its discussion as a regular part of the Oberlin curriculum would leave only "questions . . . unworthy of attention."[5] Visiting antislavery lecturers were welcomed into Oberlin classrooms and encouraged to actively participate in the lessons. James Fairchild recalled, "It was an important part of an education to hear such a man as Theodore D. Weld in the prime of his manhood."[6] Another student remembered taking "special [antislavery] courses, not published in the catalogue, that were of more importance" than any of her regular studies. These may have included one of James Thome's famous series of lectures comparing biblical slavery to American bondage.[7] Critics were not incorrect in assuming that Oberlin was truly an "Abolition School."[8]

In Oberlin's early years, differentiating between the school and the community was not only nearly impossible but largely unnecessary. On June 25, while the community was observing a concert of prayer on behalf of "the oppressed," it resolved to form itself into an antislavery society. Shipherd was selected president, and he remarked that the enthusiasm and unanimity of feeling shown by the society indicated that the organization "would *not* be a body without a soul." When the call came to demonstrate their adherence to abolitionist principles, 230 citizens and students "came up en

Partial view of Oberlin, 1838, painted by eighteen-year-old Alonzo Pease, nephew of the first Oberlin pioneer, Peter Pindar Pease (courtesy Oberlin College Archives)

masse, arm and soul to this good work of God." Shipherd predicted that all those who were absent would join as soon as possible. He, Finney, and Mahan were the first to eagerly sign their names to the society constitution.[9]

The constitution adopted by the Oberlin Anti-Slavery Society was a nearly verbatim replication of that drawn up by the Lane students the year before. The Oberlin document, however, prominently bore the names of not just students but also faculty and community leaders among its endorsers.[10] The goal of the society was to be "the immediate emancipation of the whole colored race within the United States," not only of the slave from the master, but also of free African Americans from "the oppression of public sentiment" in the North. They sought the elevation of all of the oppressed "to an intellectual, moral, and political equality with the whites."[11] The enslaved, they wrote, had been "constituted by God a moral agent, the keeper of his own happiness, the executive of his own powers, the accountable arbiter of his own choice." Bondage robbed slaves of his or her own self and free will, and in so doing, earned Oberlin's scorn.[12]

To keep Oberlin's influence pure in the world's eyes, the Oberlin Church also took decisive action on the slavery question soon after the founding of the antislavery society. The church body resolved that "as Slavery is a Sin no person shall be invited to preach or minister in this Church or any Br[other] be invited to commune who is a slave holder."[13] Oberlin students soon spread this spirit to other nearby churches and religious organizations. Thanks to their efforts, many religious Ohioans went on record to declare slavery "a violation of all rights—a heinous sin against God" and to "have no Christian communion with those who practice slavery, nor with any who justify the system."[14]

By the fall of 1835, Oberlin had quickly become a major center of antislavery activity in the West. Its population represented a virtually unbroken abolitionist unit and very likely contained more antislavery reformers per capita than any other town in America, and their beliefs were spreading. In order to capitalize on the growing abolitionist sentiment in the region, the AASS sought lecturing agents to secure the advances of the nascent movement and to continue the spread of the antislavery message.[15] Theodore Dwight Weld, in consultation with AASS executive secretary Elizur Wright Jr. determined that the bustling Oberlin Institute campus was just the place to recruit the needed men. In November, Weld headed to the Western Reserve to enroll several of the "worthies of Oberlin" as commissioned abolitionist agents.[16] Weld arrived in Oberlin from southern Ohio on the seventh of that month and quickly went to work recruiting antislavery laborers and winning over the hearts of a community already well progressed down the path of immediatism.[17] His lectures "took a strong hold upon the hearts of the old and young," James Fairchild remembered, and the subject of abolition quickly became the engrossing theme of private contemplation, public discussion, and "the burden of song and prayer."[18] Over the course of the next three weeks, Weld thoroughly "abolitionized" the Oberlin community and significantly advanced the transformation that had begun just a handful of months earlier.[19]

Weld's Oberlin "reform revival" was perhaps his most successful to date. For twenty-one frigid November nights, he lectured on abolition in one of the new buildings that had been hastily thrown up to house Oberlin's influx of students. He wrote to Lewis Tappan that his makeshift lecture hall "was neither plastered nor lathed and the only seats are rough boards thrown upon blocks." The dedication of the Oberlinites was staggering, though, and Weld estimated that some 500 or 600 students and other community members of both sexes packed the hall every night despite the lack of functional fireplaces or sufficient chairs.[20] Fairchild credited Weld with illuminating that long, dark November "with the flashes of his genius and power."[21]

Somehow Weld also found an hour or two each day to focus his most earnest efforts upon the Oberlin students who had volunteered to go out into the enemy's camp as lecturing agents for the AASS. Samuel Gould, William Allan, James Thome, John Alvord, Huntington Lyman, and Sereno Streeter received an intensive crash course "in the principles, facts, arguments, etc., of the whole subject." Of course, the entire process must have seemed quite familiar to them by that point, as it had only been a little over a year since Weld first began instructing them in abolitionist doctrine and methods while they were students at Lane. Though Weld had not enrolled at Oberlin like many of the other Rebels, and while they had been busying themselves with their educational arrangements, he had been lecturing on

Theodore Dwight Weld, ca. 1844 (from Garrison and Garrison, *William Lloyd Garrison*, vol. 2 [1885])

abolition across the region. Now, he knew better than they what worked, what did not, the best ways to win an argument, how to flee a hostile town, or confront a mob. As their mentor, Weld laid open "the treasures of his anti-slavery magazine" for their benefit.[22]

These men were to be the shock troops of a revolutionary movement, and Weld and the AASS wanted to make sure that they received the most thorough preparation possible before they went out to face a hostile nation. When Weld wrapped up his campaign in Oberlin, these "young warriors" accompanied him to Cleveland to continue their intensive training. A sympathetic local judge opened his law office to Weld and his chosen men, and they quickly converted it into "a school of abolition." Their coursework included "copying documents, with hints, discussions, and suggestions," as well as practical chemistry lessons, particularly questions "related to tar and feathers, and how to erase their stain." In this way, they passed another two weeks "in earnest and most profitable drill."[23]

A Revival in Abolitionism

When they finally packed their bags and headed out into the field as AASS lecturers, these Oberlin students were the most thoroughly prepared activists in the movement. Following Weld's example, they would enter a town and seek out a church where they would attempt to arrange with its minister permission to hold a meeting. Often, the first assembly incited an anti-abolitionist riot, and at that point, their exhaustive preparation would prove invaluable. The account of Oberlin students James Thome and John Alvord of their lecture in Middlebury, Ohio, demonstrates the dangers abolitionists regularly faced. "Last night," Alvord wrote a friend, "Midd[l]ebury puked. . . . Spasmodic heavings and wretchings were manifest during the whole day. Toward night symptoms more alarming." As Thome began his lecture that evening in the local church, all chaos broke loose: "[I]n came a broadside of Eggs. Eggs, Glass, Egg shells, whites and yolks flew on every side. Br. Thom[e]s Fact Book received an egg just in its bowels and I doubt whether one in the House escaped a spattering. I have been trying to clean off this morning, but cant get off the stink. Thome dodged like a stoned gander. He brought up at length against the side of the desk, cocked his eye and stood gazing upward at the flying missiles as they stream[e]d in ropy masses through the house." After a twenty-minute lull, a crash in the rear of the church warned the beleaguered lecturers that another volley of rotten eggs was on its way. The mob "continued the fire some time like scattering musketry, mingled with their howlings."[24]

Invariably, the church would respond by closing its doors to further agitation (and destruction), and the lecturers would move to a local store, warehouse, private home, barn, or open field (if they were not driven out of town altogether by anti-abolitionists).[25] There, the physical opposition might be just as fierce. Weld instructed his students that at the most potentially dangerous point, when the agent actually left the lecture venue and had to face the angry mobs, they should draw themselves up to their full height and cross their arms. His experience showed that crowds were sometimes hesitant to attack a man with arms in such a defensive position.[26] After two or three days of hostility, violent opposition would sometimes fizzle out, and the real process of conversion could begin.[27] If all went well, they would win antislavery converts who would then assume the burden of converting others to abolitionism and completing the organization of local antislavery societies, while the abolitionists moved on to their next appointment and began the process anew.[28]

This Oberlin student contingent formed almost one-half of the AASS's lecturing cadre in 1835–36, and even more were preparing to follow in their footsteps. After a visit to Oberlin in late 1836, Ohio Anti-Slavery Society (OASS) financial agent Edward Weed reported that another large group of "young men of talents" and "skilled in the subject they are about to present" were preparing to enter the field as antislavery agents. They would be joined by several of their Oberlin professors in their labors. Weed rejoiced that these Oberlinites were precisely of the sort the movement most hoped to mobilize—"men of devoted piety—stimulated and urged on in the efforts they are about to make in behalf of suffering humanity, as I trust, by a pure and holy benevolence."[29]

As the decade wore on, dozens of Oberlin students and professors served as agents for the AASS in Ohio, Michigan, Indiana, Pennsylvania, and New York. They were so numerous and successful in Ohio that the national society was able to recall Weld to administrative duties in New York after his time in Oberlin in 1835. Elizur Wright Jr. realized the vital importance of the western region in the antislavery struggle and informed Weld that he believed that "the band going out from Oberlin is more for the west than all our forces in the east." They were recruiting legions of antislavery converts and participating in the formation of local antislavery societies on a scale unknown to the movement to that point and that would not be equaled in the future. Wright undoubtedly brimmed with pleasure as he wrote Weld, "We never before had so much to encourage us."[30]

One noteworthy aspect of the efforts of the abolitionists from Oberlin of the mid-1830s was their appearance before individuals and communities whose only previous exposure to organized abolitionism was what they had heard or read secondhand about the archradical publisher of the *Liberator*, William Lloyd Garrison.[31] The journalistic practice of the early nineteenth century was for newspaper editors to exchange copies of their journals with other publications that could then be excerpted to fill copy space, and Garrison regularly sent copies of the *Liberator* to over a hundred other editors, North and South.[32] However, proslavery and anti-abolitionist publishers often selectively quoted Garrison's paper, exposing readers to only the most radical of his writings. These excerpts were often inserted alongside crudely exaggerated commentary. One Northern paper on Garrison's exchange wrote under the heading "Incendiary Publications": "We have frequently adverted in terms of censure to a publication issued in Boston, entitled the Liberator, and edited by *a fanatic of the name of Garrison*. The object of this publication appears to be twofold—the emancipation of the blacks from slavery on the EXTERMINATION OF THE WHITES."[33]

Since the Oberlin students and townsmen were also immediatists and official representatives of the same national organization as Garrison, they had a unique opportunity to elaborate personally on the principles of immediatism and hence mitigate misconceptions. To be sure, the greatest obstacle abolitionists from Oberlin had to confront in their efforts was the naked intolerance of many of their listeners. However, among those whose racism did not place them completely outside the reaches of the abolitionists' argument, a great many had historically been turned off of the idea of immediate emancipation because of a misunderstanding of abolitionists' basic purposes. Due in large part to the misrepresentations of proslavery ideologues, many Americans were under the mistaken conviction that abolitionists intended immediatism to mean the instantaneous emancipation of the enslaved and a resulting "discharge from all political restraints and obligations" of those who were thus freed.[34] Abolitionists' challenge was to disabuse people of these sensational notions and bring them to a more accurate understanding of just what ends immediatists sought. As early as 1833, it was clear to abolitionists in Ohio that they must win over those who were prepared "to give up their 'gradualism' and their colonization as a remedy for slavery" but who could "not give up their grudge against Garrison!"[35]

What many people misunderstood about Garrison's immediatist standard, much like perfectionism, was that it was a constant striving rather than a fait accompli. Few abolitionists approached Garrison's moral example, and the average citizen was even further behind. To convert the skeptics, Oberlin abolitionists placed themselves somewhere between Garrison's harshness and the citizens' hesitancy. James Thome's method of stilling the disquiet of a hostile audience was representative of their style. He had been invited to lecture in Akron, Ohio, but found that when he arrived, the whole town planned to "prove, to a demonstration, the absurdity and danger of Abolition."[36] Placed in the tricky position of having to first justify the appropriateness of his lecture before presenting it, he began by explaining the true "*principles and designs of Abolitionist Societies*," as opposed to the prejudiced notions of which his listeners came already convinced. "First," he recalled, "I was particularly careful to *disclaim* certain things which are confounded with abolitionism; such as social intercourse, amalgamation, etc. I further stated that we did not claim for the slave the right of voting, immediately, or eligibility to office." His frustration was somewhat eased when the lawyer appointed to rebut him "expressed his astonishment at the *disclaimers* which [he] had made." Disarmed, the man declared that he was not quite ready "to go *all the lengths*" with Thome, but he admitted that the Oberlin man was "a NEW abolitionist" and had presented him with a perspective on abolitionism than he had known before. Thome then "proceeded to state what abolition *was*," and in his report to Weld recalled, "I blazed and threw sky-rockets, talked of human rights, touched upon the Amer. Revolution and brought heaven and earth together."[37]

Though his speech had partially contradicted the AASS's mission statement, the constitution of the Oberlin Anti-Slavery Society, of which he was a founding member, as well as his own personal beliefs regarding African Americans' place in society, Thome had distilled immediatism down to its essence in order to bring more converts to the cause.[38] By setting aside more controversial topics ("bear-skins" and "a man of straw" he called them), Thome and those like him made immediatists of men and women first, then set them down the "striving" path that could eventually make them more consistent abolitionists.[39]

Their method of spreading their antislavery gospel also gave the movement a critical boost. The evangelical missionary impulse helped this new generation of abolitionists mobilize larger numbers of people in the countryside, far away from the urban centers favored by earlier reformers.[40] In their abolitionist revival, these speakers left nothing to be misunderstood. Their antislavery "sermons" steadily drove home their message, and like the best revivalists, they tenaciously wore down their opposition until they achieved conversion. As their critics accurately declared, they "pervade[d] the land, preaching up to nightly crowds a crusade against slavery." They were described as "infuriate zealots" who "unfurl[ed] the banner of the cross as the standard to which the abolitionist is to rally."[41]

Often, almost as soon as one lecturer of group of speakers left a town, another arrived to take their place, or the same speakers would make a return visit later to discourage backsliding. Thus every word of every speech had a cumulative effect, reinforcing arguments made earlier or introducing new ones to then be reinforced themselves within a short period of time. As one modern rhetorician puts it, the early Ohio abolitionist campaigns of the Oberlin band, even if spread across a wide area, "were not isolated acts, but rather separate battles in a campaign with each battle representing another step toward the fulfillment of the campaign's objective."[42] Indeed, the reformers from Oberlin described their efforts in similar military terms and even described the area of their abolitionist canvass as "a battle-field in the war with human slavery."[43] Finney would have called it "spiritual warfare," but whatever terminology was used, it was truly a "revival in abolitionism."[44]

A Breakwater against the Surges of Skepticism

Once these lecturers had a chance to settle misunderstandings by clarifying their dedication to peaceful change (despite the militaristic rhetoric of their letters), abolitionism appeared to some formerly hostile opponents as a reasonable movement. As historian Paul Goodman suggests, just as they had earlier been deceived by colonizationists, people discovered that they had also been misled by groundless prejudice against immediatism. Especially in direct debates with colonizationists, these abolitionists were able to convincingly demonstrate the impracticability of sending millions of African Americans back to Africa, the opposition of free blacks to the scheme, and the concealed proslavery bases of colonizationist leaders.[45]

From late 1834 to early 1836, Oberlin lecturers had been concentrated in Ohio, New York, and Massachusetts, and nearly two-thirds of all AASS auxiliary societies had been formed in those states. Conversely, states like Pennsylvania, Connecticut, and New Jersey, places where abolitionists had made few inroads, contained only thirty-two, fifteen, and six societies, respectively. Noting the connection between the organized lecturing campaign (the agency system) and the unmistakable growth of abolitionist sentiment, the executive committee of the AASS cut their publications' budget by more than two-thirds and directed their most aggressive efforts toward swelling their force of agents.[46]

The expanded agency system was to be made up of seventy men, a number of powerful biblical significance. These men were to evangelize like the seventy men Jesus called after first selecting his twelve apostles.[47] Weld had primary responsibility for selecting new recruits, assisted by the abolitionist poet John Greenleaf Whittier and Lane Rebel Henry Stanton. These men visited Northern colleges to enlist "men of the most unquenchable enthusiasm, and the most obstinate constancy."[48] They made extraordinary efforts to recruit young theological students who they believed "exhibited better specimens of intellectual and moral worth."[49]

The Oberlin Institute was the first place Weld turned to recruit more helpers in the cause. Oberlin students had proven themselves as the embodiment of "intellectual and moral worth," and their participation among the "seventy" would be key. However, when Weld appealed to Oberlin leaders for help, he ran into some unexpected resistance: Charles Grandison Finney.[50] Though he rejoiced at the results of the recent lecture tours of his students, Finney maintained (as he would the entire antebellum period) that focusing solely on abolitionism often confounded broad revivalism and that oftentimes violent responses to antislavery agitation was a prelude to civil strife that threatened to tear apart the United States.[51] However, Finney had also taught his students the value of independent thinking and refused to strong-arm students away from antislavery lecturing.[52] Moreover, Weld's own barrage of letters to his Oberlin recruits was convincing enough to override much of Finney's hesitancy.[53] In the end, most of the Oberlin lecturers who had gone out before accepted new agencies among the "seventy," and even more students joined up for the first time.[54] Among those of the "seventy" who have been identified by historians, nearly a third were from Oberlin.[55]

Agents were to be paid between $500 and $600 per year, a generous sum considering that Oberlin Institute professors' salaries never exceeded that amount in any year prior to the Civil War.[56] Still, many recruits required advances on their pay to defray their initial expenses. Since the society was then stretched financially and unable to meet these requests, some recruits could not accept their appointments for lack of funds. Oberlin's students in particular, many of them already having to work their way through college by the sweat of their manual labor, would need some considerable advances on their pay. However, Weld realized that the participation of the Oberlin contingent was vital to the success of the enterprise. When it became obvious that their involvement was in jeopardy, his high esteem for them led Weld to beg funds from AASS leaders, who were able to personally advance them each five to fifteen dollars apiece. If the executive committee remained unmovable in their decision not to advance lecturers' salaries, Weld offered to pay the Oberlin men directly out of his own pocket, an amount that would have been hundreds of dollars.[57]

Once on their feet, the Oberlin agents were some of the most widely dispersed of the group, with assignments in New York, Pennsylvania, Connecticut, Michigan, Ohio, New Hampshire, and Massachusetts. Hiram Wilson accepted his assignment as "agent to the Negroes in Canada," and James Thome sailed to Antigua, Barbados, and Jamaica to report back on the results of British emancipation, which had been declared in 1833.[58] They were also the busiest out of the gate. While the AASS agency committee called the rest of the "seventy" to New York City for a multiweek crash training session, those from Oberlin who were already alumni of Weld's 1835 Oberlin/Cleveland school of abolitionism bypassed the conclave and immediately went to work.[59]

The Oberlin agents were again frustrated to initially find themselves stymied by the effects of misinformation that had been circulated regarding William Lloyd Garrison. Before, their biggest obstacle had been overcoming exaggerated misrepresentations of Garrison and immediatism. Now, as they approached antislavery as a religious crusade to convert men and women to abolitionism, Oberlin's abolitionist agents had to explain to potential converts Garrison's broad censure of the churches and clergy. Many Americans considered these institutions to be the very loci of spiritual authority and guidance. Yet the conservatism of church governing bodies with regard to the slavery question proved to be one of the most formidable obstacles to the abolitionist agenda, forming, as James G. Birney famously declared in 1840, "the bulwarks of American slavery."[60]

Garrison openly criticized the institutional churches and the clergy that led them for their refusal to speak out against the institution. National church bodies often included members and even ministers who were slave owners. However, while they sternly rebuked those with whom they were in communion for sins such as drunkenness, seduction, murder, or other grave sins, few Northern churches or their leaders spoke out against slavery in a similar way. While Southern pulpits were used to defend slavery, Northern ones seldom pointed out their errors, and, by their silence, actually tightened slavery's grip. In fact, many Northern clerics encouraged a patently anti-abolitionist agenda and used their authority to stifle debate over the slavery issue. For the sake of national denominational unity, ministers attempted to quiet antislavery agitation in their churches. When it became an issue, they attempted to shut it down by barring their doors to antislavery speakers and criticizing them in the press and by passing resolutions at national conventions recommending for punishment those who circulated or subscribed to antislavery publications.[61]

As he had promised in the *Liberator*'s first issue, Garrison did not "equivocate" in meeting this opposition.[62] His description in the *Liberator* of one Ohio church body as a "CAGE OF UNCLEAN BIRDS, AND SYNAGOGUE OF SATAN" after it wavered on an official statement regarding slavery was not unique.[63] If they would not at least allow abolitionists a hearing, to say nothing of outwardly denouncing slavery, Garrison asked, "What then is 'the Church' but the synagogue of Satan, and 'the great mass of the clergy' but hirelings, dumb dogs that cannot bark.'"[64] His intent was to raise the standard of Christian revolt against "the powers of darkness," and he increasingly characterized those church leaders who compromised with social evil as being under "Satanic influences," perhaps even more so than slaveholders themselves.[65] In doing so, however, he potentially alienated many religious Americans who represented the abolitionist lecturers' most likely converts.[66]

By the 1830s, Garrison was also well on his way to a conclusion that the church and its attendant institutional hierarchy stood in the way of the divine order that God intended; the slavery issue simply made it more obvious. Garrison charged that by frustrating churchgoers from the chance to

William Lloyd Garrison (from Grimké, *William Lloyd Garrison* [1891])

live their lives in obedience to God's moral law, denominational hierarchies were exercising a despotism similar to that of the slaveholder.[67] To those that would label him an infidel, Garrison replied that he was so "only in the same sense in which Jesus was a blasphemer, and the apostles were 'pestilent and seditious fellows, seeking to turn the world upside down.'"[68]

Nonetheless, Garrison's logic was lost on most Northern church leaders. He and the *Liberator*, though not speaking officially on behalf of the AASS, stood for abolition generally in many ministers' minds. The Massachusetts and Connecticut Associations of Congregational Clergymen passed resolutions effectively closing their churches to all "itinerant agents and lecturers" who threatened to disturb the peace of their church and their authority as leaders.[69] This, in turn, made it harder for abolitionists to make headway with already skeptical audiences. Abolitionists from Oberlin attempting to penetrate into New England often found "many of the friends of Christ" arrayed against them. The initial hurdle of trying to explain why religious bodies appeared opposed to their message threatened to undercut their effectiveness.[70]

Still, although initially having to spend valuable time explaining how the antislavery movement could possibly have God's support despite the apparent opposition of the church, abolitionists from Oberlin were largely successful in playing down the fears of churchgoing audiences who had come to equate abolitionism with fanaticism and infidelity. Like Garrison, they appreciated the power of the clergy over their flocks and held the same opinion of what organized churches ought to be. However, his belief that "the Church, so called," must "be dashed in pieces" was incompatible with the emphasis Oberlinites placed upon the need to reform it from within through "bold preaching of the truth as they saw it, and for plain dealing with the brethren whom they thought unjust and misguided."[71] They sensed that Garrison's idea of a proper ecclesiology ignored the need for a united community of believers and feared that, alongside the destruction of church bodies that winked at slavery, he also sought "the annihilation of the *true* Christian church." Ecclesiastical abolitionists did not always accept the validity of existing denominational structures, but they still acknowledged the need for sanctified abolitionists to worship together in purified churches of their own.[72]

Oberlin abolitionists became well known for "arresting or preventing the infidelity which has, in some cases, been associated with anti-slavery and other reforms." Wherever they went, they attempted to appear as both Christians and abolitionists. Their lives and labors, alumnus Timothy Hudson wrote, were "an unanswerable demonstration that the Gospel makes men true reformers, and that the doctrine in which extreme conservatism and infidel radicalism seem agreed, that Christianity and reform cannot go together, is an arrogant lie." As ecclesiastical abolitionists, Hudson concluded, "Oberlin [community members have] erected a breakwater against the surges of skepticism, which has saved many souls from ruin."[73]

Though the abolitionists from Oberlin were just as disappointed as the most radical Garrisonians in their frustration with churches and their leaders, they registered their disapproval through earnest pleas to repent. Certain actions or individuals aroused their scorn, but they saw little use in damning those who were only vicariously associated with the "bad seeds."[74] Indeed, Oberlin Institute student John Alvord saw the prospects for abolitionist conversion much more likely through "a *few words* ad[d]ressed to the warm heart of the convert or to a broken down church" rather than "*many words* when poured upon the flinty rock."[75] Professor James Monroe compared Garrison's view of the church to the traveler who found his way blocked by a fallen rock. Rather than sensibly finding men and leverage enough to dislodge the rock from the road, the traveler insisted upon remaining "stock still" until he had devised a universal solvent that would dissolve every bit of rock "of the globe that we inhabit." Monroe deemed such a method "a slow way to reach the end of the journey, to say nothing of the question whether we can afford to lose the granite."[76]

Oberlin abolitionists wanted to make the churches the bedrock of the movement, purifying and organizing them as antislavery societies unto themselves, saving souls and slaves all at once.[77] They approached their largely religious audiences through terms to which they would instantly relate rather than through diatribes that might implicate the majority of the gathered spectators. When a hostile crowd made it necessary, they would gradually work their way into an abolitionist lecture by beginning their address as a sermon on the religious duties of evangelicals. This would sometimes allow them to form an important connection and familiarity with their listeners, especially church members, before moving on to the more controversial duties perfectionism imposed on Christians with regard to abolitionism. This approach allowed lecturers to do more for the cause than might have been accomplished by a more direct effort, though even the indirect course often met harsh resistance.[78]

Especially since most of their opponents would have been much less informed regarding the issues than the trained lecturers, an early and clear demonstration that the Bible opposed slavery sometimes converted those who were "almost totally ignorant, not only of slavery, but of the principles of abolition which [they] had come to oppose."[79] To be sure, proslavery advocates regularly quoted scripture to suggest a biblical support for slavery. However, Oberlin abolitionists, almost all of whom were students trained by theologians like Finney, Mahan, Cowles, Morgan, and others, brought a scholar's knowledge of the Bible to the table, and used it with a revivalist's determination to convert. In their hands, the Bible offered conclusive evidence of the sinfulness of slavery. Often, as William Allan stated, "the result was good for the truth," and local antislavery societies formed in abolitionists' wake.[80]

Every Man and Woman Must Be an Agent

In the late 1830s, the contingent of abolitionists from Oberlin had played a vital part in spreading what slaveholding Kentucky senator Henry Clay called the "contagion" of abolitionism across Ohio, the West, and even parts of New England and the Mid-Atlantic.[81] As in revivals, the antislavery lecturers seldom left towns unaffected. Sometimes, an abolitionist revival would result in the formation of a local antislavery society that would continue the crusade to convert others to immediatism. By 1836, Ohio alone claimed more than a quarter of all abolition societies in the nation.[82] By 1837, there were eighty more local societies formed in the state, bringing

Ohio's collective membership roll to at least 20,000 active abolitionists. Whenever the Oberlin Anti-Slavery Society held its meetings, it did so as one of the largest auxiliaries to the AASS in the entire nation.[83]

Oberlin abolitionists were also able to deal heavy blows to the ACS in the West. In 1838, a colonizationist in Ohio wrote to the secretary of the national society begging him to send competent agents to his region immediately. He wrote, "We have been struggling for the last four or five years, against the current of abolition which has been setting strong upon us." Ohio, he continued, had been "literally flooded with abolition agents and publications," the source of which he traced to "*Oberlin Institute*, where they manufacture the *article* by wholesale." He complained that they "spring up like mushrooms, and overspread the land."[84] They had nearly paralyzed the efforts of the society, and the local auxiliaries that had not "deserted" had essentially ceased to function. The writer feared that if the ACS could not "make inroads upon the enemy," this "hot-bed of abolitionism" could spell its doom.[85]

A key tactic lecturing agents often used in their appeals for support was to have audience members sign an antislavery petition to be sent to lawmakers, urging them to use the power of their elected positions toward particular antislavery measures or to prevent the passage of those they believed had proslavery motives behind them. Similar efforts had played an important role in the Northern emancipation movement in the late eighteenth century, and a steady trickle of antislavery memorials had made their way to the nation's capital through the 1820s, including several from Founding Fathers as influential as Benjamin Franklin. The 1833 constitution of the AASS had admonished its members to influence Congress to end the domestic slave trade and to abolish the institution everywhere it had the constitutional power to do so, especially the District of Columbia and the Territories.[86] Oberlin professors Henry Cowles and Timothy Hudson also incorporated similar language into the constitution of the OASS in 1835, binding members to their "imperative duty" of extending their influence as far as legally possible.[87] Since the most logical way to accomplish this was by directly appealing to congressional representatives, abolitionist agents used the petitioning strategy to their advantage.

The activities of the large numbers of antislavery agents in 1835 initiated the first major stream of antislavery petitions to Congress numerous enough to merit any sustained discussion regarding them among lawmakers. South Carolina Senator John C. Calhoun complained that the new wave of petitions was far greater than anything previous. He rightly believed that they were a Northern attempt to disable the South's most important institution, and he considered their discussion before a national body unacceptable. He pronounced the petitions as "the most daring attempt against American liberty, that has yet been brought forward in Congress, since the foundation of the Republic" and moved that the Senate refuse to receive them altogether.[88]

Calhoun's proposal inspired spirited debate in the Senate, but it did not pass. After weeks of similar discussion in the House, however, a special committee recommended that all petitions relating in any way or to any extent whatsoever to antislavery be laid upon the table without discussion.[89] Though opponents immediately denounced the resolution as unconstitutional and contrary to the rules of the House and the spirit of free discussion, a majority pushed it through, and it was re-passed in similar form at each session until it became a standing rule in 1840.[90]

This immediately became known as the infamous "gag rule," and even more than moderate abolitionists' elucidation of the nuances of immediatism, this act of Congress suggested to many Northerners that antislavery was not just Garrisonian radicalism. Antislavery, or at least the abridgement of every citizens' First Amendment rights that the denial of antislavery petitions represented, became an issue that affected every American. Oberlin's biweekly newspaper, the *Oberlin Evangelist*, pointed out that Congress acted against the wishes of most Americans when it refused to consider the passage of even "righteous laws."[91] Though prominent congressmen called the petition issue "a mere abstraction" and despite the congressional gag (often *because* of it), abolitionists continued to flood lawmakers' offices with antislavery petitions. Some even assured the men to whom they addressed their grievances that they would submit the same petition over and over until it was finally acknowledged from the floor of Congress.[92]

In abolition centers like Oberlin, antislavery petitions circulated continuously. For there not to have been a petition effort under way at any given time would have seemed peculiar. However, in areas not so fully abolitionized (which remained the vast majority), agents often ran into difficulties gathering signatures. Petitions typically demanded the end of slavery and the slave trade in Washington, D.C., and the ending of slavery and nonextension where the federal government had jurisdiction. This meant subscribing one's self to many of the most important aspects of the AASS platform. While ending the embarrassment of slavery in the nation's capital may not have been a hard sell to many Northerners, the remainder of the petition would have been a bitter pill to swallow for men and women who still felt like they had little or no personal investment in the national slavery issue, and who may have doubted the ultimate expediency of a general emancipation in the first place.

As shorthanded agents continued to be overwhelmed, they began to request appropriate literature to help them spread the message and convince any possible holdouts. They wanted solid treatises on slavery and abolitionist ideology to supplement their own efforts when their time was spread thin or to leave behind in a locality after it had already been canvassed. To meet this need, Weld quickly put together some thoughts on abolition and congressional powers that he published under the pseudonym Wythe in the *New York Evening Post* and later collected as a fifty-five-page pamphlet, *The Power of Congress over the District of Columbia*, as well as an anonymous pamphlet titled simply *The Bible against Slavery*.[93]

Oberlin abolitionists lent their efforts to helping with the compilation of some of the more substantial works to meet the literary demand. James Thome assisted Weld with the writing of his most important work, *American Slavery As It Is: Testimony of a Thousand Witnesses*, and contributed his own first-hand experiences with Kentucky slavery to the text.[94] Weld and the executive committee of the AASS so valued Thome's contributions that he was retained to do most of the research and writing for their 1841 publication *Slavery and the Internal Slave Trade in the United States of North America*.[95] In addition to his work with Weld, Thome collaborated with Horace Kimball, his traveling companion to the West Indies, on *Emancipation in the West Indies*, an extremely influential book that demonstrated the practicality, efficiency, and safety of immediate emancipation as demonstrated in the British example. After exhausting himself as one of the first and most active of the AASS lecturing agents in the mid-1830s, Thome struggled for months with serious throat ailments and extreme fatigue. The AASS leadership badly wanted to include Thome among the "seventy" lecturing phalanx, but officials feared that the demanding work might result in the loss of Thome's powerful voice or even "induce pulmonary consumption terminating in death."[96] Still, fellow Oberlin alumnus and AASS executive Sereno Streeter could not allow that such a powerful advocate be lost to disability. On Streeter's recommendations, the society sent Thome to the West Indies, thought to be a much healthier climate where his influential pen rather than his voice would be put to good use. "The wounded soldier must prepare ammunition for those who can fight," Streeter wrote, and Thome's efforts in the Caribbean would be "a most powerful auxiliary in advancing the cause of emancipation by collecting and transmitting facts."[97]

Horace Kimball, it seems, was in worse shape than Thome. Though only in his mid-20s, he was ill most of the voyage and finally succumbed to tuberculosis in 1838.[98] Thus, Thome shouldered most of the burden of turning their observations and interviews with Caribbean missionaries, public officials, and former slaves into a nearly 1,000-page manuscript.[99] He hoped that his work would break the silence that the proslavery press had attempted to maintain regarding the results of British emancipation, the episode Thome described as the "great experiment of freedom."[100] His illumination of the successful emancipation in the British Caribbean was a valuable and revolutionary tool in the efforts to convert those wary of the effects of immediate emancipation. Henry Stanton believed the book contained "truth enough to convert the whole nation," and Weld credited Thome's work with having advanced the antislavery cause more than any other literary effort published in the United States to that point.[101] It would, another booster proclaimed, "abolitionize the world" and "remove all objections but such as spring from negro-prejudice."[102] Demand for the book was so intense that readers quickly snatched up the 2,500 copies of the first edition, and the AASS contracted for the printing of a second edition of 100,000 copies later in 1838.[103]

The growing emphasis that was being placed upon antislavery petitions and memorials, supported by the growing body of antislavery literature that abolitionists were producing, made the need for lecturing agents less urgent. In their wake, lecturers often left considerable numbers of genuine antislavery converts, and they always left abolitionist literature.[104] Once a town had been abolitionized and a lecturer had moved on, a clutch of books by Thome or Weld put into the right hands served nearly the same purpose as the presence of an actual agent. The best of the antislavery literature well explained the doctrines of abolitionism. Though nothing completely took the place of on-site exhorters, these "anti-slavery libraries" were useful in keeping a locality's abolitionism at a fever pitch when lecturers were not immediately available.[105] The petitioning process also gradually became a local, grassroots endeavor, with community organizers able to manage the process from start to finish.

As abolitionists nationwide shifted their efforts to blanketing policymakers with antislavery petitions, Oberlin also sent fewer agents into the field as official representatives of the AASS.[106] Indeed, the shift to petitioning was a fortuitous development. After the financial collapse of 1837, the national society simply could no longer support its army of agents. Now, it was imperative to abolitionists from Oberlin and elsewhere that "every man and woman must be an agent" to "make the most of our abolitionism by bringing it all into use."[107] Statistics of the petitioning efforts after 1837 demonstrate that abolitionists on the local level rose to the challenge. In 1838, the AASS forwarded petitions to Congress bearing over 4,000 names. By 1840, more than two million men and women had signed antislavery memorials that made it to Washington. Moreover, a lion's share of the petitioning labor was done by women, whose involvement tripled the number of petition names secured previously by paid male agents.[108]

As the ranks of salaried agents thinned, abolitionists asserted that "nothing can be made a substitute" for the "*neighborhood influence*" local petitioners offered in their door-to-door canvasses.[109] Indeed, the unsung heroes of the late 1830s were local antislavery workers who went to out-of-the-way places where editors and busy lecturers could not.[110] Since petitioning had become the primary method of agitation by many abolitionists, the local nature of the endeavor increasingly made central authority unnecessary. Once a town had been visited by an antislavery agent or two, anyone could quickly master the skill of petition circulating, especially since they were often armed with an array of supporting abolitionist literature and since most petitions were of a simple, similar form and printed locally.[111] After being shown the way, local centers of abolitionism were more than capable of sustaining themselves. Moreover, antislavery petitions were increasingly being sent directly to Congress, bypassing central AASS offices, since there was no postage charged on constituents' correspondence with their representatives.[112] Many abolitionists believed that the national society was becoming a victim of one of its chief successes.[113]

As state and county auxiliaries began to shoulder the burden of antislavery organization, they increasingly came into conflict with the national society over financial matters. Local societies were becoming self-sufficient and self-contained. Many had their own newspapers, agents in the field, and central offices, and often, their own independent agendas for antislavery agitation. As abolitionism became more localized, abolitionists began to balk at arrangements that bled their precious resources from their own community. The national society attempted to curtail these defections in 1837 by requiring state auxiliaries to pledge a definite amount.[114] However, state contributions were slow coming in that year, and the societies also objected to the intrusions of national agents into their fields of influence. At the national anniversary meeting in 1838, the states managed to push through a resolution that barred all AASS financial agents, unless acting in cooperation with local organizations, from their borders, leaving the national society dependent on the payments of individual pledges that were becoming fewer and farther between.[115] In the year following the 1838 convention, not a single state auxiliary met its annual pledge, and some paid none at all.[116] Moreover, some members of the AASS Executive Committee, once the financial bedrock of the society, had suffered massive individual losses in the financial crash of 1837. President Arthur Tappan went bankrupt, and with his riches also went his practical influence in the organization.[117] By 1839, the AASS could not count on even its most generous benefactors to sustain it, and reigning in the independent-minded state societies seemed equally hopeless.[118]

Oberlin was struggling financially as well. The school had always been supported almost exclusively by the philanthropic donations of American abolitionists. By the late 1830s, however, they sat $50,000 in debt and did not even have funds enough to support the faculty.[119] And just as the AASS was suffering from Arthur Tappan's financial ruin, so too did Oberlin, to whom he had pledged thousands of dollars every year. The most he was able to do after the crash was to cancel the outstanding notes he held against the school.[120]

Still, abolitionists across the country agreed that the Oberlin Institute seemed to be weathering the financial storm better than most abolitionist strongholds.[121] The school's administration as well as its traveling agents put their faith in God to provide, and as it always had, Oberlin refused to fold.[122] John Keep wrote to Levi Burnell urging him to tell the faculty to "hold up good courage—hold on—We will not give up the ship. If *possible*, they shall have their bread—& when on trial it shall appear that the means *cannot be had* then, & not till then, shall we say, God calls us to shepherd our school."[123] President Mahan and the trustees even proposed that the faculty work on a "faith mission" concept of dividing in appropriate amounts whatever funds agents were able to collect.[124] After all, God had led them this far and placed Oberlin at the head of a movement to prepare for His millennium. Moreover, adversity was not unexpected. As Shipherd had made clear at the colony's founding, Oberlin had before it "a mighty work, difficult of accomplishment." Armed with the knowledge that "when any one goes about a great and good work Satan will roll mountains in his way," Oberlin would survive.[125] The world remained to be saved, and no hardship would stand in the way.

CHAPTER THREE

A City upon a Hill
Utopian Oberlin

The Oberlin community did not limit its reform agenda to just antislavery. Much like theology professor Charles Grandison Finney, Oberlinites saw abolitionism as an essential yet partial element of their perfectionist Christianity. John J. Shipherd and Philo Stewart had undertaken their Oberlin enterprise to found a bulwark against sin in all its forms; it was to be a center for reform in the most fundamental sense of the word. Even before the addition of the abolitionist faculty, Oberlin had been founded as a community and school to re-form the world.

The founders had consciously sought out the most pious people in America, and the new gathered community drew up a covenant by which all colonists should live and govern themselves. They shared elaborate plans to live lives that strove toward perfection and to send out the educated products of this environment to help the young nation down the path of regeneration and prepare it for the coming reign of God on earth. Their plan was to cast race, class, and gender by the wayside of the triumphant march of progress and to serve as a beacon of Christian reform. As Shipherd wrote in 1834, "If the ch[urch] in gnl. is a city set upon a hill, Oberlin is on the pinnacle of that hill, both to observation and temptation; for Satan wars against us with a vengeance."[1]

* * *

EARLY OBERLIN DEVELOPED as a utopian community similar to many of the other utopian experiments that popped up across the nation in the 1830s and 1840s. At least 100 of these ventures came into existence between the American Revolution and the Civil War. Though their foundational bases included a wide range of motivations, all strove in some way for a radically new social order. Historian Christopher Clark, in his study of the Northampton Association, writes that utopian communities "were part of a crucial moment in American history, a moment in which ideas about society, culture, and religion were tested and reshaped."[2]

Utopia was a deceptively unreachable ideal—a society where all physical, social, and spiritual forces worked together to fulfill mankind's greatest and most worthy aspirations. In this ideal world, citizens lived and worked together in a social order that was both self-selecting and self-perpetuating. As sociologist Rosabeth Kanter points out, in a utopia, "what people want to do is the same as what they have to do; the interests of the individuals are congruent with the interests of the group." Nineteenth-century communitarians sought comfort and security in the notion that their social order eliminated the need for competition and self-interest and replaced them with mutual responsibility and reliance.[3] Yet this unforgiving and complete dependence on disinterested human agency also made these communities precarious assemblages.

Oberlin was a town and college that not only rebuked the dominant American society but, as an intensive training ground, sent out reformers to change the perceived problems in the world at large. The Christian life that Finney urged his listeners to follow was not just inward-looking, as some important utopian communities were. In Oberlin, Christian perfection would not be accomplished by simple self-reflection and inaction—it had to be continuously nurtured by constant action on behalf of God and the rest of His universe.[4] Finney reminded the residents of Oberlin of their exceptionalism. As part of Oberlin, they possessed responsibilities far beyond the civic duties of most Americans. In the *Oberlin Evangelist*, he declared to each of his readers, "You are a professor of the religion of Jesus Christ. Your profession of religion has placed you on high, as 'a city that cannot be hid.' The eyes of God, of Christians, of the world, of hell are upon you."[5] The allusion to God's chosen "city upon a hill" as well as the religious mission of the Pilgrims was not lost on many who were part of the Oberlin community. Similar references frequently occurred in residents' correspondence, student compositions, and antislavery orations.[6] One resident described Oberlin Institute, the most tangible result of Oberlin's errand into the wilderness, to William Lloyd Garrison as "the Pilgrim School. It is so, most emphatically."[7]

The Oberlin community's utopianism, like that of its Pilgrim forebears, was that of an intentional community. Unlike most communities, which began spontaneously, the Oberlin community was created as a deliberate effort to realize a specific goal or set of goals, in this case, the salvation of the world. To be operational (not to mention durable), such a community had to present a unique agenda that would attract and then retain its followers. To that end, and also similar to their Puritan predecessors, Oberlin was a self-governing, self-selecting body committed to an explicit agenda in the form of a covenant to which all early settlers had to affix their names. Colonists were recruited based on the degree to which their personal aspirations aligned with those set out in the covenant. The goals of the community were more likely to be realized if it were peopled with those who intrinsically exhibited adherence to the terms of the covenant rather than those whose obedience required coercive enforcement.[8] Shipherd and Stewart unfolded their covenant in several private letters early in the planning process.[9] The entire document sought to check particular obstacles to Christian regeneration, and the pledge covered a multitude of potential sins. Colonists did not hold up one section as more important than another; everything came down to each subscriber choosing to do right by one another—to live by the biblical injunction to love one's neighbor as one's self.

Keeping to any one part of the covenant necessarily meant much more than simply following a single rule, and the connections between the covenant and Oberlin's attempt to rid the world of sin and the proslavery mindset were legion. For instance, living as a community of property holders but holding only so much as could be legitimately put to good use discouraged greed, the impulse abolitionists placed behind slavery. A society that lacked such avarice and materialism would be a society that knew no class distinctions. Moreover, working one's own lands would inculcate an increased respect for the value of labor and the desire that everyone, white or black, free or enslaved, should realize it. Avoidance of strong drink and other stimulants or depressants precluded addiction and therefore its deleterious effects on personal relationships, clarity, and purity of thought. The requirement of modest clothing and bland foods supposedly curtailed lust and temptation, strengthened families, and encouraged respect among community members as equals.[10]

Residents clearly sought a God-centered life and heaven on earth, and the town was a religious community even as it became the headquarters and ideological crucible of abolitionism in the West. Its basic antislavery views were a product of its religiosity. Once Oberlin had procured the brilliant theological minds of Asa Mahan and Finney, it also became possible to develop a particular theological expression of the perfection toward which they strove. Oberlin thinkers rejected the extreme Calvinist doctrine of election and advocated individual salvation and free will. As free spiritual agents, men and women were able as individuals to either accept or reject the salvation of Jesus Christ and live their lives while consciously and constantly rejecting sin. Together, Mahan, Finney, Henry Cowles, John Morgan, and others arrived at what would become known as the Oberlin doctrine of Christian perfection, or complete sanctification.[11]

Briefly (since this will be treated in more detail later), Oberlin perfectionism held that just as God forgave one's sins after sincere repentance (justification), so too could He give one the ability to conquer temptation and lead a sinless life if one truly let Him (sanctification).[12] God would allow the truly faithful to solidly grasp righteousness and would consecrate their will to do good. This sanctification, or second "baptism of the Holy Ghost" meant the attainment of a life totally pleasing to God.[13] The sanctified shifted their behavioral allegiance from sinful selfishness to altruistic actions. The continuous and conscious decision to follow God's law would help keep the sanctified from sin and would guide the righteous toward perfection and help establish God's kingdom on earth.[14] Recently, abolitionist scholar John Stauffer has termed this "sacred self-sovereignty," the idea that the kingdom of God was not beyond this world but that each individual had immediate access to divine inspiration and guidance, that God resided within each person.[15]

Oberlin perfectionism confronted the free spiritual agents in Oberlin with the same guidance as the Oberlin Covenant, only each person's relationship was more explicitly with God rather than the community. Still, community members dedicated to serving God through right living necessarily retained their obligations to one another. By the 1840s, Oberlin's brand of religious perfectionism had replaced the covenant in the daily regulation of citizens' lives, since its ideas governed not just a handful of enumerated rules but every decision of a person's life. The last signature appended to the original covenant was added in 1839.[16] Perfectionism, however, remained a constant striving in the community for many more decades.

For the Oberlin community in its strivings against sin, the most pressing evil that stood in the way of American regeneration and "liv[ing] together in all things as brethren" was selfishness and the resulting artificial distinctions between members of American society.[17] These included not just slavery but gender and racial discrimination, as well as the closely related greed and class conflict that were dividing the nation. Once Oberlinites understood God as indwelling within each of them, they could completely dismiss societal hierarchies as sources of order or meaning.[18] They believed that true liberty could only flourish among people living in relative equality, stripped of all artificial obstacles standing between each person and his or her natural right to personal liberty and moral agency.[19] As Finney commonly expressed to his Oberlin audiences, God was "no respecter of persons" and was "interested in the happiness of every individual."[20] Thus, Oberlinites were urged to treat all people "as members of the government of God," even to the extent they should not be thought of as a man or woman, black or white, just a person made in God's image.[21] Oberlinites wanted to fully truly democratize society and hoped to begin that process by blurring the lines that presently divided it. As Professor James Fairchild wrote, "What men most require for the cultivation of fellow feeling, is to look at each other fairly in the face."[22]

Cheek by Jowl: African American Oberlinites

Although the Oberlin Institute came to a strained sense of racial egalitarianism reluctantly, it was still significant. The Oberlin Institute was one of the few establishments of higher learning in America open to African American students. Oneida continued to accept male black scholars into its ranks until it closed its doors in February 1844, but it was a lonely exception. Indeed, Beriah Green, Oneida's abolitionist president, began sending black students to Oberlin even while his own school continued to operate.[23] Not until the mid-1840s, when a few colleges had been founded by men with Oberlin connections or modeled after the Oberlin example, were opportunities for African Americans of both sexes to gain a college education significantly expanded.[24] However, though the Oberlin Institute's uniqueness attracted negative attention from proslavery advocates and racist enemies, even they could not deny the results of black education when these students were given an opportunity to blossom. Oberlin African Americans always believed that education was "the most potent means for the redemption of the Half-Free and the Slave," and their own institution developed into one of the preeminent colleges of the era.[25] Oberlin's African American students celebrated the fact that, unlike at Harvard or Yale, "the blackest child of the poorest parents may drink of the healing stream" of higher education.[26]

While the school and community never became "the pool of Bethesda for the sin of prejudice," as two alumni remembered in 1864, it still came closer "than any other place in the United States" to reaching complete racial acceptance.[27] Black alumnus Samuel Watson declared Oberlin to be

A class photo from the 1855 preparatory department (courtesy Oberlin College Archives)

"about as near the colored man's paradise as any place in the country."[28] This anticipated the conclusion of historian James Brewer Stewart that Oberlin "explored the furthest boundaries of egalitarianism allowed by their age."[29] Over the years there were instances where white students expressed an uncomfortable degree of racism, but these were relatively few and far between.[30] Professor Henry Cowles declared Oberlin's "great business" to be "to educate mind and heart," and he and other leaders would have little reason to be proud of their successes if they failed to eradicate "the notion that 'nature' has made any such difference between the colored and the white 'classes' that it would be wrong for either to associate with the other."[31]

The admissions policy that the Oberlin Institute approved in 1835 was designed "to elevate [African American students] to a common platform of intellectual, social, and religious life" as that available to white students across America. The faculty realized that simply offering African American students the chance to study at an all-black school would only result in the perpetuation of a caste barrier that "a false system has reared between the races." Though they admitted that to found such a school would admittedly be better than no school at all, Oberlin leaders hoped to meet the more difficult challenge of actually maintaining an institution in the breach itself and creating a unique learning environment where students of any race would feel comfortable.[32]

Oberlin's color-blind admissions policy predictably met with disapproval in many places outside of Oberlin. As censure spread from northern Ohio and was distorted, many critics came to believe that the Oberlin Institute was actually pushing out its white students so that only African Americans would attend. One correspondent informed Shipherd that if he did not keep the white and black students segregated to avoid charges of "amalgamation," the whole Oberlin enterprise would "be blown *sky high*" and he would be left with "a black establishment there thro' out!"[33] Satirist Charles Farrar Brown (under the nom de plume Artemus Ward) wrote, "Its my onbiassed 'pinion that they go it rather too strong on Ethiopians at Oberlin." To support his assertion, Brown claimed that on rainy days, white Oberlinites could not find their way through the streets without lamps, "there bein such a numerosity of cullerd pussons in the town."[34]

In fact, African American students at the Oberlin Institute always made up but a small percentage of the student body.[35] By the end of 1835, only three black students had enrolled at Oberlin. In any given year before the Civil War, contemporary estimates suggest that only between 2 to 5 percent of Oberlin's student population was African American (students' racial designations were not recorded in official Oberlin records).[36] Of the approximately 8,800 total students who attended Oberlin College in the antebellum period, only slightly more than 3 percent were black. However, though a small absolute number, more African American students were educated at Oberlin before 1860 than at all other American colleges combined, and the numbers increased almost every year.[37]

Former Lane Rebel James Bradley was the first African American to arrive in Oberlin, and, in 1844, Pittsburgh native George Vashon was the first African American to earn his college degree from the Oberlin Institute. In 1842, Sarah Watson became the first black woman to enroll at Oberlin, and eight years later, Lucy Stanton became the nation's first African American woman to earn a four-year degree. Most African Americans, of course, enrolled in Oberlin's preparatory department.[38] Oberlin never turned away a qualified applicant in any department, regardless of race or gender, but there were certain minimum expectations for admission to the collegiate program, including a rigorous examination in Latin, Greek, and Algebra.[39] Black students were not accorded any special considerations in the classroom if they could not handle the academic rigor at Oberlin. There were equal expectations for everyone.[40]

African American students hailed from all corners of North America, the Caribbean, and Africa. Some of these black scholars were sent directly to Oberlin by abolitionists hoping "to elevate the colored race to a position above 'hewers of wood or drawers of water.'"[41] Black education at Oberlin was also a family affair. Thirteen families accounted for nearly a third of all African American students enrolled at Oberlin before 1860.[42] These included the abolitionist Langston brothers: Gideon, Charles, and John, as well as the Edmonson sisters, Emily and Mary, who had been rescued from the slave ship *Pearl* and supported at Oberlin with funds provided by Harriett Beecher Stowe. The Jones family (originally from North Carolina) is perhaps the best example of how highly many black Oberlin families valued education. Alan Jones made sure that four of his sons graduated from the Oberlin Institute before 1860, a record equaled by few white families in the nineteenth century.[43] When the first of these sons to enter the Oberlin Institute spoke seriously about withdrawing, Alan Jones roughly led him to the back of their Oberlin house, gestured to an ax and chopping block, and told him to "take your choice. You go back to college or you lay your head on the chopping block and I chop it off."[44] The elder Jones would have agreed with John Vashon in wanting his son to be counted among "the smartest youth in the world."[45]

This was the hope of most people in the Oberlin community. The day-to-day operations of the Oberlin Institute and town aimed to demonstrate the absurdity of racism and distinctions based on color to the outside world. Northern African Americans outside Oberlin's borders were segregated in church, refused entry into schools that white children attended, blocked from all employment that white workers could also perform, and almost entirely excluded from the civic process. Moreover, the amount and degree of racial discrimination was steadily increasing, yet, as Boston abolitionist Lydia Maria Child pointed out in the year of Oberlin's founding, few whites where "really aware of how oppressive the influence of society is made to bear upon [free] blacks."[46] The Oberlin community consciously set out to force Americans to think. John C. Calhoun had once remarked that "if there could be found a Negro that could conjugate a Greek verb, he would give up all his preconceived ideas of the inferiority of the Negro." To this, black Oberlin student Fanny Jackson Coppin declared, "Let's try him."[47]

The only distinctions made between white and African American students were those based on "character" and "those founded on mental and moral worth."[48] Oberlin's dining halls, classrooms, and religious exercises were fully integrated.[49] Students were completely free to choose their own seating arrangements and were never forced by administrators to sit beside someone not of their choosing.⁵⁰ However, black students, especially former slaves, were said to often be the most sought after dining hall or classroom companions, a situation that, owing to black students' relative scarcity, often led to intense competition and jockeying for position by white students, both male and female.⁵¹ Though it does not appear that students of different races ever lived in the same room, it was not because any college policy prohibited it (Oberlin's two main dormitories, Tappan and Ladies Halls, could only accommodate approximately 200 students, usually in single rooms). Since dorm space was limited, most young scholars lived in private homes in town, often with prominent citizens or professors' families.⁵² Here, too, the color-blind spirit prevailed. Finney was said to have "never been without a colored student at his table," and the John Mercer Langston household included at one point not only his wife and five children but three mulatto sons of a Louisiana planter and a young boy from Africa.⁵³ The 1850 census shows twenty-nine African Americans, many of them students, living in eighteen white households.⁵⁴ This level of integration was exceptional in antebellum America, and in a state of affairs that would have been truly scandalous elsewhere, it was not unheard of for African American male students to board in the same house as their white female classmates.⁵⁵

Though there was not an African American faculty member in the antebellum decades, select black students were among those chosen to mold young minds as teachers in the fully integrated preparatory department. Fanny Jackson Coppin was one of these instructors in 1864 and 1865. She remembered that some of her students were surprised when they first saw their teacher, yet there were no signs of insubordination. Eventually, her class became so popular that it had to be divided into four sections. Coppin well remembered the delight of principal Edward Fairchild when he had to subdivide her class once enrollment topped eighty. She summed up her Oberlin teaching experience as "an overwhelming success."⁵⁶

African Americans were elected to leadership positions in prestigious student literary societies such as the Union Society, Theological Literary Society, and the Young Ladies' Literary Society. Here, African Americans played an important role in shaping the opinions of their white classmates. Besides exposing them to a perspective belonging uniquely to antebellum African Americans, black students often actively criticized their white counterparts' arguments and helped develop them into thorough, practical, and inclusive approaches to reform and education. In the preparatory

Fanny Jackson (Coppin)
(from Coppin, *Unwritten History*
[1919])

department, similar discussions fascinated outsiders. "I listened to quite a discussion . . . between the tutor a white lady, and a colored man," one journalist wrote. "Much greater freedom between pupils and teachers is allowed here than at any other institution."[57] In the more rudimentary educational environment of the Liberty School, established in 1844 for the elementary education of black adults, even newly free former slaves felt entirely free to express their opinions, challenge their white instructors, and actively participate in interracial dialog, discussion, and debate.[58] These debates were signs of interracial vitality, since critique and discussion were welcomed and encouraged, and they occurred without students losing respect for each other. Indeed, these encounters often resulted in enduring friendships.

In intimate encounters like these, black and white Oberlin students learned to fully trust one another and developed a sense of empathy based on shared experience and mutual understanding. Though these experiences were of great consequence to young white Oberlinites, they were life-changing to their black classmates. As a boarder in Professor Henry Peck's household, Fanny Jackson was "regarded as an honored member of the family circle." Though she credited her white roommates with having "a great influence upon her life" and as "a potent factor in forming her character," her influence on them was perhaps greater. Jackson was born a slave, and her stories of bondage helped her budding abolitionist sisters develop an uncommon and powerful empathy that brought them to tears. For Jackson, that demonstration of not just sympathy but compassionate identification "seemed to wipe out a little of what was wrong."[59]

John Mercer Langston remembered his close interactions with white classmates as "the most interesting and pleasant portion of my life." One of the fastest friendships he made as a young scholar was with a white student named Henry Howe. They both had rooms in Tappan Hall in 1849, and the Sunday before the commencement of the term, Henry stopped by Langston's room and invited him to play checkers and read Latin back in his own room on the fourth floor. This simple gesture of kindness "astonished" Langston, since he "had never before had a young white friend who was willing to treat me as his friend. . . . I felt as Topsy felt when Eva spoke a word of kindness and love to her." He wrote to Henry, "I can not begin to tell how much your conduct then led toward making me what I am. It led me to feel that after all there might be something in me. This is the feeling that begets effort. This is the feeling that brings success to effort."[60]

The Oberlin community also encouraged its nonstudent African American residents to excel and play prominent civic roles, and they did not shrink from the challenge. In fact, this widely known aspect of the community was one of the magnets that drew African Americans there in the first place. In other Northern communities, as one abolitionist remarked, black residents might "form a very small portion of the population, and are dependent, they receive protection and favors," but when they begin to "increase and compete with the laboring class for a living, and *especially when they begin to aspire to social equality,* they cease to be 'interesting negroes' and become 'niggers.'"[61] This, however, was not the case in Oberlin, where the large proportion of African Americans in the community competed as businessmen with their white townsmen (who also, importantly, often called them "Sir" or "Mr." when addressing them).[62]

Of course, black Oberlinites had a long way to go to catch up with their white neighbors economically. Most of them had arrived in Oberlin with little more to their names than the clothes on their back, and none, with the exceptions of John Mercer Langston (a lawyer) and perhaps grocer John Watson, could be considered well-off. Accordingly, most African Americans lived in the southeast quadrant of town where rent was cheapest, and they seldom had bank accounts or large estates.[63] Nonetheless, as one observer wrote, "The usual prejudice against Black tradesmen exists here in a very slight degree, if at all. . . . A man is regarded in Oberlin, to a great extent, according to his personal worth and not for his color."[64] When added to the perfectionist atmosphere already impelling Oberlinites to self-reliance and excellence in all they did, Oberlin's progressive stance on race fostered a class of African American citizens that were able to stand as a rebuke to racist arguments claiming that they were incapable of fending for themselves in a modern society. The inevitable contrasts that Southern observers would be forced to make between educated free African Americans in the North and the "degraded" slaves of the South would help "burn slavery out by the roots."[65]

Indeed, black Oberlinites became so self-confident that they simply ignored those who did not show them what they believed to be an appropriate degree of respect, and comported themselves in a way that, were some racial insult to be directed at them, it would be the insulter who would clearly be made to look the fool.[66] Oberlin's racial relations seemed to prove that, as black alumnus John Mercer Langston declared, African Americans and whites could truly live "cheek by jowl" in freedom and equality if simply given the chance.[67] And their identity as "equals" would have strengthened their identities as "Oberlinites." Progressive whites journeyed over hundreds of miles and through countless hardships to join the community. Determined African Americans did that (and more) for the same reason. Together, they formed an uncommon bond based on trust, empathy, determination, and shared struggle. In a world that hated African Americans for the color of their skin, there did exist an exceptional community where blacks and whites could actually trust one another, love one another, and embolden each other toward greatness.

The Work of Female Education

Women were also welcome to enroll at the Oberlin Institute and claim their own privileged place among Christian Americans. In the first college circular, Shipherd announced that one of the primary goals of the Oberlin Institute was "the elevation of the female character, bringing within the reach of the misjudged and neglected sex, all the instructive privileges which hitherto have unreasonably distinguished the leading sex from theirs."[68] Just what Shipherd meant by "all instructional privileges" remained unclear. Philo Stewart, Shipherd's earliest Oberlin associate, believed that while women's education was vitally important for the success of the Oberlin enterprise, it was also crucial for the health of the nation. "The work of female education must be carried out in some form," he wrote, "and in a much more efficient manner than it has been hitherto, or our country will go to destruction."[69] The Oberlin founders intended to provide a measure of fair play in the education of America's women.

Professor James Fairchild frequently advocated the Oberlin coeducational experiment, and his views are instructive in attempting to pinpoint the intentions of the founders with regard to women. His two main arguments in support of Oberlin's course were that society had a sacred obligation to educate its women as the full human beings that they were, and that they would ultimately be a "civilizing influence" on Oberlin men, well-preparing them for their public ministerial lives after graduation.[70] Fairchild presented the Oberlin position that in a coeducational environment, the "animal man" was kept subordinate in the presence of "these higher beings." Fairchild believed coeducation to be the most efficient way to make men out of boys and "gentlemen of rowdies."[71]

However, women studying at the Oberlin Institute did not limit themselves to training as adjuncts to future husbands' utopian dreams. Perhaps their greatest contribution to the perfectionist and utopian mission of the Oberlin community was their active involvement in the abolitionist movement. Many Oberlin ladies arrived with a solid abolitionist background, and these women were instrumental in shaping the antislavery ideology of the other female students. For instance, Betsey Mix Cowles had spent many of her pre-Oberlin years working on behalf of antislavery through the Ashtabula Female Anti-Slavery Society.[72] Lucy Stone was an ardent Garrisonian by the time she enrolled at Oberlin. She kept a picture of Garrison in her room throughout her Oberlin tenure and promoted the *Liberator* and other antislavery periodicals on campus.[73] Others arrived in Oberlin with unimpeachable abolitionist pedigrees. Sallie Holley's father, New York abolitionist Myron Holley, was a founder of the antislavery Liberty Party in 1839. Frances Russwurm's father, John Russwurm, was the abolitionist editor of *Freedom's Journal*, the first African American owned and operated newspaper in the United States.[74] Rosetta Douglass was the daughter of Frederick Douglass and had assisted his abolitionist efforts at home and at the offices of the *North Star* before she enrolled at Oberlin.[75]

Perhaps one reason for the extra zeal and effectiveness of the Oberlin ladies in their antislavery efforts came from their intimate contact with former slaves. Many members of female groups like the Young Ladies' Literary Society (YLLS) and the Oberlin Female Moral Reform Society were positioned in ways that allowed them unique and direct access to men and

Sarah Margru Kinson, Oberlin student and the youngest of the Amistad captives (from *American Phrenological Journal and Miscellany* [1850])

women born into slavery. These contacts, as historian Stacey Robertson notes, "were transformative experience[s]," and they "awakened women to the real life horror of the institution."[76] The YLLS held its first meetings in the home of a former slave, the mother of one of Lucy Stone's pupils.[77] Stone was also a teacher in the Oberlin Liberty School.[78]

Since the Oberlin Institute was the only American college open to females for several years, many female students had been born in or had lived for a considerable amount of time in the South. Indeed, many of the Oberlin women had been previously enslaved. Antoinette Brown Blackwell remembered one of her classmates who had arrived in America onboard a slave ship. Though she had been rescued from bondage and was receiving a college education, she often rose at YLLS meetings to discuss the horrors of slavery. "My people, my poor people" was her poignant refrain.[79] Fanny Jackson had moved her white friends to tears when she spoke of her slave past.[80] Sarah Margru Kinson, who had been the youngest of the Amistad captives, had been enslaved in Africa in 1839 at age six and was marched 100 miles from her home to the slave pens of the coast. Her Oberlin compositions offered chilling glimpses into kidnapping and the African slave trade.[81] Connections such as these undoubtedly played a crucial role in the YLLS's decision to empty its "budget box" to aid needy "fugitives" when they came through Oberlin.[82]

African American women were particularly important in the aggressive stance of Oberlin's female abolitionists. These well-educated black women were able to develop more articulate arguments against the peculiar institution, and their often times intimate connections with slavery, many as former slaves or just a generation removed from bonds, allowed them to strike at both the core of proslavery racism and the hearts of ambivalent listeners like few others could. One of these most able of these women was Lucy Stanton. Though born free in Cleveland, Stanton was never far removed from the specter of slavery. Growing up, she lived in an abolitionist household that functioned as a busy shelter on the Underground Railroad, so she often found herself in the midst of dozens of fugitives at a time, all with stories to tell.[83] Her graduation essay, "A Plea for the Oppressed," was one of the most passionate addresses offered by an Oberlin woman in the cause of antislavery, and the most touching parts of her essay were her identifications with the enslaved: the horrors of a slave mother sold away from her children; the terror of a sexually violated slave girl; and the numbness of the same girl after she had been splattered with the blood of her brother, shed by the master's hand as he tried to protect her dignity. Yet Stanton's plea was not the lament of a defeated race. Her address ended with the expectation of deliverance, sure and soon. Hers was a promise, shared by all the Oberlin ladies who concurred in her address, to do all in their power to bring about complete emancipation. That done, it would not be long before "the shout of joy gushes from the heart of earth's freed millions!" "How sweet," she wrote, "how majestic . . . float those deep inspiring sounds over the ocean of space! Softened and mellowed they reach earth, filling the soul with harmony, and breathing of God—of love—and of universal freedom." Despite the fact that applause had been discouraged at the ceremony, the crowd roared its approval at the close of Stanton's address.[84]

Oberlin women were also conspicuous in the town's annual First of August celebrations, observed each year to mark the anniversary of British West Indian Emancipation in 1833 and as an alternative to an often hypocritical (from the standpoint of abolitionists) Fourth of July holiday. The *Oberlin Evangelist* called West Indian Independence Day "a more interesting time to the friend of human rights, than the anniversary of American Independence, so long as the principles of the declaration of that independence are so utterly disregarded by our slave holding and pro-slavery citizens."[85] In fact, as historian David Brion Davis points out, the celebration was not only condemnatory of slavery itself but intended to remind the world that Britain, "the tyrant symbolically overthrown every Fourth of July," had much to teach the United States about the meaning of freedom.[86] The day's festivities were planned by the town's African American leaders, and the proceedings

Lucy Stone (from *Illustrated News* [1853])

were very often a chance for black leaders and Oberlin ladies to demonstrate their "reciprocal supportive relationships" that they had developed in their close connections over the years.[87] It was clear to the young organizers that some of the most zealous advocates of the African American cause in Oberlin were, in fact, those women who were busy breaking the traditional mold of the woman's sphere in the cause of the slave. Thus convinced, black leaders like William Howard Day and Daniel Seales extended invitations to Oberlin ladies, including Lucy Stone, Antoinette Brown, Emiline Crooker, and Mary Crabb, to address the First of August crowds on relevant topics. On platforms that sometimes included only a single white male participant, multiple white and black Oberlin women passionately spoke out against the iniquities of American bondage.[88]

One such occasion was Lucy Stone's first public address. Leading up to the event, the gravity of what she was about to do set in. Here she was, a woman, and she was soon to speak publicly on one of the most explosive political issues of the day. Her "siege of terrible headaches" betrayed her trepidation, yet when the time came for Stone to address the massive crowd, she did so with a powerful command and confidence that impressed her audience.[89] Her speech, though a bit melodramatic and naive, was a prospectus of her abolitionist efforts to come. She pointed out that a "rectified public sentiment" must be the primary remedy for evil. It did not matter, she further noted, that "the strong arm of the law may be around systems of wrong, nor though they may be as hoary with age as guilt. Let but the indignant frown of a virtuous public be concentrated upon them, and they must inevitably perish." She concluded her first public speech by comparing West Indian emancipation to Christ's resurrection.[90]

A Cleveland newspaperman in the audience was especially impressed. Stone's speech, he wrote later, "gave evidence that a mind naturally brilliant had not been dimmed, but polished rather" by her Oberlin education. He recognized her as "one of those who believe that neither color nor sex should deprive of equal rights, and true to her principles, she ascended the stand and in a clear full tone read her own article."[91]

That Mental and Manual Toil

For all Oberlin students—black and white, male and female—the institute's manual labor system best exemplified the convergence of the community's utopian ideas. This ultimate leveling experience instilled respect for all classes of people, reverence for the opposite sex, appreciation of all races, and empathy with those in bonds.[92] Moreover, Oberlin initially required all of its students to work as many as four hours a day at manual labor, with no exceptions.[93] "If a student will not work and study," Shipherd wrote, "he leaves Oberlin." In his first official report, the founder stressed that manual labor was indispensable to a complete education since it underscored the equality of students, "all of both sexes, rich and poor," preserved health, promoted clarity of thought, allowed some pecuniary advantage, formed habits of industry and economy, and established in all students a familiarity and respect for "common things."[94]

Administrators procured an 800-acre "farm" to employ the labor of its students. This in itself initially provided all the working effort that students could offer since only about 50 acres of the 800 were cleared and under cultivation. Students undertook the heavy toil of felling trees, clearing land, and plowing fields. As pasture expanded, the school obtained livestock and beasts of burden to provide both sustenance and more tasks for the students.[95]

Oberlin had not been alone among American schools in experimenting with such a system. Lane Seminary, had incorporated manual labor into its curriculum, and its student body was made up of a large number of Oneida Institute alumni, a school founded on manual labor principles in upstate New York by Finney's mentor George Gale. However, by the mid-1830s, what historian Paul Goodman describes as a "manual labor boom" in American schools had ended.[96] For most, the benefits of labor and study simply did not outweigh the costs. In the volatile economic environment of the late 1830s, most schools were not willing to pay more for farms, workshops, etc., than they were able to offset with profit. One by one, manual labor institutions like Andover, Knox, and Denison dropped the department from their operational plans, and in the process, cut off poorer students' only access to a quality education.[97]

The Oberlin community, however, refused to reduce its labor system to ciphers on a balance sheet. As the rest of the country moved beyond the fad of manual laborism, Oberlin's stubborn adherence to the system demonstrated its rejection of the social order of the outside world as well as its sharp distinction between moral and material progress. Though manual labor received less emphasis as years went by, it was never completely abandoned, and the motto "Learning and Labor" remains emblazoned on the official college seal. Manual labor embodied nearly everything that Oberlin stood for, and Shipherd early on equated the survival of the community's and institution's basic ideologies with the health of its college labor system.[98] Their program was far from profitable, but profit was never the ultimate goal (though the diminishing of expense was always welcome). Rather, as Weld put it, the "grand design of the system" was to enable the student "to expand his views, to elevate his aims, to ennoble his purposes," demonstrating obedience to God's plan and perfecting the moral state of each individual and the society of which he was a part.[99] Henry Cowles agreed that these qualities caused God to "*smile on the enterprise,*" since the system, as Oberlinites and Weld understood it, met the most pressing "*wants of the age.*"[100]

The practical effect of Oberlin's scheme was to eliminate the gap between the developing white- and blue-collar classes that was obtaining in American society as a whole. The haves and the have-nots outside of Oberlin were increasingly classified by their proximity to physical toil. Elites North and South did not dirty their hands in manual drudgery. Lower-class whites, free blacks, and slaves were those who earned their livelihoods by the sweat of their brows. To be sure, bourgeois culture in the North gave lip service to its commitment to and respect for free white labor, but in reality it had become an implicit part of the American Dream to move as far beyond the toiling masses as one could on one's way to wealth.[101] At Oberlin, however, regulations requiring manual labor applied equally to scions of wealthy Southern planters, daughters of Northern merchants, and former slaves. Even the faculty and administration did their share of labor for Oberlin when needed.[102] One observer in 1849 recognized President Asa Mahan "setting the example in this particular." As Mahan drove his work wagon through the college square on the way to the institute's farm, he had "his coat off, holding the reigns in one hand and a hoe in the other with a negro sitting on each side of him, and two white men behind."[103] He was always eager to pitch in, "especially when any 'dirty work' was to be done. . . . Its necessity made every form of labor honorable."[104] Another early visitor to Oberlin described the school as "emphatically a PEOPLE'S COLLEGE" where industrious students are not "made to feel that poverty and labor are disgrace; . . . each one is made to feel that labor is honorable, and idleness a disgrace, to the rich as well as the poor."[105]

Of course, the common brotherhood encouraged by Oberlin's manual labor system included African Americans, who had long been the innocent victims of racist connections between labor, race, and servility. The Aristotelian supporting logic for this view was best articulated in the 1850s by James Henry Hammond of South Carolina. In his famous "mudsill" speech, Hammond summarized the long-standing Southern mind-set that held that there was, and always would be, a lower, "mudsill" class for the upper classes to rest upon. These most degraded workers performed the menial work that allowed the higher classes to properly advance "civilization." In America, this drew a sharp line between the slaves (and by extension all African Americans), who "required a low order of intellect and but little skill" in performing the most laborious manual labor, and those who, in their rightful and natural exemption from labor, managed them and pursued more "civilized" and refined pursuits with their time.[106]

Especially in Ohio and other free states where the existence of slavery did not create an automatic division between such "honorable" and "dishonorable" labor, the desire to remove one's self as far as possible from drudgery and the stigma of slavery was strong.[107] The pattern established in the South whereby African Americans did the work nobody else would do and every white man sought to be the oppressor of the one beneath him was easily transferable to the North.[108] It did not help that Hammond and other proslavery spokesmen described Northern white wage workers as hardly distinguishable from slaves.[109]

To Henry Cowles and other Oberlinites, this mind-set was "one of the giant evils of the civilized world," and any sensible student of history must agree. The contempt shown toward labor and the laboring classes by people like Hammond "abstracted from the race the spirit of selfishness to reign rampant over human hearts!" In fact, Cowles argued that the very essence of slavery was an "anti-labor aristocratic spirit." It would be "a rank absurdity," he believed, to educate young republicans in such a manner as to leave that spirit intact, then to hope to "set them to redeem society in our age from the crushing evils of oppression."[110]

Early Oberlin's utopian society created men and women bound by a perfectionist faith to make bare the faults of the world and do whatever it took to correct them. Their neighbors were their brothers and sisters, everyone was welcome, and their basic rule was the golden one of the Bible. They had, as other utopians had tried to do, attempted to create a microcosmic model of society, maintained and supported by "the sacred ideals of equality and liberty." In their isolation, they held off the harmful influence of worldly things and ideas and sought to realize their own version of heaven on earth.[111] Consider the "Oberlin doctrine" as set out in 1839 by Finney, Mahan, and J. P. Cowles. To the question "Why ought I love my neighbor?," Mahan answered, "Because I perceive intuitively that it is right." Cowles thought to add that it was because "my love will be useful to my neighbor." Finney encapsulated both answers in the comprehensive theory that all moral beings intuitively know their obligation to "choose the welfare of all sentient existences." Finney's answer was, "*I ought to love my neighbor because his welfare is valuable.*"[112] Each moral agent had the ethical choice between love and sin, utopia and the world. This was the Oberlin mantra: live the righteous life and love your neighbor as yourself so that, by your example, others may do the same until the certain commencement of the millennium.

CHAPTER FOUR

A Hotbed of Abolitionism

After his expulsion in 1837, disgruntled student Delazon Smith described Oberlin's isolated setting as a "mud-hole, frog-pond, morter-bed, swamp," so remote that he could not fathom why otherwise intelligent students continued to flock to such an "impolitic and very unnatural location."[1] In his old age, Charles Grandison Finney also recalled that during Oberlin's infancy, the community was mired in the midst of the wilderness. After his tenure in cosmopolitan New York City, Oberlin appeared to him "unfortunate, ill-considered, hastily decided upon; and had it not been for the good hand of God in helping us at every step, the institution would have been a failure because of its ill-judged location."[2]

However, James Fairchild, Oberlin alumnus, professor, and president after Finney's retirement in 1866, remembered the peculiar site quite differently. Echoing the philosophy of the founders, Fairchild suggested during the college's fiftieth anniversary celebration that upon closer consideration, it was not difficult to appreciate that Oberlin had developed in the best location possible. As for its isolation, he believed that "the result must be accepted as a vindication. The desirable thing was to secure a community around the college in general sympathy with its educational work, and with little attraction for other interests which might bring in undesirable influences." As he considered the half century of unprecedented intellectual ferment and reform agitation that Oberlin had produced, Fairchild concluded, "To a great extent the world has yielded the Oberlin tract to the uses for which it was selected and consecrated."[3]

Alone in the Ohio wilderness and with community members firmly united in their missionary enterprise, Oberlin was a place, unlike any other in America, where free discussion and legitimately open debate were allowed and encouraged. It was a singular community where ideas that otherwise would have to be carefully stated, if discussed at all, and that were likely to be received with outrage elsewhere could be expressed and debated with complete freedom. The Lane Rebels had insisted upon this guarantee in 1834, and it was also the principal demand of Finney, Mahan, and Morgan before they agreed to sign on to the Oberlin project. In Oberlin, there was no need to shock an audience's sensibilities to be noticed, and neither was there the need to adhere to narrow and limited definitions of various outsiders' notions of what it meant to be a "true" abolitionist.

"Students here are encouraged to search for truth," a group of Oberlin student-abolitionists wrote in 1839, "& to receive no doctrine simply because it is supported by great names, & to reject not simply because it lacks such support."[4] The Oberlin community attracted and welcomed people of all backgrounds into its fellowship. Together, community members calmly and methodically worked through the most vexing questions before the antislavery movement. The most distinguished abolitionists in America went out of their way to visit Oberlin, and as one alumna remembered, the community welcomed all reformers on the understanding "that their theories must stand the test of open and free discussion." "Oberlin," she concluded, "would prove all things and hold fast only that which was good."[5]

* * *

IN FEW PLACES BESIDES OBERLIN could one find such a motley assortment of men and women who were so able and willing to collaborate on the development of antislavery strategy. Oberlin's community included the children of Quakers and slaveholders, former slaves, political organizers, nonresistants, and radical Garrisonians, yet no one was denied a seat at the debate table. Visitors to Oberlin were commonly invited to participate in the college's cross-question classes.[6] Even Stephen Foster, a radical Garrisonian described by one historian as "undoubtedly the most aggressive and humorless reformer ever to grace the antislavery stage," and author of the book *The Brotherhood of Thieves; or, A True Picture of the American Church and Clergy*, was invited to speak his mind in Oberlin multiple times.[7] Despite Foster's assurances during one visit that the Oberlin Church was connected to the Southern slaveholders' churches in a single unbroken "covenant of Hell," Asa Mahan welcomed the debate that took up the evenings of a full October week in 1846 before huge audiences in the college chapel.[8]

Formal discussions of issues such as the "effect of slavery upon the free people of the north," "Would it be the duty of Abolitionists to join the colored people in case of an insurrection," "Would it be practible [sic] to extend the right of suffrage to the colored man of this nation, were they all emancipated," and "the proper sphere of woman" augmented the innumerable private debates that all combined to produce a well-reasoned and practical abolitionist ideology.[9] Speakers never assumed that their positions would be received without thorough consideration, discussion, and critique by the community. Debates on even relatively straightforward issues like support for antislavery newspapers and "popular prejudices" were described as "animated." The YLLS even organized a debate on the "necessity of reading and counseling other opinions than our own."[10]

The members of the abolitionist vanguard coming out of Oberlin were diligent in their adherence to Finney's injunction to always back up words with deeds. As many of them had at Lane, they continued in their efforts at "practical abolitionism" by serving as teachers of Northern African Americans, especially former slaves. "Every candid mind," the *Oberlin Evangelist* reported, "must see that the degradation of the colored man at the north is one of the strongest bulwarks of slavery at the south." The editor identified the most common justification "of the negro-hater, whether found in the northern apologist or southern slaveholder," in support of slavery as the natural condition of African Americans, most of whom were barred from educational opportunities because of an assumed intellectual capacity.[11] Each winter, dozens of Oberlin students spent their only break of the year teaching in schools across the region. They looked especially for opportunities to head up a school for young African American scholars. By the fall of 1840, Oberlin could boast that at least thirty-nine of its most accomplished and able students were engaged in teaching at such academies. Few of these tutors received any compensation for their efforts beyond the necessities of room and board. To support themselves, they were often forced to also lead evening classes at local schools for white children after their African American students went home.[12] The Cincinnati *Philanthropist* advised readers that schools for African American students that sought qualified and dedicated teachers should make their applications directly to Oberlin.[13] The college, the editor pledged, would provide zealous student-educators who possessed the "firmness compounded with much enthusiasm" necessary to lead these academies.[14]

Augustus Wattles and Amzi Barber, Lane Rebel and Oberlin alumnus, respectively, served as general agents of the Ohio Ladies' Society for the

Education of Free People of Color through the 1840s, and they often noted the frustrations that many of these Oberlin student-teachers faced.[15] One young man built with his own hands the schoolhouse for his fifty scholars, mostly former slaves, in Brown County, Ohio. He felt the need to sleep in the building all winter for fear that local whites would otherwise burn it. A derisively designated "amalgamation school" in Pike County was led by an Oberlin woman who was threatened with tar and feathers by a drunken "cut throat" mob if she did not abandon her efforts.[16] George Vashon, Oberlin scholar and son of a prominent Pittsburgh African American family, remained faithfully at his own Pike County teaching post even after all but four black families had been forcefully driven away and his schoolhouse vandalized and eventually burned to the ground.[17]

Perhaps the most notable of these Oberlin-trained teachers was Hiram Wilson, a former Lane Rebel and member of the "Seventy" lecturing phalanx. Immediately after completing his theological degree at Oberlin with the other Rebels, he left for British Canada with nothing to his name but the gift of twenty-five dollars from Finney. His mission was twofold: Wilson hoped to explore the western province of Canada to determine the needs of its black population, most of whom had fled there from bondage in the American South. More immediately, he was to accompany a new friend, a man who had escaped from slavery and made Oberlin one of his last stops on the Underground Railroad from the South, on the last leg of his journey to free British soil. When they arrived in Canada, the men discovered tens of thousands of refugees from slavery who were in desperate need of both material and educational support.[18]

Wilson spent the rest of his life working among the black residents of Canada West. With the help of other Oberlin students, he hoped to found a series of schools in Afro-Canadian communities.[19] His greatest desire was to establish a manual labor school for former slaves patterned after what he had experienced as a student at Oberlin.[20] His dream was realized at the Dawn settlement near Dresden, where refugees who had often suffered at the hands of unscrupulous Canadian whites could learn agricultural methods, mechanical skills, and domestic arts, in addition to receiving a thorough and useful education.[21] Students would labor three to four hours per day in addition to studying to be properly prepare to go forth as teachers and abolitionist missionaries. One former slave involved in the project realized that the program Wilson helped establish "would train up those who would afterwards instruct others" and enable Afro-Canadians to gradually become independent of whites for their intellectual progress and physical prosperity.[22] Wilson intended Dawn to "bring forth upon the Anti-Slavery battle ground Colored champions who will wage a successful warfare."[23]

Hiram Wilson could not possibly meet by himself the challenges with which the hundreds of eager students met. For assistance, he turned to the richest source for empathetic reinforcements he knew: Oberlin.[24] Within the first five years of Wilson's efforts at Dawn, he and his students availed themselves of the services of at least forty-three college scholars, most of whom were Oberlinites he described as "good Samaritans."[25] At least three of his dedicated Oberlin assistants lost their lives to the fierce Canadian frontier elements. Those that lived to return to Ohio most often did so with empty pockets and severely weathered constitutions.[26]

Back at Oberlin, the community members also championed efforts to educate their neighbors who had spent most or parts of their lives in bondage. Though Oberlin's schools were always open to its African American residents, the influx into the town of self-emancipating bondsmen in the late 1830s and early 1840s necessitated the organization of a special school for adults who were just beginning their journey toward literacy.[27] In 1844, the community erected a schoolhouse where those who "were moved by the desire and purpose of elevating themselves educationally and morally," very often elderly heads of households, would be taught by Oberlin Institute students.[28] This "Liberty School" was one of the first things the young John Mercer Langston noticed when he arrived in Oberlin. He described it as the "Faneuil Hall" of former slaves, "in which the negro made his most eloquent and effective speeches against his enslavement."[29] Oberlin student Lucy Stone was a popular teacher in the school, and the speeches to which Langston referred also moved her with their power.[30] Even after spending all day in intense study, these same former slaves would gather in the Liberty schoolhouse again in the evenings to share the stories of their wrongs in slavery that compelled their escape to the North. Langston did not recall many dry eyes among the storytellers or those who listened to their tales.[31] Indeed, it was the testimony of Lucy Stone's formerly enslaved students that most inspired her to continue to battle for emancipation after her graduation from Oberlin in 1847.

Yet a life in bondage left deep psychological scars. One of Stone's pupils in the Liberty School remained so depressed during his early days in Oberlin that he was hardly able to perform the simplest academic tasks. "Robert" rarely raised his heavy eyes from his desk, never spoke in class, and seemed incapable of learning his lessons. This behavior frightened Stone at first, but she made a point of speaking compassionately to him every day.

Gradually, Robert began to shed the pall that he had acquired in slavery. Soon the two could be seen walking together to Liberty School classes, and as they strolled, Robert did much of the talking. He shared with his teacher and friend tales of his painful experiences in slavery, as well as his dreams for the future, and she offered in return an empathetic ear and the promise to do all within her power to correct the evils that had so scarred him.[32]

Stone called Robert "one of the warmest and truest friends I had," and credited him with giving her an education as valuable as the one she offered him at the Liberty School.[33] In her hometown of West Brookfield, Massachusetts, Stone's abolitionism had been informed by an abstract notion of what slavery was and the experiences of the men and women so enslaved. In Oberlin, however, former slaves like Robert gave her a firsthand appreciation for the plight of Southern African Americans and nurtured a genuine empathy that few abolitionists ever acquired. "When I saw how they were *dehumanized*," Stone wrote a family member, "I wondered, that in the wide universe of god, one tongue could be found, that failed to utter its indignant rebuke against all that pertains to so execrable a system."[34]

An Unwelcome School of Abolitionism

Outside the town limits of Oberlin, however, most Americans refused to raise their voice against slavery. Even Oberlin's crusade to educate free African Americans was viewed by many Ohioans as a bothersome cause that hindered their state's advancement. The influence wielded by colonizationists and proslavery advocates during Ohio's first four decades of statehood led a majority of residents to oppose African American influx on all terms. The promise of a college education for black students, especially considering the numbers already enrolled at Oberlin, seemed to many Ohioans an unwanted magnet to members of a "despised" and "degraded" race.[35] To them, Ohio was to be a white man's country, populated by the best and brightest white sons and daughters of the older states. As the local Colonization Society auxiliaries decreased, its members were forced to confront the likelihood of permanently having to contend with the presence of African Americans. Thus many colonizationists shifted their energies to a vigorous support of Ohio's Black Laws in order to head off any further African American immigration into the state. Slavery itself was sometimes opposed, but usually only upon racist grounds and only insofar as it applied to their own state and as a way of preserving the racial status quo.

"Good" Ohioans were those who kept the best interests of their home state in mind and did not just tolerate the institution in slave states but actively encouraged it. One of Ohio's earliest historians, Caleb Atwater, echoed the now-classic refrain of the colonizationists in 1838 when he instructed his fellow Ohioans that "it is our interest, in Ohio, to have slavery continued in the slaveholding states, for a century yet, otherwise our growth would be checked." The wide and deep streams of "wealth, numbers, enterprise, youth, vigor, and the very life blood of the slave-holding states" then pouring into Ohio would be dammed up, "and even roll back to their sources, rendering those states, not merely our equals, but even our superiors, in numbers, wealth, and political power." Their duty as "patriotic citizen[s] of this most prosperous of states ever founded, on the surface of this earth," according to Atwater, was to encourage the institution's incubuslike survival outside its borders. The secret of Ohio's growth depended upon the slave states ignoring good business sense and leaving Ohio to develop manufactures and gather a critical mass of the nation's best minds and most able citizens.[36] Ohio's dependence on slavery was even deeper than Atwater admitted; Ohio farmers fed Kentucky's slaves and depended on the Southern market for their livelihood.[37]

It should come as no surprise, then, that Ohio lawmakers recognized the threat that the town and its college supposedly posed to the state's prosperity and quickly moved to nip the emerging menace in the bud. As James Fairchild remarked, Oberlin had become "the propagandist of . . . new ideas; and thus was the world's quiet disturbed."[38] Over the next several years, Oberlin's opponents in the Ohio legislature undertook a fierce and unprecedented campaign to destroy the growing college and deny official recognition to the town that nurtured such "offensive" abolitionist ideologies. The Oberlin community had taken an enthusiastic stand against Ohio's twin ideological pillars of racism and support for Southern slavery. Enemies sought to punish it and make a dramatic example of its case.

The original charter granted by the Ohio legislature to the Oberlin Collegiate Institute on February 2, 1834, was apparently granted without opposition from lawmakers.[39] Though the founders' ambitious missionary dreams may have struck many as foolish visions with slim prospects for success, there was nothing so offensive about the school to merit legislative resistance. It would not be popularly associated with antislavery until 1835, and its explicit championing of coeducational principles was as yet a moot point, since no women would seek admission into the collegiate course until 1837.[40] Moreover, the Oberlin Institute's primary stated goal was to labor unceasingly for the benefit of western souls, a worthy enterprise for an officially chartered school.

With the clear turn to abolitionism after the arrival of the Lane Rebels and the subsequent national celebrity that the school and town attained, reformers from Oberlin stayed below the radar of what would prove to be a tremendously hostile state legislature only for a short period. In December of 1835, residents of Oberlin commenced their determined campaign to effectively be a thorn in the side of the Ohio legislature by sending in their first petition for the repeal of the state's Black Laws.[41] From that point forward, their relationship with the state government would be an extraordinarily turbulent one.

As the Oberlin Institute grew in late 1836 and early 1837, it sought authorization from the Ohio legislature to expand their board of trustees.[42] However, this was also in the midst of the period when abolitionist missionaries from Oberlin were barnstorming across Ohio in the most intense blitz of antislavery agitation in the United States to date. By 1837, leaders of the Oberlin community had also made themselves odious to conservative politicians by their willingness to exert their influence to sway local elections.[43] When Whig senator John Allen presented the request of his Oberlin constituents to expand their college's board, his bill ran into spirited resistance on the part of several influential Democrats. Opponents rationalized their opposition to an ostensible procedural formality on the grounds that the Oberlin Institute was "under clerical control to a highly objectionable extent." More significant, however, was that the school was commonly known as "a hot bed of abolitionism in that part of the State"—a place where people of all races interacted as equals.[44] Opponents brashly declared that the only recognition they would be willing to give such a dubious institution would be through an outright repeal of their charter. Senator Allen, in his futile defense of the Oberlin bill, urged tongue in cheek that the increase in trustees might actually make it more difficult for the school to hide "their evil practices from the public."[45] Nonetheless, the proposal was indefinitely postponed.[46]

The next month, the Oberlin Institute sought documents of incorporation for their Sheffield Manual Labor School, another branch of the college that had already been opened nearby in Lorain County to accommodate the overflow students who had swelled the main campus beyond its capacities.[47] Included in this group were African Americans James Bradley and Charles and Gideon Langston. Again, the same Ohio Democrats who had led the attack on the trustees bill took the forefront in opposition to this proposal, predicting that the Sheffield campus would become no more than an obnoxious extension of Oberlin and therefore become yet another unwelcome "school of abolitionism."[48] Only after the addition of amendments that limited the school's income and barred nonwhite students from enrolling (which, for unexplained reasons, did not appear in the final version of the bill) could Democratic opposition be overcome.[49]

At the same time, a House bill to incorporate the town of Oberlin arrived on the Senate floor for debate, and as Oberlinites might have expected, it was indefinitely postponed by another lopsided vote.[50] Allen wrote to Levi Burnell, secretary of the Oberlin Institute, that a large majority of the Senate were very hostile to the "abolition doctrines of the North and East and to every thing in reference to them." This was clearly another instance where anti-abolitionists conflated the characteristics of many eastern reformers, which they found repellant, with abolitionists as a whole. Try as they might, abolitionists from Oberlin could not always escape comparisons with their more outspoken and radical counterparts. Allen, however, recognized the distinction, and he described their opponents in the Senate as being "as ultra on one side as I think a section of the abolitionists are on the other."[51] He also lamented what impressed him as the utter impossibility of passing any bill through the legislature that would alter the state's "unholy" Black Laws or any proposal that appeared to favor abolitionists in any way.[52] Oberlin's incorporation bill met with especially harsh criticism because, as Allen complained to Burnell, "the name was Oberlin, and . . . you are considered especially friendly to the blacks."[53]

By the late 1830s, "Oberlin" had become the most powerful political symbol exploited by the enemies of abolitionism in Ohio. The community's reputation was due partially to exaggeration and outright fiction, but there was a great amount of truth in the accusations of its critics. The Western Reserve college and town offered an unambiguous example of all that was supposedly wrong with abolitionism—they threatened the racial social and economic order of Ohio and all the free states. Most ominously to conservatives, Oberlin's and the town's abolitionist missionary advance guard revealed their threat continuously and tenaciously, despite ongoing attempts to crush their spirit. This, of course, only raised their star higher in the eyes of abolitionists across the North. One antislavery editor from New Hampshire even invoked the Romantic poet William Wordsworth, describing Oberlin as "a champion cased in adamant" for the abolitionist cause.[54]

Perfectionist Politics

As Oberlin increasingly took the brunt of political anti-abolitionist abuse in the West, they also learned a trick or two from their tormenters. Despite the increasing legislative attacks, Ohio lawmakers' worst fears regarding Oberlin's potency seemed to be justified as the town and school joined the vanguard of abolitionists who were increasingly turning to the political realm as another potential remedy to the contagion of American slavery. Hostile Ohio lawmakers could only watch in frustration as the tiny Ohio community once again began to influence a shift in the national antislavery movement far beyond what its absolute numbers would suggest.

The transformation among abolitionists from moral suasion and limited organized political involvement to a systematic antislavery voting strategy came about just as the Great Revival of the Second Great Awakening was losing momentum. As religious leaders sought new strategies and tactics to consolidate the gains made in the revival decades, many abolitionists were also considering new approaches and lines of attack in their fight against slavery. To a significant degree, these developments overlapped, resulting in, as historian Douglas Strong terms it, a sort of "perfectionist politics."[55] The process of Oberlin's espousal of political antislavery as an aspect of their abolitionism is an instructive example.

All observers agreed that revivals had been steadily dropping off since 1835.[56] The early successes of Finney and a host of other revivalists had resulted in their emulation by even larger numbers of enthusiastic and persuasive exhorters, yet the end result was often one itinerant following upon the heels of another, often presenting audiences with conflicting messages. This was, as historian Nathan Hatch shows, a thorough process of democratization in American spiritual life, but it also meant that it was a period of rapid religious fragmentation.[57] In such an environment, hopeful revivalists had to set themselves apart from others to retain authority, and quite often this was done through appeals to greater and greater emotionalism and sensationalism. Finney was especially concerned about issues of revival quality and especially of backsliding converts.[58] He would remember in 1845 that the revival fire that swept behind his efforts in 1830 and 1831 was "more superficial" than was truly necessary for thorough conversion, and that it had often degenerated into a spirit of "fanaticism and misrule."[59] Conversion based entirely on emotion and outward performance had no substance. Superficial revivals were producing superficial converts whose safety from eternal damnation seemed inevitably ephemeral.

The solution to the problem as several Oberlin professors saw it around 1840 was to translate emotional conversions into settled conviction. Most significantly, this plan included the teachings and writings of Finney, Mahan, and others on entire sanctification (also called Oberlin perfectionism). Individuals genuinely concerned about the fate of their immortal souls could undertake a lifetime of deliberate living, and by choosing holiness in each of their actions, Christians could sustain their salvation while they avoided the peaks and valleys produced by a series of superficial revivals. They also expressed a sentiment that religious authorities across the nation were articulating—it was time for consolidation. As historian Charles Hambrick-Stowe points out, Finney "envisioned a grand partnership of settled pastors, lay men and women, and evangelists working to develop mature congregations of Christians committed to serving God and doing good in the world." Not surprisingly, he sought an extension of the environment he oversaw in Oberlin.[60]

Oberlin perfectionism helped its followers to locate the channels God would use to effect His plans in a post-Revival America, plans that most assuredly included the abolition of slavery. The greatest antislavery efforts during the Revival had concentrated on reshaping the national conscience through moral appeals. Oberlinites had first sought a spiritual revolution through mass Christian conversion, a process that they believed had to be accomplished before any sort of more worldly antislavery movement could be successful. Some among them, Finney included, believed that right-minded political action would be a direct result of a universal awareness of the sinfulness of slavery. It would literally be God's government on earth, and few abolitionists before the mid-1830s saw much point in debating the merits of political strategies, since the whole question would be rendered moot by the Lord's approaching millennium.[61]

Widespread and uncontrollable revivals had proven themselves imperfect tools for saving souls and bringing about God's reign on earth. Many Oberlinites recognized that the moral government of God was also highly dependent on human choice—that is, the aggregate of worldly opinion, human government. Their meticulous study of the Bible showed conclusively that God regularly exerted moral influence through the instrumentality of worldly governments and actually commanded His people to obey magistrates and rulers. Moreover, Finney taught that every person who possessed the franchise or any degree of moral influence over others was bound to exert that influence in the promotion of virtue and happiness. "As human governments are plainly indispensable to the highest good of man," Finney believed, "they are bound to exert their influence to secure a legislation that is in accordance with the law of God."[62] He had long assured his congregants that God witnessed even their most secret political actions and would bless or curse them according to the choices they made.[63] Since contemporary governmental bodies had proven themselves some of the most obstinate opponents of the Oberlin community's antislavery message, while at the same time demonstrating the considerable force they could wield toward obstructionist ends, the friends of the slave in Oberlin realized that a meeting on their opponents' home territory was necessary.[64]

Finneyite revivalism taught that one's salvation depended on a genuine and independent decision to perform the acts necessary to become saved. However, that salvation also came with obligations, the most important of which was for the newly born Christian to do everything within his or her power to save others and to assist in the salvation of the entire world. This led evangelicals operating within the budding political antislavery environment to approve of an activist state, one that was capable of supporting reform movements like antislavery. Slavery was a wicked and unacceptable social institution; Christians had the ability and ceaseless obligation to eradicate all evil. Therefore, antislavery politics seemed to many abolitionists a legitimate venture.[65] In Oberlin, the heightened religious atmosphere kept its citizens motivated to act in ways consistent with the obligations undertaken from the moment they were saved.

Finney was explicit in his instructions regarding what he believed to be the political duties of Christian abolitionists. "Christians," he preached, "can no more take neutral ground on this subject, than they can take neutral ground on the subject of the sanctification of the Sabbath." He likened antislavery ambivalence to an enemy of God who claimed that he was neither a saint nor a sinner. The deception lay in his declaration to take neutral ground "and pray, 'good Lord and good devil,' because he did not know which side would be more popular."[66]

Except for the nonresistants of the Garrisonian camp, it was difficult for most abolitionists to disagree with Finney's reasoning. Since they had gained nothing from the South besides abuse, nothing from the North besides mob violence and laws that proscribed the lives of Northern African Americans, and little from Congress besides "gag rules" and censure, many abolitionists increasingly came to the conclusion that moral suasion, questioning of candidates, and petitioning were not nearly enough by themselves. Alvan Stewart, a man courted by the Oberlin Institute in the mid-1830s to join its faculty as professor of law and political economy, complained, "We might as well send the lamb as an ambassador to a community of wolves. I would not lift my hand to sign a petition to Congress, to be insulted by that body."[67] Many abolitionists were coming to recognize that since slavery was established and sustained by law, it had to be overthrown through the ballot box and the election of antislavery lawmakers.

Abolitionists realized with regret just how deeply ingrained the nation's anti-abolitionist tendencies were. Though the resulting frustration did not lead them to declare that moral suasion was no longer tenable, it was clear to many reformers that it could not stand alone as the only means of overthrowing slavery. Oberlin abolitionists heeded Finney's charge to "meddle with politics . . . for the same reason that they [were] bound to seek the universal good of all men."[68] They embraced the spreading notion that political action held a powerful religious significance as a manifestation of divine will; perfection justified many abolitionists' entrance into an arena many once considered profane and morally treacherous. Perfectionists across the North followed similar advice. As Theodore Clarke Smith notes of abolitionists' entrance into antislavery politics, "Expediency saw in such action[s] a way to impress obdurate politicians; impatience expected in this course a shorter road to abolition than through mere moral protest."[69] As Robert Fogel points out, the broadening of the antislavery appeal was largely a process of secularization, yet the secular arguments never entirely supplanted the religious ones precisely because so many of the principal leaders of the political movement were deeply religious men and also because evangelicals were a huge political constituency that would never be converted to the antislavery argument through strictly secular appeals.[70] Abolitionists' moral emphasis would not to be jettisoned but rather expanded after intense introspective examinations of their duties as perfectionists led them to think of progressive politics as a moral obligation in itself.[71]

As the 1830s came to a close, mainstream politicians were closing ranks to crush any antislavery influence from within, convincing large numbers of Ohioans of the complete bankruptcy of the two major parties.[72] Many Northern Democrats had endorsed bigotry and mob violence and were thus anathema to abolitionists. Whig leaders appeared only slightly more acceptable, often mixing nominal condemnations of "mob rule" with criticisms of abolitionists as "amalgamationists."[73] Thus committed antislavery men were becoming, in historian James Brewer Stewart's estimation, "self-consciously estranged" from the majority of the white North.[74] So while a few politician-abolitionists like Joshua Giddings, Thomas Morris, and Salmon P. Chase continued their frustrating crusade to inject antislavery into politics, abolitionists from Oberlin and like-minded reformers sought some means to channel this frustration into a positive force for antislavery.

Even as early as 1837, abolitionists from Oberlin were including a recognizable political appeal in their antislavery agitation, pressing their converts to protect everyone's natural and civil rights and to secure "correct principles" through the political process.⁷⁵ Enemies outside of Oberlin already blamed the community for improperly influencing local elections. At one point in 1837, a dozen thugs volunteered to travel to Oberlin to "tar and feather Mr. Finney" for his decisive role in swaying voters.⁷⁶ From the late 1830s through the Civil War, there was nothing in the political atmosphere at Oberlin that rivaled slavery and antislavery in importance.⁷⁷ With many other abolitionists, Oberlinites were turning a corner toward greater political action. Still, their main thrust remained a religious one. In Oberlin, the movement was still fundamentally perfectionist, but after the late 1830s, it expressed its religiosity in a more collected and organized fashion. There would be no perpetual revival to keep the most important reform issues before the eyes of the nation but, instead, a cumulative effort by godly individuals among the body politic to effect God's will and realize critical change. Finney preached to a New York audience in the late 1830s that "if you will give your vote only for honest men, the country will be obliged to have honest rulers," and the parties "will be compelled to put up honest men as candidates."⁷⁸

However, this proved to be wishful thinking.⁷⁹ As the establishment demonstrated its conservatism, abolitionists realized the need for a more precise plan of political attack. Petitions, though they had served a valuable purpose, would no longer suffice on their own. Often, questioning of politicians and bartering of blocs of votes for candidates' pledges on antislavery issues seemed more promising. In 1839, the OASS pledged its support to a Whig candidate for the state legislature, but only upon his solemn promise that he would use his seat to abolish the state's Black Laws.⁸⁰ Democrats were quick to blame the Oberlin community for their candidate's resounding defeat. An Elyria man wrote in to the *Ohio Statesman* that "Oberlin with her array of abolitionists was against us. It was thought the whigs [sic] would not bow to Oberlin, but we were mistaken." It was all too clear to Ohio Democrats that "the requisitions of Oberlin were complied with, to the very letter."⁸¹

However, once abolitionists' support served the purposes of the party, the politicians often brushed their desires aside and forgot campaign promises.⁸² Though some Northern Whigs did not support this duplicity, the increasing control of the party by its Southern wing made it more and more odious to antislavery voters.⁸³ Thus Ohio abolitionist voters in the late 1830s faced a crisis that they shared with political antislavery agitators across the North. Few antislavery politicians were prepared to abandon their familiar and secure positions within one of the two major political camps in order to strike out independently through a third party. Even the Whig Party, that of John Quincy Adams, Giddings, and Edward and Benjamin Wade, was severely tainted by its proslavery Southern contingent who demanded silence on the slavery issue as the price of national unity.

James G. Birney spoke for a growing number of fed up Ohio abolitionists when he declared that consistency demanded "that discarding every name of party, we vote for men of *principle*—the friends of LIBERTY, of LAW, of ORDER."[84] By 1838, the annual meeting of the OASS (presided over by Oberlinite William Dawes) and many local Ohio auxiliaries demanded that politicians demonstrate firm antislavery principles and profess a desire to do away with all laws and regulations based on race in order to win the support of antislavery voters.[85] Especially on the Western Reserve, abolitionists interrogated candidates for state and local office and sent them questionnaires seeking their opinions on the important antislavery questions of the day. Still, they stopped short of naming independent nominees, even when none of the other candidates measured up to their standards.[86]

The election of 1838 was a veritable revolution in Ohio antislavery politics. Many antislavery men came to the polls with Democratic ballots, hoping to strengthen abolitionist senator Thomas Morris's chances for reelection. Perhaps more important, however, was the fallout over Ohio's Whig governor Joseph Vance's conduct in the Mahan affair. John Mahan was an Ohio minister who had been indicted by a Kentucky grand jury for allegedly assisting a slave's escape to freedom. Vance used his influence to have Mahan arrested and turned over to the Kentucky authorities, and nothing else he could have done would have as disastrous an effect on his chances for reelection.[87] Once-wary abolitionists and sympathetic enemies of the Slave Power rushed to the polls to register their outrage over Ohio's capitulation to slaveholders, and when the dust settled on Election Day, the results were disastrous for Vance and the Whigs. The governor, who had been elected by a majority of 6,000 four years earlier, was trounced by more than 5,000 votes. Across the board in Ohio, Whig candidates for the legislature where either defeated by Democrats in their bids for reelection or elected by slim majorities.[88]

Abolitionists never doubted for a moment that the turnaround was due to their contribution, and Whig newspapers conceded that their boasts were probably correct. Friendly publications were euphoric. The *Philanthropist* sang the praises of abolitionist voters in Ohio, commending them for being the first demonstrably strong antislavery voting bloc in the North. The *Emancipator* put the change in the election returns for the Ohio legislature at

25,000 owing to abolitionists' support for Morris. Reports of their political maneuvers and successes generated an outpouring of encouragement from the eastern antislavery press as well.[89] Though the Whig losses left the Democrats in power, the united mass of antislavery voters in Ohio had demonstrated the consequences of betraying their trust. Whigs could no longer take these votes for granted, and thereafter would have to actively earn the valuable support of antislavery men.

The Principles of Immutable Justice

However, the antislavery electoral successes of 1838 made the frustrations of the next year more frustrating. That winter, Oberlin and Ohio abolitionists lost all hope that moral suasion alone would convert the South to emancipation or that reform within the two major parties in the North was a realistic possibility. Although Ohio had always had a symbiotic relationship with Kentucky, on January 12, 1839, the state legislature seemed to go out of its way in its attempts to conciliate the complaints of the slaveholding states, particularly its southern neighbor. The Ohio legislature passed a series of resolutions that denied congressional jurisdiction over slavery in the states, condemned all antislavery agitation, and declared abolitionists' activities fanatical acts that would lead to the disruption of the union. However, editors of the *Oberlin Evangelist* singled out two additional resolutions as the most insulting and galling. The first resolved that the repeal of the state's Black Laws was both impolitic and inexpedient and would only encourage the African American population of all the other states to flock to Ohio. The other, anticipating the logic of the *Dred Scott* decision eighteen years later, declared that "the blacks and mulattoes who may be residents within this State have no *Constitutional right to present their petitions to the General Assembly for any purpose whatsoever.*"[90] The editors of the *Oberlin Evangelist* could only express "*grief and sorrow of heart*" that legislators so blatantly trampled upon "the principles of immutable justice."[91]

The January resolutions were followed by events and the passage of legislation even more infuriating to Ohio abolitionists. That same month, two Kentucky politicians, a Whig and a Democrat, arrived in Columbus as commissioners from their state legislature.[92] They had been sent to Ohio on an errand designed to gather support for an Ohio fugitive slave law to assist Kentucky slaveholders in reclaiming their escaped bondsmen. On February 12, the governor personally delivered the commissioners' request for such a law to the legislature, where it was referred to the Judiciary Committee with favorable instructions. The Kentuckians' bill then passed the House and Senate and became law in February.[93] In both houses, the only opposition to the bill came from northern Ohio. The state threw a public feast in honor of the Kentucky commissioners, and after gorging themselves on the free-labor-produced bounty of Ohio's farms, they returned home in March to report on their unqualified success.[94]

Though a federal fugitive law remained in effect, Kentucky had demanded "more effective" protection of its slave property.[95] Ohio lawmakers complied and imposed even stiffer penalties on all those who would oppose the new law. Any person found guilty of harboring, concealing, or interfering in any way with the recapture of an alleged fugitive or frustrating in any way the smooth operation of this 1839 law could be fined as much as $500 and imprisoned for up to sixty days. Conviction would qualify as both a state and a federal offense.[96]

The new statute subjected Ohioans to legal obligations that other Northerners would not have to confront until 1850 (when the more famous national fugitive slave law was adopted). In a town like Oberlin, which had always held a sober respect for governmental authority, some citizens were unsure of their obligations under it.[97] Charles Finney, however, was not. To him, slavery had always stood between the enslaved and his right to independent moral agency. As the Fugitive Act was passing through the Ohio legislature, Oberlin's most powerful shaper of public opinion was busy excoriating it in the pages of the *Oberlin Evangelist*. "To enslave a man," Finney wrote, "is to treat a man as a thing—to set aside moral agency; and to treat a moral agent as a mere piece of property." The new law did just that—it reduced men to chattel, and as such, it was abhorrent to God and Finney's own moral sensibilities. "To be a slave," he explained, "is to be under the necessity of choosing between two evils," that is, choosing either to remain in abject bondage or to be brutally punished for attempted escape. The fugitive law was meant to force free men to aid in entangling more tightly the fleeing slave "in a course of life not chosen for its own sake" and without real options.[98]

By demonstrating how slavery had a negative effect on the lives of all Northerners, abolitionists from Oberlin and Ohio were able to draw broad political support for the antislavery cause. They were able to gain a degree of encouragement, albeit potentially selfish and not necessarily humanitarian, for their cause.[99] To combat the usurpation of the Slave Power of moral and political authority, Finney, more than a decade before the more widely publicized public statements of William Seward or Theodore Parker, invoked a doctrine of "higher law" for Americans to follow. The eastern antislavery press

Charles Grandison Finney in the 1850s (courtesy Oberlin College Archives)

reprinted excerpts of Finney's editorial, lauded it as a "stern and settled defiance of wicked law-makers," and congratulated Finney for "setting a lesson for the whole country, and preparing the way for emancipation" in the South.[100]

Within days of the passage of Ohio's Fugitive Act, Finney and the editors of the *Oberlin Evangelist* began explaining their theory of civil disobedience. Finney declared that "whatever is contrary to the law of God is not law, is not obligatory upon men." Man's laws that stood in contradistinction to God's laws were void, and Christians were bound to disobey them if they wished to please the Lord.[101] Since laws did not execute themselves, and since they could never be successfully executed if public sentiment made their enforcement impossible, Oberlin residents saw it as their duty to "have *moral* power" and set the example of noncompliance from which the rest of society could learn.[102]

Ohio lawmakers who had been empowered by antislavery votes in 1838 apparently saw little inconsistency with their answers to abolitionists' interrogations in October and their support for the 1839 fugitive bill. The resulting loss of abolitionist confidence in the efficacy of their political activism to that point was profound. These developments seemed to be the worst-case scenario imagined by the Ohio abolitionists, who in the report of their state antislavery society in 1839 lamented, "We have trusted that the paternal character of our institutions, the leniency of our laws, and the purity of our political creed, would so effectually secure the affection and confidence of the people." Naively, they had hoped that in the passage of time they would "advance from point to point, until all our institutions, based on the principle of eternal right, should become the admiration of the nations."[103] The editors of the *Oberlin Evangelist* could only take solace in the fact that delinquent legislators would "stand condemned at the bar of their own conscience, and at the bar of God."[104]

However, the events of that winter emboldened Finney. He was neither shocked into stagnancy by the stalled antislavery political movement nor willing to let the minions of slavery off without a thorough rebuke for their treachery. Finney had already expressed his anger at the Fugitive Slave Act (he refused to legitimize it by calling it a "law") and carried his fury to the OASS's May anniversary.[105] As Professor James Thome predicted, Finney's opposition to the fugitive bill was the defining aspect of the convention.[106] After being selected as the convention's chairman by the 300-plus official delegates, Finney moved for the adoption of nine successive resolutions condemning the fugitive bill.[107] Ever the educator-minister, Finney accompanied each resolution with a detailed and clear explanation of its meaning and implications. He further elaborated on his "higher law" doctrine in two of the resolutions, declaring that no human law "can annul, or set aside, the law or authority of God," and so far as man's fugitive law violated God's authority, obedience to it would be "highly immoral."[108]

James G. Birney was in the audience to hear the oration and was awed by his zeal. Birney praised Finney to an eastern friend and predicted that the new Ohio law would be "totally inoperative."[109] The editors of the *Oberlin Evangelist* agreed, calling it, among other things, "contrary to the law of nature, contrary to the law of God, contrary to all righteous municipal or civil laws, contrary to the constitution of Ohio, and contrary to the constitution of the United States." In their opinion it would be "wholly inoperative while it exists, and will be speedily abolished."[110]

The Path Straight Forward

The demonstration of Ohio's subservience to the Kentucky Slave Power caused mass confusion among most politically-minded Ohio abolitionists.

Western Reserve Whigs who opposed the legislation had limited power within their party.[111] Democrats rolled to even more dominating majorities statewide, yet the abolitionists could not claim responsibility for the landslide as they had a year earlier. This time around, their votes had been split between the two parties or withheld altogether in frustration. Democrats had proven untrustworthy, and many Whigs lined up in support of the Fugitive Slave Law and laughed at abolitionists who had been "gulled" by the Democracy in 1838.[112] Taking advantage of Democrats' increased majorities in the legislature, the state Democratic convention in January of 1840 set the tone for the coming session by condemning abolition societies.[113] The Ohio House resolved later that month that they considered "the unlawful, unwise, and unconstitutional interference of the fanatical abolitionists of the north with the domestic institutions of the southern states as highly criminal," and that all citizens were duty bound to denounce the abolitionists "in their mad, fanatical and revolutionary schemes."[114] They went on to declare that "the conduct of the abolitionist is calculated to incite insurrection among the slaves, and is (if not directly) indirectly a guarantee on the part of the abolitionist, to assist the slaves in the indiscriminate butchery and murder of the slave-holders."[115]

It was within this atmosphere that the Oberlin Dialectic Association, a student literary society, sought incorporation from the legislature early in the session. Its bid was soundly defeated, but ambitious House members also used the opportunity to "[distinguish] themselves by their opposition." They urged several amendments, including one to prohibit abolition lectures within the society, and another, proposed by Knox County Democrat Byram Leonard, to strike the word "Oberlin" from wherever it appeared in the documents of incorporation and replace it with the word "Abolition." This, Leonard said, would satisfy his desire to avoid having the statute book "disgraced" by the name Oberlin and simultaneously make it easier for readers to understand "what institution was meant."[116] Leonard went on to declare that he "did not like the knowledge that emanated from that institution," since it "sent out scholars, who as school teachers, instilled their abolition doctrines into the minds of our children."[117]

After another legislative session emphasized the inadequacy of the Ohio abolitionists' political strategy, some were finally ready to take the next step toward organized political action. Oberlin students and townspeople busied themselves debating these vital points.[118] By now, there was little question in their minds about the propriety of voting, yet what seemed a forgone conclusion in Oberlin, much of the Northwest, and upstate New York was doing its part to rend the eastern movement in two. However, as the Garrisonians battled the political faction back East, the issue hardly induced any debate in the West.[119] A July meeting of the Oberlin-led Lorain County Anti-Slavery Society had already resolved that "it is the duty of abolitionists to use their influence to secure the nomination for office of men who are the friends of equal rights," and that "it is their duty to attend the polls and vote for such men."[120]

Assuming that they would vote *somehow*, western abolitionists were forced to confront two other questions by the rapid approach of the 1840 presidential election. Could they vote for anyone except a declared abolitionist? The Lorain County Anti-Slavery Society boldly offered its opinion in no uncertain terms: "To give your suffrage for a man who denies the fundamental principles of free government . . . would betray a mental imbecility."[121] Still remaining, though, was the second great question: what was to be done if Martin Van Buren were pitted against the likes of a Henry Clay or William Henry Harrison, all proslavery men, for the presidency?

An attempt to resolve the issue was made at an August 1839 AASS meeting at Albany, New York, specifically called to address antislavery politics.[122] After a long and animated debate, the assembly's majority resolved to neither vote for nor support the election of any man to public office who was not in favor of the immediate abolitionist of slavery.[123] The editor of the Cincinnati *Philanthropist* called this resolution "wrong in principle and inexpedient" since, he claimed, it demanded arbitrary qualifications in a candidate. Rather, editor Gamaliel Bailey believed, "requirements should be limited by the constitutional responsibilities of the office they seek."[124] Many Ohio societies agreed and took the same position by resolving to demand only such pledges as candidates could be reasonably expected to offer. Local conventions in several Ohio counties joined with a general Western Reserve convention in resolving, "That abolitionists ought not, and we *will not*, vote for any man for any legislative or executive office who is not heartily opposed to slavery and who will not openly meet and honestly sustain all constitutional measures calculated immediately to restore to the oppressed their rights."[125]

The quandary of what to do with two equally unsuitable candidates remained, however. On October 23, 1839, a special meeting of the AASS convened in Cleveland to address the issue once again.[126] Of the 400 abolitionists in attendance, a powerful majority were from Ohio, including, as one Democratic paper sarcastically remarked, "all the black and white negroes of Oberlin . . . headed by Mahand and Fininey of the Oberlin Institute."[127]

These Oberlinites had publicly resolved to "rescue the political power of this country from the hands of the present [Democratic] party."[128] After the sessions were opened with a prayer from Mahan, several Garrisonians presented an argument to deny the propriety of any sort of political action. After a "long and zealously devised" rebuttal by Oberlin delegates Mahan, Finney, and Edward Wade, two resolutions were adopted by an overwhelming majority: first, to vote for no opponents of abolitionism; second, to "neglect no opportunity to record their votes against slavery when proper candidates in all respects are put up for office."[129]

New Yorker Myron Holley's resolution was more radical. It demanded that when existing parties directly opposed or purposefully overlooked the rights of the slave, it was time to form "a *new political party*," of which the candidates for president and vice president would be nominated by a specially appointed committee. After a full day's debate, Holley's resolutions were tabled. Mahan and Edward Wade then offered their support for an amendment that authorized the calling of a nominating convention, providing the nominees of the two major parties proved unacceptable. However, this too was blocked.[130]

Henry Stanton called these deliberations some of the most interesting debates on political action that he had ever witnessed, despite the fact that the overall sentiment remained against independent nominations under the then-current circumstances.[131] However, Elizur Wright Sr., father of the AASS secretary, thought a great opportunity had been missed. He had brought a group of sixteen Oberlin students to the convention and believed that Holley's resolution would have passed if "a few aspiring ones [among the delegates] who are seeking promotion" from eastern abolitionist leaders had not been afraid to support such a controversial issue. "I think," Wright wrote, "that these gentlemen have yet to learn that the path *straight forward* is the road to honor."[132]

The final show of support for Holley's resolution was also undertaken without the defense of the man who could have been one of its most able advocates. Finney, the acknowledged leader of the significant Oberlin contingent to the convention, had to leave Cleveland before the Holley resolution or the proposed amendment was thoroughly discussed and voted upon. Before being called away, Finney admitted that he was ready to defend the resolution since he could not personally "vote for an enemy of God & man to legislate for any people." Though in disgust he had often remained aloof of politics in the past when there was no suitable candidate, Finney declared that he would go to the polls if an antislavery party put forward its own candidate.[133]

From the East, Garrisonians cried foul, accusing the political faction of trickery and attempting to pack the convention with political westerners. Other critics identified a logical flaw in the Holley argument. They accused him and his followers of attempting to turn the AASS into a political party, yet by the founding principles of the society, such a transformation was impossible. The primary object of the AASS as stated in its 1833 Declaration of Sentiments had been the abolition of slavery in the states; it had grudgingly admitted the inability of Congress to directly act outside of territory it controlled. The Philanthropist argued that a national political party contemplating as its object the abolition of slavery, particularly on the state level, was a manifest absurdity.[134]

However, on November 13, a convention in Warsaw, New York, led by Myron Holley formally nominated former Lane Rebel James G. Birney to head an independent abolitionist ticket in the 1840 presidential race, but he declined the nomination for the time being.[135] By the first few weeks of 1840, the exasperating notion of the Whig ticket led by the slaveholder Harrison against the incumbent Democrat Van Buren was leading many who had formerly questioned the wisdom of independent action to reexamine their views.[136] In February, Holley issued a call for a "National Third-Party Anti-Slavery Convention" to meet in April.[137] Though the Philanthropist remained cool to the idea of political action, many of the letters it received from its subscribers betrayed a developing momentum in the opposite direction.[138]

The convention met on April 1, with more than nine-tenths of the delegates were from New York State. Birney was again nominated for the presidency. However, with Ohio only represented by some of its closest New York friends like William Goodell and Alvan Stewart and by the correspondence of some of its citizens, the Philanthropist warned its readers not to get "carried away" in the new movement or too caught up in the excitement.[139] Besides the ideological objections of the nonresistants, most disagreements on the issue were mainly based on pragmatism. Some abolitionists believed that a third-party foray was destined for a resounding defeat. If abolitionists concentrated their votes into a losing cause, the other parties would have no reason to court the favor of antislavery voters. Many also believed an independent nomination was tactically unwise since by voting as a bloc for those candidates they considered friends of the slave, abolitionists might hold the balance of power in close elections and thus represent the votes that could force Whigs or Democrats to concede to some of their demands.

The Oberlin community again offered its town and college as a forum to debate the wisdom of running a third-party ticket in the upcoming national election. There, public discussion on the issue began just days after the April nominations.[140] The editors of the *Oberlin Evangelist* weighed in by admitting the inevitability of "the last resort" in an editorial titled "Alarming Facts—The Slave Power Triumphing," and urged their readers to either cast their votes for Birney and Thomas Earle or avoid voting altogether.[141] Not all abolitionists from Oberlin actually considered a third-party loss a forgone conclusion. Writing from England, John Keep expressed to his wife the pleasure he would take in bragging to his English friends about the great changes that would follow the election when Birney and the new party supplanted the Democrats and Whigs, "each charging the other as a crime, that it is friendly to Abolition!!!"[142]

On September 1, 1840, in "a fine specimen of the *real* abolitionism in Ohio," the state's first Liberty Party convention convened.[143] Almost 200 political abolitionists gathered and voted, by an almost two-to-one margin, that both the Whig Harrison and the Democrat Van Buren had "forfeited all claims" to abolitionist support. Van Buren's allegiance to the Slave Power had long been a forgone conclusion to many Ohioans, and after the *Oberlin Evangelist* ran a three-page exposé on Harrison's proslavery attitude, "as orthodox on the subject . . . as Mr. Van Buren," abolitionists could not help but agree that both candidates for the presidency presented "a most humiliating spectacle."[144] That being the case, the state convention voted to back the national Liberty Party's ticket of Birney and Earle.[145] In doing so delegates subscribed to a platform that the Oberlin community had stood firmly upon since at least 1835: an endorsement of the principle of immediatism, the acknowledgment of congressional power to abolish slavery in the District of Columbia and the Territories, and the general opposition to human slavery "to the full extent of Constitutional power."[146] The *Philanthropist* also fell into line, enthusiastically jumping into the cause. Despite the editor's fear of failure, the newspaper began flying the names of Birney and Earle from its masthead.[147]

Nonetheless, the "Tippecanoe and Tyler Too" hullabaloo retained a disconcerting hold on Ohio's Whig antislavery politicians.[148] With few exceptions, the most powerful antislavery politicians, the individuals one historian describes as the men who would soon represent "the personification of political abolitionism" were not yet ready to break ranks with their old party in 1840.[149] Giddings, Benjamin and Edward Wade, Leister King, Samuel Lewis, and Salmon P. Chase all threw their support to Harrison in the 1840 contest. Even the Western Reserve majority voted Whig.[150] Perhaps many Ohioans did as one minister quoted in the *Oberlin Evangelist* did when

Henry Cowles (from Fairchild, *Oberlin: The Colony and the College* [1883])

he announced to his congregation, "I shall vote for—, and I trust God will forgive me for so doing."[151] Some Oberlinites, however, showed little mercy and blamed the Whig faithful for wrecking the abolitionist cause in the election. "The Whig candidates for Congress," one wrote, "did us more harm than any other men on the Reserve. They had nothing to fear for themselves and stumped it for Harrison, for weeks, throwing out insinuations against [the Liberty Party] as an affair got up in certain quarters to help Van Buren, &c."[152] And though the majority of Oberlinites supported the independent Liberty Party ticket in 1840, there was still a Whig presence in the town.[153] Professor Henry Cowles, who abandoned the party that year, had to forbid his son from attending a Whig parade that marched from Wellington to Oberlin with a brass band at its head. A group of Oberlin women did join in the procession, causing one partisan to declare that "the *ladies* are not backward in the good cause."[154]

It was clear that many antislavery vacillators remained with their old party. Since the Liberty Party did not make any nominations apart from its presidential ticket, many abolitionists who had formerly voted Whig brought Whig ballots to the polls without scratching out Harrison's name at the head of the ticket. Many others, intent on voting for Birney, could not find the appropriate ballots or did not know the names of the third-party electors. Others simply stayed home and left the Election Day commotion to others.[155] In Ohio, only one-third of one percent of voters cast ballots for the abolitionists. Overall, national returns showed that not one in ten of the thousands of abolitionists who had resolved to act without regard to party ties actually cut those connections.[156] Locally, Democrats accused the Ohio abolitionists of lacking any semblance of consistency or honesty for not supporting the ticket they themselves had nominated, and for offering only "a beggarly account of empty boxes."[157]

To be sure, Birney's 902 Ohio votes in the election were a far cry from what political abolitionists had originally desired, but third-party supporters were not overly disheartened. Ultimately, a foundation for further antislavery political action had been established. "Where," asked the editors of the *Oberlin Evangelist*, "is the man of this 'glorious minority' who regrets his vote? We have heard of none."[158] The returns from Lorain County, of which Oberlin was a significant part, were a major reason that the ten counties of the Western Reserve cast almost a full half of the state Liberty Party total. This geographic concentration of votes reflected both the foundation of a body of antislavery voters in Ohio and an indication of the future course of antislavery growth in the state.[159] Moreover, despite their seemingly small numbers, Ohio's third-party voters now represented the powerful voting bloc many of them had anticipated prior to the election. By 1840, Ohio had emerged as one of the most crucial states in the political battle over slavery. It was the third most populous state in the nation, and in that year, Ohio controlled more electoral votes than all other midwestern states combined.[160] However, from the 1830s through the early 1850s, control of the state legislature was generally shared evenly between Democrats and Whigs.[161] Several instances of abolitionists affecting the results of Ohio elections have already been mentioned, but the birth of a party that potentially held the balance of power in one of the most important states in the union raised eyebrows among the political establishment. Because of the issue of abolition, Ohio's third-party voters, led by Oberlin and the Western Reserve, were a political force to be reckoned with in state politics long before they polled even a plurality in any election.

Accordingly, the inauspicious beginning of the national Liberty Party effort did not scare away those who had cast ballots for Birney and Earle in 1840. The *Oberlin Evangelist* declared that every one of the Ohio Liberty Party voters of 1840 could "*be depended upon . . . in the coming struggle.*"[162] Slavery had proven itself a fixture of American politics, and since Liberty Party abolitionists felt a moral imperative to participate in the process, the independent party offered them the best path toward their goal of immediate emancipation.[163] Oberlin's leaders already predicted an energized Western Reserve where enthusiastic Liberty Party conventions would be attended by more "than the whole Freeman's vote in Ohio" of 1840.[164]

These earliest Liberty Party reformers were firm in their abolitionist values and continued to see the third party as an effective way to reconcile moral suasion and political action. Many drew a parallel between their ideas of entire sanctification and antislavery voting. As historian Douglas Strong argues, a vote for an abolitionist candidate recorded a person's spiritual choice against sin and in support of holiness. A Liberty Party ballot, he writes, "became a practical and definitive way for ecclesiastical abolitionists to exhibit their sanctified resolve."[165] The *Oberlin Evangelist* suggested as much when its editor unashamedly commended the "men [who] did not bow the knee to Baal" in the 1840 election.[166] "Passing events are pregnant with omens of promise," Professor Henry Cowles declared in the aftermath of the election, "and a thousand eyes are striving to pierce the destinies of the future."[167]

CHAPTER FIVE

All the Truly Wise or Truly Pious Have the Same End in View

Oberlin and Abolitionist Schism

The remarkable growth and expansion of the abolitionist movement also contained within it the seeds of discord. Reformers weighed the value of moral suasion in their agitation, and those who found it insufficient as an antislavery tactic began to consider new means and to set new goals in the fight against slavery. Others began to expand abolitionism to a program of universal emancipation from all unjust inequalities. As abolitionists' reform agendas diverged, the possibility of enduring antislavery unity seemed increasingly unlikely. Eastern leaders, including William Lloyd Garrison, Lewis and Arthur Tappan, and James Birney, became embroiled in internal ideological and personal battles that led to the dramatic division of the AASS in May 1840.

However, away from the East Coast, the "schism" among abolitionists was not felt nearly as acutely. The ideological heterogeneity that Oberlinites had encouraged and many others had adopted had helped Ohio and the West grow into a fecund abolitionist stronghold to rival eastern centers. The region was much better able to accommodate the differences that disturbed eastern antislavery unity in 1837–40. Even before Oberlin professor

John Morgan led the OASS to a position of neutrality relative to the warring eastern abolitionist factions in June of 1840, reformers from the Oberlin community had endeavored to make abolitionism acceptable to the widest constituency possible. Though this may have sometimes been at the expense of strict ideological consistency, these men and women hoped to avoid being sidetracked by debates over "proper" or "pure" means by prioritizing the ultimate goal of emancipation.[1] To be sure, this approach was moderate compared to that of most radical abolitionists of the era. Still, Oberlinites and those like them appreciated their responsibility of bringing the growing antislavery forces in line behind the radical shock troops. As one close Western Reserve ally of the Oberlin community declared to a group of Garrisonians, "You beat the bush . . . and I will catch the birds."[2]

* * *

WITH STRAINED RESOURCES in the late 1830s and early 1840s, the Oberlin community remained alert to the importance of continued vigilance. Despite the fact that the national antislavery movement seemed to be "paralyzed for want of funds," the editor of the *Oberlin Evangelist* reminded abolitionists that "slavery is still the same sin against God—its horrors are the same—the majority of our citizens still manifest a determined hostility to the principles of liberty—the churches still close their ears at the cry of the needy—the Congress of the U.S. and the Legislature of Ohio, yet trample down the suffering and the dumb." The financial downturn had not lessened the suffering of the slaves, and the abolitionists of Oberlin believed that worldly considerations should have no affect on the biblical injunction to "*remember them that are in bonds as bound with them*" or to "do to others as we would have them do to us."[3]

In the immediate financial crisis, and even amid ideological battles that seemed to threaten the national society from within, the Oberlin Institute and community became a powerful symbolic standard around which abolitionists could rally. When Oberlin commissioned William Dawes and John Keep in late 1839 to make a last-ditch appeal to English philanthropists for the survival of their college, American reformers of all backgrounds joined together and enthusiastically offered their support. Amasa Walker wrote to English abolitionist George Thompson that the "Oberlin Institute is beloved by all those of every denomination who love Geo. Thompson and W. Lloyd Garrison, & is hated deeply & sincerely by all those 'gentlemen of property and standing.'"[4] Philadelphia Garrisonian James Forten commended the Oberlin Institute's color-blind admissions policy in glowing terms to an

English correspondent, while dietary reformer Dr. Sylvester Graham wrote to Londoner Peter Roget that Oberlin was "perhaps more closely associated with all the best interests of intellectual & moral men, & the highest hopes of the human family than any other literary institution in our country."[5] Garrison's friend Elizabeth Pease declared to an English correspondent, "The [Oberlin] Institute may be almost considered a nursery for Abolitionists."[6] Lewis Tappan assured George Thompson that the school had "the entire confidence of Abolitionists throughout the country. It is a nursery of Anti-Slavery Lecturers, Agents, & Preachers."[7]

Theodore Weld drafted a circular to present Oberlin's cause to the world, and in it, he encapsulated its crucial contributions to abolitionism and American reform. Thirty-six abolitionist leaders as diverse as the Tappans, Garrison, Angelina Grimké Weld, James Birney, John Greenleaf Whittier, Gerrit Smith, Maria Weston Chapman, Wendell Phillips, and Joshua Giddings endorsed Weld's appeal. In doing so, American abolitionists put aside their mounting sectarianism and united behind Oberlin's role as an antislavery institution, a bulwark against human bondage. The document's introduction read in part:

> In all its features, this Institution is opposed to Slavery; and is a practical and standing exhibition of the great doctrine of immediate emancipation, producing its legitimate and beneficial results; youth are admitted to all its privileges, without regard to colour, or nation, and there is a department for the instruction of females. It is thoroughly evangelical in its spirit and character, is free from all sectarian partialities, discards the prejudice of caste in all its various and disgraceful forms, and has already become a terror to the slaveholder, and a shield and a solace to the victim of the white man's tyranny. By uniting the youth of all colours in the same course of academical training, it furnishes a practical method of elevating the African race, of abolishing the tyranny of caste, and of operating an effectual door through which the black and the free-coloured man may attain the rights of citizenship, and the blessings of a quiet and protected home.[8]

The "Appeal" praised the effects of Oberlin's manual labor system, as well as the school's self-sacrificing cadre of abolitionist professors and students who had "excited not only the bitter hostility of the upholders of slavery, but also a large proportion of the professing church." Though "called to pecuniary sacrifices, such as modern times have rarely witnessed," the abolitionist men and women of Oberlin were driven on by "a solemn conviction of duty towards God and their fellow-men." Weld reverentially asserted that "their acts will stand out in the history of a progressive benevolence, as a pattern for the church's imitation."[9]

This was no small praise from perhaps the ablest abolitionist to trek a lecture circuit in the 1830s, yet many of the esteemed abolitionists who endorsed Weld's plea felt further compelled to write their own testimonial of support to be carried throughout England by the Oberlin delegation. They wrote that they felt "solemnly moved by duty, and sweetly constrained by love to the truth, and honour in its faithful avowal" to give their "emphatic testimony in favour of the Oberlin Institute." They praised "the spirit that pervades the Institution" and wrote of "the mighty influence, young as it is, which it is already putting forth." The Oberlin Institute, they wrote, was "accomplishing more for freedom of thought, speech, and conscience, more for the great cause of human liberty and equal rights, the annihilation of prejudice and caste in every form—more to honour God, to exalt his Truth, and to purify a corrupt church and ministry, than any other Institution in the United States."[10]

By the time Keep and Dawes reached England in late 1839, their school and community represented to many there the great hope of abolitionism and human rights in America.[11] British abolitionist Harriett Martineau had gone to great lengths to publicize the vital leadership in the antislavery movement of her American friends connected to what she simply called "the Oberlin." Their arrival was followed a few weeks later by "An Expression of Sentiments of the Colored Students of the Oberlin Institution," who felt it their duty to officially commend their school to British supporters and to thank those who offered their generous financial backing. The principles upon which the Oberlin Institute was conducted, they wrote, allowed them with "unshaken confidence" to endorse it as one of the most efficient means of elevating African Americans "from the state of moral degradation in which they have been placed by their oppressors."[12] One British minister told Keep, "No doubt you have a good & Christian school at Oberlin—but this merely will not give you favor among us in England—for there are many important Christian schools in your Country & this." Rather, it was Oberlin's stand against the "abominable system of slavery" that would "excite the feelings of the Englishmen."[13]

Keep encouraged the view of Oberlin as a universal stronghold rather than just an American institution, one that sought to "ameliorate the condition

"Father" John Keep (from Fairchild, *Oberlin: The Colony and the College* [1883])

of all men" by standing "where Christ stood."[14] The Oberlin enterprise, he told one English audience, "has been brought up by the peculiar exigencies of the times, & properly belongs to the world." Moreover, Keep and Dawes took great pains to show how Oberlin deliberately avoided sectarianism and concentrated their greatest efforts upon effecting emancipation. Their efforts were not in vain, and resulted in $30,000 of pledges from supporters in England, and even the memorialization in verse by a young man in Derby:

> America needs you,
> Ye heroes arise and gird you anew for the strife,
> For her falls have re-echoed the groans of the slave,
> Her rivers have swallowed his life,
> Her forests & prairies no refuge afford,
> Excepting one holy spot:
> 'Tis Oberlin's walls;
> The only retreat where the white man injures him not.[15]

While in England, the men also made a memorable appearance at the inaugural 1840 World's Anti-Slavery Convention in London. Keep made several speeches during the conclave, routinely condemned the American slave system, and touted Oberlin as "a new seminary," where all races and both sexes were welcomed and where abolitionism was taught alongside traditional subjects. He informed his listeners that in Oberlin, they were training an abolition phalanx to reach out to the nation's African American population, "sympathize with him, stay with him, weep over him, pray with him, teach him, comfort him, pour oil into his wounds, and raise him to the dignity of a man."[16]

Although Keep and Dawes hoped to represent American abolitionism as a respectable religious enterprise, they regretted that most of the rest of the American delegation "did not appear well as *Christians*." "Much harm," Keep wrote, "has been done by this."[17] When convention officials decided not to seat the female delegates from the United States, Garrisonians protested, publicly called the officers "enemies of freedom," and promised to let loose a "moral hurricane" if *all* delegates were not welcomed on equal terms.[18] A spirited debate ensued on the convention floor. Wendell Phillips and George Thompson argued for inclusion, while James Birney, one of the Garrisonians' most vocal opponents on the political question at home, disputed the Americans' right to dictate procedural matters at a British convention. Though an occasional English voice was heard, the most vociferous contest on the first day of the convention was among Americans, disputing many of the same issues that divided them across the Atlantic.[19]

At tea following one day's deliberations, Keep observed that Garrison and Henry Stanton "were injudicious in introducing some things not appropriate." Garrison "brought forward some of his peculiar views & made much confusion" and criticized a long history of "English foibles." The once-friendly gathering was then overcome by an "uproar" that Keep described as "so great that no one could hear him [Garrison], for 10 or 15 minutes—& yet on he went & had his say out." Stanton also attempted to force his partisan ideas into the conversation. "The effect of his speech & of Garrison's was unhappy," Keep wrote. "I felt both ashamed & grieved." Though no one recorded his exact words, some who heard Garrison's harangue hoped they would never have to suffer through another meeting with him. Keep wrote to his wife that the "weak sides of the Abolitionists were seen—their dissentions, &c—Still I am inclined to *hope* that the effect was good."[20]

However, the Oberlin delegation could not conceal what was transpiring across the Atlantic. With the 1840 spring thaw in the Northeast, the AASS finally cracked. At the May anniversary meeting in New York City, the nomination of a woman to the business committee capped the mounting inability of all abolitionists to work together under a single organization.

Issues like political action, women's rights, nonresistance, and anticlericalism combined in an ideological ferment that seemed to render a unified antislavery agenda all but impossible. A significant number of men under the leadership of Lewis Tappan withdrew to form the rival American and Foreign Anti-Slavery Society (AFASS), or "New Org," as it would also be called (to distinguish it from the rival AASS, "Old Org.")

Although the split appeared incredibly bitter and occasioned a war of words in the eastern antislavery press, the fragmentation of the AASS only marked the end of a progression toward expansion and decentralization. Moreover, as historian Ronald Walters rightly argues, rather than discouraging abolitionists or retarding the movement, the diversity of antislavery after 1840 actually encouraged the maximum number of people to enlist in the cause. It shifted the locus of antislavery activity away from the national society and to the local level, made leadership positions more numerous and accessible, and led to the creation of organizations to serve nearly every ideological persuasion.[21] The supposed "split" ultimately allowed abolitionists to promote antislavery by whatever means they deemed best and most appropriate. This was the path of independent antislavery thought that Oberlinites had been blazing since the community's founding. Rather than follow any particular leaders or strictly adhering to any narrow ideology, Oberlin reformers selectively adopted whatever means they believed offered the greatest hope for success.

By the time of the AASS schism, Oberlin-led Ohio abolitionists were already some of the most independent in America. The Philanthropist boasted in 1838 that "Ohio abolitionists would feel themselves degraded by identifying the cause of anti-slavery with *names or institutions*; nor have they so far forgotten the respect due themselves, and their devotion to the *slave*, as to descend to personal squabbling, sectarian conflict, or humiliating strifes for the mastery." Ohio abolitionists, the Philanthropist editor wrote, "'*are of age*'; they are in the habit of judging and acting *for themselves*, without any *reverential* reference for what the Spectator, or Liberator, or Philanthropist may choose to say . . . we are glad of it."[22]

The degree of partisan infighting among many eastern abolitionists did not replicate itself beyond the Alleghenies. As Oberlin abolitionists pointed out, they were determined to rise above the divisions distracting their "eastern brethren" since they and other westerners were situated "too near the great evil of slavery, and have too much abolition work to do, to cease contending with the common foe, for the sake of turning our weapons upon each other."[23] As historian Stacey Robertson points out of Ohio abolitionists in general, more-common interactions with fugitives from just across the Ohio River made political or ideological conflicts among abolitionists there seem trivial in comparison.[24] The editors of the *Oberlin Evangelist* had long expressed their earnest hope that the fragile national society could remain intact "till the last fetter is broken from the last slave." The editors believed that *any* agitation on behalf of abolition was of great value.[25]

Never Has There Been a More Friendly Schism

In Ohio, the debate over independent political action continued, yet there were few overt signs that the movement was in disarray. Over 500 delegates arrived at the annual meeting of the OASS in June determined not to let ideological differences divide the western movement in two.[26] Official news of the national split had arrived only two days before the convention, and Oberlin men led the way in attempting to avoid the fatally divisive quarrels that had undone the national society. The result was, as one observer noted, a "very happy" meeting. Those issues that vexed easterners seemed "happily laid aside" in Ohio. In response to a letter from Lewis Tappan explaining the schism, the OASS resolved to withdraw from being an auxiliary to the AASS while "disclaim[ing] all intention of censuring the old organization." Significantly, they also stopped short of approving the new organization, "or expressing any opinion on the merits of the controversy between them." Oberlin professor John Morgan argued at length in favor of the resolutions, and after "some of his best remarks," they were adopted without debate.[27] One delegate concluded his account of the convention by declaring that the abolitionists of Ohio were "united, zealous, unfaltering, determined never to relax in effort, till the last chain be broken, and the shout of the redeemed bondman tell that slavery has expired."[28]

Nonetheless, in 1842, the executive committee of the AASS dispatched its general agent John Collins on a mission to reclaim Ohio for the "Old Org."[29] Eastern Garrisonians viewed the Ohio society's decision not to affiliate itself with either faction more from the perspective of withdrawal from the parent society than as a declaration of neutrality. Since prominent Garrisonians believed that "Ohio is to the West what Mass. is to N.E. in point of influence," they decided that it was time that blurred lines of allegiance be clearly redrawn between western abolitionists.[30] Collins concentrated his efforts on playing up ideological differences between strict nonresistance and moral suasion on the one hand, and the pronounced shift of the OASS toward open support of antislavery politics on the other. A minority of members were swayed by Collins's "wily arguments and plausible sophistry," as William Birney put it. Several joined together at the 1842 annual meeting in a motion to re-annex the OASS to the AASS. When that measure was defeated, they withdrew from the society to form their own organization, the Ohio American Anti-Slavery Society (OAASS), and renewed their auxiliary connection to the parent society.[31]

However, John Collins did not remain long in Ohio, and he returned to New England late in the year.[32] In the absence of the divisive eastern influence, the Ohio split remained cordial. Representatives of the old society admitted that "certainly never has there been a more friendly schism since the separation of Abraham and Lott." The 1842 annual report of the OASS stressed that only a single point of difference distinguished the two organizations: "one is auxiliary to the American Anti-Slavery Society, the other is not auxiliary to any society."[33] The two organizations agreed not to publicly discuss any differences that may thereafter arise between them, and leaders reached an understanding whereby the points on which they did disagree would be "left nearly out of sight" so that they could "labor shoulder to shoulder, for the advancement of the anti-slavery cause" in pursuit of the measures upon which they mutually agreed.[34] In addition, the new society agreed to help pay off the old society's debt, and the *Philanthropist* was to become the shared newspaper of both organizations.[35]

By 1843, the dual societies' meetings could hardly be distinguished from each other. Representatives of each shared lecture platforms, and conventions met across the state with no mention of which of the two organizations was the sponsor. In most, members of both groups cooperated in the gatherings. In the summer of 1844, the *Oberlin Evangelist* recommend that its readers attend a series of antislavery meetings, one nearly every night, to be addressed by Oberlin professor and "New Org" adherent Timothy Hudson, Garrisonian and former slave Henry Bibb, OAASS agent and Liberty Party leader Samuel Brooke, Oberlin alum Amos Dresser, and others.[36]

Despite the fact that differences over the role of antislavery politics in the movement ostensibly contributed to the relatively painless split in the Ohio ranks, even correspondents for the *Liberator* admitted that the issue was not nearly as divisive in the West as in the East. Its coverage of the 1842 anniversary of the OASS concluded that "third party in that region is altogether a different thing from third party in New England."[37] The day that some members of the OASS defected in 1842, the president of the state's Liberty Party actually joined them and donated a considerable sum to their cause.[38] At a highly publicized county meeting in the OAASS's Salem headquarters members resolved in March 1845 to do all in their power to reunite the two Ohio societies.[39] The Garrisonian auxiliary in Ohio even elected an avowed Liberty Party activist as its president that year, and its membership continued to include Garrisonians as well as "warm Liberty party men" for the rest of that party's life.[40] To those who thought that there "ought to be a regular pitched battle between the Ohio American Society and the Liberty Party," Gamaliel Bailey declared, "there should be none, if I can help it.... I would rather any time shake a friend by the hand, than knock him over the noddle."[41]

Even with the friendliness among Ohio abolitionists after the national split, Oberlin abolitionists undertook further attempts to smooth over any differences and allay the suspicions of some westerners that they would eventually have to choose sides in the conflict or adopt a rigid antislavery ideology with which they were not completely comfortable. The statement of one Western Reserve man in 1844 is instructive: "Abolitionism is quite popular among us. Nearly every man is an abolitionist of some sort. We have modern abolitionists, old fashioned abolitionists, political abolitionists, and religious abolitionists, enthusiastic or hot-headed abolitionists, deliberate abolitionists, immediate and gradual abolitionists, ultra and radical abolitionists, subtle and Bondite abolitionists, and to cap the climax, we have quite a popular class of do-nothing abolitionists."[42]

Spokespeople from the Oberlin community stressed that the means one chose were far less important than the desired end every true enemy of slavery shared. As Finney declared to his Oberlin followers, "All the truly wise or truly pious have one and the same end in view," and the thoughtful consideration of that fact would necessarily lead abolitionists to what they genuinely believed were the most appropriate methods. Both ultraradicals and conservatives, Finney believed, misunderstood the true spirit of the reform.[43]

Yet for years after the 1840 split, whenever Oberlin abolitionists advocated principles that resembled the line laid down by "new organizers," Garrison pounced upon them without reserve in the pages of the Liberator. He and many other eastern abolitionists would not countenance neutrality, and when members of the Oberlin community continued as the West's most vocal advocates of independent abolitionism, the town and all its residents became a favorite target. Even though they had never sought out such a confrontation, Oberlin abolitionists now faced unrelenting opposition not only from enemies of abolitionism in their own region but from the eastern radicals as well.

Garrison's greatest objections in the early 1840s in numerous *Liberator* articles bore out Oberlin professor John Cowles's observation, even before the split, regarding radical Garrisonians in general that "if a man cannot swallow Garrison whole, hook and all, they give him over to Satan forthwith, that he may learn not to blaspheme the name in which they rejoice."[44] Most Oberlinites were committed to perfecting the admittedly flawed government through their sanctified votes, and their belief in a religious duty to vote and support human governments was by no means meant to be a provocative jab at nonresistants but was the result of careful study and protracted consideration.[45] However, Garrison, under headings such as "Protestant Popery," ridiculed Oberlin's perfectionist politics. Mahan and Finney, he wrote, were utterly devoid of "moral courage and firmness."[46] By even recognizing the constitutional authority of the president of the United States (who was a slaveholder), Oberlinites faced Garrison's cynical dismissal of their "*anti-slavery* piety." Finney, he charged, likely felt "delight" to see a "man-thief . . . in the Presidential chair."[47] In another column, Garrison derided Finney's arguments that human government was a divine institution and described such reasoning as "spectres of logic, and legal apparitions . . . sophistry and metaphysical parade."[48]

Still, Oberlin remained above ideological quarrels and refused to fight a war of words with Garrison. Finney articulated the belief that whenever anyone, regardless of how much truth they had on their side, possessed a "wrong spirit in the proclamation and defense of it," they could expect God to "give them up to defeat." "The needed reformation," he wrote in a widely circulated essay, "can never be brought about by contending for truth in a wrong spirit."[49] Oberlin professor and proud Garrisonian Amasa Walker gently reproved Garrison's attacks upon his school, writing to him, "I know you would not wish to excite any unjust prejudice against Oberlin. It is a place where, above all others I ever saw, the colored man enjoys his rights." "I trust you must feel friendly to Oberlin," he concluded, "and be very unwilling to do any thing that should operate to its injury in the public mind."[50] Others simply left matters to God; "Oberlin will live while truth lives," one defensive resident wrote directly to Garrison; "let its enemies say and do what they may."[51]

Eastern Garrisonians continued to worry about the direction that Oberlinites were leading Ohio's movement. Abolitionists like Lucretia Mott had long held a paranoid fear that the influential Oberlin community would "be New organized" and take all of Ohio with it.[52] Others believed that they should do all they could to wrest Ohio abolitionists from the grasp of "the pro-slavery priest and the aspiring demagogue," their dismissive description of Oberlinites and all but the strictest Garrisonian abolitionists.[53] In 1844, under pressure from the eastern radicals, the OAASS began to purge its executive committee of members who might slow a deliberate move away from strict Garrisonianism, even dismissing its general agent. Samuel Brooke, who was also concurrently serving as a financial agent for the Liberty Party, was charged with being unable to serve "with such divided loyalty."[54]

Most prominent in the overhaul was the executive committee's invitation in 1845 to Abby Kelley, the woman one historian terms "the flying wedge of Garrisonian policy," to assist in the restructuring.[55] Kelley had earlier informed one Ohio correspondent that she and the AASS were "making arrangements to cut out the tongue of the Son of the Father of Lies, *New Organization*, alias, Third Party, in this state," and it seems as if her mission to Ohio was just so calculated.[56] Though she could not carry the June anniversary convention to adopt Garrison's declaration that the Constitution was "a covenant with death and an agreement with hell," the delegates did give support to the motto "No Union with Slaveholders." Also, over the strenuous protest of Oberlin's John Keep, Kelley helped pass through resolutions that unmistakably distanced the OAASS from any connection with political abolitionism.[57] Along with her fiancé Stephen Foster and fellow New Englanders Giles Stebbins, Benjamin Jones, Elizabeth Hitchcock, and Parker Pillsbury, Kelley helped establish the *Anti-Slavery Bugle* in Salem to avoid sharing the *Philanthropist*'s pages with "new organizers."[58] The *Bugle*'s lead article in the inaugural issue was written by the famous nonresistant Adin Ballou and titled "The Superiority of Moral Over Political Power."[59] As an exclamation point, the executive committee changed the name of the organization to the Western Anti-Slavery Society (WASS), to demonstrate that "all parts of the country, west of the Alleghenies . . . could be reached by the agents of the American Anti-Slavery Society."[60]

Although the attempts of Oberlin abolitionists to avoid a practical division in Ohio were tested when the OAASS remade itself as the WASS, their continuing influence within that body kept it from ever becoming an exact mirror image of the AASS or Abby Kelley's unrestricted radical domain. The year after the organization of the WASS, Oberlin alumna Betsey Mix Cowles, herself a close confidant of Kelley, issued a call in the *Bugle* for an independent abolitionist meeting and invited "all friends of the slave '*of every persuasion*'" to gather together to work toward their shared goals. Cowles addressed all possible critics—"Those who call us Abby Kelleyites . . . come and see what a company of such 'ites' will do; only think of it, if one creates such a stir in community—what will a whole company do!" To Garrisonians she urged, "Take your shield in hand; carefully peep over or under it; see how such 'oos' look." To political abolitionists, Cowles suggested they "buckle on the whole political armor; come and stand your ground manfully."[61] Besides Cowles, other Ohioans with Garrisonian leanings no doubt agreed with Oberlin student and Garrisonian Lucy Stone in feeling sorry whenever true friends disagreed, "for 'Union is strength,' and the poor slave suffers by disunion."[62] Despite grumbling from the outside leadership of the new society, it was apparent that everyone was welcome at the Ohio abolitionist table.

Eastern Garrisonians did not understand how members of their Ohio auxiliary could simultaneously support them and the Liberty Party and political abolitionism all at once. Abby Kelley angrily informed Cowles that the "Liberty Party, with Father [John] Keep at its head, is trying to appropriate to itself the entire fruits of our labors."[63] Yet Keep and many other Oberlinites were also familiar faces at meetings of the then-OAASS. Giles Stebbins, one of Kelley's lecturing partners in Ohio, wrote to Garrison of his surprise when they refused to waste time bickering. These particular abolitionists, he wrote, "manifested a fairness and candor that would put to shame their brethren in the East." Stebbins found "less blinding prejudice, than farther East, and of course more willingness to discuss fairly, and with a wish to arrive at the truth."[64] This, of course, was the Oberlin way, and as one alumnus remarked years later, their "recognition that means, as well as ends, has their place in morals" represented a purifying and equalizing force in their abolitionism.[65] Put simply, their quarrel was with slavery, not other reformers.

Many Ohioans began, when possible, to maintain membership in and attend the meetings of both organizations in addition to their continuing involvement with the Liberty Party.[66] Within two or three years after the 1842 split, the old OASS had for all intents and purposes merged with the Liberty Party.[67] The new organization paid off its final debts, its newspaper became a shared organ, and abolitionists of all stripes began to use the names Ohio American Anti-Slavery Society, the Ohio Anti-Slavery Society, and the Ohio State Anti-Slavery Society interchangeably to denote the surviving moral abolition organization in Ohio. Both the Liberty Party and the antislavery society continued to gain members, but their respective membership lists shared many of the same names.[68]

This overlap was demonstrated in the farewell meeting held to honor Abby Kelley and husband Stephen Foster's 1846 Ohio lecture tour. The

Portrait of Abby Kelley Foster, by Charlotte M. Wharton (courtesy of the artist [1999])

meeting was held in Salem, the headquarters of the WASS, and though organizers expected only a few curious people to turn out, a huge crowd filled the meetinghouse to hear the speeches of the Fosters and other antislavery luminaries. However, it was not just Garrisonians who made up the assembly but a wide variety of abolitionists who came simply to celebrate the absolute advance of antislavery sentiment in Ohio and to acknowledge two of the holy warriors who played important parts in it. Thus it should not be surprising that the same meeting at which Stephen Foster presented an address on "the pro-slavery character of the Constitution, and the sinfulness of those who stand in political connection with the slaveholders" was also treated to a speech by a Western Reserve man with Oberlin connections who described the Liberty Party as "the abolitionist's staff of accomplishment, and the ballot-box the means of salvation to the slave."[69]

We Are as a People, Chained Together

Unlike white abolitionists who might lament wasted effort while attempting to fight slavery on an ideological plane, Oberlin's black abolitionists brought to the table a different picture of slavery and freedom, one informed either by their own experiences as bondsmen or by daily exposure to racist America.[70] Slavery was quite real to them, and as William Howard Day reminded his brethren, "It is more than a mere figure of speech to say, that we are as a people, chained together." "We are one people," he declared in an 1848 address, "one in general complexion, one in common degradation, one in popular estimation—As one rises, all must rise, and as one falls, all must fall."[71] Alumna Sara Stanley also discounted isolated or individual action. "Let unanimity of action characterize us," she urged a black gathering. For her, only "a radical, utilitarian spirit" would do "in the common cause."[72] Oberlin's black abolitionists treasured their town and school's empathetic commitment to practical abolitionism and concern for the ends that must be met rather than the means used to achieve them.

The handful of black activists in Oberlin formed the nucleus of an aggressive group who constantly kept community members at a brisk pace of reformist agitation and helped steer them clear of abolitionist infighting. Indeed, they quickly became the radical conscience of the Oberlin community that refused to allow its antislavery vanguard to rest. In his first commencement address as Oberlin's president in 1866, James Fairchild credited the school's black students with having "saved us from stagnation during the generation past . . . and left a lasting impression upon the vast majority of the thousands that have been gathered here."[73] In the words of black Oberlin leaders, they were "lovers of liberty and of our country" who resolved to use the benefits they gained from their Oberlin experience on behalf of the "oppressed colored citizens of the United States," of which they were but "a portion."[74] William Howard Day urged all similarly situated African Americans that with "our feet on the rock of freedom, we must drag our brethren from the slimy depths of slavery, ignorance, and ruin." "Every one of us," he wrote, "should be ashamed to consider himself free, while his brother is a slave. The wrongs of our brethren should be our constant theme."[75]

That African American students were so scarce in Oberlin's early years actually amplified their sense of racial responsibility.[76] One female graduate remembered that each and every one of her actions at Oberlin College was charged with a significance far beyond its immediate consequence. She recalled that she felt as though she had "the honor of the whole African race" upon her shoulders during her class recitations.[77] Yet, as Sara Stanley pointed out, though African Americans lacked sheer numbers, "the race is not always gained by the swift, nor the battle by the strong."[78] Historians William and Aimee Lee Cheek suggest that the presence of the uncommon Oberlin African American student was akin to that of the fugitive slave on a lecture platform. Both were powerful agents for the abolitionist conversions of the white population that surrounded them.[79] Still, they were more common at Oberlin than at any other school, so their numbers, though small, brought them into close and regular contact with white students. "A single colored student in each class, unconsciously to himself," one professor noted, "stood there in his own right 'a man and a brother,' more effective than all the Anti-Slavery sermons that Oberlin could have brought to bear."[80] Intimacy was a powerful tool of conversion.

Come-Outism and Come-Outers

It was largely through the demands of Oberlin African Americans and a handful of radical women that the faculty were convinced to allow Abby Kelley and Stephen Foster, the "come-outerism twins," to debate their theories in the Oberlin Church.[81] The two were perhaps the most notorious of the Garrisonians who strictly followed the biblical injunction "Come out of her, my people, that ye partake not of her sins, and that ye receive not of her plagues."[82] Although some Northern churches condemned slaveholding as a sin, their counterparts in the South more often acknowledged it as a benign and moral institution. Thus membership within a national church body technically made one a member of an organization that in some way approved of slavery. Come-outers demanded that these churchgoers withdraw from all fellowship with churches that refused to completely sever connections with slaveholders or that sanctioned them.

They applied the same logic to the U.S. government and argued that support for a government that was not a pronounced enemy of slavery was no different than the outright support of a proslavery authority. Although the words "slave" or "slavery" did not appear in the Constitution, come-outers interpreted it as a proslavery document. Its clause that allowed three-fifths of "all other persons" besides free men to be counted toward congressional representation, its articles governing fugitives from labor, and its authorization of the use of federal troops to "suppress insurrections" (presumably slave rebellions) damned the nation's foundational document in their eyes. Garrisonian come-outers like Kelley and Foster instructed their listeners to immediately come out of "corrupt" churches, to renounce the authority of clergy and constitutionally elected officials, and to do all in their power to accomplish the Garrisonian motto "No Union with Slaveholders."[83]

Despite the respect Oberlin abolitionists held for governmental authority and their manifest reverence for organized churches, they recognized the kernel of truth within the come-outer argument. Professor James Thome admitted that no reform ever set out with higher pretensions and applauded its "lofty heroism, its uncompromising positions, its double portion of the martyr spirit, its parade of logical withal, and its specious eloquence." Yet he also pointed out that "all is not gold that glitters. It is not the mill that clatters most that grinds the best grist."[84] The Oberlin community itself practiced a form of religious come-outerism. Its single church steadfastly refused communion and fellowship to slaveholders and remained congregational in governance. When the institute's graduates went forth to preach in other churches that had some distant connection to a slaveholding congregation or congregant, they did so hoping to reform these church bodies from within rather than choke the life from them by withdrawal.

To Oberlinites, the role of the churches was not merely to be an abolitionist tool. Though the antislavery crusade was most decidedly a religious one, and though they believed that the churches must lead the way, abolition was not their sole function. This was the same creed that Finney espoused even before Oberlin's founding—the eradication of slavery was an important though not controlling factor in complete Christian regeneration.[85] Thus, a church that exerted its influence in a sinful way should be condemned, but Thome wrote that "this is a case which calls not for proscription, extermination and destruction, but for patience, kindness, forbearance and instruction."[86] By abandoning a potentially reformable church over a single issue, come-outerism came dangerously close to fabricating a religion of its own, a Christianity that was "to all intents and purposes devotion to the slave."[87] Accordingly, slavery seemed the only sin worth acknowledging. This also branded all members of national churches or ministers of the gospel worse sinners than actual slaveholders, the "corollary from the position that the Churches in the free states are the bulwark of slavery."[88]

Oberlin abolitionists and many of like mind did not deny that slavery was a sin—"the sum of all villainies." Yet they could not grant that it was the *only* sin worth illuminating, or that everyone but the most estranged come-outer shared equally with planters and slave-dealers the guilt for the survival of slavery in the United States.[89] Oberlinites appreciated that there were a significant number of antislavery people in the nonslaveholding states who might also exert "a vast and most salutary influence." Moreover, they also rightly believed that their beneficial influence was rapidly increasing, and that "incessant blows, both political and moral, are telling prodigiously upon the battlements of oppression." Even assuming for argument's sake that the denominational churches of the free states *were* bulwarks of slavery,

Thome recognized that it was only because they wielded an immensely powerful influence that they should be appropriated rather than alienated. He asked if the slave would truly thank come-outers "for destroying a mighty engine of influence when they might by pursuing a different course have secured it entirely to his interest?"[90]

Kelley and Foster were in the midst of their 1846 Ohio lecturing tour when they approached Oberlin. They had left a long trail of agitated audiences in their wake, as slavery, the Liberty Party, the Constitution, and the "New Org" came in for equal amounts of abuse.[91] Betsey Mix Cowles wrote Professor Henry Cowles before the Kelley-Fosters arrived in Oberlin. She admitted that "the tide of prejudice is strong against them," but she had faith that Oberlinites would allow them the opportunity to argue their case. "If they are propagating error," she said, "there is mind enough with you to grapple with it & free discussion is in accordance with the principles of us all."[92]

However, when the Garrisonians made it to town at the end of February, the Oberlin community was in the midst of a powerful religious awakening. "A revival, as usual," Kelley complained to a friend, "was in progress when we arrived."[93] The *Oberlin Evangelist* reported that "this visit of our friends occurred at a time when many souls among us were anxiously inquiring the way of salvation, when many were just entering upon the peculiar trials, vicissitudes, and joys of a life of faith and consecration to God." Many Oberlinites felt that they could not afford to have their minds or those of their families and friends diverted from the revival, even in favor of abolitionism.[94] Still, the couple was warmly greeted at the depot by Oberlin student and former Garrisonian lecturer James Monroe and welcomed into the home of President Asa Mahan.[95]

Abby Kelley spent much of her time in Oberlin attempting to illuminate its church's connection with slavery and endeavoring to show that the Constitution was a proslavery document that ought not be supported by voting or holding public office under its provisions. She later claimed that she had made Oberlin's religious connection "with the vile system . . . considerably clear."[96] Regarding the Constitution, she argued that though its preamble expressed some of the egalitarian sentiment embodied in the Declaration of Independence, it must be dismissed as nothing more than "a signboard over a store door, which often tells untruths." The wisest solution to constitutional inconsistencies, she avowed, was to reconcile them through disunion and the complete separation of the North from the slaveholding South.[97]

However, members of her Oberlin audience concluded that Kelley's rhetoric was far superior to her reasoning. Though her argument was "perhaps as good as can be made in proof of such a position," she failed to convince her listeners that they held the wrong views regarding the church or their national compact.[98] As they saw it, one of the Garrisonians' chief argumentative flaws was their apparent lack of practical solutions to the problem of slavery. Timothy Hudson complained that "they tried to convince us how the work could not, rather than how it could, be accomplished." The Kelley-Fosters berated the organized churches and their members, disparaged constitutional government, and criticized compromising politicians, "yet failed to point out a more excellent way." "I for one," Hudson declared, "have yet to be convinced that the Liberty Party is not the heaven-appointed means for the overthrow of that most-vile & heaven-insulting system of slavery."[99]

Most of Hudson's fellow townsmen agreed. They had no problem supporting the Liberty Party and its place in the governmental system because they did not believe that the Constitution was necessarily a proslavery document. Rather, they subscribed to the constitutional arguments of abolitionists like Lysander Spooner and William Goodell, who both famously argued that the Constitution was actually an antislavery document that could and should be used to abolitionists' advantage. Strictly interpreted, there was no reference to "compromises," "guarantees," "slaves," "slavery," or "property in man." Instead, there was the explicit guarantee to citizens of life, liberty, and property of the Fifth Amendment. Since African Americans were either citizens or aliens (and if aliens they could be naturalized), they were entitled to the same rights as white Americans. Thus slavery was unconstitutional as were the various state laws that supported the institution.[100]

Overall, the impression that the Kelley-Fosters made upon Oberlin minds was similar to the opinion held by Hudson. Of Kelley, he reasoned that she possessed a "powerful mind" and deep devotion to the slave. Moreover, her efforts in behalf of abolitionism were doing great good in the region. However, when moved to consider the logic of her argument, he could not admit that her positions were all sound or that she was at all times charitable, kind, or fair.[101] Helen Cowles, wife of Professor Henry Cowles, remarked on Kelley's look of "contempt and scorn upon her countenance" before she ever began to speak. Cowles wrote that the first address matched her appearance. "I left while she was speaking," Cowles reported, "and though she spoke twice more, that was the last I wanted to hear from them."[102]

For her part, Kelley was not generous in her impressions of the Oberlin community. She characterized the logic of Mahan and John Morgan as "flimsy," and when community officials refused to indefinitely extend the debates alongside the ongoing revival, Kelley exclaimed "in the language of the Church[,] 'Good Lord deliver me from the tyranny of superstition—'tis the most cruel of all tyrannies.'"[103] Garrison used Kelley's account as another opportunity to disparage Oberlin, which had now been a favorite target of his journalistic barbs for several years. Under the heading "Refuge of Oppression," a column in the *Liberator* in which he specially reserved "to make permanent record of the various forms of hostility to the anti-slavery cause, its faithful advocates, and the free colored population," Garrison excoriated Oberlin's reception of the Kelley-Fosters and the *Oberlin Evangelist*'s explanation for it. He mocked the community's "*pious*" pronouncements, even subtitling his critique "Piety Versus Humanity."[104] There, in the same column where he publicly rebuked the various Southern legislatures, colonizationists, slave dealers, and other proslavery forces, Garrison inexplicably wrote off the Oberlin community as no better than a den of slaveholders. By calling the *Oberlin Evangelist* a "refuge of oppression," he dismissed its messages just like he would countless other "tyrant's plea for grasping his victims."[105]

However, even some of Garrison's friends could not stomach the denunciation of one of abolitionism's most important strongholds, especially one trying so hard to bridge the movement's ideological divides. Massachusetts abolitionist Isaac Stearns fired off a letter to Garrison claiming that he could not see any harm in the *Oberlin Evangelist*'s story, "unless the honor and rights of the slave, or anti-slavery, is paramount to the rights of God or his government." Stearns scolded Garrison, writing that "God is greater and more worthy of honor than all other beings put together." If God was in fact at Oberlin at the time "*manifesting* his presence . . . to have those of his sinful creatures who do not appreciate such things, come in to avert their attention to an inferior subject, I consider an indignity offered to God himself, and of baneful tendency."[106]

It seemed that no one was completely satisfied with the Garrisonians' February visit, and Kelley soon began campaigning for another invitation later that year. Some members of the Oberlin faculty, reflecting on the disruptive nature of the couple's first visit, suggested that Kelley and Foster were "unsafe advocates of the slave" and should not be encouraged to return. Kelley complained to Lucy Stone that the decision was "all because we are infidels." She believed that Oberlin's community leaders would rather "attack us in our absence, and send the cry 'Infidel' on our heels, all over the country, but give us no opportunity to refute the vile slanders."[107] Ultimately, the spirit of free discussion prevailed. A meeting of black Oberlinites characterized the Kelley-Fosters as "true and honest friends of the oppressed" and their leader Garrison as the "Leonidas of the Anti-Slavery Movement."[108] Oberlin officials reluctantly agreed and invited the two back, though they would have to present their arguments in the old chapel in Colonial Hall so that they might not "defile" Oberlin's church.[109]

The bulk of the several days' discussion consisted of what Kelley described as a "brawling debate" between her husband and Asa Mahan, an adversary whom she said "exhibited a recklessness of principle I was not prepared to witness."[110] The men again took up the topics of the Constitution and come-outerism, and their debates were the biggest draw in town. The Oberlin Musical Association even interrupted its meetings "to accommodate the discussion then in progress . . . on disunion in church and state organizations."[111] Lucy Stone concluded that some of the faculty were pleased with the lectures. The events "set the people to thinking," so much that she imagined that "great good will result."[112] The editor of the *Oberlin Evangelist* was not as convinced of a change of opinion in his town. "The discussion is now over," he wrote, and "we are not aware that disunion and come-out-ism have made one new convert." In fact, public opinion in Oberlin appeared to set more powerfully against come-outerism than it had before the Kelley-Fosters' visit. The pair had been "weak in argument—strong only in vituperation."[113] The editor wondered how they ever hoped to secure the respect of an intelligent community while pursuing such an adversarial and illogical course.[114] Finney was even more negative in his assessment. Kelley wrote that "Professor Finney said the Spirit of God left the place immediately on our entering it."[115]

In 1847, the general agent of the WASS led Garrison on his own lecture tour of Ohio, accompanied across the state by Frederick Douglass, Stephen Foster, and Oberlin student George Vashon (Abby Kelley had taken a temporary leave from lecturing for the birth of a daughter).[116] Though no abolitionist lecture circuit in the West was complete without a stop in Oberlin, Garrison worried that he and his companions would make little headway there. They had only scheduled one day in town, Garrison wrote, and he believed that "a good deal of prejudice is cherished against me on account of my 'infidelity' and 'comeouterism.'" Nonetheless, he believed that "if there was a spot on the globe where [I] would be welcome to speak [my] freest thought, that spot was Oberlin."[117] He maintained that he and his cohorts were nonetheless prepared "to give our testimony, both in regard to the Church and State, whatever may be thought or said of us."[118]

When Garrison arrived in Oberlin for the first time in August of 1847, he expressed a "lively interest in its welfare." "Oberlin," he wrote to his wife,

Asa Mahan (courtesy Oberlin College Archives)

"has done much for the relief for the flying fugitives from the southern prison-house.... It has also promoted the cause of emancipation in various ways, and its church refuses to be connected with any slaveholding or pro-slavery church by religious fellowship." He thought that Oberlinites' political associations "diminish[ed] the power of their example," but he held out hope that he could convince them of the error of their ways.[119]

Garrison and his colleagues arrived in time to witness the Oberlin commencement ceremonies. His most likely advocate among that year's graduates, Lucy Stone, did not present a commencement address because, as a woman, she would not be allowed to read it publicly. However, the eastern visitors did listen to young and zealous platform speakers who denounced "the fanaticism of Come-outerism and Disunionism." Finney, perhaps spying his distinguished guests in the audience, then took a turn at the rostrum and advised the graduates that "denouncing Come-outerism on the one hand, or talking about the importance of preserving harmony or union in the church, on the other, would avail them nothing." He commended them to go "heartily" into all reforms of the age and, in language similar to Garrison's, to be "anti-devil all over." If they were not prepared to do this, Finney informed them, their future avocation should be anything but reform or the ministry.[120]

The next day, thousands of people from across the region crowded into Oberlin's First Church to hear the lively antislavery discussions. Garrison and Douglass did most of the talking for the easterners. Foster, curiously, said "but little." Garrison described Mahan's follow-up comments as "perfectly respectful . . . with good temper and courtesy." That evening, the group was entertained by Oberlin Institute treasurer Hamilton Hill and Professor Hudson. Though their tight schedule could not accommodate Mahan's invitation to dine with him the next day, Garrison and his associates were able to spend time mingling with some of the students, many of whom made favorable impressions on the visitors.[121]

Oberlinites, if not won over by Garrison's ideas, were thoroughly impressed by Garrison the man. For most of them, their only knowledge of him had been what they had read in the pages of the Liberator, and they were taken aback by the charming, polite gentleman and his associates they met in person. John Morgan, for one, finally understood the source of Garrison's charismatic influence over his eastern followers. He also heaped praise upon Frederick Douglass's shoulders, calling him "one of the greatest phenomena of the age . . . full of wit, human[ity] and pathos."[122] Still, Oberlinites lamented the fact that even such a powerful advocate for the slave as Douglass seemed constrained by the need to adhere to a particular abolitionist dogma in order to remain a member in good standing among his colleagues. Morgan noted that Douglass was "sometimes mighty in invective," the result of his being too much "under the influence of the Garrisonian clique."[123] The Oberlin community continued to believe that the antislavery movement was one of individuals who must each formulate his or her own personal ideology. After all, one's own conscience was the ultimate arbiter in determining right and wrong, wise and foolish. The goal was emancipation; there were many legitimate paths to that end.

Though some radicals like the Kelley-Fosters continued to earn notoriety by their militant efforts to "out-Garrison Garrison" in their demands for dogmatic adherence to a strict ideology, even the Liberator editor increasingly became more receptive to the practical efforts of abolitionists of the Oberlin school and respectful of antislavery tactics other than his own, especially during and after his Ohio tour of 1847.[124] Though he continued to remind politically-minded reformers that there was a higher moral position to be obtained by them, Garrison hailed the political antislavery movement "as a cheering sign of the times."[125] He believed that those abolitionists like the Oberlinites who eschewed conformity but did not "lose sight of the true issue" and who sincerely believed their chosen path to be the best hope for abolition deserved his earnest "commendation and sympathy."[126]

Frederick Douglass emerged from that Ohio summer impressed and even more transformed than his mentor. He summed up his tour of Ohio's Western Reserve by declaring the region "in a healthy state of Anti-Slavery agitation." "The West," he wrote, "is decidedly the best Anti-Slavery field in the country.—The people are more disposed to hear—less confined and narrow in their views, and less circumscribed in their action by sectarian trammels, than are the people of the East."[127] "Agreeing with or differing from you of the same religious faith or politics, or differing from you in both, it makes no difference," Douglass remembered. "Once make him feel you are an honest man and you are welcomed with all the fullness of genuine hospitality, to his heart and his home."[128]

Within weeks of concluding his Oberlin visit, Douglass publicly embraced the independence with which the Oberlinites had so thoroughly impressed him, distanced himself from the controlling Garrisonian influence (both ideologically and geographically), and established his own abolitionist newspaper in western New York.[129] In the first issue of the North Star, Douglass acknowledged the role of "that infallible teacher, experience" in convincing him to establish "a newspaper, devoted to the cause of Liberty, Humanity and Progress." In his very first editorial, addressed to his "oppressed countrymen," Douglass vowed not only to "boldly advocate emancipation" but to do so unconstrained by dogma. "Among the multitude of plans proposed and opinions held, with reference to our cause and condition," Douglass declared, "we shall try to have a mind of our own, harmonizing with all as far as we can, and differing from any and all where we must, but always discriminating between men and measures."[130] His promise to "cordially approve every measure and effort calculated to advance [the] sacred cause, and strenuously oppose any which in our opinion may tend to retard its progress" earned the high praise of the abolitionist editor of the Oberlin Evangelist, Professor Henry Cowles, who called the paper "an honor to the colored race."[131] His community had advocated that same independence for years before Douglass ever gave his first public speech. As antislavery reformers across the free states noticeably reconsolidated their efforts to achieve a practical abolitionism, the influential Oberlin community continued to be in the vanguard.

CHAPTER SIX

The Tyrant's Grapple by Our Vote, We'll Loosen from Our Brother's Throat

Oberlin, Free Soil, and the Fight for Equal Rights

As one of the principal issues that divided the AASS, the question of antislavery politics remained a primary point of contention among reformers later in the 1840s. Nonresistant critics of political action pointed to the gradual dilution of antislavery demands in the third-party platforms for the sake of popular appeal. The compromises necessary to be a force in politics, they argued, destroyed the pure moral essence of abolitionism. Even if antislavery politicians were successful in their objectives, strict moral suasionists worried that they would only superficially injure slavery while leaving intact the underlying racism that sustained it. For their part, abolitionists who hoped to effect emancipation through politics valued any advance, however small, toward the eradication of slavery. They well realized that their political involvement dulled the radical edge that had originally inspired them to appeal to the electorate. Still, there were also those like the abolitionists from Oberlin who attempted to bridge the gap between politics and moralism, and these were often the reformers who achieved the most lasting and significant results.

Though these Oberlin abolitionists were directly involved in politics, they remained true to the principal tenet of the original Liberty Party platform and even the 1833 "Declaration of Sentiments" of the AASS. By bringing political as well as moral weapons into the fight with slavery, Oberlinites believed that they could at least check the growth of the institution. Further, by breaking the stranglehold of the Slave Power over the federal government, even incrementally, they believed that they could direct slavery toward extinction. They also appreciated the degree to which politics could be successfully utilized toward the other significant facet of their abolitionism: equal rights in the North. As other abolitionists quarreled over the appropriateness of moral suasion versus political antislavery, the Oberlin community embraced them both and employed them to the full advantage of African Americans, North and South, free and enslaved.

Their goals remained emancipation and equal rights. The means to those ends remained whatever strategy offered the best hope of success. An illustrative example of the Oberlin community's evolution may be found in the various editions of Oberlin alumnus George Clark's popular antislavery songbooks. From a collection of just a handful of tunes in the late 1830s, Clark's songbook went through seven editions titled *The Liberty Minstrel* before being renamed *The Free Soil Minstrel* in 1848. The book's preface was constantly altered to reflect the transitions from Liberty Party to Free-Soil allegiances (and later, Republican), but it always retained its moral core. Clark repeated verbatim in each edition the same universal declaration of intent: "An ardent love of humanity—a deep consciousness of the injustice of slavery—a heart full of sympathy for the oppressed, and a due appreciation for the blessings of freedom." Clark's melodies were songs with lyrics written by Garrisonians, "new organizers," and even slaves, and were to be sung "wherever music is loved and appreciated—Slavery abhorred and Liberty held sacred.[1]

* * *

AS THE OBERLIN COMMUNITY continued to grow in influence in both the abolitionist movement and in local politics after 1840, the opposition it faced because of its abolitionism increased as well. Even in the face of criticism from within the abolitionist movement in the late 1830s and early 1840s, Oberlinites' stiffest censure came from the swelling numbers of their political enemies. When the Democratic-majority Ohio legislature convened in the winter of 1841, one of its first orders of business was the reception of petitions signed by hundreds of anti-abolitionists from different counties in the state whose primary demand was the extermination of the Oberlin Collegiate Institute.[2] A letter to the *Ohio Statesman* from Richland County gives some indication of the reasons the Oberlin community continued to trouble conservative Ohioans. The writer described the Oberlin Institute and its faculty and students as seditious troublemakers who were more dangerous than any other group of reformers in the nation. The writer considered their abolitionist activities "a matter of public notoriety—so notorious that almost every person in the State knows more or less about it." He had "*no doubt* that the majority of them are *at heart* Traitors to the nation, and will prove themselves such. . . . Hence their charter ought to be repealed."[3] Even Ohio's largest Whig newspaper called the persecution of the Oberlin community "but a fair return for the favors thus received," referring to the fact that the town's Liberty Party votes in recent elections had drawn support away from the Whigs and helped the Democrats to the majority.[4]

Though the legislature took up the bill several times that session, final consideration was postponed until the beginning of the next.[5] When debate resumed in January of 1842, it appeared that the recess had not lessened the animosity many lawmakers felt toward all that Oberlin and the community stood for. Lorain County senator Josiah Harris wrote to his wife late in 1842, telling her that she could not possibly conceive "of the opposition and prejudice existing against Oberlin College in the Legislature."[6] Opponents wasted little time before striking. On the first day of the session, Representative Caleb McNulty introduced a bill to repeal Oberlin's charter, a move Representative Thomas Earle told Asa Mahan was "introduced and sustained by the leaders of the Locofoco [Democratic] party in the house."[7] In the rush to discredit everything connected with "Oberlin," Democratic lawmakers called the town and its inhabitants bandits, lawbreakers, "a foul stench in their nostrils," and "a nuisance and a disgrace to this state."[8]

Progressive Whigs offered some defense of the community. For them, however, it was mainly a self-serving countermeasure to Democratic abuse. These lawmakers described the Democrats' charges as "vague and indefinite—but violent and vindictive in their character."[9] A Muskingum County representative asked for proof of Oberlin's infractions and a more precise definition of what Democratic lawmakers meant by "infamous."[10] Hocking County's Legrand Byington arose and boldly answered him, "Why Sir, the evidence of the iniquitous character of that institution is as broad as the light of day; and those who control it, glory in their villainy." "Such being the fact," he argued, "it was folly to waste time" debating details.[11]

The bill initially seemed certain to pass the House.[12] It was referred to a standing judiciary committee, and on December 23 Democrat Legrand Byington reported that a majority of the committee recommended passage without amendment.[13] The next day, Representative Caleb McNulty introduced a copy of recently expelled Oberlin student Delazon Smith's sensationalized *Oberlin Unmasked* to that body. This book was, in classmate James Fairchild's estimation, "a scurrilous pamphlet," and in the words of another Oberlinite, "a choice collection of venomous lies; lies of the filthiest order."[14] McNulty, however, rather enjoyed the work and vouched for its accuracy with a document signed by ten residents of Brown County who testified to the "good standing and integrity" of the author.[15] However, when he moved for a final vote, several key Democrats were absent, and the House quickly adjourned. Later, he moved again for the final vote but could not rally enough support to push the bill through. Thomas Earle was finally able to win indefinite postponement of the measure by a vote of thirty-six to twenty-nine.[16]

One reason for the aggression of the Ohio political establishment was the Oberlin community's growing clout in state politics. Though its votes in 1840 registered little impact in state elections, by 1842 Oberlin voters had combined into a solid voting bloc that strengthened the Liberty Party in Ohio. In the governor's race that year, Russia Township, of which Oberlin was the main part, gave Liberty candidate Leicester King a 240 percent advantage over his closest competitor, and King's vote total was 35 percent higher than the *combined* total for the Whig and Democratic candidates.[17] Over the next two years, with a single exception, Oberlin delivered a plurality of their votes to Liberty Party candidates, and only the fear of Texas annexation in 1844 pushed a small number back into the Whig camp.[18]

Still, the political allegiance of most Oberlinites was not to a party but to the interests of the enslaved and equal rights. The single exception where the majority of Oberlin voters did not support the Liberty Party ticket referred to above is instructive. In 1843, abolitionist Edward Hamlin of Elyria ran for Congress as a Whig. Russia Township propelled him to victory by giving him a convincing majority of its votes.[19] The editor of the Warren *Liberty Herald* scolded Oberlin's voters for throwing their support to the Whig over the Liberty Party candidate. He named "President Mahan, Professors Finney and Whipple, and Mr. Taylor of the *Evangelist* . . . as among those who had assented to the anti-slavery pretensions of the whig party [sic], and would yield them their support." Hoping to lay a great insult upon them, he asked, "On what common ground have the Oberlin abolitionists and the Clay Whigs of Lorain been enabled to meet in loving embrace at the polls?"[20]

However, Hamlin's pledge to the Oberlin voters had been to *oppose* the slaveholder Henry Clay's nomination and election in the upcoming presidential campaign.²¹ The editor of the *Oberlin Evangelist* defended his town's course in the election by boldly asserting, "We have not changed our action since 1840. We vote for the slave, and for the man, let him belong to what party he may, who will do his full duty to the slave." Nonetheless, Oberlinites would always sustain the nominations of the Liberty Party, unless someone else could foreseeably do more than the Liberty nominees. To *Oberlin Evangelist* editor Horace Taylor and the independent Oberlinites he spoke for, their path seemed "perfectly plain in principle. In just such circumstances we were placed at the late election."²²

Veni, Vidi, Vici

Unlike the major parties that ascribed vital importance to a litany of different issues in their platforms, the Liberty Party initially limited itself to a single issue: slavery. In offering candidates for office who prioritized the slavery issue, the Liberty Party believed that it simultaneously offered abolitionist candidates whose values would inform all other important decisions in a consistent manner. A true friend of equal rights would always side with the best interests of the people. By not busying itself with fashioning planks concerned with what it viewed as less consequential issues, the Liberty Party believed that its representatives, from an equal rights perspective, would be best qualified to decide all other issues after discussion on the floor of Congress, utilizing the collective wisdom of its members.²³

Predictably, the antislavery party suffered from lack of appeal to a large constituency. It simply was unable to convince a critical mass of people that slavery and its extension were the most pressing issues facing them at election time. The issues of the national bank, public lands, internal improvements, and the tariff still registered strongly with many voters and were hotly debated across the nation. Yet the issue of Texas annexation gave the Liberty Party a slavery-related political issue that would demand attention. The subject had been lurking in the shadows of mainstream political discourse since the mid-1830s and was increasing annually. Southern slaveholders had been emigrating to Texas since the 1820s with the approval of Mexico. However, when Mexico decreed a plan of gradual emancipation, Anglo-American residents declared their independence. They fought a bloody war with Mexico and founded the Republic of Texas in 1835 hoping for a speedy annexation to the United States.²⁴ By the late 1830s, it seemed almost certain that Texas would come into the union, potentially as four separate slave states.²⁵

Oberlin abolitionists, like many Americans, feared that they had been unwillingly swept into a new, more ominous era in the nation's history. "Annexation is now the greatest word in the American vocabulary," Oberlin student John Alvord declared in an antislavery speech. He warned that "*veni-vidi-vici* is inscribed on the banners of every Caesar who leads a straggling band of American adventurers into the chaparral of a territory which an unfortunate war has given them the right to invade."[26] Many Americans would have agreed with Alvord that their nation seemed to be moving toward an age of conquest and military adventurism at the whim of the Slave Power.

The South appeared united across party lines in favor of annexation, while the North was divided. Whigs opposed it; most Democrats favored it. Though Northern Democrats dismissed the potential Liberty Party threat as miniscule, Whigs realized the danger that they faced from mounting deserters to the Liberty standard over the issue. Moreover, when President William Henry Harrison died of pneumonia in April 1841 just a month after taking office, Whigs found themselves under the party leadership of a man who did not accurately represent the majority of his followers. John Tyler of Virginia had been a longtime Jacksonian Democrat before his addition to the Harrison ticket in 1840. He was a slaveholder, an enemy of Henry Clay, and a strong states' rights advocate. Within five months of his assumption of the presidency, all but one of Tyler's Whig cabinet members had resigned in disgust. By the end of the year, prominent party men were demanding that Tyler pledge not to seek reelection, and progressive Whigs began defecting to the Liberty Party in droves.[27] Steadfast "Conscience" Whigs, though a small minority in their party, attacked the upstart independents, maintaining that it was their position in a powerful national party that offered the only possible protection against Texas annexation and the resulting expansion of slavery.[28]

When the Democracy nominated the slaveholding Tennessean James Polk for the presidency in late 1843 and came out unequivocally for annexation, "Conscience" Whigs ratcheted up the force of their attacks. Most Whigs viewed the Liberty Party men as vote poachers, and some Ohio party members accused them of actually being tools of the proslavery Democrats.[29] Lorain County Whigs implored Liberty men to "reflect before they cast a vote that will be equivalent to one vote for the loco-foco ticket."[30] In a more direct critique, another Lorain County Whig newspaper accused the Liberty Party of adopting a policy of "DIVIDE and RUIN." The paper emphasized the role of several unnamed Oberlin professors who had allegedly declared it the duty of all Liberty Party men to "do all the mischief [they] could to both the political parties."[31] Even the Democratic press in Ohio admitted that the Liberty approach seemed suicidal to their own interests. The Whigs, the editor of the *Lorain Republican* wrote, had always been the Liberty Party's closest allies, and "*now stood ready and willing to co-operate with the abolitionists in their undertakings.*"[32] Nonetheless, state election returns in October showed a marked increase in the third-party vote over the previous election. Lorain County set the pace, producing the largest proportional Liberty Party vote of any county in Ohio. The *Cincinnati Philanthropist and Weekly Herald* declared, "Well done Lorain!" and dubbed Oberlin's home territory "the banner county of the State."[33]

Following the elections of 1843, the national Liberty Party convention in Buffalo again nominated James G. Birney to head its presidential ticket and passed a series of resolutions laying out the party's bare-bones antislavery platform. Curiously missing from these position statements was any mention of its stand on the Texas issue. As it became clear on the campaign trail that the proslavery interests were pushing for annexation and the Whigs were moving into a position of opposition, the attitude of the Liberty Party, in Ohio and elsewhere, remained ambiguous and confused as to how best to counter Whig strength. Members who had reluctantly left the Whig Party for the Liberty banner were particularly vexed. The unexpected and generally unappreciated appearance at the convention of Abby Kelley and Stephen Foster, who were seemingly bent on castigating any and all political positions, did not help in solidifying the Liberty Party approach.[34]

On the one hand, it did seem as if the only thing between an expanded slave South was an act of Congress and the signature of a Democratic president. There seemed to be something to the Whig argument that anything short of those Liberty Party members' support of the Whig candidate could result in a Democratic victory. To a point, the Whig logic was on target; realistically, they were the only hope against Democratic success and Texas annexation. Their fatal flaw, however, was their selection of Henry Clay as their presidential candidate. Had they selected anyone remotely resembling a man with antislavery principles, the continued existence of the Liberty Party would have been threatened.[35] In Clay, however, the Whigs had selected the man just duplicitous enough, in abolitionists' eyes, to be the most undesirable candidate imaginable. Clay was a slaveholder, an obvious disqualification for abolitionist support. Moreover, his public ridicule of abolitionists (presumably to court Southern favor) made his selection utterly repulsive to antislavery appetites.[36]

Ohioans were unrelenting in their attacks on Clay. In *Philanthropist* editor Gamaliel Bailey's estimation, Clay had earned his ill-treatment by having done more to extend the domination of the Slave Power than anyone else. He was, in Bailey's opinion, "the guardian angel in the interests of slavery."[37] Asa Mahan excoriated Clay to Oberlin audiences, calling him "a most bloody duelist, and a man who sustains the vilest character." On one occasion, he criticized Clay to the point where one out-of-town observer characterized the Oberlin Institute president as more resembling "a street brawler" than a minister.[38] Professor Timothy Hudson undertook a lecture tour where, a Whig paper protested, he "abused the Whigs and Mr. Clay most shamefully . . . after the most approved Locofoco style."[39] A group of Oberlin clergymen passed on to their readership the warning, "He who votes for a SLAVEHOLDER, endorses the system. . . . In a word, he who votes for an IMMORAL MAN,—A LAW-BREAKER, is at war with Jehovah's government."[40]

An Ohio Liberty Party convention on February 7 sustained the hurried pace of preparations for the upcoming elections by nominating presidential electors and naming Leicester King as its candidate for governor. The delegates resolved to do their duty to supply candidates for every election, from local coroner to the president of the United States.[41] In October, though their votes did not add up to victory, they did give the Liberty Party the balance of state political power. Again, Oberlin cast its majority for King.[42] Ohio abolitionists could not yet directly pull the levers of government, but their influence in deciding elections was growing. Put into perspective, had Oberlin filled its First Church to only two-thirds of its capacity with Whig voters, the Democratic governor-elect would have been sent home rather than to Columbus.[43]

In November, the Liberty Party had the bittersweet victory of swaying the presidential election. Polk was elected the eleventh president of the United States, and the Liberty vote total of 62,054 far exceeded Polk's margin of victory over Clay. Much has been made over the Liberty Party vote being the deciding factor in the New York results, giving Polk the edge and clinching the electoral advantage overall. However, the state of Ohio also accounted for twenty-three electoral votes, the third weightiest state in America. The Buckeye State was the only other state in the union where the margin of victory was less than the Liberty Party total, giving those voters the balance of power in that state as well.[44]

The election of 1844 was a pivotal moment in the life of the Liberty Party and Ohio independent antislavery politics. The party had proven itself a force to be reckoned with on the national scene, yet at a steep price. The influential *New York Tribune* thundered that these "third-party wire-workers" had forced Polk upon the nation rather than helping to elect the only anti-Texas candidate who could have realistically won. The editor laid "the curses of unborn generations" upon their heads. "Riot in your infamy," he wrote, "and rejoice in its triumph, but never ask us to unite with you in anything."[45] In an election that turned largely on the issue of Texas annexation, the Liberty Party had assured the election of the worst possible candidate in the Whigs', and admittedly their own, eyes. As they had in 1840, accusations began to fly that Birney and the Liberty Party were actually Democrats in disguise bent on subsidizing Polk's election.[46]

The Oberlin community refused to allow such accusations to stand. The town cast its vote almost entirely for Birney in 1844, and residents would have agreed with some Ohio Democrats who asked, "Why do the Whigs accuse the 'Liberty party' with defeating Mr. Clay? Can not the Liberty party, with some propriety charge the Whigs with defeating Mr. Birney, and electing in his place Mr. Polk, a slave holder?"[47] Of the *nineteen* Clay supporters that a Whig newspaper claimed to have identified in Oberlin, many were too young for the franchise, and even more had repented of their ways by the time of the election.[48] In the end, Oberlin residents lamented the glaring corruption of the major parties but resolved to let their consciences rest easy, trusting that the ultimate outcome would be in their favor. "*Do right, and leave the issue with God*," the *Oberlin Evangelist* counseled.[49]

Still, when Texas officially became a state in 1845, the Oberlin community trembled at the thought of what lay in store for America. The Mexican government had warned that the annexation of Texas would be cause for war. Upon Texas statehood, the nation immediately broke off diplomatic relations with the United States, and both sides prepared for war. Although Oberlin students had formed a Peace Society some years earlier, and the student Dialectic Society had debated such topics as "Would it be our duty, should there be a levy, to take up arms?" and "Do the interests of our country demand the proposed standing army?" they mainly opposed unjust and selfish wars while recognizing the necessity of defensive battle.[50] Polk's war for expansion was unacceptable by Oberlin standards, and when U.S. forces invaded Mexico in 1846, Oberlin citizens gathered in a meeting of protest. They resolved that the U.S. government had, "by an unconstitutional and outrageously unjust annexation of Texas . . . plunged the country into a war in which the God of justice and the common sentiment of the world are against us, and in which every blow struck on the part of this nation will be an act of robbery and murder."[51] The *Oberlin Evangelist* warned, "Wars of aggression like this we not only deprecate and deplore, but most unqualifiedly condemn. The conscience of the world and the court of heaven are against us, and we should not be disappointed if bitter woes betide our nation for it, to befall us ere all is over." Polk's war was especially heinous in many Oberlinites' eyes not simply because it appeared to be a war of aggression but because the outcome would likely bolster America's slave system, extending its reaches to the far West and potentially adding representatives from several new slave states to the national legislature. Henry Cowles reminded his *Oberlin Evangelist* readers that "it costs blood and treasure to sustain American Slavery. Our nation has only begun to foot these bills."[52]

Free Soil, Free Speech, Free Labor, and Free Men

At the conclusion of the Mexican War in February 1848, Oberlinites mourned the inevitable expansion of slavery. While much of the nation celebrated America's resounding victory, Oberlin grieved for its implications. Finney, Mahan, and a handful of other Oberlin leaders asserted in a Cleveland newspaper that the main ambition of America's true "friends of freedom" should have been "the total prevention of the extension of Slavery over any of the territories now under the jurisdiction of this Government."[53] Henry Cowles suggested that bonfires and congratulations were absurdly inappropriate "in the present crisis." A more fitting response would include only "confession, humiliation, sackcloth, and ashes."[54]

The only positive outcome of the Mexican War, from an antislavery perspective, was the advancement in the North of segments of the Whig and Democratic Parties toward slowing the expansion of slavery into new territories obtained through the Mexican cession. To be sure, this was most often the product of white supremacists' objections to the presence there of any African Americans, slave or free, rather than humanitarian impulses. Accordingly, the Oberlin community continued to embrace the Liberty Party. Even Garrisonians like Lucy Stone cheered the efforts of the independent party. "I wish God speed to all they do," she wrote, "which is calculated to hasten the day of release to the wretched bondman. . . . I am glad to have *anything* done for the poor, downtrodden slave, and do not care whether it is by the Old Organization or New Organization, for the oppressed."[55]

At a rally in Oberlin in the summer of 1848 the Liberty Party pledged its allegiance to the third party because it embraced many of its valued antislavery principles, including abolition in the District of Columbia, the divorce of the federal government from all involvement with slavery, the exclusion of slavery from the Territories, and the repeal of all state Black Laws, "and [made its] success the specific and paramount aim of its efforts."[56]

However, the Oberlin gathering also made its support contingent on the party standing "on some higher application of its principles," especially "its old and vital ones"—including immediate emancipation. It clarified that "we love the Liberty Party only as an instrument for the enforcement of these principles and the success of these measures." Whenever any new party should arise that embraced the same, it continued, "we shall rejoice to see the Liberty Party merged in this new party, whenever the hope of success is rationally increased thereby."[57]

The Whigs' nomination of slaveholder Zachary Taylor for the presidency was more than many progressive party members could stomach. Henry Cowles detected strong feelings of disgust and defeatism among Whigs passing through Oberlin on their return from the Cleveland convention. The utter powerlessness they felt at the hands of the Slave Power seemed to affect them "with a kind of dumb ague."[58] Some of the most prominent among them, however, refused to resign themselves to the fate of a "conquered people." This included Western Reserve congressman Joshua Giddings, who had declared even before the nominating convention, "Sooner than this right arm (lifted above his head) fall from its socket and my tongue cleave to the roof of my mouth that I will vote for Zach. Taylor for President."[59] Within a week of Taylor's nomination, every county of the Western Reserve hosted a "people's meeting," without regard to party, to demand an independent national antislavery, anti-extension candidate.[60] The official call for a convention of "Friends of Freedom, Free Territory and Free Labor opposed to the election of Cass or Taylor" was issued by a meeting of the "Friends of Free Territory of the State of Ohio," to be held August 9 in Buffalo.[61]

The *National Era*, Gamaliel Bailey's new paper in Washington, reported that there was not enough room in its pages for even brief notices of all the Free-Soil meetings in Ohio. The people there seemed to be "cutting loose, *en masse*, from the old party organizations."[62] In Oberlin, a meeting of Liberty Party faithful recommended that its members attend the Buffalo convention to press forward its radical party goals. Just before the Buffalo gathering, Charles Grandison Finney, Henry Cowles, Asa Mahan, and other Oberlin notables highlighted in the Cleveland *True Democrat* the importance of cooperation among "friends of freedom of all parties" at the upcoming convention. A "true Abolitionist," they maintained, was any person "who sincerely holds chattel slavery, in all its forms, to be intrinsically wrong, and who is heartily devoted, in the use of all the means which he honestly judges to be lawful and wise, to its total extinction."[63] Right then, the primary attention of antislavery voters should be the divorce of the federal government "from the dominion of the Slave Power" as well as the extension of slavery in territory over which it had jurisdiction. They believed that these were the "*great issues of the approaching presidential election*," and to meet them, "all the friends of freedom should unite in a patriotic forgetfulness of former party pledges, party ties, and predilections."[64]

When the Buffalo convention assembled under the "Great Oberlin Tent," which Finney had first brought with him to Ohio in 1835, its membership was made up of Liberty Party men, "Conscience" Whigs, and "Barnburner" Democrats who were opposed to slavery's extension.[65] Delegates were rightfully uncertain whether groups as diverse as the abolitionist Liberty Party contingent could find common ground with Democrats whose claim to an antislavery position rested primarily on white supremacy. Moreover, the Barnburners and Liberty Party had already nominated candidates for the presidency, Martin Van Buren and John Hale, respectively. The Whigs had a slate of hopefuls themselves including Giddings and Charles Francis Adams, son of the late president and congressman John Quincy Adams.[66]

The Oberlin delegation was headed by Asa Mahan, who, according to Pittsburgh's Martin Delaney, was one of the most prominent speakers at the convention.[67] The delegates brought with them their charge by the Oberlin Liberty Party to represent its interests, and to pledge to the convention and its nominees its support only if their platform and candidates "ably and adequately represent[ed] them."[68] It became clear early on that the Barnburners, the most numerous of the various blocs, would not accept any presidential nominee but their own. Although Van Buren bore a name that Oberlin men had historically considered "synonymous in the history of this country with servility," the Liberty Party contingent supported his nomination on the condition that the convention adopt a platform that more closely aligned with their own demands than those of the Democratic defectors.[69]

Thus the first ever convention of the national Free-Soil Party put forward the ticket of Van Buren and Adams upon a "national platform of freedom in opposition to the sectional platform of slavery." Delegates demanded that the government abolish slavery where it possessed the constitutional power to do so and to prohibit its extension into the Territories. They resolved their motto to be "Free Soil, Free Speech, Free Labor, and Free Men," under which they would "fight ever, until a triumphant victory will reward our exertions."[70] "Henceforth," the editor of the *Oberlin Evangelist* rejoiced, "there will be in reality but two great political parties in this country—the party of the South, composed of Southern slaveholders, and a few Northern office expectants with Southern principles, on the one hand—and the FREE DE-MOCRACY of the nation, and especially the North, on the other."[71]

This sentiment certainly saw the Free-Soil glass as half full from an antislavery point of view. In fact, Free-Soil in 1848 was far less progressive than most Oberlinites cared to admit. To be sure, the party was the only one that refused to explicitly endorse slavery, but the complaint of the majority of its members was against the dictates of the Slave Power rather than slavery itself. The Buffalo platform pledged no interference with slavery within the limits of any state. Although the convention resolved that the original policy of the nation was "to limit, localize, and discourage slavery," it was far from a commitment to abolitionism.[72] Rather, it was the manifestation of the antislavery limits of the Free-Soil Party: the majority of its members were former Democrats who still shared the racism of their old party. They were willing to leave the institution of slavery alone, so long as those who continued to practice it limited the institution (and the presence of most African Americans) to the South. As historian Henry Mayer notes, to consider slavery bad policy because it threatened the prosperity of white workers was quite different from considering slavery a sin because it infringed upon God-given freedom. In fact, the logic of many Free-Soilers smacked of the same spirit that sustained the Ohio Black Laws.[73]

This struck many abolitionists as an abandonment of their antislavery principles and a precipitous retreat from the former Liberty Party standard. Even Gerrit Smith, perhaps Oberlin's greatest antebellum financial supporter, lamented that "but few are left to govern their votes by such considerations as I govern my own." He predicted that of the 70,000 people who belonged to the Free-Soil Party, not 1,000 would insist that their candidates be abolitionists. "When I see such wise and good men, as compose the Faculty of Oberlin Institute, adopting their ethics to the emergency," Smith wrote, "I expect nothing better than but here and there one will be found able to keep himself from being carried off in the flood of defection."[74]

Most Oberlinites did not see any problem with addressing their immediate concerns "to the emergency." Indeed, the emergency in the late 1840s and early 1850s was the battle over the extension of slavery into western territories. They believed that the type of ideological consistency demanded by Smith, Garrison, and others would not immediately free any slaves. Restricting one's self to the support of only those antislavery strategies that exclusively demanded immediate emancipation, however desirable in an ideal world, promised few immediate positive results. However, a political party that could hold the balance of power in national and state elections at a critical moment when the issue of slavery extension was before the nation had much more potential for tangible consequences. Better attempt to limit slavery now than miss the best opportunity to check its advance across the continent.

Henry Cowles explained in the *Oberlin Evangelist* that when "the principles and aims of a party are only good, and involve nothing morally wrong, we go with it heart and soul." Even though he realized that his readers could not hope to immediately gain all that they may have wished, they were, as always, willing to follow the path that offered the most realistic potential under the circumstances.[75] After the Buffalo convention, the *Oberlin Evangelist* declared the Free-Soil movement in harmony with God's will and agreed with one Oberlin delegate that "God is moving the elements, and moving in them, and will doubtless bring his own truths to accomplish whereunto He has sent it."[76] Moreover, the faculty pointed out in their article in the *True Democrat* that antislavery men elected now would form a core of leadership for future reinforcements to rally around, making the ultimate goal of total emancipation possible at a later date.[77] Just as a line from one of Oberlin alumnus George Clark's antislavery songs from that year proclaimed: "Huzza for Free Soil! Free Soil evermore, / Till its boundaries embrace on our land every shore; / And should traitors essay the foul curse to extend, / Shall it any less speedily come to its end?"[78]

Oberlinites were only slightly put off by nonresistant Garrisonian critics who pointed out the compromises necessary to succeed in the political world and considered the Free-Soilers insufferably conservative. When it came to agitating the slavery issue, Oberlin abolitionists continued to appreciate the value of the most radical reformers, just as they had in the 1830s. These agitators' uncompromising moral appeals pushed the limits of the debate. As the radical extreme advanced, so too could the center; the radicals enlarged the realm of the possible for the politicians. The more extreme the strictly moral agitator's demand, the more reasonable and attractive the propositions of more moderate antislavery politicians appeared. Moderate abolitionists were the ones to shepherd the growing centrist body of those sympathetic to abolitionist and antislavery measures into a popular movement with the power to effect truly radical changes to the government from within.

It would be a mistake, however, to always consider the moral agitators and the politicians as mutually exclusive groups. Most Oberlinites were immediatist moral agitators who also happened to seek change through politics. Their commitment to abolitionism sprang from their perfectionist understanding of moral law, developed in their churches and antislavery societies, and applied to their political agenda. The obligation for men to obey and participate in human governments, Finney wrote, "while they legislate upon the principles of the moral law, is as unalterable as the moral law itself."[79] Though many of the Free-Soilers in 1848 would have settled for far less than complete emancipation, Oberlin abolitionists and most other former Liberty Party supporters would not. Rather, they hoped to secure whatever victories they could, such as nonextension, abolition in Washington, D.C., or the repeal of Black Laws, while they continued in their demands for immediate and full emancipation.

The Oberlin community's African American members were also fully involved in the political and reform movements of 1848, and they played a significant role in influencing their white neighbors in their embrace of antislavery politics. In early September 1848, Oberlin sent a proud delegation of its citizens, students, and alumni to the National Colored Convention in Cleveland. Besides the performance of a rousing "Liberty song" from Oberlinites Sabram Cox and William Howard Day at the opening of the second day's session, the Oberlin contingent used its numerous positions of leadership in the convention to shape the direction of the national African American reform agenda.[80] Delegates firmly resolved that "slavery is the greatest curse ever inflicted on man, being of hellish origin, the legitimate offspring of the Devil" and pledged themselves "to use all justifiable means for its speedy and immediate overthrow." When it came to the question of just what those means included, the members of the business committee, headed by Day and Charles Langston, revealed their proclivity toward the brand of political action encouraged by the Oberlin contingent and the new Free-Soil Party. With the realization that abolitionists in Ohio and the West viewed political involvement in a much more favorable light than some of their fellows nationwide, committee members resolved that though their efforts would remain moral in their tendency, it was no less the duty of every member of the convention to take notice of the Free-Soil Party and counsel it in the "course which shall best promote the cause of Liberty and Humanity."[81]

The convention adopted a resolution to recommend the Free-Soil Party and the Buffalo platform to the support of African Americans everywhere.[82] Still, Langston, Day, and others could not secure the passage of their resolutions that recommended that all African Americans who possessed the franchise use it to secure the Free-Soil candidates in office. Their enthusiastic characterization of the party as one that was "bound together by a

Charles Langston (courtesy Oberlin College Archives)

common sentiment expressing the wish of a large portion of the people of this Union" and that represented "the dawn of a bright and more auspicious day" was rejected by the majority of the convention's delegates.[83] The "common sentiment" of the Oberlin delegation was in advance of that of the convention as a whole.

Oberlinites, black and white, had reached the conclusion that in a country where suffrage was widespread and slavery established and upheld by the law, a national reform could not be carried without votes. As Professor James Monroe wrote, even if the standards of the Free-Soil Party were not as demanding as Oberlinites may have desired, abolitionists had a responsibility to constantly attempt to elevate them. Langston, Day, and Monroe had not declared the Free-Soil Party to be perfect but rather deemed it the best political option available and a satisfactory starting point for more promising advancements to come. If the Free-Soil Party did not embrace every measure committed abolitionists desired, the party embraced a great many of them, and in doing so potentially gained the numbers necessary to implement them all. In Monroe's words, most Oberlinites were willing that antislavery principles be brought forward a few at a time, if, by doing so, a party could be secured strong enough to give each successive principle a triumph: "first the blade, then the ear, and then the full corn in the ear." "Hungry men," Monroe figured, "might wish that the full corn in the ear should be produced at once, but the constitution of nature is otherwise."[84]

Free-Soilers were disappointed by the November election returns, though they did show much stronger than the Liberty Party had in 1840 and 1844. Lorain County was one of six counties in Ohio to cast a plurality of its votes for Van Buren.[85] The Oberlin community once again balanced the sting of defeat with faith in ultimate victory. Finney grieved the outcome of the election, especially the fact that so many Northerners accommodated themselves to the demands of the Slave Power. In an emotional and teary Thanksgiving sermon just days after the presidency had been decided, he prayed that the arrogant Southern aristocrats would continue to "*spit in the dough-faces* of the North until they provoked them to put an end to slavery."[86] When the *Oberlin Evangelist* announced Taylor's election, the editor expressed hope that "whatever wrath, or guilt, or error of man may be involved in it, the Lord will over-rule to his own praise, and the remainder thereof, will restrain."[87]

Our Elevation, Moral, Intellectual, and Political

Throughout the clamor of the political season, the Oberlin community continued to press the other goal of their abolitionism, equal rights for free African Americans. This had been an important plank in the Liberty Party platforms of 1840 and 1844, and though the more conservative majority of the Free-Soil coalition dropped the demand in 1848, it had remained a vital consideration as Oberlin voters selected local and statewide officers. Yet while Oberlin's politicians had been forced to compromise in the presidential campaign and sacrifice, politically, the demand for immediate emancipation and equal rights to free soil nationally, the town's African American population led the radical moral push to maintain the link between antislavery and black rights.

After the National Colored Convention in September, the leaders of Oberlin's black community hoped to advance their cause even further on their home turf of Ohio. Immediately following the national convention, Charles Langston issued a call for a state convention to be held in Columbus in January 1849. The main objects of their deliberations would be "our elevation, moral, intellectual, and political," with special attention to be

William Howard Day (from Richings, *Evidences of Progress among Colored People* [1902])

paid to Ohio's Black Laws.⁸⁸ After Langston was selected the convention's president, a business committee including Oberlin alumni William Howard Day, John Mercer Langston, and John M. Brown drafted a series of resolutions, many of which appear to have been drawn directly from a meeting of Oberlin African Americans that was held the previous month.⁸⁹

The delegates to the Ohio convention resolved to do all within their power to repeal not only their state's Black Laws but any state and federal laws that made distinctions based on color. Towns were asked to contribute to a fund to support black lecturers in their crusade to bring the evils of the laws before the populace. They expressed their patriotism and rejected all colonization schemes, insisting that with the proper education and training, African Americans could compete with anyone of any complexion.⁹⁰ Any person, black or white, who "failed to treat other colored men on terms of perfect equality with the whites in all cases" was to be judged "as recreant to the dearest cause, and should be esteemed outcasts."⁹¹

Significantly, the Ohio delegates also hoped to push African Americans nationally toward an endorsement of physical resistance against the Slave Power in the North and South. Quoting the familiar verse of Lord Byron, the Oberlin-dominated business committee declared that one "who would be free, himself must strike the blow." For several years, growing segregation, racial violence, and other discrimination, not to mention the continued health of slavery, convinced many Northern African Americans that moral reform had failed. Despite acknowledging its continuing intrinsic worth, black leaders were becoming increasingly more militant.[92] Convention leaders eagerly urged the Southern bondsman "to leave immediately with his hoe on his shoulder, for a land of liberty" and use whatever means were at his disposal to gain freedom. They also called for free African Americans to do whatever they could to aid "our brothers and sisters in fleeing from the prison-house of bondage to the land of freedom." All were advised to keep a sharp lookout "for men-thieves and their abettors," and when found, to warn them that no person claimed as a slave would be taken from their midst "without trouble." This was not the old nonresistant strategy of relying on surrogates (the slaves themselves) to use violence to implement their goals but a clear step toward accepting violence as a legitimate means to encourage emancipation.[93] In an acknowledgment of two African American prophets who had urged forceful resistance ahead of its time, the convention recommended that 500 copies of David Walker's 1829 "Appeal to the Colored Citizens of the World" and Henry Highland Garnet's 1843 "Address to the Slaves of the United States" be "gratuitously circulated."[94]

This meeting was a watershed moment for Ohio African American abolitionists. The *Oberlin Evangelist* lauded the Oberlin community's leadership of the colored conventions of 1848 and 1849, and declared that the meetings "served to give impulse to a mass of mind too long and too cruelly crushed, and also to give character before the world to their determined efforts for real improvement."[95] Moreover, the convention requested and was granted permission to address the assembled legislature on the evening of January 11. The convention appointed William Howard Day, the man responsible for much of the forceful language adopted by the delegates, as chairman of the business committee to present their case to lawmakers. He had been preparing for such an opportunity for weeks, undertaking exhaustive and meticulous research on the state of African Americans in Ohio. However, once tapped by the convention, Day had but one day to complete his address. With the help of Oberlin friends John Mercer Langston and Lawrence Minor, Day polished his arguments through the night and right up until the hours preceding his speech. This would be the address of an elite African American orator, and it would be thoroughly infused with the spirit of Oberlin abolitionism.[96]

Day's address to the legislature dwelt upon the history of abuses suffered by African Americans. He pointed out the racist perversions of the constitutions of Ohio and the United States and the denial of their voting rights and lack of representation despite their status as taxpayers, decried the state's negligence toward providing equal education for African American children, and placed much of the blame on the very body he was addressing. Then, before stepping away from the podium, the twenty-three-year-old offered a brief message to his fellow African Americans of Ohio. He advised them to "come out, as soon as possible, from situations called degrading—encourage education—... resist every species of oppression—serve God and humanity." Still ostensibly addressing his black audience, Day concluded with words also intended for the hearing of his white listeners. "Let us go to work," he charged them, and "inform our opposers that we are coming—coming for our rights—coming through the Constitution of our common country—coming through the law—and relying upon God and the justice of our cause, pledge ourselves never to cease our resistance to tyranny, whether it be in the *iron* manacles of the *slave*, or in the unjust written manacles of the *free*."[97]

With the exception of the expected hostile reception Day's address received in the conservative press, the Oberlinite was feted as a black champion. His speech was comparable to, in the words of the *Oberlin Evangelist*, "the labored efforts of men of far greater fame and far higher pretension."[98] The *Cincinnati Gazette* congratulated him for having "found the white folks guilty, and then enumerated the number of rebels (meaning black citizens) in the United States, and what they could accomplish."[99] Frederick Douglass called it "an incident in our history well worthy of reflection and remark. The colored man has been allowed to come up, without insult and without reproach—to enter into a place hitherto deemed sacred to the white man alone, and standing there to plead his right to be deemed a man and a brother ... to say 'our God,' and to beg permission to say 'our country.'"[100]

The constant agitation and pressure of Oberlin's black alumni, students, and town residents against the state's Black Laws was a key reason that "repealism" remained an important adjunct of the Oberlin community's abolitionism.[101] This was the case even when arguing against these laws brought criticism from abolitionist friends or threats of violence from less friendly quarters. Though Oberlin alumna Betsey Mix Cowles was a close friend of Abby Kelley and considered herself a solid Garrisonian, she refused to shy away from the promotion of antislavery politics, especially since she believed it offered the clearest way to remove the legal disabilities of Ohio's African American population. In 1846, she used funds gathered at the annual meeting of the Ashtabula County Female Anti-Slavery Society to begin publication of a newspaper she called A *Plea for the Oppressed*, devoted to agitation, largely political, against the Black Laws. Though the sheet survived only a short run, it was a powerful voice against discriminatory legislation and was enthusiastically supported by both Liberty Party members and many Ohio Whigs.[102]

However, despite support from political abolitionists and even many Garrisonians in Ohio, eastern nonresistants heaped criticism upon Cowles and her project. Since Cowles had presented her prospectus at an antislavery society meeting that met concurrently with the Liberty Party, Parker Pillsbury criticized the *Plea*'s supporters in Ohio as being under the control of those who ought to have been their adversaries, the political abolitionists.[103] Maria Weston Chapman wrote to Kelley from Boston afraid that Cowles' efforts "went to build up our worst foe," and if that was the case, "it had better never been." The rumor that the Whig candidate for governor endorsed the *Plea* caused Kelley to regret even the appearance "that Slaveocrats use our money."[104] Although Garrisonians advocated racial equality, many eastern leaders argued that campaigns (like Cowles's) against the Black Laws, Underground Railroad work, and schools for African Americans did not *directly* challenge slavery. The editors of the WASS's *Anti-Slavery Bugle* pointed out that "we condemn none of these benevolent enterprises . . . but they never can redeem the slave . . . not a slave chain will be broken thereby." Pillsbury said the *Plea* and its anti–Black Law campaign had "no more to do with Anti-Slavery, than with the man in the moon."[105]

The "petty bickering" over the *Plea* may have led Cowles to distance herself from eastern Garrisonians, and they from her.[106] Still, she continued to work tirelessly for the repeal of the Black Laws through the Garrisonian WASS. Her open-mindedness on all things antislavery encouraged Oberlin professor Timothy Hudson, on behalf of the "New Org," to ask her for data that she gathered for the *Plea* to be used in an AFASS pamphlet toward that end.[107] As the slavery issue was increasingly agitated in the public's mind, the AFASS also hoped to "fix the eyes of the people of the free states on their own legislation" since "a large portion of the voters even in the free states, are ignorant of the enormities even of their own laws."[108]

"Friendly fire" was not the only risk abolitionists faced in their crusade against the Black Laws. Reminiscent of the dire straits in which Oberlin's abolitionists were placed in the 1830s, those men and women who urged racial egalitarianism upon an often resistant populace faced violent reactions to their message.[109] Late in May of 1848, Charles Langston, on a lecture tour with Martin Delaney, stopped in the central Ohio town of Marseilles to

Betsey Mix Cowles (from Howe, *Historical Collections of Ohio* [1889])

convene a meeting in opposition to slavery and the Black Laws. As the two men began their walk to the meeting place that evening, they were followed by a gang of young men who taunted and directed curses at them. Once they reached the venue, Langston overheard the plans of between forty and fifty ruffians to violently disrupt the meeting.[110]

The abolitionists could not speak before such a hostile and potentially dangerous crowd, and after one of the ruffians stood and declared, "I move that we adjourn, by considering this a darkey burlesque," Langston and Delaney left the hall to the continuing cries of "'darkey burlesque!' with many other epithets of disparagement." Later, as the two abolitionists looked out their hotel window, they witnessed a gathering crowd who were raising a commotion with "a brass drum, a tamborine, a clarionet, violin, jaw-bone of a horse, castanets, and a number of other instruments, or whatever would tend to excite and rally a formidable mob." The crowd included "well nigh all of the men and boys in the neighborhood who were able to throw a brickbat."[111]

Delaney recalled that failing to find sufficient tar for a proper tar and feathering, the mob simply set the empty pitch barrel aflame along with empty boxes that produced a blaze big enough to be seen for miles. When this failed to draw out the abolitionists, the crowd decided that they would instead break into their room, handcuff them, and immediately take them south where each of them, as slaves, might bring $1,500 cash. This Delaney and Langston determined to resist to the death, since they were "not slaves, nor will we tamely suffer the treatment of slaves, let it come from a high or low source, or from wherever it may."[112] Eventually the mob tired after several hours of what the abolitionists could only describe as "ferocious blackguardism," having become drunk and run out of objects to burn. They did admonish the bellhop to beat their drum if the abolitionists attempted to escape in the night, and declared within their hearing that they "would neither eat nor drink, till they took our lives." When the men left town that morning, however, they found only six sleeping ruffians remaining in the street and were able to escape Marseilles with only a few stones hurled at their buggy on their way out of town.[113]

The Elevation of the Colored American, Half-Free

The national Free-Soil platform was not friendly toward "repealism." However, the party's local success in Ohio was what finally led to the end of the laws in that state. The Free-Soil ticket had sent eight men to the Ohio House of Representatives in 1848, including Oberlin Institute trustee Norton Townsend and John Morse, another abolitionist with strong Oberlin connections.[114] When the weighty questions of organizing the House and deciding two contested elections arose as the first orders of business, all of the Ohio Free-Soilers but Morse and Townsend split back into their former parties. For nearly a month, Whigs and Democrats battled for the quorum necessary to control the legislature.

Salmon P. Chase wrote to another politician that he feared the rising bitterness would result in the dissolution of the legislature, and perhaps even bloodshed, had not the Free-Soilers intervened. Townsend was named to a committee of three to decide the fate of the contested offices. He had been sent to the legislature by the Free-Soil citizens of Lorain County with the charge that he "act with any party, or against any party, as in his judgment the cause of freedom should require."[115] To that end, he proposed a deal by which he would support whichever party promised to support a bill for the repeal of many of Ohio's Black Laws. Whigs, angry at what they saw as Townsend's defection, were cool to the proposals, but the Democrats, eager to gain power in the state, expressed interest.[116] Townsend cast the deciding vote that gave the surprisingly cooperative Democrats control of the disputed seats.

Even with the two seats in the Democratic column, neither major party possessed the quorum necessary to organize the House. To this end, Morse,

Townsend, Democratic leaders, and Free-Soil organizer Chase struck a deal by which Morse and Townsend agreed to help the Democrats organize the House. It would give the Democrats the speakership and all the valuable powers of patronage that entailed. In return, the Free-Soilers were given the assurance that their man, Chase, would be named Ohio's senator.[117] Townsend and Morse also insisted on their most important demand for their cooperation: the repeal of the most galling of the state's Black Laws. These included prohibitions on publicly funded schools for black children, a $500 bond requirement for African Americans entering the state, the requirement of a certified freedom certificate, a bar to employment without properly recorded freedom papers, and the exclusion of black testimony in court when white litigants were involved.[118] Townsend and Morse demanded a written pledge from all those who would benefit from their support that these infamous laws would be wiped from the books that session.[119]

Townsend's actions in the House brought upon him the scorn of many Ohio Whigs and Whig-leaning Free-Soilers. One "independent" Free-Soiler wrote that it "would require an act of omnipotence to bring [him] . . . up to the level of a Judas Iscariot."[120] Townsend's sin lay in his bucking the racist Free-Soil majority to seek equal rights for African Americans.[121] Predictably, Townsend had to constantly defend himself before his colleagues. After one barrage of insults by Whigs and Free-Soilers in May, he turned the other cheek and declared, "My blows shall always be reserved for the enemies of freedom, and not expended upon its friends, however severely they may feel disposed to condemn any action of mine." He believed that it was his fate to be regarded as a "political Jonah, who must be thrown overboard, to secure the safety and preservation of the Free Soil bark." Still, he enthusiastically welcomed his ostracism and declared that he cared infinitely more for freedom than for his own standing in the Free-Soil Party. Townsend considered himself under no obligation to vote according to the demands of a handful of men who had until just recently been faithful Whigs, and who continued "to give quite unmistakable evidence of the lineage whence they sprung." He pledged his only allegiance to voting blocs formed to abrogate racist laws, prevent the extension of slavery, and the divorce the government from all connection with it.[122]

Oberlinites, however, heaped praise upon Townsend for boldly doing the job they sent him to Columbus to do: act independently for the downtrodden, whatever the path and whatever the consequences. A meeting of the Lorain County Free-Soilers resolved that Townsend had "met fully all the reasonable expectations of genuine Free-Soilers, and is still worthy of their confidence, and entitled to the plaudit, 'Well done, good and faithful servant.'" They maintained that the true principles of Free-Soil had been advanced more than ever before in the state, and that Townsend was entitled to a large share of the honor of forcing those principles upon an often unwilling legislature.[123]

In February, Oberlin's African American students and residents celebrated their newly acknowledged rights and spent an entire day in praise, worship, and commemoration of the events that had brought about the change. Their songs acknowledged the help of white allies like Townsend but were mainly offered to recognize their own efforts in the repeal campaign. Six black speakers spent the day developing the theme of self-improvement and what they could accomplish through their own agitation efforts.[124] They resolved that "Love to God, Love to each other, Purity in ourselves, and Fidelity to our great cause, is the motto which we ought to and will urge upon ourselves and our people."[125] It was black Oberlinites and other Ohio African Americans, Frederick Douglass wrote, who were "stemming the current of the most raging floods, combating every opposition, resisting every obstacle until at length they have forced the dominant class in their own state to notice and respect their efforts."[126]

Even after the repeal of most of the Black Laws in 1849, the prohibition on African American voting remained on the books. The Ohio Supreme Court had ruled in 1842 that "all men, nearer white than black, or of the grade between the mulatto and the white" were entitled to vote as "white male citizens" under the 1802 constitution.[127] In Oberlin, African Americans may have voted long before this decision. William Howard Day reported that William Newman had been the first black voter in Lorain County, implying that he had cast a ballot long before others could legally do so.[128] John Mercer Langston told an audience that in and around Oberlin, "we have gone so far as to say that anybody that will take responsibility of swearing that he is more than half-white, shall vote. We do not care how black he is."[129] Oberlin did have a handful of conservative Democrats, including innkeeper Chauncey Wack, who patrolled the polling places to assure the "purity" of the vote. Yet in 1842, when John Ramsey, a self-emancipated giant of a man, attempted to vote, Wack challenged him, and election officials dutifully questioned the potential voter. When asked how white his father was, Ramsey replied, "I should think, about as white as Mr. Wack." By that point, an audience had gathered who excitedly cheered Ramsey on, and Wack finally conceded, dejectedly exclaiming, "Let him vote, let him vote! I have nothing more to say."[130]

But in other parts of Ohio, African Americans had considerably less support. Even those men who qualified under the 1842 court decision could be challenged before an election judge. State and national black conventions proclaimed that a race-blind suffrage law was their main goal. The leadership of the 1850 Convention of the Colored Citizens of Ohio included John and Charles Langston, Day, James Monroe Jones, and John M. Brown, all Oberlin alumni. In the words of Day, they had "one principle object—the securing for the colored man a vote in the State."[131] Delegates voted that he prepare and deliver an address to the Ohio Constitutional Convention that would convene in May.[132]

That convention had been called to revise the long-outdated document of 1802 and to make the state's governance more "democratic" in nature. Despite the fact that the convention's majority were conservative Democrats, the state colored convention believed that "by vigorous and energetic action," they could induce the delegates to alter the constitution to give all citizens, without discrimination, "this heaven bestowed and inalienable right" to vote.[133] However, similar revisions of state constitutions in Pennsylvania and New York had resulted in either the complete disfranchisement of their African American populations or severely restricted suffrage. In neighboring Illinois, constitutional restructuring had resulted in an outright ban on black immigration.[134] On the other hand, Ohio had just repealed the majority of its Black Laws, and as a result of abolitionist agitation and controversy that surrounded the resolution of the Mexican War, the issue of slavery and racial oppression was again squarely before the eyes of Ohioans. It seemed to those who had the most to gain and lose, the state's African Americans, that the occasion was pregnant with possibilities, both good and evil. The Ohio Colored Citizens Convention resolved that "it is the duty of every colored man, to do every thing in his power, to secure to himself and brethren, their political rights. . . . We will *fight and fight ever* until these privileges are *granted to us.*"[135]

Langston and Day were also appointed to the executive committee of a newly formed "Ohio Colored American League," the object of which was to be "the liberation of the slave and the elevation of the colored American, half-free." Oberlin had already formed a similar organization in anticipation of the national convention "to advocate *the right of the colored man to vote.*" It employed Day as its agent, and he informed the state organization that, at least as far as he was concerned, the direction of both Colored American Leagues would follow the direction of the Oberlin reformers. The leagues concentrated on supplying a cadre of lecturers across the state to circulate petitions to be laid before constitutional convention delegates and to speak out on the subjects of equal rights and the voting franchise for all Ohioans, regardless of color.[136] Agents would be appointed to canvass the state, lecturing to all those who would listen, and making a special attempt to reach those who would not. Thus, as John Watson told the convention, "If they do take our rights from us, they shall take our rights from us in our presence."[137]

The eyes of all Ohio African Americans were on Columbus when the constitutional convention convened on May 6, 1850. Immediately, it seemed as if the worst fears of black reformers would come to pass. Once the convention was organized and brought to order, the first substantive matter of business was the presentation by Benjamin Stanton of Logan County of a memorial asking the convention to authorize an act to provide for the extradition of all African Americans from the state.[138] Over the course of the nearly yearlong convention that followed, petitions signed by over a thousand Ohioans were presented in opposition to African American enfranchisement, demanding that African Americans be barred from entering the state, and moving that those African Americans currently living in the state be expelled.[139]

As the constitutional convention stretched on, the Convention of the Colored Citizens of Ohio held its annual meeting in January in the same city. John and Charles Langston served together on the executive committee that asked the constitutional convention to "give every citizen, irrespective of color, a right to say at the ballot box who shall make and execute the law by which he is governed."[140] In a direct appeal to the lawmakers at the convention, Day, Charles Langston, and Charles Yancey offered a veritable resume of qualifications upon which African Americans were entitled to full citizenship. They cited African American participation in every American war, legal opinions by prestigious jurists, as well as the U.S. Constitution and Declaration of Independence. Moreover, they marshaled statistics to show that African Americans freely paid more than their fair share of taxes in support of a government that considered them less than full men. "In your hands," they humbly wrote to the delegates, "our destiny is placed. To you, therefore, we appeal. We look to you."[141]

The all-white constitutional convention, however, would only disappoint their hopeful black counterparts. When Norton Townsend attempted to introduce a memorial written by Day requesting the franchise be extended to all persons regardless of color, it was immediately challenged by William Sawyer of Auglaize County. Sawyer flatly demanded to know whether that particular petition was one "from colored people." Townsend replied that the petition was signed by only one individual, who was a legal citizen of the state. "As to the person's color," Townsend remarked, "he was very nearly white, having less black blood in him than a mulatto." Regardless, Sawyer declared that he wanted give the convention advance notice that he would object to all similar petitions that might be thereafter presented. His reasoning was suggested by his contention that "he objected to this petition, more especially than any other."[142]

Townsend had not imagined such vehement opposition would be offered to the mere *reception* of his constituent's petition. He defended Day as one who "has what is called African blood in his veins, and is therefore identified in feeling with the oppressed colored people of this State," but who was also entitled to the right of suffrage and all the rights and privileges of citizenship under the then-present constitution as interpreted by the state supreme court. Day, he said, was a man who had worked tirelessly to elect him as a delegate to the convention, as well as someone who possessed the same right to be heard as the constituents of any other delegate. Moreover, Townsend asserted that Day, "colored though he be," was well educated and as much of a gentleman as any man who opposed the reception of his petition. "I venture to say, also," he went on, "that if anyone here wished to discuss the propriety of granting the prayer of this memorial, the gentleman from whom it emanated will be ready to meet them anywhere, and I know he will be found abundantly able to sustain himself."[143] In the end, and though many conservatives supported the propositions, the eight petitions against African American immigration and the five for extradition were rejected by the convention. African Americans were constitutionally barred for the first time from participation in the state militia, but provisions for white-only public schooling were dropped, leaving the final decision to be made by the legislature at a later date.[144] With regard to African American enfranchisement, three petitions were presented in favor and three against. The committee on the elective franchise offered its report in December, and its draft conferred the vote on "white male citizens" only.[145] Again, Townsend arose as "the champion of negro rights" in this battle and objected to the use of the qualifier "white." "Humanity," Townsend argued, "does not consist in the color of the hair, or eyes, or skin, or where a person may have been born, or what his origin or capacity—these peculiarities may be changed indefinitely, but a man is a man for all that."[146] He noted that in Oberlin, there was less prejudice, not because Oberlinites did not know any African Americans but because they *did*.[147] Still, Townsend included even himself among the members of a privileged racial class and noted one particular right that all white Ohioans possessed: "'the right of the strongest,' a right always recognized, I believe, among robbers, but not usually recognized among honest men."[148] Despite the efforts of Townsend and some other Northern Ohio delegates, the convention voted overwhelmingly to deny the ballot to everyone but white men.[149]

Though the constitutional convention had not been a complete disaster for Ohio African Americans, the events of 1850–51 had been disheartening overall. Both federal and state lawmakers seemed committed to keeping all blacks in thralldom. Still, at the end of their own deliberations in 1850, Ohio's steadfastly patriotic African Americans joined together in a resounding rendition of a song written by Oberlin alumnus Joshua Simpson, "Liberia Is Not the Place for Me."[150] Defeatism would accomplish nothing; there were even greater battles to be fought, and soon. "A mountain of Prejudice is to be surmounted," John Mercer Langston told one audience. "A Herculean task is before us."[151] Indeed, other abolitionists from Oberlin sensed a great struggle in the immediate future. "The time is plainly coming, and is even now at the door," the editor of the *Oberlin Evangelist* declared, "when the great question is to be tried, and settled. Either slavery is soon to be riveted on this nation, while the nation shall stand, or it is to stand rebuked and chained under the withering eye and in the giant grasp of the genius of Freedom. . . . The time for ill-starred compromises is past and gone, we trust forever."[152]

Before Ohio's equally ill-starred constitutional convention had even adjourned, the *Evangelist*'s prediction seemed to have partially come true. The time for compromise, however, seemed to remain very much in the present. African Americans in Ohio and all of the supposedly free states faced a threat even more grave than the denial of the franchise. With the passage of the Compromise of 1850 and its infamous Fugitive Slave Law, the United States of America suddenly became one massive slave territory. Langston was right to call the task before abolitionists at the turn of the decade "Herculean," yet he and his colleagues would not rest while they remained "half-free" in the North and a single slave remained in bonds in the South. As the Slave Power attempted to tighten its grip over the nation in the 1850, Oberlin abolitionists would be there to fight them at every step.

CHAPTER SEVEN

We Must Watch and Improve This Tide

Oberlin Confronts the Slave Power, 1850–1858

The decade of the 1850s was a period both pregnant with possibilities for abolitionist advancement and full of crushing setbacks to their cause at the hands of the Slave Power. No abolitionist victory seemed secure before an election, act of Congress, or judicial decision forced a reevaluation of their tactics and strategies. However, reformers in Oberlin viewed the events of the decade as a triumphant march toward emancipation, believing, in the words of an Oberlin student newspaper, that the course of truth "is ever accumulative of power" and the moral force of abolitionist gains could never be beaten into submission.[1] As Oberlin's abolitionist musician Joshua Simpson wrote in his popular 1852 songbook *The Emancipation Car*:

> The Tyrant-host is great and strong;
> But ah, their reign will not be long . . .
> Stand up, stand up my boys,
> The battle field is ours:
> Fight on, Fight on, all hearts resolved,
> To break the Tyrant's power.[2]

* * *

IN SEPTEMBER OF 1850, John Mercer Langston and Charles Langston addressed a cheerless letter to Senator Salmon P. Chase. As they wrote, the Ohio Constitutional Convention was presenting them and other African Americans with one disappointment after another and their faith in the United States was wearing thin. They perceived Chase as a shrewd politician, a man with a sensitive finger on the pulse of the populace. Rumors were circulating in Oberlin and elsewhere regarding another congressional compromise measure over the slavery question, and the Langston brothers were pessimistic.[3] They asked Chase if he thought the public sentiment of the country was such as would preclude the successful attainment of their political rights or any vestige of civil or social equality. They pled for his advice regarding the best course to pursue, and even wondered whether the federal government might allow disfranchised African Americans a land grant in the Territories where they might peaceably settle and enjoy the rights already held by most Americans. Should they abandon the land of their birth, they wondered, or remain until "the great principles on which our Government was founded shall exist in practice as well as in theory?"[4]

By the time the Langstons posted their letter, Congress had already passed several of the component parts of the Compromise of 1850, measures intended to offer a final solution to the slavery problem in the United States. The first parts bailed out a debt-ridden Texas in return for the transfer of a large territory to the federal government, organized the New Mexico and Utah Territories (with slavery being allowed or banned based on local option), and admitted California as a free state. Though the compromise also banned the slave trade in the District of Columbia, its fourth provision, passed just six days after the Langstons wrote their letter to Chase, would prove itself one of the most controversial laws ever passed by the U.S. government. Abolitionists considered the compromise's Fugitive Slave Law the most odious edict to ever disgrace the federal statute book. Of all the measures, it was the greatest concession to the slave states, meant to bolster the largely unenforced fugitive clause of 1793. This 1850 law shifted responsibility for the recapture of alleged fugitive slaves from the states to the federal government. Now, in any state of the Union, a slaveholder's testimony as to the identity of his absconded slave was to be taken as indisputable fact by federal officials. A person apprehended under the act had no right to give testimony in his or her behalf and no right to a trial by jury and was barred from the right of habeas corpus. Commissioners who remanded a "fugitive" back to slavery received ten dollars for their efforts, while those who upheld the freedom of the accused earned but five. Moreover, all bystanders were subject to being deputized by marshals or conscripted into a "*posse comitatus*" to aid in the capture of alleged runaways. Anyone guilty of refusing such service or acting in any way so as to frustrate the execution of the law could face imprisonment up to six months and a fine up to $1,000.[5]

John Langston described the operations of the law in personal terms. He had never been a slave (though his mother had), and he realized that if he or others like him were kidnapped with no white witnesses to vouch for their freedom, they risked being enslaved on the word of someone who did not even have to be present. The Fugitive Slave Act, he thundered to a large African American audience, "strips man of his manhood and liberty upon an *ex-parte* trial . . . declares that the decision of the commissioner, the lowest judicial officer known to the law, upon the matter of personal liberty—the gravest subject that can be submitted to any tribunal, shall be final and conclusive." Mostly, however, Langston protested that the law struck down "all the great bulwarks of Liberty" since it "kills alike, the true spirit of the American Declaration of Independence, the Constitution, and the palladium of our liberties."[6] Another black Oberlin alumnus, William Newman, expressed to their mutual friend Frederick Douglass his belief that the bill had been inspired by the direct influence of "his Satanic majesty" and was "the climax of his infernal wickedness."[7]

Across the North, the negative reaction among whites was also strong. For the first time, *all* Northerners risked a patent and often unwilling complicity in enslaving fellow men and women, not to mention fines and imprisonment if they balked at assisting in the process. It seemed that the federal government had not only openly declared its commitment to slave hunting but also commanded all its citizens to join the business as well.[8] A September meeting of outraged Oberlinites denounced the act as "belonging to a dark age and a tyrannical government" and lamented the appearance that barbarism and oppression had triumphed over the spirits of liberty and progress. Their meeting was but one of many across the free states that blasted the pretensions of the Slave Power. Though those gathered stopped short of espousing outright separation from the offending states, they did admit that "a union which brings us under the law of slavery, and enjoins upon us the loathsome work of slave-catching" was not counted "among our precious things."[9]

Oberlin patriarch John Keep rightly read the gauge of Northern public opinion. He wrote to Finney in November urging him to immediately return to Oberlin from a revival sojourn in England to help guide the rising sentiment against the Fugitive Slave Act toward abolitionist grounds. The "diabolical legislation," Keep wrote, had greatly aroused the nation, and he reported that sympathy for African Americans in the North was at a new high. The law seemed to be backfiring on its supporters and was creating "new interest, & great important tendencies toward Oberlin." Keep advised Finney that "we must watch and improve this tide."[10] He well understood that as a powerful symbol of abolitionism, many eyes across the country would be upon the Oberlin community observing its response to the passage of the legislation and following its example in opposing it.

As it did in other Northern reform centers, the Fugitive Slave Law brought Oberlin's black and white abolitionists together as never before. White residents' empathy was augmented now by a real sense of shared oppression, though clearly differing in degree. The community first responded by affirming and strengthening its commitment to those already among them who risked reenslavement at the hands of federal marshals. The September Oberlin meeting solemnly insisted that "while our fugitive brother remains in our midst, we will stand by him to the last, to protect him by all justifiable means in our power."[11] A similarly indignant meeting of African Americans in Columbus that same month listened as Charles Langston urged slaves to continue to flee for the "land of liberty," pledged his support and that of every Northern African American for their protection, and warned them to be constantly prepared to defend their newly won freedom at all costs. That meeting also appointed a five-man vigilance committee to protect Columbus's "fugitives" from seizure by slaveholders or their agents.[12] Nearly all of Oberlin's population was so zealously guardful of their black neighbors already that no such dedicated committee was necessary there.[13]

Still, across Ohio and the North, some free African Americans, whether fugitives from slavery or not, began an exodus to locations where the iniquitous Fugitive Slave Law had no force. Untold numbers moved their families to other locations in the United States (like Oberlin) where they felt more secure.[14] Oberlin's black population, the majority of which would be considered fugitives, swelled by nearly 300 percent between 1850 and 1860 as people who felt vulnerable to slave hunters flocked to what many considered the safest location in America (and, conveniently, a place only a few miles from Lake Erie's access to Canada).[15] According to some historians, between 15,000 and 20,000 African Americans left their home country for British Canada between the passage of the Fugitive Slave Act and 1860.[16]

African American leaders used the forum of the 1851 Convention of Colored Citizens of Ohio to continue their critique of the legislation. John Langston was the first to address the convention on the issue, calling the Fugitive Slave Law the "abomination of all abominations." The public outcry across the free states was to be expected, he said, if one assumed that mankind had not yet been entirely divested of its humanity. Moreover, the enactment possessed "neither the form nor the essence of true law" and was nothing more than "a hideous deformity in the *garb* of law."[17]

The discussion of the constitutionality of the fugitive law opened up another important debate among the delegates when Ford Douglass of Cleveland attempted to put the convention on record as affirming the Constitution as a proslavery document under which African Americans could not consistently vote. Oberlin alumnus John M. Brown quickly moved to indefinitely postpone Douglass's resolution, and former classmates William Howard Day and Charles Langston arose to support him and take issue with Douglass's logic.[18] Both Day and Langston acknowledged that the Constitution, as it had been recently construed by lawmakers and federal courts, *did* sanction slavery as well as the return of self-emancipated men and women to bondage. However, they stressed that it was not that peculiar construction under which they voted. Day likened the Constitution to the Bible, another document that had commonly been appropriated to uphold slavery. Should they also discard the Bible, he asked, or should they rather "discard the false opinions of mistaken men, in regard to it?" "If [the Constitution] says it was framed to 'establish justice,' it, of course, is opposed to injustice," Day argued. "If it says plainly that no person shall be deprived of life, *liberty*, or property without due process of law, I suppose it means it, and I shall avail myself of the benefit of it."[19]

This debate encapsulated the commitment of Oberlin's abolitionists, particularly its black reformers, to practical abolitionism. Instead of ideological exclusivity, men like the Langstons and Day appreciated the value of *anything* that could be used to their advantage and as an emancipatory tool. Of course the Constitution was framed by slaveholders for the benefit of slaveholders. Yet unless black reformers were prepared to give up their claims to citizenship and the attendant rights and protections they claimed under its terms, it could be a most valuable weapon. As Day reasoned, as an oppressed African American in the North, and especially as a representative of the millions of slaves in the South, he must not only hold every instrument precious that guaranteed him liberty but vow to continue his appeal to the American people for the rights thus guaranteed.[20] Charles Langston's reply to Douglass was even more direct. Just as he would encourage slaves to stop at nothing, even violence, to achieve their freedom, so too would he vote under the Constitution if he thought it could advance the cause. "Sir," he thundered at Douglass, "I have long since adopted as my God, the freedom of the colored people of the United States, and my religion, to do anything that will effect that object."[21]

In February of 1851, Day and the Langston brothers were among a delegation of Ohio African Americans sent by the colored convention to attempt to thus expand their liberties at an important and unprecedented meeting with Ohio's Democratic governor, Reuben Wood. The group hoped to extract a written endorsement from Wood in favor of black enfranchisement to be presented to the ongoing state constitutional convention.[22] Wood expressed a surprised yet condescending delight that African Americans were showing an interest in the political machinations of the state, and he voiced some vague concern for "the welfare of the colored." The majority of his reply, however, was described by disappointed abolitionists as a "shuffling, evasive, cowardly answer" to a sincere appeal.[23]

John Langston voiced his determined frustration to an African American audience not long thereafter. The chronic shortsightedness of the self-appointed gatekeepers of citizenship was obstructing the recognition of African American rights. It seemed clear to him that black advancement would ultimately have to be through their own efforts, with the help of their closest allies. "We struggle against opinions," he declared, and reminded his listeners, "Our warfare lies in the field of thought. Glorious struggle! Godlike warfare!" He realized that many Americans despised their black neighbors because of what they viewed as a long history of submissiveness, yet Langston pledged "before the world and in the face of Heaven" to "manfully" continue the struggle for advancement in civil and social life.[24] The time for strictly moral appeals to those in power had long since passed.

Langston decided to attack the flawed American legal system from within. Though refused admission into any law school on account of his race, on the recommendation of Professor John Morgan, he began theological study at Oberlin in 1851 as the best available course for a young black man to train for a legal career.[25] With Langston back in the familiar role of Oberlin student, his radical spark reinvigorated his colleagues. He was elected secretary of the Theological Literary Society in his first year. There, he and other members assiduously debated the pressing issues of the day, including the various fine points of the Fugitive Slave Law, as well as the related but not-so-fine question, "Ought Daniel Webster be hung?"[26]

John Mercer Langston in his 1853 theological department portrait (courtesy Oberlin College Archives)

In September, Langston was elected chairman of the new Oberlin Young Men's Anti-Slavery Society, open to students, faculty, and town residents and dedicated solely to "the social and moral elevation of the colored race."[27] At the society's organization, Langston also assumed the role of student agent in charge of arousing support among the western black population for their educational welfare.[28]

By the time the 1852 Convention of Colored Freemen of Ohio met in Cincinnati in January, the outrage over the Fugitive Slave Law and the emphasis on African American self-reliance had reached a fever pitch. Charles Langston served on the business committee that, in the first resolution of the convention, declared that "colored people can do more to elevate themselves and break down the illiberal prejudice, which bears upon them as a millstone to blight their prospects, by an honest truthful effort, than can, or will be done, by any or all other agencies combined."[29] At a September meeting in Cleveland, African American abolitionists, including Oberlin notables Sabram Cox, William Howard Day, and John Mercer Langston in various leadership roles, stepped up the forcefulness of their rhetoric and resolved that the only way to mitigate the iniquities of the fugitive law was for everyone, "singly and collectively," to enforce their right to liberty and the pursuit of happiness, regardless of means employed, when threatened with enslavement. Moreover, in another explicit turn away from the pacific roots of white antislavery toward the increasingly aggressive rhetoric of black abolitionist leaders, meeting attendees resolved to "in no case . . . deal more mildly with the robber of body, than with the highwayman or the assassin."[30]

Though Sojourner Truth, who was present at the meeting, tearfully urged the delegates to continue on the path of "peace and forbearance," it was clear that many Ohio African Americans had already taken up as their own Patrick Henry's revolutionary motto "Give me Liberty or give me Death."[31] It was alumnus William Newman who had quoted the patriot leader while declaring it his intention to kill "any so-called man" who attempted to enslave him or his family. To do that, in defense of personal liberty, would be to Newman an act of the highest virtue. White Americans, he concluded, would prove themselves hypocrites if they disagreed with his declaration that "thrice armed is he who hath his quarrel just."[32] At an earlier antislavery meeting, Charles Langston had called "on every slave, from Maryland to Texas, to arise and assert their liberties, and cut their masters' throats if they attempt again to reduce them to slavery."[33] As historian Leslie Alexander points out, the use of force was no longer an abstract philosophical debate among abolitionists, especially African Americans, who increasingly had little patience with reformers who recommended nonresistance to those who were denied the protection of equitable laws.[34]

In Oberlin, the recognition of the expediency of using violence to destroy slavery was not particularly controversial by this point (as it still was in many other communities and antislavery organizations). Even in its earliest days, Oberlin's abolitionist community members had not considered themselves thorough nonresistants. As James Fairchild recalled, "the right to repel by force injustice and outrage, under proper conditions, was vindicated in the Oberlin philosophy, and maintained as a practical principle." However, most white abolitionists in early Oberlin had little expectation that the antislavery struggle might "afford occasion for any application of the principle." Not until African Americans arrived in larger numbers in the 1840s, made slavery truly "real" to the community, and began fostering empathy in their white neighbors did they realize that violence to protect and even advance freedom might also be condoned and encouraged. Once forceful resistance to slavery became a common thread in the antislavery arguments of Oberlin's black reformers (and even as an offensive tactic operating in the South), the notion that it would be acceptable if it produced, in Fairchild's words, "useful result" gained support.[35] African Americans themselves were less timid in their embrace of militancy. In an 1856 antislavery address, alumna Sara Stanley invoked the warrior tradition of the ancient Spartans when she urged black male abolitionists, "Bring home your shield, or be brought upon it."[36]

Oberlin and the Free Democracy

The presidential election of 1852 was the first since the passage of the Fugitive Slave Law, and the measure was at the heart of the campaign. Democrats pledged to uphold the fugitive law and to strenuously oppose "all efforts of the Abolitionists or others, made to induce Congress to interfere with questions of slavery." Whigs endorsed all parts of the Compromise of 1850 "as a settlement in principle and substance of the dangerous and exciting questions which they embrace" and pledged to demand their strict enforcement. Like the Democrats, they deprecated all further agitation of the slavery question "thus settled" as dangerous to the nation's peace.[37] Finney's précis in August of the parties' positions exposed their unmistakable mutual foundation: "Both parties," he preached, "concede to the South all they ask."[38]

When the news reached Oberlin that the Democrats had nominated Franklin Pierce for the presidency in June, the small handful of local Democrats convened an impromptu ratification meeting. However, a much larger group of Oberlinites joined the meeting to mock the Democratic candidate and shout Free-Soil slogans whenever they could.[39] Included in the crowd was a group of young African Americans, sarcastically described by an observer from Cleveland as being "of *very* Democratic principles." As the first politician took the stump to praise the prospect of a President Pierce, his words were drowned out by calls from the crowd demanding that John Langston offer some remarks instead. Langston complied and fit many of his declarations to the occasion of the rally—by sharply attacking the Democratic Party. Moreover, he also vented his frustration with the Whigs and their candidate, Mexican War hero Winfield Scott, who had done little to differentiate themselves from the rabidly proslavery Democracy. After Langston's speech concluded to loud cheers, the meeting adjourned with three groans for the Democrats.[40]

The former Free-Soil Party, newly renamed the Free Democracy, held its August nominating convention in Pittsburgh. Delegates selected John Hale of New Hampshire as the party's presidential candidate to run on a ticket with the radical George Julian of Indiana. The tone of the convention was set early on by the Ohioans, as Buckeye delegates paraded around the hall with a banner reading, "NO COMPROMISE WITH SLAVEHOLDERS OR DOUGHFACES," a jab at the backsliding Barnburners of 1848.[41] Though they would miss the numbers Van Buren's supporters had brought the party, the Free Democrats used the defection to radicalize their platform. They unabashedly denounced slavery as "a sin against God and a crime against man" and dropped their earlier denial of congressional power to interfere with slavery in the states. Delegates excoriated the Fugitive Slave Law and its supporters, called for the official recognition of the Republic of Haiti, and, in "a mighty protest against the absurd, unnatural, and wicked prejudice that exists so universally against the man of color," selected Frederick Douglass as an officer of the convention.[42] Though they noted the party's shortcomings, even the Garrisonian WASS admitted that the convention had taken a "bold and defiant" position against the Slave Power.[43]

Finney had played an important role in the development of the Free Democratic platform, and upon his return to Oberlin, his account of the convention thrilled eager listeners.[44] His first *Oberlin Evangelist* article published after the convention was a scathing attack on slavery, its supporters, the fugitive bill, and the hopelessly proslavery Whig and Democratic Parties.[45] Oberlinites also had the opportunity to hear from other delegates on their return trips from Pittsburgh, including Douglass, Gerrit Smith, and their former professor Amasa Walker, now the secretary of state of Massachusetts.[46] John Langston, as chairman of the Oberlin Young Men's Anti-Slavery Society, welcomed Salmon P. Chase and candidate John Hale himself to Oberlin in October for a series of lively and well-received speeches.[47]

The Oberlin community campaigned hard that fall for Hale as well as town favorite and Oberlin trustee Norton Townsend, who had been nominated for a congressional seat. Black Oberlinites were especially active on the stump, and as the events during one such speech in French Creek, Ohio, showed, the Oberlin name still bore a particular connotation, especially because of the new black vanguard that carried it. Langston was one of three speakers scheduled to speak on behalf of the Free Democracy and Townsend. The first two speakers, both white, struggled through their addresses while hostile listeners shouted provocative insults and incendiary questions. In fact, the second man could not make it to the conclusion of his remarks because of an insistent local Democrat in front repeatedly shouting the question "Are you in favor of *nigger* social equality?" The speaker's obvious discomfort and hesitation to respond fed the audience's animus, and their storm of hand clapping, foot stomping, and hissing made his continuance impossible.[48]

Langston would not be so intimidated. He quickly arose and restated the heckler's question, answered it in the affirmative, and declared that "it was only the enemy of human rights" who would object so vehemently to "equal freedom." Stymied, the critic resorted to what Langston would later remember as the most reliable of insults in antebellum Ohio—he screamed, "You learned that at Oberlin!" "You learned another thing at Oberlin!" the man went on, "You learned to walk with white women there!" Langston, with a wide grin on his face, walked to the very edge of the platform, right up to the heckler, and replied, "If you have in your family, any good-looking, intelligent, refined sisters, you would do your family a special service by introducing me to them at once." Stung, the critic was shouted back to his seat by the howling and newly supportive audience, one of whom shouted, "Joe Ladd, you d—d fool sit down! That darkey is too smart for you!" The township, described by Langston as formerly "anti-negro and of positive detestable pro-slavery character in its hatred of such a community and college as those of Oberlin," cast a large majority of its votes for Townsend in the general election.[49]

However, those votes would not be enough to send Townsend to Congress, and despite Ohio casting more votes for Hale and Julian than any other state, the national Free Democratic ticket went down to defeat as well.[50] The *Oberlin Evangelist* expressed grief at the Democratic triumph with a now-familiar sentiment. "Our chief consolation," editor Henry Cowles wrote, "is that Jehovah sitteth on a yet higher throne, making the utmost use of even the misrule of men." Still, the West proved itself the most steadfast in its third-party support, and even though the loss of the Van Buren voters of 1848 was regrettable, "truer and more reliable men" had cast their ballots for freedom in 1852, "and on better and more enduring principles."[51] In fact, Cowles found much in the election to suggest hope for the antislavery cause. For one, the Whig Party appeared to be in shambles, maybe even in its death throes. Its only hope for survival, he wrote, would have been to take decided ground against slavery. That done, the Whigs could have possibly carried the "heavy free states," yet they "foisted the monstrous pro-slavery plank into her political platform, to conciliate the South, and hoped by her choice of the least offensive of her Presidential candidates, to conciliate the North." In trying to please everyone, the Whig Party pleased nobody, "and her monstrous compromise plank proved a millstone to her neck as she launched off upon the political sea. May her doom be a warning!"⁵² At the same time, "freedom rejoice[d]" in the election to Congress of abolitionists Joshua Giddings and Edward Wade of Ohio and Gerrit Smith of New York. "The great political men of the past are gone—Calhoun, Clay and Webster!" Cowles wrote, and he eulogized the South, who "sits in her widowhood, without one great mind to lead her . . . glad to fawn upon a fourth rate man of the North, if he will only save her from ruin." The election of a cadre of abolitionists seemed clear proof that antislavery sentiment was on the rise. "Dare anyone deny," Cowles asked, "that the tide of Anti-Slavery feeling is rising with a deep mountain swell, to ebb no more till the whole land is swept and bathed in its power?"⁵³

No More Compromises

However, the Pierce administration was largely successful in keeping discussion of the slavery issue to a minimum in its first year, despite the constant prodding of abolitionists. Finney challenged his congregation, "Shall we let this entire subject alone, and go in for contention of the other issues as if they had any importance worth naming in the comparison?"⁵⁴ Langston frankly told a New York audience in 1853 that despite the efforts of Congress and the administration to stifle it, they could not check antislavery agitation. "Go," he urged his audience, "and padlock all the whites at the North—go padlock all the mouths of all the slaveholders at the South. . . . Still you cannot check agitation. . . . As long as there remained a vestige of Slavery, so long there would be agitation."⁵⁵ Langston's words were prophetic, because beginning in late 1853, Illinois senator Stephen Douglas's attempt to organize the Nebraska Territory would make sure that more than just a vestige of slavery discussion would engross the United States.

Douglas's plan was originally meant simply to organize the territory above the 36°30' line of the Missouri Compromise to expedite the completion of a transcontinental railroad. However, he soon found that to achieve passage of his bill, he would have to finesse powerful Southerners in the Senate. The result was the introduction of legislation that repealed the 1820 Compromise and opened up the Territories to slavery if residents so voted under a "popular sovereignty" provision. This could have potentially created slave states from territories formerly declared beyond the reach of the institution. When Pierce made support of the bill a test of party loyalty, many northern Democrats, Whigs, Free Democrats, and abolitionists all geared up for an aggressive fight.⁵⁶

Immediately after Douglas introduced the Kansas-Nebraska Bill, Oberlin residents convened a meeting to express their burning indignation at the government's audacity in attempting the "atrocious" repeal of the Missouri Compromise with a new "nefarious scheme."[57] Professor James Fairchild stressed that the area in question was the very territory to which the 1820 compromise was meant to apply. He figured that since the South had gained all the advantages that it could expect from that bargain, it now hoped to annul it and "rob freedom of what was granted."[58] The attendees resolved that "the eternal condemnation of all honest men should forever attach to every member of Congress who speaks or votes for this abominable measure." They further declared that "a bolder or more reckless attempt to seal the fate of Government as a Republic, has never been made; we look upon it with horror and pray God it may never succeed."[59]

However, Douglas's stout efforts pushed the bill through both Houses, and in May it became law. Quickly, though, many abolitionists realized that the bill's passage might not be the horrific event they initially predicted and indeed might contain a silver lining. Langston, for one, scolded America for its past blindness to the iniquities of slavery but expressed hope for the impetus that the act might give the antislavery cause. In an address at the AASS's 1855 anniversary meeting, Langston observed that now there was not a single American who could truly say, "'I have my full share of liberty,'" and he predicted that such dissatisfaction would create valuable political allies.[60] The bitter taste of the Fugitive Slave Act still lingered in the mouths of many Northerners, and yet another concession to the Slave Power offered a chance for abolitionists to shepherd anti-Nebraska sentiment into a new political movement. As James Monroe wrote, the widespread disgust finally enabled "the dullest Northern men to see that the country could not continue to exist half slave and half free—that slavery and freedom were, as they always must be, engaged in mortal conflict, and one or the other must perish."[61]

Oberlin's initial response to the "consummated iniquity" was to hold a series of meetings to explore proposals to divorce the federal government from slavery, "and put[ ] it actively on the side of Freedom." A July meeting of voters in Oberlin reaffirmed its resolve to accept "no more compromises—no yielding to the South."[62] Another political meeting in Oberlin the next month took the opportunity to clarify its "Anti-Slavery Platform" in light of the Kansas-Nebraska Bill, legislation, the attendees declared, that had proven again their insistence that the contest between slavery and freedom was a "war of extermination." These were antagonistic principles between which there could be no harmony, common interest, or compromise. "Our war," the platform read, "is with Slavery itself, as well as all its usurpations and aggressions," and delegates vowed to seek the destruction of the institution where it already existed and to stop its expansion. Moreover, they demanded the repeal of the Fugitive Slave Law, the prohibition of slavery in the Territories and District of Columbia, the abolition of the coastwise and interstate slave trade, the denial of statehood to any territory that allowed slavery, and the employment of "the entire moral power of the Government at home and abroad" toward emancipation. "The time has come," they concluded, "when the people of the North should rally and combine their energies, not only to prevent the spread of slavery, but to crush the system itself."[63]

Even though the rising anti-Nebraska tide was forming into an antislavery political association with an antiblack element similar to that which had haunted the Free-Soil Party, Oberlin abolitionists, even its black reformers, had faith that it could eventually coalesce into a party of freedom. William Howard Day and John Langston stumped for anti-Nebraska candidates across Ohio and the Northern states, and conservatives noted the men's successes as portents of things to come: "negro stump-speakers! negro voters! negro jurors! negro office-holders!"[64] Many in Ohio were already calling supporters of the new party "Republicans," and as an old man, Langston would proudly recall, "I was present at the party's birth. I helped to dress it."[65]

The success that anti-Nebraska politicians found after the passage of the act was staggering. In Ohio, the gauge of public opinion was initially most evident in the widespread condemnation of Stephen Douglas. Realizing that his legislation was pulling the national Democratic Party apart along sectional lines, Douglas set off on a conciliatory tour across the Northwest at the end of the congressional session. However, he found only furious crowds awaiting him at nearly every train stop. "All along the Western Reserve of Ohio," Douglas remarked, "I saw my effigy upon every tree we passed."[66]

As state election returns accumulated in October, the *Cleveland Leader* confidently declared "Ohio All Anti-Nebraska!"[67] Voters elected "an unbroken Anti-Nebraska delegation" to Congress, including Elyria abolitionist and Langston's mentor Philemon Bliss, who pulled to victory on overwhelming majorities from the town of Oberlin, Russia Township, and Lorain County.[68] The next year, Russia Township voters gave the local candidates of the Republican Party proper a majority of nearly 400 votes, and the *Oberlin*

Evangelist declared the results "an Anti-Slavery Triumph."⁶⁹ It was, the editor declared, a clear mass movement "to rebuke the slavery propagandism of our times—an omen of the certain triumph of Freedom in her present conflict against Slavery—the inauguration of an era in which corrupt politicians must give place to men of known moral principle!"⁷⁰

God Go with Them

The fact that the fate of slavery in states carved from the Territories would be decided by the votes of its citizens encouraged thousands of partisans from across the nation to emigrate there in an attempt to swell support for their particular side of the slavery debate. On August 21, 1854, the Kansas Emigrant Aid Association of Northern Ohio (AANO) organized in Oberlin, structured around the Oberlin Emigrant Aid Company that had been organized four months earlier.⁷¹ Its basic mission was similar to that of other emigrant aid companies, to swell free-soil ballot boxes in the Territories, yet it was not to be a profit-oriented venture. Moreover, the AANO's emigrants were selectively chosen for their avowed abolitionism, as opposed to most other emigrant's outright hostility to African Americans.⁷² Most easterners would have agreed with the New York man who urged the AANO to avoid "rash and hasty" antislavery statements. He believed they would be best served by taking a position that would "enable the conservative men of the North to act with and aid us."⁷³ However, the selection of abolitionists with Oberlin ties such as Norton Townsend, James Thome, James Fairchild, Timothy Hudson, Henry Peck, and John Reed to the executive committee of the association suggested a radically different path. "Spirited" abolitionist speeches by Asa Mahan, John Langston, Peck, Townsend, Thome, and others left no doubt as to the true motivations of the Northern Ohioans.⁷⁴

"A great crisis is upon us," the delegates to the AANO organizing convention declared. "Let Slavery triumph now, and the fate of this nation may be sealed." If Kansas was lost, the effect would be to embolden proslavery advocates and discourage the "friends of Liberty," so that "even with more rapid strides, despotism will march forward in the consummation of its avowed end, viz.: the entire subjugation of the nation." They enthusiastically held up two plans of action: to elect true-hearted men to Congress, and to begin sending into Kansas a committed antislavery population. They pledged, "To the consummation of an end so important, we will give both our time, our means, and our untiring energy."⁷⁵

Corresponding secretary John Reed left Oberlin to canvass northern Ohio to organize auxiliary societies and recruit emigrant families of the abolitionist stripe.[76] On October 23, 1854, the first company of forty-three emigrants set out from Oberlin.[77] In all, the association sent out at least seven groups of emigrants of between twenty and more than a hundred people each during the Kansas crisis from 1854 to 1860.[78] When they reached Kansas Territory, the companies from the AANO found familiar faces on the ground to help them in the coming struggles. The antislavery American Missionary Association (AMA) had begun sending missionary emigrants to the area in the summer of 1854. Some of the first volunteers for the AMA crusade were Oberlin men and women who sought to labor in the field where their influence would be "most felt for the cause of the Lord and the Slave."[79] Their initial mission was to establish abolitionist churches and schools for the families of emigrants moving west—churches, notably, that did not fellowship slaveholders and schools that taught out of "books of an anti-slavery character."[80]

AMA missionaries from Oberlin, however, were even more radical than their handlers back East thought wise. Association head Simeon Jocelyn warned John Byrd that he should not make the slavery issue "too prominent" in his Sabbath labors.[81] Nonetheless, Byrd threw caution to the wind and settled in the midst of a group of proslavery emigrants and continued to preach as he saw fit.[82] One particular sermon of his regarding the "nefarious institution of slavery" near proslavery Leavenworth nearly got him tarred and feathered, and only vigilante imprisonment by a proslavery mob could stop his crusade to convert the ruffians.[83]

The differences between the AANO and most of the other emigrant groups were remarkable. One Osawatomie settler wrote candidly of his associates in Kansas in 1855: "The community here are very nearly united on the free-state question. But the majority would dislike and resent being called abolitionists." There was "a prevailing sentiment" against admitting African Americans into the territory at all, slave or free.[84] Oberlin alumnus Samuel Adair, John Brown's brother-in-law, expressed his frustration at the racism of most Kansas emigrants. "Their Free Soil is Free Soil for *white, but not for black*," he wrote. "They hate slavery but they hate the negro worse." He concluded that the ignorance of some of those men was "most profound."[85] One traveler passing through rightly declared, "The Free State men warred not against slavery in the abstract, only slavery in Kansas." Most of them lived "in deadly terror of being termed 'abolitionists'—frightened at the mere mention of that mysterious specter—'negro equality.'"[86] "These people are intensely anti-abolitionist," John Byrd wrote, "and if colored persons are to be allowed to come in at all, they would prefer that they should enter as slaves rather than free men."[87]

Back in Ohio, people in Oberlin followed the unfolding events in Kansas with a watchful eye. A correspondent in Lawrence wrote to the *Oberlin Evangelist* that fraud and violence ruled the day at the first territorial election. Border Ruffians from Missouri "rode over the free citizens of the Territory, trampled the sacred rights of the ballot-box in the dust, and now glory in their own infamy."[88] Henry Cowles Jr. wrote home to Oberlin describing a similar scene at the next election in March. "A Missouri mob took possession of the polls," he told his father, and the free-soilers were threatened with guns and knives while the belligerent ruffians "did *all* the voting."[89] Early in 1856, Samuel Wood, by then a veteran of two tours in Kansas, told a rapt Oberlin audience of his travails in the Territory and the dangers emigrants faced at the hands of Border Ruffians. Self-preservation was of vital importance to Kansas emigrants. As he told his listeners what he had experienced firsthand at the hands of proslavery mobs, a critic described the Oberlin crowd's reaction, and remarking that "it was plain to see their meek and non-resistant spirits turning into fighting demons." Of course, the idea of such a restrictive ideology as true nonresistance never had much traction in Oberlin. This did not mean that Oberlinites did not value peace, and Wood's appeal left room for the most peace-loving abolitionist, even those "whose tender consciences would not permit of their giving to buy powder, ball, and rifles for war." These no less honorable partisans were still able to donate money and goods by earmarking it "for provision or clothing."[90] So influenced by their hometown, Oberlin's participants in the struggle were rare among Kansas emigrants in that whenever possible, they used their words as weapons and guns only as a last resort: they fought "first with the Bible, and when that failed, with Sharpe's rifle."[91]

The news of the sack of Lawrence, the free-soil capital in Kansas, by a proslavery army hit Oberlin like a bombshell. Men and women crowded into the college chapel to take part in an impromptu meeting called to voice their righteous anger against the Slave Power in Kansas. James Monroe declared himself at a loss for words over the "audacity and atrocity" of the proslavery mob's attack on the city. His colleague Timothy Hudson, however, filled any void that Monroe may have left, declaring that "the spirit of true democracy had utterly perished from the self-styled democratic party." Instead of upholding governance "*by* the people, and *for* the people, they had surrendered themselves, bound hand and foot, to the sway of a petty oligarchy."[92]

Though their support had never wavered for their friends in Kansas, the fall of Lawrence, coupled with news of the violent caning of Charles Sumner by a Southerner on the floor of the U.S. Senate, pushed the Oberlin community into a heightened sense of urgency and agitation. The words of John Langston just a handful of months earlier had never seemed so true. If slavery triumphed in Kansas, the fate of the nation would be sealed. But, should Kansas be rescued from the evils of slavery, it would "plume afresh the drooping wing of Freedom, and inspire a rational hope, that, having vanquished the slave power *once*, the North will be filled with a life which shall work out the complete redemption of our government, and the enfranchisement of the oppressed millions of our land."[93]

Again, Oberlin rose to the challenge. By late May of 1856, "Charlie" Finney and Henry Cowles Jr. were fighting for the antislavery ideals of their namesakes on the plains of Kansas.[94] Oberlin men already on the ground stepped up their agitation to the point where their names were placed on the ruffians' "hanging list."[95] In July, the elder Finney went to Buffalo on his son's behalf to the organizational meeting of the National Kansas Committee. That convention proposed establishing state and county committees to recruit volunteers and to raise money for arms and supplies to keep the free-soilers well-equipped in the field.[96] That same summer, Oberlin's senior class petitioned the faculty to grant them permission to graduate early so that they could emigrate as soon as possible. Mary Cowles remarked in her journal that the members of other classes would doubtless follow as well, and she earnestly prayed that "God go with them."[97]

As Fast as Public Opinion Would Sustain

Back in the states, the party that had coalesced around opposition to the Kansas-Nebraska Act was gaining members and influence and taking on a more definite shape. Despite attempts by a few antislavery Whig faithful to reassert their party's free-soil credentials, the new Republican Party was reaping the defections from the sectionally split national organizations and adding them to its own solid base. In 1854, anti-Nebraska fusion candidates had taken 100 of the 234 seats in the Thirty-Fourth Congress. The uproar over "Bloody Kansas" and "Bloody Sumner" would be the last straws for many antislavery Whigs and Democrats who refused to be cowed by the Slave Power.[98]

In March of 1856, organizers sent out a call for a national convention to be held in Philadelphia. Delegates were invited "without regard to past political differences or divisions" to oppose the repeal of the Missouri Compromise, the proslavery position of the current administration, and the extension of slavery into the Territories, and to support the admission of Kansas as a free state. Ohio Republicans adopted the language of the national committee in issuing their own call for a state convention that would meet approximately two weeks before the national body. Oberlin's Henry Peck was among the delegates from the Ohio convention who were selected to go on to represent them in Philadelphia and who helped pass through a platform that was quite radical in comparison with that of the Whigs and Democrats.[99]

The first national Republican platform highlighted the egalitarian principles of the Declaration of Independence, denied the authority of Congress to legalize slavery in any territory under its jurisdiction, and arraigned the Pierce administration for sanctioning the atrocities in Kansas and for committing a "high crime against the Constitution, the Union, and humanity" in the process. Still, radicals within the party were dissatisfied that the platform only denied congressional authority to establish slavery by positive legislation, rather than affirming the ability of Congress to interfere with slavery where it already existed. Its insistence that the government uphold the rights of "life, liberty, and the pursuit of happiness" only applied to "persons under its exclusive jurisdiction," thus effectively sanctioning slavery in the states and sustaining the legality of the Fugitive Slave Law.[100] Despite the view of some antislavery advocates that political antislavery had been fatally diluted since its earliest days, the fact remained that the only alternatives to the Republicans' avowedly antislavery nominee John Frémont were Millard Fillmore, now the candidate of the weak American (Know-Nothing) Party, who as president had signed the Fugitive Slave Bill into law and overseen the Kansas outrages, and Democrat James Buchanan, who pledged to uphold the act and oppose Kansas's admission as a free state.[101] John Langston, writing with the business committee of the 1856 Ohio State Convention of Colored Men, welcomed the new Republican Party, and though it clearly was not the true party of freedom that would tolerate "no law for slavery," it stood out as the only real and best hope of achieving the political goals of abolitionism that had ever existed. Despite the party's shortcomings, Langston asserted that it "may do great service in the cause of Freedom."[102]

James Monroe expressed similar sentiments when he accepted the nomination of the Lorain County Republicans for the Ohio legislature in 1855. The more progressive Republicans in Ohio wanted a representative from Oberlin in Columbus to help neutralize the conservative element of the party.¹⁰³ Monroe had twice previously rejected Free-Soil nominations for the legislature, believing that the platform left too much to be desired for a radical like himself. In 1855, though, he realized that his rightful "place" was with the men who were "constantly striving, and with a good degree of success, to elevate" the principles of the Liberty and Free-Soil heir, the Republican Party. It took votes to make political progress, and Monroe's influence would be a healthy one for the party. "If the new party were not moving as fast as I could wish," he believed, "they were, perhaps, moving as fast as public opinion would sustain."¹⁰⁴

Monroe coasted to victory with nearly 90 percent of the vote in his district, running far ahead of his ticket, which also contributed a 1,800-vote majority to Salmon P. Chase in his successful bid for governor.¹⁰⁵ Meanwhile, Ohio Democrats grew apprehensive. The *Cleveland Plain Dealer*, while not missing the opportunity to insult Oberlin, expressed its fear after the enthusiastic "Lorain fusion" of 1855. "Oberlin, her professors and students," the editor complained, "have at last got control of the universal whig party [sic] in that county." Democrats worried that the school and town that had been "so long the dictator of morals and religion for this region of the country, has now become dictator in its politics."¹⁰⁶ Reflecting on his mandate, Monroe wrote, "It was still a new thing for an old abolitionist to be elected to office, and it was certainly a new thing to me. A shower of friendly votes was a pleasanter experience than a shower of brickbats."¹⁰⁷

Still, there were considerable obstacles that progressive Republicans in Ohio and nationwide would face in their crusade for emancipation and African American civil rights. Abolitionists within the party who hoped to push the boundaries of the organization's minimalist antislavery platform had to compete with conservatives who eschewed any attempts to go beyond nominal anti-expansionism, not to mention proposed abolitionist measures that offended their often virulent racism. The views of one prominent Ohio Republican in 1858 could stand for many earlier in the decade: "The 'negro question,' as we understand it," John Greiner declared, "is a white man's question, the question of the right of free white laborers to the soil of the territories. It is not to be crushed or retarded by shouting 'Sambo' at us." To make his point even clearer, Greiner explained: "We have no Sambo in our platform. . . . We object to Sambo. We don't want him about. We insist that he shall not be forced upon us."¹⁰⁸

Monroe ran into similar resistance when he first attempted to introduce a habeas corpus bill before the Ohio House in 1856. "About one-half of the Republicans were very conservative," he recalled, "and much inclined to vote with the Democrats upon any question which looked like one of Abolitionism."[109] Monroe trod carefully. In a move reminiscent of Oberlin's decision more than twenty years earlier to admit students "irrespective of color" without explicitly mentioning African American applicants, the bill that Monroe finally forced through contained no mention of "fugitives" or "slavery" but was rather a broad guarantee to the right of the writ of habeas corpus to all men and women.[110] In his remarks in support of his bill, Monroe declared himself a staunch abolitionist but a practical man as well. "I wish to accomplish something," he admitted, "and if I cannot get what I would like, I shall not . . . refuse to get what I can."[111]

Monroe represented a large (and growing) group of antislavery politicians who, though working through a major political party with obvious limitations from an abolitionist point of view, did not limit their own political creed to an official party platform. They did not carelessly abandon their principles but rather carried them as far as possible into various legislative chambers and party caucuses to press for radicalization from within. The *Oberlin Students' Monthly* agreed that any and all moves toward abolitionists' ultimate goals were accumulative. When a "friend of truth" like Monroe made a concession to carry his point, he did not sacrifice principle but postponed acceptance until a more promising day.[112] Like-minded attendees of an Oberlin Republican gathering declared that they hoped to bring slavery to an end where it already existed as well as to oppose its extension over "territory where it is not." Moreover, where they lacked the political power to assail it directly, they pledged to "use all agencies which may be justly employed, to arouse the nation to a sense of its wickedness, its cruelties and the dangers to which it exposes." Even if a majority of Republicans claimed themselves powerless to attack slavery because of constitutional limitations, citizens of Oberlin vowed to "go to the very verge of our constitutional power" to that end. Once they reached the limits that party consensus had set, they promised to continue their advocacy of an antislavery Constitution. They would "study the instrument anew" and demonstrate to their more conservative associates "what rights and duties it teaches in regard to universal liberty, which the sophistries of slavery may have hitherto concealed."[113] This was the very message John Langston expressed to a group of abolitionists during Monroe's first term in office. "If the Republican Party is not Anti-Slavery enough," he urged his listeners, "take hold of it and make it so."[114] Langston and his brother Charles campaigned for Frémont in the style of abolitionist lectures that brooked no compromise.[115] They took the same occasions to criticize the lethargy of the Republicans

Left to right: Professors James Fairchild, John Morgan, and James Monroe (courtesy Oberlin College Archives)

and press for African American enfranchisement, all the while lifting up Frémont as the candidate who had the potential to effect the most change.[116]

Besides the Langstons, other Oberlin professors, students, and residents logged countless miles campaigning for "Frémont and Freedom," and hundreds of Oberlinites attended Republican rallies whenever one was held in northwestern Ohio.[117] In Newark, Ohio, the Democratic newspaper complained about "Oberlin darkies . . . stumping it with all their might for Frémont," and five days later noted the scheduled lecture of "a learned nigger, said to be a graduate of Oberlin, a man of piety, and a supporter of Frémont."[118] Oberlin's commencement exercises in August led a Cleveland correspondent to report that he did not hear a single speech "that was not charged to the muzzle with political abolitionism."[119] The *Oberlin Evangelist* appealed to its readers, "by all that is fearful in the pending crisis—by all that is sacred in freedom and right . . . to ensure the election of the men whose banner flings to the breeze the freemen's emphatic sign—*Free Press, Free Speech, Free Men, Frémont and Victory!*"[120] This was the constant cheer of the Oberlin Frémont parade in which Anthony Burns, the celebrated "fugitive" who was now an Oberlin student, marched "as a freeman and a brother" with other partisans.[121] For weeks before the election, the five o'clock bell that had once summoned Oberlin students to their manual labor, now called residents to "break-o-day meetings invoking aid from Almighty God in behalf of 'Freedom and Frémont.'" The day before the election, all business in town halted so that an appropriate amount of prayer and fasting could be offered on behalf of Oberlin's candidate.[122]

Oberlin did nearly all within its power (in addition to appeals to the Almighty) to win the day for Frémont. The final tally on Election Day in Russia Township showed him with more than a five-to-one advantage over Buchanan.[123] These votes contributed to a Frémont majority statewide and put Ohio in the Republican column along with all of New England, New York, Michigan, and Wisconsin. Still, Buchanan's sweep of the South and sufficiently strong showing in a handful of Northern states disappointed Frémont's presidential bid. Moreover, besides retaining the presidency, Democrats riding Buchanan's coattails managed to win control of Congress, and the Supreme Court under Chief Justice Roger Taney, a Southerner, already appeared to lean proslavery.[124]

Even in states like Ohio that were solidly Republican, the blunt conservatism of the party refused to give up its control. There, Republicans who might otherwise have followed the prodding of radicals had to immediately shift gears and consider the upcoming 1857 statewide elections. Nonetheless, Langston, Monroe, and Norton Townsend, with the support of other prominent Lorain County Republicans, undertook another concerted campaign to strike the word "white" from Ohio's voting qualifications—"the last vestige," as Langston described it, "of the old barbarous and inhuman Black Laws."[125] Langston renewed his assault as president of the 1857 Ohio State Convention of Colored Men. In an adept "Address to the Legislature of Ohio," Langston laid the groundwork for a constitutional amendment allowing black suffrage based on the spirit of the Constitution and Declaration of Independence and the "humanity and manhood," citizenship, status as taxpayers, and historically demonstrated patriotism of African Americans. Langston assured lawmakers that no unjust or oppressive legislation would ever drive African Americans from the state. Instead, the survival of "cruel and despotic statutes" would make black activists anchor themselves even more solidly to Ohio until they could successfully erase them from the books.[126]

The day after Langston's address to the African American convention, Monroe delivered a speech in the Ohio House where he proposed the constitutional amendment authorizing African American suffrage.[127] As legislators thumbed through the petitions sent over by Langston's fellow delegates at the colored convention, Monroe unfolded the argument for universal manhood suffrage. Meanwhile, Oberlin's representative in the Senate, Herman

Canfield, reported Langston's full address to the judiciary committee.[128] However, for the sake of party unity and under pressure from House leaders, Monroe did not call for the yeas and nays on the passage of the amendment, a tactic he had hoped to use in order to put each member of the House on record.[129] In its censure of Monroe's colleagues (and perhaps as a not-so-subtle chiding of Monroe), the *Oberlin Evangelist* prayed, "O give us men for rulers, upright and true to their better convictions!"[130] Even more to the point was the one-man drama performed in Oberlin by William Wells Brown in January 1858, titled "Experience, or How to Give a Northern Man a Backbone."[131]

So Unparalleled a Judicial Outrage

The *Oberlin Evangelist* editor could not have known it at the time, but beginning with the Supreme Court's decision in *Dred Scott v. Sanford* three days after the paper's lament over Monroe's timidity, Oberlin's (and much of the North's) faith in the government would progressively spiral downward until civil war seemed imminent. Taney's dicta in his *Dred Scott* opinion holding that African Americans, whether slave or free, were not citizens of the United States stunned the cautiously optimistic abolitionists. Moreover, Taney added insult to injury when he asserted that the framers of the Constitution never intended African Americans to enjoy the privileges of citizenship and that they had viewed all blacks as "so far inferior that they had no rights which the white man was bound to respect." He also ruled that the Missouri Compromise of 1820 had been unconstitutional and that Congress had no authority to prohibit slavery in any of the Territories.[132]

Across the North, the response of reformers with Oberlin connections was of a single mind. Amos Dresser declared in a religious meeting that Taney, on behalf of the Court, "wields the sword to oppress the innocent instead of protecting them" and in doing so subverted the function of civil government and became "the minister of Satan instead of the minister of God." America, he mourned, was "no longer the citadel of justice, but the defender and sustainer of crime."[133] Feeling the sting of federal insult even more personally were African Americans. Charles Langston spoke for many when, in a letter to Salmon P. Chase, he denounced the decision that he saw as "so gross, so monstrous, so unparalleled a judicial outrage." Taney's judicial opinion, Langston wrote, "overtaxes our patience, well-nigh extinguishes our hopes, almost goads us into madness."[134]

However, despite its tremendous symbolic importance, the *Dred Scott* decision would not have the same galvanizing effect on the North as did the

Kansas-Nebraska uproar. In fact, no other major judicial opinion in American history affected the daily lives of so few people as did *Dred Scott*. It supposedly annulled a law that had been rendered void three years earlier, and denied freedom to slaves in a particular area where there were no slaves. More importantly, the decision, by its very circumstances, did not allow any actual way for its opponents to openly defy it, as did the Fugitive Slave Law. Despite all the controversy, the decision only applied to proposed Republican legislation on slavery extension and the fate of a single man, Dred Scott.[135]

The Republican Party in Ohio also could not capitalize on *Dred Scott* as they may have wished because of a severe financial panic that reached full force in mid-1857. Since the Republican Party was in power during the crisis, its representatives were often blamed for the economic woes of their constituents. It did not help that the Republican treasurer had been implicated in the embezzlement of a half a million dollars from the state during the downturn that bankrupted the treasury.[136] Moreover, Democrats took Taney's opinion that the Missouri Compromise of 1820 had been unconstitutional and that Congress did not have the authority to prohibit slavery in the Territories to mean that the key plank of the Republican Party's platform, federally mandated nonextension of slavery, had become a nonissue. Emboldened, proslavery interests basked in their newfound advantage. Though Chase was reelected to his post as Ohio's governor, his margin of victory was less than one-half of one percent of all votes cast, an advantage that some Democrats attributed principally to the illegal voting of mulatto and African American residents of Oberlin.[137] An even more discouraging aspect of the conservative backlash of 1857 for Ohio Republicans was that the results of the state elections threw control of the Ohio legislature back into the hands of the Democrats.[138]

Ohio Democrats rightly believed that they now possessed the power to undo the progressive legislation of the last Republican legislature. Besides feeling muscle enough to abrogate all the laws in Ohio that protected African Americans against being kidnapped under the Fugitive Slave Law, Democrats were also rumored to be considering a renewed campaign to bring the notorious Black Laws back into full effect.[139] When Monroe attempted to present a carefully prepared speech in defense of his own 1856 habeas corpus bill that was on the chopping block, the conservative majority blocked him from presenting it.[140]

Yet most troubling for abolitionists in Ohio was the conservative shift in the Republican Party itself. Abolitionists Oliver Brown of Portage County, Elyria's Philemon Bliss, and even Ashtabula's Joshua Giddings were denied renomination to their congressional seats by local nominating committees.[141] Thomas Corwin, one of the most prominent Republicans in the state, actually endorsed the Fugitive Slave Law in his successful congressional campaign of 1858.[142] National party leaders like William Seward and John McLean seldom mentioned the Fugitive Slave Law or any other sectional issue outside of their opinions regarding the Territories. Radical Republicans worried that an "extensive effort" was under way to move the party as far away from "extreme" doctrines as possible.[143] Despite the hopeful prospects of 1856, antislavery politics was threatening to fulfill the predictions of the most radical abolitionists: men concerned more with widespread public appeal, consensus, and ambition for office than the emancipation of American slaves seemed to be rising to the top of the Republican Party. From the South, men like South Carolina's James Henry Hammond publicly celebrated what they saw as the antislavery sentiment of the North dying out.[144]

Abolitionists from Oberlin would not give up the struggle; they had worked hard for emancipation from a disadvantage since 1834, and hope did not perish easily among them. In an August 1858 speech celebrating the anniversary of West Indian emancipation, John Langston recalled the long history of the abolitionist struggle and reminded his audience that despite the gloomy portents, "whenever, wherever Liberty has made a stand against oppression . . . she has always won the most brilliant, splendid triumphs." Langston extolled giants among men, from Moses to Spartacus, Toussaint-Louverture, and William Lloyd Garrison, who had tried to show the slaveholders of the world right from wrong. Despite the discouraging events of 1857 and 1858, Langston assured his audience that champions would continue to rise. He reminded his listeners, "The anti-slavery movement has always had its representative men; men who have been its advocates, its champions, and its heroes."[145]

Though he could not know it at the time, within six weeks, Langston and a host of others from Oberlin would prove themselves the current champions and heroes of the abolitionist movement. They would help revive the sagging antislavery sentiments of the Republican Party, successfully confront the encroachments of the Slave Power as few had done before, and lay out in detail before the nation the injustice of slavery and the Fugitive Slave Law. Yet they would do so not through any new radical innovation but rather through a remarkable example of their most concrete method of practical emancipation that they had been practicing since Oberlin's founding—offering passage on the Underground Railroad to a brother "from the House of Bondage."[146]

CHAPTER EIGHT

That Railroad Center at Which All Branches Converged

Oberlin and the Underground Railroad

Nearly a half century after he first arrived as an undergraduate at Oberlin, James Fairchild remembered in his old age that the "irrepressible conflict between freedom and slavery in our land first appeared, in practical form, along the geographical line between free and slave territory." On one side of that line, the Ohio River, could be found slaves desperate to escape their bondage. On the opposite shore was the prospect of freedom, "shadowy and uncertain indeed, but sufficient to excite the hopes of an imaginative and impressible race."[1] Besides a small handful of slave rebellions in the South, only acts of individuals and small groups of bondsmen and the operation of the Underground Railroad offered physical resistance to the laws that enslaved men and women. Though the "railroad" had existed for decades before Oberlin itself, once the community became a legendary beacon for all freedom seekers, it was, by all accounts, responsible for a great deal of the success of the "underground" phenomenon.

Scholars have long disputed the myth of the Underground Railroad as a well-organized benevolent operation of mostly white heroes and passive African Americans, but the legend has died slowly, especially outside of academia.² Though it is probably the most well known aspect of the abolitionist movement, it was also the rarest by far. As historian Stacey Robertson points out, signing one's name to an antislavery petition or attending a meeting was one thing, but actively breaking federal and state laws in helping a fugitive was something entirely different and something few antislavery men or women were willing to do.³ Also contributing to a general misunderstanding of the Underground Railroad are well-documented cases of extraordinary episodes, such as the cunning escapes of Henry Box Brown or William and Ellen Craft.⁴ Yet, to a remarkable extent, the history of the Oberlin community conforms to its exceptional billing. To be sure, there are some accounts of Oberlin's branch of the Underground Railroad that are too vague or clichéd to be fully believed, but there are perhaps even more firsthand accounts that are easily verified by multiple sources.⁵ Even those various thinly documented stories in which similar elements or details appear, the kernel of truth they contain informs the tales with more solid backing.

The most common confirmations of the lively Oberlin Underground are simple comments like that of Hiram Wilson to Oberlin treasurer Hamilton Hill in 1848: "Those six fugitives who were in Oberlin when we left all got over safe into Canada by the next Monday."⁶ Another five "travelers" presented Professors James Monroe and Henry Peck with a succinct note from a Medina man who had written, "Gents, here are five Slaves from the House of Bondage, which I need not say to you that you will see to them—they can tell their own story."⁷ Their "own story," it seems, was not recorded for posterity, nor were those of countless others who passed through Oberlin under similar circumstances.⁸ These frequent but brief allusions offer few details regarding the escaping slaves themselves or exactly what events marked their passage through Oberlin. They do, however, confirm Oberlin as a busy depot on the "Liberty Line" and silently vouch for the more exceptional cases and remarkable circumstances that are described in this chapter. Though Oberlin was but a part of a vast network of participants who will never be known, the relatively well documented involvement of its townspeople in the Underground Railroad demonstrated its fundamentally practical and independent approach to abolitionism, as well as the vital importance of African Americans in the great freedom struggle.

* * *

ONE EARLY HISTORIAN OF OBERLIN suggests that the townspeople's open defiance of the Fugitive Slave Law placed them in a practical state of rebellion against the national government after 1850.⁹ Of course, these men and women had been on record for their opposition longer than most Americans since they had been subjected to the restrictions of an Ohio fugitive law twelve years earlier. As he had regarding that Ohio bill, Charles Grandison Finney refused even to recognize the 1850 federal enactment by calling it a fugitive slave law.[10] The only fugitive slave law worth obeying, he and most Oberlinites agreed, was God's "higher law" of justice and righteousness that they had maintained since the 1830s: "Thou shalt not deliver unto his master the servant which is escaped from his master unto thee; he shall dwell with thee, even among you, in that place which he shall choose . . . thou shalt not oppress him."[11]

Most Oberlinites, especially black residents, construed Old Testament law in a positive sense and vowed not only to avoid oppression but to actively assist every escaping slave and protect him "by all justifiable means" in their power.[12] As African Americans traveled the perilous route of the North Star through northwestern Ohio, the "assistance" from many in the Oberlin community took many forms. The combined efforts of the absconders and their abolitionist allies always resulted in the completion of another leg of the former slave's journey closer to freedom, without, Oberlinites were proud to point out, a single exception.

Help could be as simple as a truthful answer to slave catcher's prying questions. Abolitionists in the Oberlin community were skilled in the arts of obfuscation. If accosted by a suspected kidnapper, some were accustomed to silently listen to the man recount his entire tale and legal case, then turn just as silently and walk away after he had spent his energy. It was also possible for the Christians of Oberlin to throw off the trail of a slaveholder's agent without resorting to lies. Fairchild recalled the story of one man who was approached just outside of Oberlin and asked by a shady-looking stranger if he had seen any "fugitives" pass by his house recently. "Yes," the man answered, to which the slave hunter asked, "Which way was he going?" The man told him that he saw the man in question head north toward Oberlin, and the pursuer quickly took off in that direction. He did not feel the need to also tell him that he had seen the same man heading back away from Oberlin later that same day.[13]

Most often, the assistance rendered a fugitive slave by Oberlinites took a much more direct form. The most straightforward method was for an abolitionist to venture into a slaveholding state and, as Southerners called it, "entice" enslaved men and women to leave their owners for freedom in the North.[14] However, not everyone in Oberlin approved of such audacious efforts to help slaves escape, and even some of the most famous Underground conductors in the West disclaimed any intent of extending the Railroad into the South. Indiana Quaker Levi Coffin admitted, "I was and always had been opposed to slavery, but it was no part of my business, in the South, to interfere with their laws or their slaves."[15] James Fairchild discouraged the practice, not because it infringed on states' rights, but because it involved "too much risk" to everyone involved.[16]

However, a student wrote in 1842 that "there are few in this neighborhood that would not justify such a course."[17] There were many in the Oberlin community who were willing to risk everything so that a slave might have a chance at freedom. These men and women "expected no mercy in case of detection" and entered into their plans fully aware that if caught, "nothing but bitter hatred awaited them, and the state prison was their only hope of escape from lynching."[18] These were the abolitionists who earned the greatest respect from Oberlin's African American population, many of whom were also frequent "enticers" in the South themselves. After the death in 1846 of Reverend Charles Torrey, who was imprisoned in Maryland for attempting to help a group of slaves northward, Oberlin African Americans held a mass gathering, passed resolutions, and praised the "martyr" for obeying "the dictates which he believed reason and reason's God had given him" in helping his fellow men escape to freedom and by showing his "true devotion to the cause of down-trodden humanity."[19] In the eyes of the black community, the empathetic identification "of those in bonds" could not be clearer or more highly esteemed.

Calvin Fairbank and Delia Webster were both Oberlin students in the early 1840s and committed abolitionists who pursued all available means for practical emancipation, including going into the South to help slaves escape their bonds. Fairbank claimed to have helped liberate at least forty-four slaves "from hell" between 1837 and 1844.[20] In August of 1844, a man named Gilson Berry who had escaped from Kentucky arrived in Oberlin, and he approached Fairbank with plans to venture back to also liberate his wife and children. The two decided that it would be too dangerous for the former slave to again set foot in the South, but later that month, Fairbank set out to bring back the Berry family.[21] Once in Lexington, Kentucky, however, Fairbank discovered that he could not succeed in rescuing the family he had come to liberate. Nonetheless, he soon learned that his friend Webster was then teaching in the area. Together the two made the acquaintance of an enslaved man named Lewis Hayden, who desired his freedom because, he bluntly told them, "I am a man."[22] Late on the night of September 28, Fairbank and Webster met Hayden and his wife near the home of abolitionist Cassius Clay and

Calvin Fairbank (from Fairbank, *Rev. Calvin Fairbank during Slavery Times* [1890])

set off for Ohio. At nine o'clock the next morning, the group crossed the Ohio River to Ripley, where Fairbank transferred care of the Haydens into the hands of another Underground conductor. The newly free couple would soon reach Canada, before later returning to the United States as antislavery lecturers for the AASS.[23]

However, the Haydens' legal owner had learned the details of the escape from two slaves who had recognized Fairbank in Millersburg, Kentucky. When Fairbank and Webster returned to renew their attempt to rescue Berry's family, the Oberlinites were apprehended and jailed. Besides the slaves' statement, the only evidence used against the two was a single letter found in Fairbank's possession mysteriously addressed only to "Frater" in Oberlin, a damning connection.[24] Though Webster was "humanely" incarcerated, Fairbank was shackled with twenty-four pounds of irons and forced to sleep on the floor of the jail until trial in January of 1845. At that time, the rescuers were tried separately and both were found guilty. Webster was sentenced to a prison term of two years, but Fairbank's guilty plea, despite his appeal for "an abatement on the ground of conscientious convictions of duty," resulted in a sentence of fifteen years in a Kentucky penitentiary.[25]

Webster was soon pardoned and sent back to her home state of Vermont. Fairbank, however, remained imprisoned for more than five years, despite the "strenuous efforts" of his friends and sympathizers to have him set free. This included his father, who died of cholera while visiting Lexington.[26] Nonetheless, when he was finally paroled in 1851, one of Fairbank's first acts was to return for the rescue of a slave woman named Tamar, whom he successfully helped along the Underground Railroad north. Again, Fairbank was betrayed. This time Kentucky vigilantes kidnapped him from Ohio and brought him back into their state for prosecution. An angry judge sentenced Fairbank to another fifteen years hard labor.[27]

This time, pardon would not be swift in coming. Despite great publicity in the abolitionist press, Fairbank's appeals were ignored.[28] He was hired out to work as a convict laborer and sometimes denied food so long that he was forced to eat weeds from the prison yard. Occasionally he would be lashed to a chair and flogged with a leather strap by prison guards for no reason. Fairbank tallied 35,105 "stripes laid on" during his term.[29] Only after thirteen years of prison abuse and poor health was Fairbank pardoned by the lieutenant governor of Kentucky, a year before the end of the Civil War.[30]

Oberlin theological graduate George Thompson also spent nearly five years in a Missouri jail after being found guilty of "grand larceny" for attempting to help two slaves escape into Illinois in 1841.[31] Though no laws were actually broken, and though Thompson and two other men had been unsuccessful in their rescue attempt, they were each sentenced to twelve years' imprisonment. Nonetheless, Thompson offered to have the sentence of another rescuer added to his own if the man would be pardoned. His request was denied, and as the alleged "ringleader" in the affair, Thompson was held in prison longer than any of his collaborators to warn all the other abolitionists "not to dally with [Missouri's] slaves."[32]

Professor James Thome had been born into a slaveholding Kentucky family, and even after he became a dedicated abolitionist and convinced his father to emancipate his slaves, he continued to regularly visit his Southern kin. On one such trip, Thome was apprised of the situation of an enslaved woman who, having been promised her freedom, discovered that she was to be sold away before the promised arrangement was completed. After she fled to a safe house in Augusta, Kentucky, a group of free African American women sought out Thome to lay her situation before him. Immediately, Thome urged the woman to make her escape across the Ohio River and then to push for Canada. He became increasingly interested in her plight, and after "much prayer and pondering," helped plan her escape by which she ultimately gained her freedom.[33]

Lewis Clarke (from Clarke and Clarke, *Narratives of the Sufferings of Lewis and Milton Clarke* [1846])

Back in Oberlin, Thome took the occasion of a monthly antislavery meeting to mention a few particulars concerning Tamar's escape and his role in it. He felt completely safe with his remarks, since the gathering was among a trusted group, "the tried friends of the slave." However, one student at the meeting wrote of the incident to his family in Boston, and somehow the letter was intercepted and its contents published. Word of Thome's actions soon reached Augusta. His sister wrote him that the town "was in a blaze of excitement," and she warned that if the slaveholders could get their hands on him, he would undoubtedly be jailed or lynched. Thome's father warned his son to constantly be on his guard, lest he be seized in Ohio and dragged away into Kentucky.[34]

Being "dragged away" was an even more frightening possibility for self-emancipated men and women. However, they were some of the boldest Underground conductors, and their forays into the South and operations in the North were legendary. Lewis and Milton Clarke were two Kentucky brothers who had escaped from slavery and settled in Oberlin. Both were active in the operation of the Railroad through the town. Lewis, despite his fear of "creeping round day and night . . . in a den of lions," was determined to return to Kentucky to help another brother, Cyrus, to freedom as well.[35] Armed with twenty dollars and a crude map, Lewis set out to rescue his brother. When he crossed the Ohio River into Kentucky, the realization that he was once again on slave soil made him tremble and burst into tears. Eventually, he was able to compose himself and continue into "the lion's jaws," and his light complexion allowed him to travel with relative ease among the Kentuckians. One man even engaged him in a conversation about runaway slaves.

After Lewis located his younger brother, however, the return journey was much more difficult. Though Lewis's education in Oberlin's primary school allowed him to read road signs, the way had to be made far from roads and on foot, and fierce summer storms made the way nearly impassible. Moreover, Cyrus grew so fatigued that he began to see lions of his own in hallucinations. Only Lewis's constant urging kept the pair moving along. Cyrus agreed with his brother that freedom was wonderful but complained to Lewis that "this is a hard, h-a-r-d way to get it."[36]

Even in Ohio, Cyrus's fear and mistrust of whites forced the Clarkes to sleep outdoors or in barns as they made their way from Underground depot to Underground depot. He could not bring himself to trust white benefactors after being mistreated by slaveholders his entire life, and he remained convinced that the hospitality offered him by beneficent whites was fraught with treachery. Though Milton and Lewis remained in Oberlin for some time after the rescue, Cyrus would not feel completely safe until he reached Canada, and he was soon directed on to a friendly captain at Lake Erie.[37]

A City of Refuge

However, as George Julian, a close ally of the Oberlin community, remarked, the great majority of escapes by slaves from the South were "promoted by other causes than northern interference."[38] Usually, only after making the most treacherous leg of the journey on their own were self-emancipating bondsmen assisted by white abolitionists or free Northern African Americans. Almost from the minute "Oberlin" became a name that was known beyond the physical boundaries of the town as friendly to slaves, the town became a beacon for freedom-seeking former bondsmen. Both friends and foes alike realized this, and as abolitionists across the region directed pilgrims toward Oberlin, enemies mockingly littered the roads leading to the town with signs like one cartoonish marker that depicted "a negro running with all his might to reach the place." A tavern keeper in a neighboring town hung out a sign "on the Oberlin side . . . ornamented by the representation of a panting negro, pursued by a tiger."[39]

Samuel Adair in the Kansas cabin (courtesy Oberlin College Archives)

Most critics generally had little better to say of Oberlin's involvement in the Underground Railroad than one Ohio judge who described the town as "that old buzzards' nest where the negroes who arrive over the underground railroad are regarded as dear children."[40] In the crusade to repeal the college's charter, the most potentially damning evidence anti-abolitionists could offer were allegations of the school and town's assistance to escaping slaves.[41] Equally blameworthy in other critics' eyes was the justifiable belief that an Underground Railroad station could be located wherever an Oberlin College alumnus settled.[42] Indeed, Oberlin's theological department filled the pulpits of a large number of churches in Ohio and beyond. Most of these men (and woman) remained true to their preparation at the "activist training school" in Oberlin, including the dictates to assist those fleeing from bondage and to encourage others to do so as well.[43] Even as missionaries to Kansas in the mid-1850s, Oberlin alumni would put their Underground skills to productive use. Although she had only recently given birth, Florella Brown Adair and her husband, Samuel, opened their home on Christmas Eve in 1858 to her brother John Brown and eleven former slaves who he had helped liberate from their Missouri bonds.[44] John Byrd, too, was a man notorious among proslavery emigrants for his participation in the Kansas Underground Railroad. Byrd once entered a hotel in Atchison in broad daylight and rescued an enslaved woman and her child awaiting passage to the South. Though there were several eyewitnesses to the rescue, and though the master brought suit against him for the "theft," Byrd would only admit with a smile that "it appears that underground railroad traffic in territorial slaves is a legitimate business."[45]

In the town of Oberlin itself, residents' involvement in the Underground Railroad commenced not long after the community was founded. The first definite mention of the involvement of members of the Oberlin community in helping "fugitives" to freedom was in the autumn of 1836. An African American man named Williams appeared in Oberlin, met with community leaders, and unveiled to them his plan for enticing slaves to desert their masters and seek freedom in Canada. Williams admitted that he had nearly been captured by Southern authorities in his last venture and was forced to abandon his wagon and team to save himself. Still, he claimed to have already directed several escaping slaves to Oberlin. Moreover, he had been assisted at least once by an unnamed black accomplice who was a member of the Sheffield Institute, the Oberlin satellite school (possibly Gideon or Charles Langston or James Bradley). Together, the men had succeeded in helping to liberate fourteen slaves from a single plantation.[46]

It is unlikely that the faculty would have officially supported such a risky plan of action, but Williams is also reported to have addressed his scheme to the student dining hall. There, among the more empathetic students, he raised fifty dollars to equip his venture.[47] Later, when several students took jobs teaching in African American schools in southern Ohio, it was suggested that one of the primary reasons they did so was to act on Williams's plan and spirit slaves out of Kentucky and onto free soil. The first fruit of their efforts, "a tall athletic negro," arrived in Oberlin in the winter of 1836, and he was secreted in the college-owned Palmer House until he could continue his journey to Detroit and then Canada. Several other slaves arrived soon thereafter and were boarded with the family of President Asa Mahan.[48]

Perhaps before the Mahans' guests had left Oberlin, another group of former slaves arrived in town, this time in a wagon driven by Martin Brooks, one of the student-teachers who had spent some time teaching black students near Cincinnati.[49] As his wagon drew near, the cry went out from all directions, "Another *full load* of colored brethren have arrived."[50] News of the arrival quickly spread across campus, and hordes of students rushed to the common hall to welcome their new guests. There, the new arrivals were treated to a special feast, and nearly everyone present jockeyed for a prime position to engage them in conversation. After they rested in Oberlin for some time, the travelers set out again on May 1, 1837, as a crowd of Oberlinites gathered to see them off. Several male students armed themselves and accompanied the group to their next destination.[51] From that point, the arrival in town of refugees "from the house of bondage" was a common occurrence.[52]

However, there were never as many black residents in Oberlin as outsiders may have imagined, though many of those who were there had taken residence after escape from bondage themselves. Professor Amasa Walker suggested that many, if not most, African Americans in Oberlin were self-emancipated.[53] When John Mercer Langston arrived in Oberlin in 1844, he remarked that the "major part of the colored persons residing in Oberlin at this time were fugitive slaves."[54] Because of this remarkable fact, the community had a much different perspective on the Underground Railroad from most other abolitionists. Importantly, Oberlinites recognized that the real work and risk of emancipation was done by the "fugitive" herself. However proud Oberlinites might be at their role in helping someone to freedom, there was always the recognition that they had merely assisted in a monumental undertaking and played a tiny supporting role in the overall drama. As Milton Clarke, a "fugitive" himself, remarked, "I have assisted several [slaves] to get into possession of their true owner," but he recognized at once that the bondsmen had already done most of the work themselves and that they already possessed "the true title-deed," self-ownership that only God could grant.[55]

"Fugitives" were not described in Oberlin as passive travelers but as active agents who, though welcoming support, had fully taken their own lives into their hands and done the most arduous labor of emancipation themselves. Here, the primary claim to heroism was acknowledged as the property of the self-emancipating slave. With little conceit, just about everyone in the community was willing to welcome refugees into their homes and to do their part in assisting them. This was exceptional for any town in America, even in the North, where friends of the slave were a small minority. In Oberlin, however, the tables were turned, and proslavery men and women found little company among the united throng of abolitionists. Oberlinites prided themselves on the widespread belief that "no man in Oberlin could be trusted on the slave question." To betray a slave attempting to claim his or her freedom "would have been to lose the respect of the community, and insure lasting disgrace and odium."[56]

Russia Township regularly allocated funds "for boarding a poor stranger," for medical "services to Tr[ansient] poor," or simply for the care of "transient paupers." Notably, these vague expenditures became especially common after John Mercer Langston was elected township clerk in 1857.[57] The Oberlin Maternal Association, Female Anti-Slavery Society, Young Ladies' Literary Society, and Female Moral Reform Society all collected and distributed funds specifically earmarked for "fugitives," and the college's Prudential Committee also kept a special "Fund for Fugitives."[58] The town also earned the confidence of some of the most famous Underground conductors in the Northwest. Levi Coffin, denounced by critics as a "notorious nigger thief" and praised by admirers as the "president of the Underground Railroad," was a regular Oberlin visitor, and quite often, his business in town was to accompany escaping slaves from his home territory of Indiana into the trusted hands of some "reliable and trustworthy gentleman" in Oberlin.[59]

Oberlin residents often prepared baskets of food and left them scattered across the surrounding countryside for escaping slaves, telling inquisitive children that the food was for "the rabbits." When young William Cochrane accompanied his parents to retrieve one such basket, he was surprised to observe that the rabbits had "folded their napkins."[60] Oberlin residents donated even larger quantities of goods and supplies to other known stops all along the Underground Railroad, especially depots in Canada overseen by Oberlin alumni like Hiram Wilson and other close friends. Barrels arriving from Oberlin for the benefit of former slaves might include books, clothing, bedding, cash donations, or any assortment of items meant to ease their entry into freedom.[61] Abolitionists across the country sent money directly to Oberlin professors to be used in such a manner "that the fugitives will be benefited." One such man from Wisconsin sent money to Henry Cowles, writing, "I do not know where to send it better than to send it to you."[62]

Nearly the whole community went out of its way to assist passers-through by any means available. In March of 1853, a mother with eight children in tow arrived in Oberlin. Six of the children were her own, one was her grandchild, and one was unrelated by blood. All were born in slavery. The youngest child had been entrusted into her care two years earlier by his mother, a dying slave woman. By the time they reached Oberlin, it was clear that, in the words of the *Oberlin Alumni Magazine*, "Heaven was already making out [the child's] free papers." Residents quickly ascertained that her former master, the father of the sick child, was hot on their footsteps, and an Oberlin woman offered to take the baby and "nurture him as carefully as if he were [her] own." She promised to bring the child to the woman in Canada if he survived, or alternatively to make sure the child received a

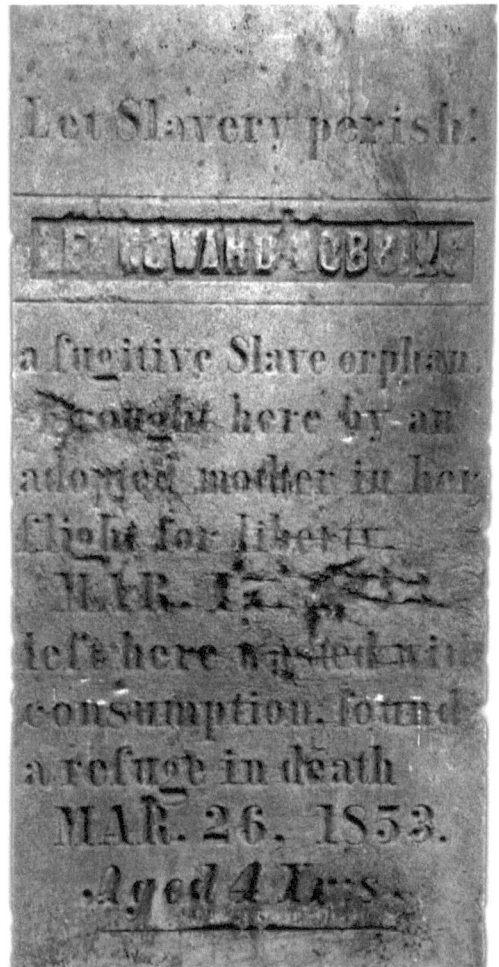

Lee Howard Dobbins grave marker (courtesy Oberlin College Archives)

proper Christian burial if he did not. Overcome with gratitude, the mother accepted the offer and quickly continued north with the other children.[63]

The child survived another nine days but eventually succumbed to his illness. Though Oberlin community members were prepared for his death, the boy's sad fate grieved them; his was a useless loss brought about by the iniquities of slavery. A craftsman specially made a small coffin for the child, and 1,000 people filled Oberlin's church to honor him. Henry Peck preached a sermon that both eulogized the innocent child and rebuked the Slave Power that extinguished his life. Congregants pondered the horrible system that denied thousands of other babies an "earthly father, save such as would chase down and sell them for the gold-value of their bones and muscles," and "how this same system tears away from its babes the mothers God gave and dooms them to more than orphanage—orphanage among human flesh-mongers!"[64]

At the close of the service, the casket was opened, and every man, woman, and child in the community passed by it and "swore between clinched teeth" to recommit themselves to emancipation on an even higher level. The student body took up a collection that was used to purchase a monument in Oberlin's cemetery. Its inscription reads, "Let Slavery perish! Lee Howard Dobbins, a fugitive slave orphan, brought here by the adopted mother in her flight for liberty, March 17th, 1853. Left here, wasted with consumption, found a refuge in death March 26th, 1853. Aged 4 years."[65]

Slave-Holders in Town!

The pursuit of the Dobbins family was not unusual. There were almost always slaveholders pursuing their "fugitive property" as they fled north. Despite the fact that no slave catcher was ever successful in returning a man or woman back to slavery from Oberlin, the town's reputation as a safe haven for escaping slaves often led the agents of slaveholders to lurk about the place they called "nigger town" in hope of a significant payday.[66] James Fairchild pointed out that in the person of each fugitive was a marketable value of approximately $1,000, which was "a sufficient motive to rally all available forces for the pursuit."[67]

In 1840, seven self-emancipated men and women reached Oberlin just minutes before slave catchers who were in hot pursuit. The slave owner's agents quickly determined in which house their human prey had been concealed and surrounded the building so that escape seemed impossible. The commotion, however, roused the attention of a large number of residents and students who quickly joined the Southerners outside the house. They did not threaten these unwanted interlopers but engaged the men in conversation as more townspeople gathered around them.

With little planning, the Oberlinites began to conspicuously enter and leave the house from all doorways, and each took with them a packet of items the slaveholders could not identify. In fact, they were secreting in bonnets, hoods, shawls, and other items of clothing that were given to the former slaves, who, one by one, exited the house indistinguishable from those who had gone in.[68] Moreover, it was not uncommon for large groups of Oberlin students, books in hand, to occupy slave catchers in "aggravatingly good natured" conversation on various scholarly subjects as these transfers were taking place.[69] In this instance, the slaveholders, distracted by the small talk, could not keep count of the large number of people about the house, and within a short amount of time, all of the "fugitives" had joined the procession and simply walked to a new location, all right under the noses of their would-be captors.[70]

Eventually, the slaveholders realized what had transpired and determined anew not to leave without their prizes. They published notice around Lorain County that there was a $700 reward for the capture of their slaves and soon found a newcomer to the area willing to act as their spy among the Oberlinites. It did not take the attentive townspeople long to become aware of this fact, though, and the wife of an Oberlin professor suggested a plan by which Oberlinites would turn the ruse against the unwelcome visitors. Customers to the blacksmith shop where the spy worked conspicuously mentioned that evening's plot for a covered wagon drawn by four horses to spirit the pilgrims to Cleveland, then on to Canada.[71]

At the appointed time, seven black students and residents, including Sabram Cox and Milton Clarke, boarded a wagon and two white men took the reins. The "slaves" were outfitted in various disguises—some had veils on; some, like Clarke, wore dresses; others were outfitted in rags. They passed the nine miles to Elyria without incident, and it seemed as if their plan was not working as intended. Nonetheless, they decided to stop at a friendly tavern for a bite to eat before returning to Oberlin. Just as they neared the hitching post, a cry went out, "There they come!" and a mob of would-be slave catchers encircled the wagon and accosted the white drivers.[72] "What do you mean by stopping honest travelers in this way?" the Oberlin men demanded. Just then, the crowd pulled back the curtains of the wagon, revealing a cartload of African Americans assumed to be the slaves in question. "O boys," Sabram Cox cried out loudly enough for all to hear, "we're in an awful scrape!" "I guess you are, for once," one man said, and the crowd pulled the "slaves" out of the wagon and took them to a nearby room where they began congratulate themselves on the "big haul" they had just made. The captors drank long into the night while the "slaves" either kept quiet or offered maddeningly ambiguous statements as to their identities.[73]

Sabram Cox had been placed near a roaring fire, and as the night grew long, he became so hot that he was forced to remove the rags that had to that point concealed his identity. As he did, another man in the room exclaimed, "By heavens! If there ain't Cox, of Oberlin!" Cox confirmed their suspicion, and after the white men vouched for them before town officials, the other African American detainees revealed themselves as well.[74] However, this was not before the powerfully built Cox directed some unrecorded remarks to the sheriff that he later recalled "were certainly not ambiguous in their nature." That night, the intimidated lawman "folded his tent and silently stole away" from the town. Overlooked in that night's drama was the wagon containing the actual slaves that passed quietly through the edge of town en route to Cleveland.[75]

Another group of Oberlinites in the early 1840s employed a similar method to divert slave catchers. When known slave hunters were noticed in town, students "Cooley" and "Whittlesey" decided to gather a group of their fellows, disguise themselves as "fugitive slaves," and stage an "escape," while the true fleeing bondsmen moved safely on to their next stop.[76] Whittlesey raced his wagon past the slave catchers toward Lake Erie, and when they gave chase, he let them gain after several miles of pursuit. When the wagon was "overtaken," its cargo leapt from the back and ran off in different directions into the woods. Cooley could not contain his laughter after a while, and though caught, his "sense of the ridiculous" led him to tear away the black silk that darkened his face and tell the disappointed Southerners, "What sublime idiots you are!"[77]

Disguises were not always necessary, for Oberlin counted among its residents the talented and widely known artist Alonzo Pease. If a man or woman needed to be spirited away from pursuers, Pease was summoned, and within an hour, his paints and skillful brushstrokes could transform a "slave" into "a very respectable Caucasian" (with the satisfaction, one Oberlin alumnus remembered in 1883, "of knowing that all the light paints could be washed off"). Thus made up, many men and women easily passed through groups of slave catchers without recognition, sometimes arm in arm with Oberlin professors.[78]

Not long after the rescues recounted above, the news that Milton and Lewis Clarke were actively engaging in Underground work caused a group of Kentucky slaveholders to attempt to reclaim one or both "of the impudent Clarkes." They directed the kidnappers to Ohio, where they ambushed and detained Milton on a rural road just outside of Oberlin. Clarke's first instinct was that he was being accosted by highway robbers, since such boldness by Southerners near the town of Oberlin would have been unexpected. However, when the Kentuckians told him, "We want not money, but *you*," he realized what was transpiring. They bound Clarke and took him before the sheriff, who had no choice but to verify his identity. What he *could* do for him, however, was argue that Clarke was actually a white man and arrest the captors on charges of assault and battery in Milton's capture. Once Clarke was ordered released by a writ of habeas corpus, the kidnappers "found themselves more surely prisoners than their late captive." At an antislavery meeting in Oberlin called specially for the occasion, Milton and Lewis Clarke gave impressive speeches, and both soon began to tour the free states as abolitionist lecturers.[79]

The Man-Stealers

The slave catchers against whom abolitionists sheltered escaping slaves became, for many, the ugly face of the South. Most often, these men were mercenaries who simply craved the monetary rewards slave hunting offered. Augustus "Gus" Chambers, a black man and one of Oberlin's most skilled blacksmiths, was not satisfied with simply calling these Southern emissaries "slave catchers" or "slave hunters." When he received word one day in 1858 that such men were lurking about Oberlin and inquiring about him, he reckoned the terms insufficient. "I don't call them *slave-catchers*," he defiantly proclaimed; "there are mighty few *slaves* around here. I call them *man-stealers*—devilish thieves!"[80]

Abolitionists in cities like New York, Philadelphia, and Boston might have wondered how Oberlin maintained such a healthy "fugitive" population without the assistance of a vigilance committee, a group of citizens specifically organized to protect townspeople from the iniquities of the Fugitive Slave Law.[81] An attempt to reclaim two slaves in 1841, however, demonstrates why such a group was unnecessary there. A man and his wife, Jefferson and Jane, had hidden in the Page family's house about a mile from the center of town. Almost immediately, their pursuers caught up with them. After they forced their way into the residence, brandished Bowie knives and pistols, and threatened the lives of the Page family, the slave hunters shackled their prey and set out east, away from Oberlin.[82]

Unbeknownst to the slave catchers, another young African American man was boarding with the Page family. When he realized what was transpiring in the front of the house, he set off as fast as he could run to the center of town. He reached the college chapel while a huge student antislavery meeting was under way, and as word spread of the outrage at the Page household, the meeting quickly adjourned and all the students went en masse in pursuit of the Southerners. Though many other students had already gone to bed, the cry "Slave-holders in town!" was put out, the chapel bell "pealed out the alarm," and the remainder of the student body dressed and joined the chase.[83]

"The Confidence Game," a drawing from the 1850s by
professor Charles Churchill (courtesy Oberlin College Archives)

The mass of several hundred Oberlinites was reportedly heavily armed. For several miles they pursued the captors, saving time by taking a shortcut through the woods. One Democratic paper reported that "the [Oberlin] negroes left their hiding places and[,] running hither and thither, some with guns, and others with clubs[,] came down upon the constable and his party with shoutings, imprecations, and yellings," while the Oberlin students "threw down their books and being joined with citizens, they hurried after, threatening vengeance to the Rebel Slaveholders, and their adherents."[84]

When the Oberlinites caught up with the Southerners at an abandoned house, the men, realizing that they were significantly outnumbered, offered no resistance. Nonetheless, they refused to abandon their "property" and demanded a hearing in court to assert their claims. An Oberlin farmer named Charles Carrier agreed that a judicial hearing of some sort was indeed necessary and told the men, "We will have justice." Though Carrier's statement may have calmed the nerves of the slave catchers, it could only have been because they did not realize what was transpiring in the meantime. While Carrier and a handful of other men stood guard over the Kentuckians until they could go before a judge in nearby Elyria the next morning, other

Oberlin men hurried to obtain a warrant for their arrest on charges of breaking and entering and assault and battery.[85]

At sunrise, an even larger group of Oberlin residents than those who gave chase the night before arrived to accompany the guards and Southerners to the county seat of Elyria. Though they knew the kidnappers would also make their own legal claims in court, Oberlinites were confident that a judge would deny them. In case the claims to the "fugitives" were upheld, the crowd from Oberlin had hatched a rescue plan. A wagon and speedy team of horses were situated near the courthouse, and the huge Oberlin contingent was to be spread out across the courtroom and nearby streets to pass the "fugitives" along. The Elyria sheriff (not, of course, the man who had fled in fear of Sabram Cox two years before) was friendly to the Oberlin community and had agreed to give the signal to start the rescue if necessary.[86]

The trial was postponed, however, and Jane and Jefferson were jailed. The kidnappers were also arraigned for breaking into the Pages' house without a warrant and assault and battery, and only after they posted substantial bonds were they released.[87] As they hurried back to Kentucky to gather more evidence, the Elyria jail, as an Oberlin source remembered, "leaked."[88] Immediately, Oberlinites were suspected of orchestrating the jailbreak.[89] Though no one from Oberlin ever admitted to it, the iron grating and bars had been pried from the second story jail windows. The former slaves were secreted for some time in the house of Oberlin's Asahel Munger before later being driven on to Cleveland by Professor Horace Taylor.[90] The mystery of the jailbreak may be partially explained, however, by the coincidence that Munger was the man in charge of keeping the Oberlin fire squad supplied with ladders, hooks, and axes to be used for rescuing residents from the upper floors of burning buildings.[91]

You-Touch-Me-If-You-Dare

The local Democratic description of the Elyria rescue makes it clear that African Americans played important and conspicuous parts in the maintenance of Oberlin's Underground line. In fact, more than any other aspect of Oberlin society, the operations of its Underground Railroad station were disproportionately controlled and led by its black residents. For those who themselves were self-emancipated, the Underground was a key survival tactic. For all Northern African Americans, their participation was a powerful political statement against the Slave Power. Black Oberlinites publicly encouraged slaves to attempt to escape their bondage, and offered their own town as a refuge, even in the face of the fugitive laws. An 1849 meeting, led by Oberlin African American notables William Howard Day, Sabram Cox, and John Watson, resolved that "no person claimed as a slave shall be taken from our midst without trouble."[92]

Once a passenger of the Railroad arrived in town, the unofficial welcoming committee was often a group of fellow travelers, those residents in Oberlin who had made parts of the same terrifying journey themselves, "guided by Freedom's star."[93] For many of Oberlin's Southern-born African American population, the town was their final destination on the Underground, and their homes became reception centers where other brave self-emancipators could rest, recover their energies, and gain motivation and encouragement from those who had experienced similar travails firsthand. Oberlin's various conductors knew to bring travelers to "the arms of their kindred . . . who had shared bondage with the wayfarers," where they would be compassionately welcomed. In one case, an Oberlin man who had once been imprisoned nearly three months for attempting to frustrate the Fugitive Slave Law transported a wagonload of former slaves to one such residence. He wrote that the heartwarming scene he witnessed more than "compensated [him] for eighty-five days of imprisonment on the fugitive's behalf."[94]

Sometimes it was impossible to safely hide people in Oberlin homes or buildings, especially when the slave catchers were in town and inquiring. In such cases, conductors in Oberlin turned their town's isolation to the advantage of the slaves. For many years, there was a dense, wooded area several miles wide between Oberlin and Elyria. Gus Chambers lived at the edge of this spot two miles northeast of town, and he oversaw the care and protection of men and women who were forced to temporarily hide there while their trail grew cold to their pursuers. Chambers, himself a former slave, served as an intermediary between Oberlin residents offering the travelers aid and the slaves within the forest who sought news of loved ones or information on the status of the slave catchers in town.[95]

Oberlin's involvement in the Underground Railroad was legendary even in its time, and one consequence was that unscrupulous men and women sometimes attempted to take advantage of the town's generosity. However, if they were discovered, there would be little question that flight from slavery was not to be made a mockery of. Imposters would be chased "with the sole object of frightening [them] so as to prevent the recurrence of such imposition."[96] In at least one case, an African American posse overtook a pretender and, in the understated words of an Oberlin reporter, "inflicted a dozen light taps on his back, whereupon he left for the West."[97]

Federal officials attempting to execute provisions of the Fugitive Slave Law met even more hostile resistance at the hands of Oberlin African Americans. Anson Dayton had served as Oberlin's township clerk until defeated at the polls in 1857 by John Langston. Stung by his defeat, Dayton abandoned the Republican Party, became an outspoken Democrat, and was soon appointed by the Buchanan administration to a patronage post as deputy U.S. marshal to enforce the Fugitive Slave Law. It was not long before Dayton began to act on his duties, but he found no success. The head of one African American family he pestered ran him off with a shotgun, firing over his head to both frighten him and notify the town of the deed. When Dayton alerted a North Carolina slaveholder to the location of his former slave in Oberlin, stonecutter James Smith, Smith confronted him in downtown Oberlin and beat him with a stout hickory stick until Dayton escaped into a nearby building.[98] A citizens' committee eventually ordered Dayton to immediately leave Oberlin, and when his retreat was not as speedy as some may have wished, five "active" African American men followed his tracks in the snow until they caught up with him, forced him to confess to his role in past attempts on "fugitives" in Oberlin and to give up his accomplices, and extracted a promise on Dayton's part to resign his post.[99]

Even though federal marshals and Southern slave catchers seemed a ubiquitous presence in Oberlin, it was nearly impossible to reclaim a free Oberlinite or "fugitive slave" from the town's protective grasp. The only instance of an alleged runaway being claimed and even temporarily jailed was the short incarceration before the Elyria jailbreak in 1841. The vigilance of Oberlin's white residents was a powerful preventative, but the instinct for self-preservation among their African American neighbors was an even greater defense. Brooklyn abolitionist William Watkins could tell that Oberlin African Americans were "not afraid of the white man." He noted "a sort of you-touch-me-if-you-dare" attitude about them and would not have been surprised by the security plans of a man like Gus Chambers.[100] William Cochrane remembered as a boy hearing Chambers declare, "If any one of those men darkens my door, he is a dead man." In his blacksmith shop, Chambers always had a hammer and iron bar at the ready for protection, and most often also had a red-hot poker in the fire. Above his door was a loaded double-barrel shotgun, and beside his bed were razor-sharp knives and a pistol. He would never kill a man, he conceded, but clarified that a "*man-stealer*" was not fully human. "The man who tries to take my life," Chambers declared, "loses his *own*."[101]

The man of whom Chambers spoke on that occasion remained in Oberlin long enough in the summer of 1858 to raise considerable alarm. The Southerner lurked around the (alcohol-serving!) hotel owned by Chauncey Wack, one of Oberlin's few Democrats. When Marshal Dayton was seen entering the establishment to meet with the stranger, it was clear to observers that the man must be a slave hunter.[102] Whether legally free or not, Oberlin African Americans acknowledged their vulnerability under the Fugitive Slave Law to being "drag[ged] back—or for the first time—into helpless and lifelong bondage."[103] They began to take special care in their nighttime travels, sometimes kept their children home from school, and whenever possible avoided venturing into areas outside of Oberlin's "citadel of human freedom." Their conversations increasingly betrayed their anxiety, and their prayers implored "the Mighty Jehovah" to save them "against all treachery and infidelity." John Ramsey, Oberlin's oldest African American, publicly prayed "that there might be found among them *no Judas*, faithless and false."[104]

Two weeks after Gus Chambers vowed to protect himself against the slave hunters, he and the rest of the town found out that the man was not actually in Oberlin to make an attempt on his freedom. Though the man was in Oberlin to reclaim an alleged fugitive, he would not make his attempt in so brash a manner as to trigger a response like Chambers threatened. Neither would he attempt to do so, as another man noted, "in bold appropriate execution of the law."[105] When the attempt was made, which would soon demand the attention of the nation, it was through the deceit of a young white boy who was willing to trade the freedom of his fellow townsman for twenty dollars.[106]

The Oberlin-Wellington Rescue

The slave hunter, Kentuckian Anderson Jennings, had been sent to Ohio in search of a slave reportedly belonging to his uncle. In Oberlin, Jennings found no trace of that slave, but he did clearly recognize another fugitive belonging to his neighbor, John Bacon.[107] John Price had escaped Bacon's plantation in Kentucky in March of 1858 and soon thereafter settled in Oberlin. Jennings immediately fired off a letter seeking the power of attorney necessary to claim him.[108] Next, he quickly ascertained who, besides Chauncey Wack, were the town's open Democrats "whom a fellow could put confidence in." With the help of a handful of proslavery Ohioans with whom he had made acquaintance elsewhere, he went out to consult with one or two locals to work out a plan for the capture of Price and yet another slave whom they thought might also be in Oberlin.[109] They met with Lewis Boynton, a Democratic farmer who lived just outside town, but Jennings was most struck by the precocity of his son, Shakespeare. At one point, Jennings followed the boy outside and offered him a cash reward to entice John Price, whom he apparently knew, into a wagon and transport him out of Oberlin where the capture could be made more safely away from abolitionist eyes.[110]

The next day, Shakespeare found John Price and lured him into his buggy on the pretext of helping him find laborers to harvest his family's potato crop.[111] When they were just outside the Oberlin town limits, Jennings's agents overtook their buggy as planned. They quickly transferred Price into their wagon. Boynton returned to Oberlin to inform Jennings of the capture, while the wagon that held Price headed South toward the town of Wellington, ten miles away. There the kidnappers hoped to board the 5:13 train to Columbus and process their claim in the much friendlier southern city.[112]

On the way to Wellington, however, the slave catchers' wagon passed two Oberlin students. Recognizing them, Price cried out.[113] One of these young men was Ansel Lyman, a staunch abolitionist who had served as one of John Brown's lieutenants in the Kansas warfare of the mid-1850s.[114] Lyman hurried back to Oberlin to alert the people, and as soon as word began circulating, all business in town screeched to a halt.[115] He instinctively went to African American John Watson's grocery store, and soon "the crowd was all rushing [there] as the rallying point."[116] Watson himself did not stay at his store very long after hearing the news. As soon as he could, he jumped into a buggy with several other black men, and they became the first to begin a mass race toward Wellington.[117] There was a rush on the livery stables in town as hundreds of residents looked for speedy mounts with which to pursue the kidnappers, and "every hack in town" was soon full of energized Oberlinites en route to Wellington.[118] Richard Winsor, Price's Sunday School teacher, was lucky to flag down a passing wagon with room enough for him and his three rifles, and as he shouted, "I am going to rescue John Price!," "shout on shout and cheer on cheer went up from the assembly."[119] Older residents not up for the chase offered their horses for freedom's service, like one Mrs. Ryder, who charged the man who borrowed her horse, "If necessary, spare not the life of my beast, but rescue the boy."[120] When there were no more horses or buggies left available in town, eager Oberlinites began the trek on foot.[121]

In all the ruckus, Chauncey Wack noticed six black men, some he suspected of being fugitive slaves themselves, loading guns and preparing shot cartridges.¹²² In addition to this unnamed group, prominent black Oberlinites, including John Copeland, Lewis Sheridan Leary, O. S. B. Wall, Charles Langston, and self-emancipated men Thomas Gena, John Hartwell, and Jerry Fox armed themselves and sought out transportation to Wellington.¹²³ Leary remembered that many of the Oberlin community's most prominent citizens and faculty members were in a prayer meeting at First Church and thus may have been oblivious to the news. He sprinted across Tappan Square and burst through the church door "all excited." Abruptly, the people in the meeting concluded their prayers and sought out swift horses.¹²⁴

John Watson's wagon reached Wellington in less than forty-five minutes. Soon the main square of the town was filled with Oberlinites and curious onlookers. The area was so packed that late-arriving wagons and horses had to be hitched some ways off from the town center.¹²⁵ By three o'clock in the afternoon, several hundred men had surrounded Wadsworth's Tavern, the Wellington hotel where Jennings and his men had holed up with their captive in an attic room.¹²⁶ Though the slave catchers would not be catching the 5:13 train to Columbus, it was rumored that they had wired Cleveland begging for military assistance.¹²⁷ As they waited, the crowd shouted, "Bring him out! Bring out the man! Out with him! Out! Out!"¹²⁸

As the situation seemed more and more desperate, the deputy U.S. marshal from Columbus (who was also with the slave catchers) made a futile attempt to demand compliance and assistance under the Fugitive Slave Law to all within hearing.¹²⁹ As the crowd pressed in upon the hotel, owner Oliver Wadsworth, a staunch Democrat and "faithful Buchaneer," closed off the building and posted guards at the doors and stairways.¹³⁰ Wellington constable Barnabus Meacham frantically tried to negotiate with leaders of both groups for a peaceful resolution, and incredibly, he allowed several Oberlin students into the hotel and up to the room where Price was being held.¹³¹ As many as twenty men were allowed into the attic at some point or another (including the students, whose presence was apparently forgotten by the slave catchers). When Charles Langston returned from a visit to the attic, he reportedly declared to the captors that if legal measures for Price's release were not successful, "*we* will have him any way." He urged the slave catchers to "give the boy up" and avoid a potential brawl.¹³² The pistol-shaped bulge in Langston's coat pocket gave his words even more weight.¹³³

Though the 5:13 train did not bring military aid, the crowd grew nervous that a later arrival would. Spontaneously, two separate groups of Oberlin abolitionists began assaults upon the hotel. The first, a racially mixed group led by Oberlin students John Cowles, William Lincoln, and Ansel Lyman, fought for several minutes past the guards and up the stairs but could not break down the door to the attic. While they pondered their next steps, a group of African Americans led by John Scott, John Copeland, and Charles Langston broke through the hotel's back door and joined the others outside Price's room.[134] Hearing familiar voices through a hole near the door where a stovepipe had formerly run, one of the forgotten Oberlin students, Richard Winsor, quietly slipped a note through to Lincoln on the outside, suggesting a way to open the door.[135] Lincoln shouted to the slave catchers inside that he would reach through the hole and shoot them if they did not open up, and as Jennings went closer to the hole to investigate, the student struck him on the head with his pistol and loosened Jennings's grip on the door, allowing the Rescuers to force their way in.[136] Within seconds, Windsor was pushing Price out the door and into the arms of others, who passed him over their shoulders and out into the open square.[137] The hotel's owner could not recall later whether Winsor touched the ground.[138]

At sunset, several hours after the first Oberlinites had arrived in Wellington, Edward Kinney, a lone straggler who had started out on foot, arrived just in time to see Simeon Bushnell, Windsor, and Price racing toward him in a buggy headed back to Oberlin.[139] The horse was "on the jump," and Windsor greeted Kinney as they passed by, waving his gun in the air and shouting, "All right!" and "All is well." As fast as they had come, most of the crowd filed in behind Price's speeding buggy and triumphantly returned home.[140] They had, in John Langston's words, rescued John Price "in the general purpose and resolution as if it were of a single fearless giant."[141]

Anderson Jennings, like all other slave catchers who attempted to reclaim a "fugitive" from Oberlin, was left with nothing but frustration and fear. One of his colleagues asked from the window of the attic room whether it would be safe for the men to leave now that Price was free. "Yes," one rescuer replied. "They will be safe now, if they are never to come again; but if they come again, no one will be accountable for their lives a moment!" As the remaining crowd shouted "Aye! Aye! Aye!" in approval, Jennings shouted down that he had only come to execute federal laws but the abolitionists had "been too much for him." One impassioned man leapt upon a box and promised Jennings that he would indeed "find us too much for 'em every time!" For men and women in Oberlin whom Southerners called "fugitives," it truly seemed that "all the South combined cannot carry him back, if we say No!"[142] Unbeknownst to the Oberlin abolitionists, the sound of that "No" would echo across the nation until it erupted into civil war.

CHAPTER NINE

This Drama of Genuine Manhood and Courage

Oberlin and the Fight for Freedom

As the sun was setting over Oberlin on September 13, 1858, one of its most prominent residents was returning from a legal engagement in an adjoining county. To his surprise, John Mercer Langston found "neither life nor stir in or about the village." The whole town seemed to have left en masse.[1] He soon solicited a quick account of the events of that day from one of the few residents left in town and headed with all haste toward Wellington, hoping "that he might arrive in time to play some humble part in this drama of genuine manhood and courage." Midway into his dash south, however, Langston was passed in the opposite direction by Simeon Bushnell's buggy spiriting John Price back toward Oberlin. Soon he was also overtaken by a host of excited Oberlinites, led by his brother Charles and brother-in-law O. S. B. Wall, returning triumphantly to town. Even without knowing all the facts of the case, the young lawyer easily realized the gravity of the situation. Hundreds of his fellow townsmen had been involved in an open and successful defiance of federal authority and the Fugitive Slave Law. The triumphant reception of the Rescuers as they gathered again in Oberlin was greater than any celebration "as had ever assembled within the limits of that consecrated town," yet Langston knew that the government's response would be both forceful and swift in coming.[2]

How the Oberlin community would handle the aftermath would have enormous consequences. Over the next few months, the town's diverse and multiracial abolitionist band carefully manipulated the rescue episode into an extraordinary propaganda triumph. In Ohio and across the North, the flagging Republican Party embraced the Oberlin Rescuers, and in the process, the resulting injection of radicalism helped rescue the party from its drift toward conservatism and directed it down the path that would ultimately lead to a national policy of emancipation.

* * *

AS SOON AS Sim Bushnell, Richard Winsor, and John Price were back in Oberlin, they sought out the few abolitionists who had not made the trip to Wellington. With Professor James Monroe and bookseller James Fitch, they hustled to the home of Professor James Fairchild. Fairchild did not personally know Price, but he already had one former slave living under his roof, and he agreed to hide John in his attic until arrangements could be made for him to leave Oberlin for Canada.[3] As these plans were being made, more Rescuers were gathering on Tappan Square to tell those who had stayed behind about the incredible events of that afternoon. When night fell, an impromptu antislavery meeting convened where Rescuers delivered speeches that attacked the Fugitive Slave Law, slaveholders, and all who would offer them sympathy.[4] Jacob Shipherd closed the festivities by calling for three groans for U.S. Marshal Dayton and three cheers for the rescue of John Price.[5]

As they had in the rescue itself, Oberlin's African American residents figured heavily in the rally as well as in related activities that followed. Before the dust had settled, John and Charles Langston had joined with other black activists in issuing a call for a state convention of the "'colored citizens' of Ohio" to reassess their struggle. Noting that "two thirds of every Congress is taken up discussing the question, 'What shall we do with the nigger,'" black leaders thought it only proper in the wake of the rescue to take their usually active role in debating "the questions in which they were so deeply interested."[6]

When the convention met in November, Charles Langston, who had quickly become an abolitionist celebrity for his role in the rescue, was chosen as its president. His remarks were said to have been "very severe on the Democracy, and very gentle toward the Republicans," as were those of his brother John.[7] The Langstons, with Peter Clark, William Howard Day, and a huge crowd of white and black abolitionists in the afternoon session, committed the convention to the formation of a new permanent statewide African American organization, and in doing so resurrected the old Ohio State Anti-Slavery Society. The new society pledged itself "to secure, by political and moral means, so far as may be, the immediate and unconditional abolition of American slavery, and the repeal of all the laws and parts of laws, State and national, that make distinction on account of color."[8] All means to the ends were left on the table, including the resort to force if necessary.

As John Langston's biographers argue, the Oberlin and Ohio African American leadership had unmistakably "thrown down the gauntlet" before the Slave Power, and Oberlin's white residents were not far behind. In the immediate wake of the rescue, Oberlinites fired off letters to newspapers across the country asserting, as one did, that "the Fugitive Slave Law 'can't be did' in this part of the Reserve at least."[9] Oberlin was clearly holding its collective head high, and at least one Western Reserve newspaper blamed the "belligerent demonstrations" of the Rescuers and their supporters for the general upheaval that followed.[10] Within days of the Cincinnati convention, the federal grand jury of the Northern District of Ohio handed down indictments against thirty-seven Lorain County men, both white and black, charging them with aiding and abetting the rescue of John Price in defiance of the Fugitive Slave Law.[11] The grand jury was made up entirely of known Democrats, including Lewis Boynton, the father of the boy who had betrayed Price. As John Langston caustically remarked, "The son betrays, and the father indicts!" Even when Judas Iscariot betrayed Christ, he went on, in his deep consciousness of guilt and shame, he had the decency to hang himself afterward.[12]

Even though John Langston was not in Oberlin or Wellington during the rescue, prosecutors nonetheless took great pains, though unsuccessful, to win an indictment against the West's most outspoken abolitionist.[13] When the U.S. marshal finally appeared in Oberlin on December 7, he carried among the dozens of notices of indictment three for more of the town's most rabid abolitionists, James Fitch, Ralph Plumb, and Professor Henry Peck, who, like Langston, were not even near Wellington the day of the rescue. Still, nearly all of the indicted Oberlinites, including the three men who never left town that day, willingly met the marshal and gave their word that they would appear in Cleveland the following afternoon. Twelve African Americans were indicted, including Charles Langston, O. S. B. Wall, John Watson, John Scott, and John Copeland. The federal official felt "as safe with their promise as their bond" regarding all the men he served with indictments.[14] Following the example of Christ, they were fully prepared to face the legal consequences for violating laws that they believed were immoral.

When the indicted Rescuers returned to Oberlin from Cleveland, temporarily free on their own recognizance, they shared what was billed as a "Felon's Feast" with their Wellington co-defendants. Hosted by the Oberlin Rescuers and their wives at the college's Palmer House, it was, as one observer wrote, "a good social dinner, followed by a real 'feast of reason and flow of soul.'" Toasts went up from all around. John Langston praised "the seed of to-day which brings the harvest of to-morrow" and predicted the approaching "reinstatement" of the Declaration of Independence and the Constitution, the first having been struck down by slavery and the second by the Fugitive Slave Law. Rescuer Ralph Plumb took time to toast "*the Alien and Sedition Law of 1798 and the Fugitive Slave Act of 1850*—Alike arbitrary, undemocratic, and unconstitutional." "As did the one," he hoped, "so may the other rouse the country to a political and moral revolution."[15]

Not Guilty, on Behalf of All

The trials of the Rescuers were set to begin in April, and the battle lines were clearly drawn between the higher and lower law, none too evenly, as it turned out. Without exception, every person connected with the court and prosecution, "from the judge on the bench down to the claimants of the fugitive," was a Democrat, and as James Fairchild remembered, within the courtroom, "the Fugitive Slave Law held full sway."[16] The prosecution's opening remarks declared, "This Oberlin 'higher law'—which I call 'Devil's law'—as interpreted by the Oberlin saints, is just what makes every man's conscience his criterion as to right or wrong. The true 'higher law' is the law of the country in which we exist, and there would be no safety for the whole world or community, a perfect hell upon earth would prevail, if this Law was carried out. It gives all to the black man, but the devil take the white man!"[17] John Langston angrily declared that every aspect of the trial was organized and constituted "*to convict*," and the first two of the thirty-seven to be tried were found guilty, to the surprise of no one.[18] Sim Bushnell, the white driver of the getaway buggy, was the first to stand before the court and was quickly convicted. Charles Langston was next to be tried. Though his case was not as clear-cut as Bushnell's, prosecutors hoped to make a clear point in Langston's trial by demonstrating the dangers of "nigger social equality" as practiced in Oberlin. They also wanted to deal a weighty blow to those whose trials remained, causing them to "cease fighting" and "plead guilty."[19] Despite the defense's plea to jurors to lay aside all political biases or prejudices, to forget Langston's color, and to decide his case as though he were one of their equals, "as he is, a man," he was convicted after only a half hour of deliberation.[20]

After the two convictions, Bushnell was sentenced to sixty days' imprisonment, court costs, and a $600 fine. Langston was thus able to anticipate his own fate.[21] When the judge asked him if he had anything to say on why the law should not also be pronounced upon him, Langston arose and gave one of the most effective antislavery speeches of the antebellum period. He called the Fugitive Slave Law "an unjust one, one made to crush the colored man" but said that he cared little for debate over its constitutionality or his innocence on such grounds. He had not been taken as a *slave* under that law but indicted as a *citizen* for violating it, and he decried the denial to him of a trial before "an *impartial* jury" of his peers. As he saw it, the men gathered to hear his case in Cleveland were neither impartial nor his peers. Rather, they were perfect examples of men infected by "universal and deeply fixed *prejudices*" that grew out of the belief that African Americans had willingly consented for 200 years to be enslaved—to be "scourged, crushed, and cruelly oppressed." This prejudice repulsed most Americans, who honored those who rebelled at oppression and despised those who meekly submitted to it. So long as African Americans were believed to submit as a people, Langston argued, they would "as a people be despised." His jury, he went on, "came into the box with that feeling. . . . The gentleman who prosecuted me, the court itself, and even the counsel who defended me had that feeling."[22]

Langston believed that the time for such beliefs had passed. His speech was both a demand that black militancy be acknowledged and a call to others of his race to strive toward his standard. He and every other African American who had gone from Oberlin to Wellington that day had done so aware that they possessed no rights "which white men are bound to respect." There was no place in America, not even the nation's capitol, where he could tell a U.S. marshal "that my father was a Revolutionary soldier, that he served under Lafayette, and fought through the whole war, and that he fought for *my* freedom as much as for his own" without risking being "clutch[ed] . . . with his bloody fingers" and told that "he has a *right* to make me a slave!" In view of all the facts, Langston concluded, he would always "fall back upon those last defenses of our rights which cannot be taken from us, and which God gave us, that we need not be slaves." African Americans would no longer be found "meekly submitting to the penalties of an infamous law."[23]

Though John Langston's legal eloquence in defense of his brother was described as being "distinguished by the highest moral tone . . . delivered in captivating, attractive style and manner," it was Charles's statement that turned out to be, in John's words, the most "powerful and matchless address, wonderful in the breadth of his views, masterly and unanswerable in his logic and law, and commanding and irresistible in its delivery and effects."[24] At the end of the speech, the packed courtroom erupted into cheers and applause. Once order was restored, the judge charged Langston with having done "injustice to the Court," though his wrong lay only in thinking that nothing he could have said could mitigate his sentence. The judge had been so moved by the defendant that he sentenced him to the "comparatively light" punishment of twenty days in jail and court costs. Even this slap on the wrist prompted John Langston to wonder "how the United States officials will collect the fines imposed upon these men."[25]

Langston wrote that his brother's speech had "carried this case to the ends of the earth, and immortalized not only the name of its author, but impressed his sentiments of liberty, justice, humanity, and sound religious duty, as illustrated in the teachings of Christ, upon every hearer and reader of his words." As a spokesman "in the interest of the Abolition cause, at the time and under the circumstances," the younger Langston declared his brother "without doubt, the best qualified man of his race for such service."[26] The speech was reprinted in journals across the country, from the Western Reserve to New England.[27] William Nell and Lewis Hayden offered resolutions before a meeting of black Bostonians "commend[ing] to the reading of the entire nation the manly, thrilling, and eloquent speech of Charles H. Langston . . . deserving high prominence in the annals of this the second revolution for liberty in the United States."[28]

Still, the Rescuers remained in jail, resolved to suffer together until freed by the "due course of law" and to refuse any terms "short of a righting by the Court of the indignity and wrong which they had suffered at its hand."[29] Their first application for a writ of habeas corpus was denied in April when the Ohio Supreme Court upheld to be perfectly constitutional the Fugitive Slave Law under which the men were held.[30] However, by mid-May, the indictments of all the men from Wellington had been nolled, the district attorney having admitted that he viewed their cases differently than the Oberlinites who traveled several miles just to rescue John Price.[31] This left only the Oberlin men imprisoned, and it cleared the way, as Henry Peck noted, "for the prosecution to work that spite against the Anti-Slavery sentiment of Oberlin, which its enemies have long entertained, and which they have

The Oberlin-Wellington Rescuers at the
Cleveland jail (courtesy Oberlin College Archives)

often threatened to gratify."[32] One unnamed Rescuer noted in late April that the Cleveland jail then contained "some fifty-five prisoners, classified as follows: Horse thief, 1; counterfeiting, 1; murder, 1; drunkenness, 1; assault and battery, 1; grand larceny, 7; petit larceny, 8; burglary, 3; and believing in the higher law, 20."[33]

Almost immediately, the court then went into recess until the July term, which resulted in another two months of confinement for the prisoners in the sweltering Cleveland jail. At this point, state attorney general Christopher Wolcott initiated another habeas corpus proceeding on behalf of Langston and Bushnell. Wolcott warned the court that "weightier consequences never hung upon the arbitrament of any tribunal." He argued, "The strain of the Federal system has come, and your honors are to determine . . . whether under that system there can be any adequate protection for the reserved rights of the states, or any sufficient safeguards for the liberty of the citizen. The cause of constitutional government is here and now on trial. God grant it a safe deliverance."[34] By a vote of three to two, however, it was not so delivered.[35]

Many observers had by this time begun to agree with the imprisoned Oberlin men that the national administration was not so interested in upholding the Fugitive Slave Law as it was intent on punishing western abolitionism's most powerful symbol, Oberlin. The *Oberlin Evangelist* realized that "Oberlin stands conspicuous for its hatred of oppression and its love of liberty." The editor remarked, "[The] bitter war against Oberlinites is only a deadly blow aimed at the very vitality of liberty. Proslavery federal usurpation cares nothing for Oberlin as such. It is her *love of liberty and hatred of oppression that must be crushed out*."[36] This was not simply Oberlin paranoia, either. The *Norwalk Reflector, Cleveland Herald, Ashtabula Sentinel, Cleveland Independent Democrat, Portage County Democrat, Western Reserve Chronicle,* and *Ohio State Journal* all published similar editorials in May of 1859. The *Cleveland Leader* concluded, "No intelligent man can resist the conviction that this is a political trial, with no other object than to make political capital for a set of fellows in Northern Ohio who use this as a means of advancing their party against the Republicans generally."[37] The Democratic press was no less convinced. "Oberlinism," the *Cleveland Plain Dealer* concluded, "was Abolitionism boiled down to the quintessence of bitterness."[38] The *Ohio Statesman* agreed, reporting that the convictions "would have a very salutary effect on the ferocious abolitionists of that classic vicinity."[39] All these suspicions were confirmed after the Wellington prisoners were released. "The Oberlinites are the ones the Government wishes to punish," the district attorney flatly declared. "We mean to make a point of Oberlin."[40]

Until the Great Result Be Accomplished

While the second habeas corpus case was still pending, a mass Republican convention was called to meet just outside the Cleveland jail to capitalize on the Rescuers' plight.[41] On May 24, a crowd estimated at 12,000 people, including a delegation of approximately 1,300 from Oberlin (nearly two-thirds of the town's population), gathered in the public square to hear speeches and addresses from antislavery dignitaries, including Joshua Giddings, Benjamin Wade, Salmon P. Chase, Cassius Clay, and other "worthies of the Anti-Slavery Movement."[42] Oberlin's contingent marched in step with its own famous Oberlin Brass Band "playing the 'Marseillaise,'" and with an elderly abolitionist "bearing aloft the 'stars and stripes' with the inscription '1776.'"[43]

James Fairchild pronounced many of the speeches that day to have been "radical, almost revolutionary."[44] Giddings pledged to all present, So long as I have life and health, I will use all my influence and all legal means to oppose the execution of this [Fugitive] law. And when all such means fail, then so long as I have strength to raise and wield an arm, so long I will resist unto death, and will work and pray for liberty with my last breath."[45] John Langston announced from the same platform that "he hated the Fugitive Slave Law as he did the Democratic Party, with a deep, unalterable hatred." A conservative Cleveland newspaper even offered Langston an backhanded compliment when it wrote that his listeners "forgot that he was a black man—he spoke a white language, such as few white men can speak." To cheers, Langston reached out to his largely white audience and demanded of them: "If you hate slavery because it oppresses the black man in the Southern States, for God's sake hate it for its enslavement of white men. Don't say that it is confined to the South—here it is on our neighbors and citizens, and shall we say that slavery does not affect us? As we love our friends, as we love our God-given rights, as we love our homes, as we love ourselves, as we love our God, let us this afternoon swear eternal enmity to this law. Exhaust the law first for these men, but if this fail, for God's sake let us fall back upon our own natural rights and say to the prison walls 'come down,' and set these men at liberty."[46] At this, Asa Mahan rose to give thanks that the Oberlin men in and out of the prison, "whom he had instructed in years past and taught them principles of liberty, were still true to their duty." Their actions assured him that "he had not lived in vain."[47]

While the Oberlin prisoners baked in the Cleveland jail, they passed the six weeks as productively as possible. The jailer, a man about whom an Oberlin gathering declared, "God made a man before he made a jailer," allowed the Rescuers an incredible amount of freedom while imprisoned.[48] Though he fulfilled his duty to keep the Oberlinites within the prison walls, John Smith allowed them use of his own apartment in the prison, as well as the adjoining furnished rooms. When many of the Rescuers' wives expressed a desire to share their husbands' imprisonment, Smith agreed and helped make their terms as comfortable as possible. Oberlin students were allowed to receive their schoolbooks from visitors, and they continued their studies without interruption, no doubt aided by the presence of James Monroe, one of their esteemed professors, sharing their incarceration.[49] The bookseller James Fitch obtained a printing press, and with the help of his colleagues, established an abolitionist newspaper, *The Rescuer*.[50] The different mechanics procured tools and materials and continued their work as best they could and advertised their wares in the pages of the *Rescuer*, while Henry Peck gave sermons on "higher law" to as many visitors as could pack the jail and the audible area outside.[51] One visitor expressed his surprised belief that "President Buchanan hardly holds greater levees than did these men on Saturday afternoon."[52]

Besides via the *Rescuer*, the Oberlin prisoners and their friends did everything that they could to keep the case before the public eye. They posed in the prison yard for the cover photograph for the May issue of *Frank Leslie's Illustrated Weekly*, and they also kept a flurry of letters in the post to abolitionists and various antislavery newspapers from Ohio to New England.[53] Those friends on the outside wrote public letters and articles and gave countless speeches on behalf of the imprisoned.[54] Abolitionists in Oberlin and elsewhere across Ohio founded chapters of the revolutionary "Sons of Liberty," who, like their forefathers who tossed tea into Boston Harbor and upheld a popular movement for freedom, pledged themselves to even more strenuous resistance to intolerable government usurpations.[55] Lorain County "Sons" made banners emblazoned with the slogans "Here Is the Government, Let Tyrants Beware" and "Resistance to Tyrants, Obedience to God!"[56]

However, before a second issue if the *Rescuer* could make the press, the Lorain County Court of Common Pleas acted. Stymied by the decisions of the Ohio Supreme Court that denied habeas corpus to its citizens, Lorain County judge James Carpenter, on the request of several Oberlin representatives, did the next best thing: he issued his own indictments—charges of kidnapping against all those involved in the capture of John Price. This would have forced the Southerners to face a Lorain County jury, one made up of "fanatics and Abolitionists," who would supposedly be "vigorously instructed in the doctrine of the unconstitutionality of the Fugitive Slave law."[57] This move set off intense discussions between officers of the two courts and of all the parties involved and ultimately resulted in a prisoner exchange—Kentuckians for Oberlinites.[58] So ended, as one commentator wrote, "the most stupendous, unjustifiable and outrageous proceeding ever presented and prosecuted against any American citizens."[59] A Cleveland Democratic newspaperman expressed his disgusted astonishment at the deal and sympathized with the Kentuckians. The editor of the *Plain Dealer*, "finding no law in Lorain but the higher law, and seeing the determination of the sheriff, judge, and jury to send them to the penitentiary anyway," lamented the fallout that would undoubtedly follow. The federal government, he wrote, "has been beaten at least, with law, justice, and facts all on its side; and Oberlin, with its rebellious Higher Law creed, is triumphant." Fearing the worst, he concluded, "The precedent is a bad one."[60]

Back in Oberlin, abolitionists agreed with the *Plain Dealer*'s assessment that the Fugitive Slave Law had been defeated, but not with its gloomy conclusion. "At last the Higher Law was triumphant!" John Langston wrote excitedly.[61] At the news, hundreds of guns were fired off into the air near Cleveland's lakeshore, and "Hecker's band" played "Home, Sweet Home" as it led the procession of the Oberlin prisoners to the train depot for their long-awaited ride home.[62] There, they were welcomed back in high style.

The fire company and hook and ladder team marched in sharp uniform behind the Oberlin Brass Band from the depot to First Church, where prayers and speeches were offered.

The nationwide press reported on the July 6th "Great Oberlin Jubilee" that followed. Until midnight, a crowd of nearly 3,000 joined to celebrate the Rescuers. First Church resonated with the notes of a 125-voice choir, and many of the former prisoners offered impassioned and triumphant speeches of gratitude.[63] In place of his brother, who could not attend the Oberlin gathering, John Langston offered "high and proud tribute" to Charles's speech before the Cleveland court and tendered some "fearless and startling words" of his own in opposition to the fugitive law. He thanked all of those involved at all stages in the process, "in his character as a negro—as a white man—as one in whom the blood of both races joined—as a *man*—and as an American citizen." One newspaper correspondent wished that the entire world could have witnessed Oberlin's celebration, with abolitionists, young and old, black and white, "pouring forth . . . noble, manlike and godlike thoughts."[64] Oberlin's excitement had hardly subsided when Sim Bushnell was finally released on July 11, setting off another round of merriment no less intense than the first.[65]

A Perfect Revival of Anti-Slavery Zeal

John Langston concluded that the events of the Oberlin-Wellington Rescue unmistakably announced that the downfall of slavery was at hand.[66] The case was the crowning insult in a long line of proslavery affronts, and it capped the Northern indignation that had been steadily accumulating with each since 1850. As Langston's biographers note, the perceived threat to liberty and self-governance that took firm hold of the Northern consciousness reached its peak in 1858–59. The Fugitive Slave Law, the Kansas-Nebraska Bill, "Bloody Kansas," "Bloody Sumner," *Dred Scott*, the increasingly audacious and fiery rhetoric of proslavery Southerners, and countless other affronts gave tangible form to the arguments of abolitionists and Republicans that the South was determined to force slavery onto the entire country and would stop at nothing to control the government.[67]

Though Langston admitted that the antislavery spirit remained largely concerned with the sanctity of the rights of white men, he rejoiced that those privileged men "had determined that the enemy of their freedom must die." He appreciated that in its destruction, "it was easy to discover the approaching life of negro freedom."[68] A friend of Rescuer Henry Peck from Michigan told him about the "perfect *revival* of anti-slavery zeal in that state in consequence of [the Rescuers';] troubles," and even William Lloyd Garrison weighed in on the great importance of the rescue in shaping public opinion in a letter to James Monroe. "This very prosecution," he wrote, "will give a fresh impetus to our noble cause."[69] Moreover, the African American contribution to the escalation of antislavery sentiment could no longer be downplayed. The editors of the *Anti-Slavery Bugle* recognized that African Americans' "moral power" on the question was not exceeded by any other class, and went on to suggest that they carried in their hands "the key of our American Bastille."[70]

Ohio Republicans were certainly revitalized by the rescue hullabaloo. Just days after the Ohio Supreme Court denied the Rescuers' second habeas corpus request, the state Republican Party commenced its annual convention in Columbus. The 1859 convention drew its highest attendance ever, and many of the delegates were determined to nominate a strong, more radical ticket and wrest the platform away from conservatives.[71] Lorain County's cadre, headed by Monroe, led the way in expressing "the indignation of Republicans" by refusing the renomination of Chief Justice Joseph Rockwell Swan, a "cowardly and miserable sham conservative" who had delivered the majority opinion against the Rescuers' habeas corpus appeal by upholding the constitutionality of the Fugitive Slave Law.[72]

Even though the state platform was developed partially in response to the supreme court's decision in the rescue case, it still fell short of the standards of most Oberlinites by not explicitly guaranteeing African American citizenship rights and suffrage. Nonetheless, most were pleased with the party's insistence on the repeal of the fugitive act. It was the most radical stance yet taken by the young state organization, and James Fitch expressed his conviction to a correspondent in New York that "the weak back of our Republican Party in Ohio has been strengthened."[73]

In June, over 1,200 Western Reserve Republicans met in Oberlin to hear reports of the Columbus convention and listen to addresses by Monroe, Joshua Giddings, and John Langston. The multiracial aspect of the speakers' platform was also reflected in the Oberlin crowd, who, no doubt, were used to such an innovation by that point. The conservative *Ohio Statesman* reported, "The white and colored Republicans were mixed up in the meeting, Sambo spreading himself and participating largely in the meeting. We do not wonder that the colored Republicans at Oberlin were happy on the occasion. They certainly had a great triumph at the State Convention."[74]

Ohio's antislavery voters had been waiting impatiently since the rescue trials began to express their righteous indignation through the ballot box. Indeed, it seemed that at each setback in the proceedings, many of the more progressive papers held out this avenue of redress as a manifest duty. At the nadir of the trials in May, the *Cleveland Leader* instructed its readers, "The free people can only take an appeal through the ballot boxes, State and National. This they will do. The struggle between Freedom and Slavery, Liberty and Despotism is but begun."[75] Regarding those elected officials who publicly opposed the progression of liberty, even the conservative *Painesville Telegraph* wrote, "God help them in their blindness."[76]

An estimated 74.5 percent of eligible Ohioans turned out to vote in October of 1859, more than ever in the history of Ohio's state elections to that point. Republican William Dennison won the governorship with almost 24,000 more votes than Salmon P. Chase had polled in victory two years earlier. The Western Reserve sent a cadre of antislavery men to the state senate, including the "Radical Triumvirate" of Oberlin alum Dolson Cox, Professor James Monroe, and future president James Garfield, who in turn helped send Chase to Washington as Ohio's senator to join Ben Wade in 1860.[77] It truly seemed, as one Western Reserve Republican put it, "the Democracy have nothing left to do but to catch runaway fugitives."[78]

For the Cause of Freedom

John Langston could say with authority to an Ohio audience in 1858 that the abolitionist movement "knows no complexional bounds." "This identification of the interests of the white and colored people of the country," he said, "this particularly national feature of the anti-slavery movement, is one of its most cheering, hope-inspiring, and hope-supporting characteristics."[79] One particular man who had always identified the interests of all races as one was former tanner, sheep herder, surveyor, and Kansas freedom fighter John Brown. Brown's family had moved to the Western Reserve when he was five years old, and the boy grew up in a strict religious, abolitionist household. John's father, Owen Brown, had been a founding member of the Western Reserve Anti-Slavery Society as well as a trustee of Oberlin Collegiate Institute. His was one of the votes in favor of the admission of students "irrespective of color," and in 1841, Owen had arranged for John to survey several thousand acres of Virginia land that Gerrit Smith had donated to Oberlin.[80]

His abolitionist pedigree contributed to his involvement at an early age in the Underground Railroad, and in 1837, Brown dedicated his life to the abolition of slavery.[81] He was the most (in)famous of the free-soil fighters in Kansas in the mid-1850s, and by 1857, he had developed a plan for "troubling Israel," that is, the South itself, over the slavery issue. Brown revealed to his closest confidants that he planned "to make an incursion into the Southern states, somewhere in the mountainous regions of the Blue Ridge and the Alleghenies," and hinted at some large-scale Underground venture.[82] The final plan would be an assault upon the federal arsenal at Harpers Ferry, Virginia, after which slaves, whom Brown assumed would rush to his aid, would be armed and sent back into the mountains as a guerrilla force to free more of their brethren and repay in kind slave owners for the miseries they had inflicted on other men.

In 1858, John Brown busied himself planning a revolutionary provisional government to be put into place after the successful capture of the arsenal and the establishment of an African American state in the surrounding countryside. He called a meeting in Chatham, Canada, for May 8th to lay out the outlines of his plan, ratify a constitution, and elect officers. It is probable that John Langston and several others with Oberlin connections were invited, and at least three made it to the meeting and affixed their names, "John Hancock bold and strong," as black Oberlin alumnus James Jones described it, to Brown's "Provisional Constitution."[83] It read in part: "We . . . the Representatives of the circumscribed citizens of the United States of America, in General Congress assembled, appealing to the supreme Judge of the World, for the rectitude of our intentions, Do in the name, & by authority of the oppressed Citizens of the Slave States, Solemnly publish and Declare: that the Slaves are, & of right ought to be as free & as independent as the unchangeable Law of God requires that All Men Shall be. . . . We mutually pledge to each other, Our Lives, and Our sacred Honor."[84] Delegates to the meeting would be the parliament; Brown was elected commander in chief.[85]

After the Chatham meeting, a close friend of Brown took the constitution to William Howard Day's printing shop in St. Catharine's, Canada West.[86] Day had moved from Ohio to Canada to work with refugees at the St. Catharines terminus of the Underground Railroad and had been a confidant of Brown either during his Oberlin days in the 1840s or through his work with Ohio's abolitionist movement. Brown considered Day his "Chairman, C[anada] W[est]," and only lack of funds, Day later wrote Brown, had kept him from attending the Chatham meeting.[87] Over sixteen days alone his cramped office, Day painstakingly set Brown's constitution in fifteen pages of type, carefully hand-stitching each copy. Even more carefully, he published the document with no title page—no printer or author.[88]

Brown's attack was delayed after some of his plans were exposed by a former associate.[89] Unable to immediately proceed from Canada to Virginia, Brown returned to Kansas for another year of slave-raiding in Missouri.[90] In March of 1859, however, Brown was in Cleveland, arriving just prior to the commencement of the Oberlin-Wellington Rescue trials. He was returning from Canada with the horses he had just used to help liberate eleven Missouri slaves.[91] Brown was in the Reserve for nearly two weeks, and during that time, besides auctioning off all of his "confiscated" livestock (now good "abolitionist" horses, he said), he also joined in the activity surrounding the trials of the Oberlin men then taking place.[92] Though Brown was already a known "outlaw" with a price on his head for his activities in Kansas, he walked fearlessly past U.S. marshals in Cleveland, and even paid a visit to Charles Langston in jail.[93] He also gave a public lecture on the Fugitive Slave Law, audaciously telling his audience about his own recent Missouri-to-Canada rescue, and instructing those present that "it was the duty of every man to liberate slaves whenever he could do so successfully."[94] Among Brown's hearers that day was Lewis Sheridan Leary, an Oberlin Rescuer who had managed to avoid indictment.[95]

There were more overlaps between the Oberlin men and John Brown's circle of friends during the Cleveland trials. John Henri Kagi, a reporter for the *New York Tribune* and *Cleveland Leader*, was a close friend of Brown who had fought with him in Kansas (once nursing him to health at the home of Samuel and Florella Brown Adair).[96] Kagi was also an acquaintance of John Langston, and he gave more than just sympathetic coverage to the Rescuers' plight.[97] On their request, Kagi traveled to Columbus so that he could give them firsthand accounts of the habeas corpus proceedings. When their request was denied, Kagi actually offered to orchestrate a jailbreak, an offer the Rescuers refused.[98] Another man, Charles Tidd (aka J. M. Greene), had been one of Brown's lieutenants in Kansas, and though his role is not as clear Kagi's, he was sufficiently involved in the rescue aftermath to merit special thanks in Jacob Shipherd's compiled history of the proceedings.[99] Kagi, at least, was actively recruiting several of the Rescuers to join Brown's band of liberators.[100]

Another man calling himself John Thomas was also recruiting men for Brown on the Reserve around the same time, and in late August, he paid a visit to Oberlin. Thomas anxiously sought out John Langston, who had been lecturing on behalf of the Ohio State Anti-Slavery Society most of that month. When Langston arrived back in town, Thomas approached him and expressed his desire to discuss some business. As the men walked from

Lewis Sheridan Leary (from Hinton, *John Brown and his Men* [1894])

Langston's law office to his house, Thomas revealed his true identity to be John Brown Jr., the son of "John Brown of Ossawattamie." He informed Langston that he was in town to see him "upon matters strictly secret and confidential." The elder Brown, he said, "proposes to strike at an early day, a blow, which shall shake and destroy American slavery itself."[101]

At this, Langston invited the man into his house for dinner and a full discussion of the matter afterward. After dining in Langston's parlor, Brown disclosed his father's plan for his assault on Harpers Ferry and asked his host for his assistance in finding and influencing "any men willing and ready to join in the enterprise, and, if need be, die in connection therewith, in an attempt to free the American slave."[102] The Browns had taken a great interest in the rescue cases, John Sr. being present in Cleveland for the trials and John Jr. through correspondence with Rescuer Ralph Plum.[103] Though Langston (like Frederick Douglass) feared Brown's plan was bound to fail, he realized that it would nonetheless take the nation one step closer to the ultimate overthrow of slavery. Accordingly, he suggested two men whom he believed were willing to make the necessary "moral investments" that Brown's plot might demand of them: Lewis Sheridan Leary and John Copeland.[104]

Langston believed that "no man of greater physical courage could be found than Leary" and commended Copeland for his role in John Price's rescue as well as his committed work in Oberlin's Underground Railroad.[105] Leary actually may have already been on board by this point, and his letters to Kagi from Oberlin show that he was solidly committed to Brown's plan and that he believed his nephew Copeland was "a hardy man, who is willing and every way competent to dig coal," a coded reference to their plans. In the same letter, Leary informed Kagi that he believed he could "get an outfit from parties interested in our welfare in this place," and he put faith in "Mr. P," Rescuer Ralph Plumb, to assist in that effort.[106]

John Brown Jr. left Oberlin happy with the results of his visit. By the time all of Brown's lieutenants had left the Western Reserve in late August (Brown Sr. had left for Canada again by early April), they thought that they had four or five committed recruits, though Leary wanted to make sure his family in Oberlin was provided for before he joined them.[107] Charles Langston, who Brown Jr. believed was also on board, paid a special visit to Leary some time in August, apparently to make sure the man maintained his enthusiasm for the cause.[108] John Langston and Plumb were also to be counted upon to "work hard."[109]

Their expenses paid by Ralph and Samuel Plumb, Leary and Copeland left Oberlin in early October under the pretense of looking for extra work. They learned that Charles Langston was in Cleveland, and they stopped to consult with him there. On the 15th, they reached Brown's rented farmhouse near Harpers Ferry, Virginia.[110] That night, Brown told his men that the revolution would begin the next day. At 8 o'clock the night of the 16th, Brown announced, "Men, get on your arms; we will proceed to the Ferry."[111]

From the beginning, the assault was a failure. The first casualty was actually a black civilian, and when Brown inexplicably allowed a train to pass by the arsenal, word of the attack quickly spread. Marines under the command of Robert E. Lee soon had the men surrounded in the arsenal.[112] In the mayhem that followed, Sheridan Leary was shot and killed while attempting to escape across the Shenandoah River.[113] John Copeland was with his kinsman as they attempted to avoid the carnage but was captured and barely avoided being lynched on the spot by Virginia troops.[114] A week later, Brown, Copeland, and three other survivors were indicted for treason, murder, and inciting slaves to insurrection. According to *Dred Scott*, African Americans were not U.S. citizens and therefore could not be tried for treason, but though Copeland could not be charged with being a traitor, he and all the other defendants were sentenced to death for their roles in the attack.[115]

Copeland used much of his time in prison writing to his family back in Oberlin. He urged his parents not to grieve his impending doom but

John Copeland (from Hinton, *John Brown and his Men* [1894])

rather to "remember the *cause* in which I was engaged; *remember it was a holy cause*, one in which men in every way better than I am, have suffered and died." "If I am dying for freedom," he wrote, "I could not die for a better cause—*I had rather die than be a slave!*"[116] He was content, he told his family, and believed that God was working through him to bring about a greater good.[117] Back in Oberlin, even Copeland's mother agreed, and on the day her son was hanged, she declared to the gathered mourners, "If I could be the means of destroying slavery, I would willingly give up all my menfolks."[118]

Once the actual perpetrators were sentenced and several Oberlin connections were uncovered, a portion of the blame for the siege logically fell upon this bastion of abolitionism.[119] Several of its residents, including the Plumbs, were wanted for questioning by federal authorities for their role in the events. Others, at missionary or teaching posts in the border states, were jailed for merely possessing letters from Oberlin.[120] To the east, a Philadelphia newspaper did not mince words in its accusations of guilt directed toward the college and town: "Oberlin is located in the very heart of what may be called the 'John Brown tract' where people are born abolitionists and where abolitionism is taught as the 'chief end of man' and often put in practice." The town was "the nursery of just such men as John Brown and his followers," and it was Oberlin in particular where "younger Browns attain their conscientiousness in ultraisms, taught from the cradle up, so that while they rob slaveholders of their property, or commit murder for the cause of freedom, they imagine they're doing God's service."[121]

Shocked, a few Oberlin residents initially attempted to put as much distance between Brown and themselves as possible, and even some of the most committed abolitionists admitted that they were "not perfectly unequivocal on the subject of John Brown's career."[122] African Americans from Oberlin, however, did not hesitate a moment in their praise of "the noble and Christlike John Brown."[123] Charles Langston even placed an advertisement in a Cleveland paper denouncing those who held back their support for Brown. Abolitionists like Gerrit Smith, John Hale, Joshua Giddings, and others had unequivocally denied their involvement in the scheme, but Langston, believing his reputation to be as valuable as those prominent white men's, declared, "I must like them publish a card of denial. . . . But what must I deny? I cannot deny that I feel the very deepest sympathy with the Immortal John Brown in his heroic and daring efforts to free the slaves.—To do this would be in my opinion more criminal than to urge the slaves to open rebellion."[124]

On December 2, 1859, John Brown was executed. Despite the town's earlier hesitancy to praise him, Oberlin commenced a period of deep mourning for the martyr and those who would follow him to the gallows in the days to come. At the time of the execution, as in countless churches across the free states, the bells of First Church tolled for an hour. Prayer meetings throughout the day were packed to capacity. Later that week, James Thome returned to his alma mater to deliver a funeral sermon for John Brown, after which money was raised to erect a monument to honor the Oberlin men who also lost their lives in Virginia.[125] Across the North, other alumni were among the countless abolitionists who praised Brown and swelled the antislavery tide.[126]

As many Oberlinites listened to Thome's funeral sermon for John Brown, others prepared for the reception of John Copeland's body and a funeral of his own.[127] James Monroe went to Virginia to attempt to retrieve the man's corpse from the Winchester Medical College, where it was taken for dissection after the execution.[128] Though the governor of Virginia had sent a telegram authorizing the recovery, Virginia soldiers were posted all along the train routes looking for "'*a damned abolitionist*." If any who looked "as though they preferred liberty to Slavery" were found, they were seized and taken from the cars.[129] It was quickly apparent that Monroe's errand into the South would end in failure.[130] When the expected train arrived in Oberlin without Copeland's body, his father was heartbroken. One witness to his grief wrote that "it seemed to make him feel worse than the intelligence that his son was dead."[131] Nonetheless, on Christmas Day, Henry Peck preached a memorial sermon in honor of Copeland and his "associate martyrdom" to 3,000 mourners in First Church.[132]

The Approach of a Cruel, Deadly Storm

At the turn of the New Year a week later, it seemed as if all Americans' eyes now turned to the 1860 national elections. The Oberlin-Wellington Rescue and John Brown's raid and execution had lit the political atmosphere on fire, and men and women from Oberlin put all of their weight behind the Republican Party.[133] Despite the party's lingering conservatism, it remained, in the words of the *Oberlin Evangelist*, "honest indefinitely before their competitors." "We wish with all our heart," the editor proclaimed, "the Republican party were better than it is." They would give their support despite the party's antislavery shortcomings, while promising "to do all we can to elevate its moral tone, and bring it more fully into sympathy with freedom and righteousness and the cause of the oppressed."[134] Despite their reservations, Oberlin speakers went out in force to stump for the Republicans while others preached politics at home.[135] James Monroe gave over thirty speeches around Ohio in the weeks leading up to the election, and Charles Finney was overheard at family prayers beseeching God to "annihilate the Democratic Party."[136]

Monroe was unable to attend the Republican National Convention in May, so Norton Townsend took his place among the Chicago delegates who nominated Abraham Lincoln for the presidency.[137] When word of the nomination reached Oberlin, the community first received the news "rather coolly," since many believed Lincoln to be too conservative on the slavery issue. "We wish with all our hearts," the editor of the *Oberlin Evangelist* wrote, the convention "had tried their hand upon a better man."[138] Nonetheless, a group of students decided to make "a big bluster" and formed a torchlight parade that was marshaled around Tappan Square. Gradually, the community warmed to the news, and musicians came to the square, formed a band, and marched with the torch carriers around a huge bonfire that had been lit in the center of the square. Once over a thousand people had gathered, speeches were offered in support of Lincoln, who now seemed their "first and only choice."[139] In conclusion, Oberlin's church bells were "rung like mad."[140]

The Republicans rolled to victory in Ohio. The state elections in October were a Republican blowout and proved to many that the Democrats were doomed in the next month's national elections. The *Ohio State Journal* declared it "the most brilliant [victory] ever achieved in the state by the Republican Party."[141] In November, Lincoln racked up a majority of nearly 47,000 votes statewide as close to 90 percent of eligible voters turned out to cast ballots. His vote share was 80 percent in Oberlin, which, however, did not officially include several dozen Oberlin women who turned out at the polls and "offered to vote."[142] As election returns came in, some in Oberlin still held back enthusiasm because slavery had not been eradicated in the election. The "tangible results from this election in the way of help to the slave," the *Oberlin Evangelist* proclaimed, "we may expect too much." Still, the editor rejoiced "that its boundaries are at length set."[143]

Early in 1861, however, the venom spewing from the South caused many Ohioans to predict secession and war. As John Langston remembered, "All could feel . . . the approach of a cruel, deadly storm."[144] In February, a community meeting produced an "Oberlin Manifesto" that praised the Union, while delegates offered prayers for wisdom and guidance for themselves and national leaders.[145] However, when shots were fired on Fort Sumter on April 12, the fears of many Oberlinites were realized. At the news, an *Oberlin Evangelist* editorial accompanied the call for a "great Union Meeting," and asked, "Who knows but that the throes of mortal strife which began at Sumter are the signs of our country's regeneration?"[146] As historian David Brion Davis writes, even the most radical abolitionists came to believe that "the Union cause was their own, a providential agency designed to destroy the Slave Power." Slave owners had been "rebels against the United States as well as the abolitionists' God."[147] On the 17th, over 2,000 men and women gathered in Oberlin for the assembly, and any and all divisions that may have existed within the town before hostilities commenced were quickly put aside for the sake of the support of the Union. In fact, in an incredible show of unity, Lewis Boynton, the formerly Democratic father of rescue villain Shakespeare and member of the 1859 federal grand jury, was selected as a convention vice president alongside a handful of abolitionists and that first Oberlin pioneer, Peter Pindar Pease. Professors Peck and Fairchild, James Fitch, Ralph Plumb, and John Langston gave stirring speeches in support of Union and in opposition to treason.[148]

Two days later, the students called a meeting in the college chapel to "rally to the defense of the Union" and enroll volunteers for the army. The faculty hastily suspended a long-standing rule against students serving in the military and prepared to review the list of young men hoping to enlist. Only those eighteen and older or with a parent's permission would be allowed to enlist.[149] Before students could officially sign up, however, Professor Monroe gave a short address to further "stir up the students and people of Oberlin to the duty of the hour." When he laid the roll on the desk, a crowd of students rushed to affix their names to it.[150] Before nightfall, a group of Oberlinites had gone into the woods and brought back the tallest tree they could fell, dragged it into the center of town, and ran up an American flag. That night, half of a company enlisted and citizens pledged several thousand dollars to sustain the volunteers. The next day was a Sunday, and many prayerfully considered the task before them. As the Sabbath passed, those who feared the rolls might fill before Monday morning sent in their names. The first company did fill, and by Tuesday morning, Oberlinites had filled a second. Both began drilling together in earnest upon Tappan Square.[151] Nearly two-thirds of the college men enlisted that weekend, and even more students left campus soon thereafter to enlist in their hometowns since only one of the Oberlin companies was initially accepted into service.[152] One resident noted with satisfaction, "Oberlin, which has been first in bringing about the state of feeling that produced this crisis now wishes to bear her share of meeting it."[153] Another enlistee put it more bluntly: "We must now put up or shut up."[154]

Town business came to a halt for the next two days as Oberlin residents joined forces to outfit their companies as quickly as possible.[155] Forgotten were their demonstrations against the government of just two years before. In this fight, it was clear to all that, despite the explicit disclaimers of the federal government, they were on the side of freedom against slavery. That war-torn April, "Oberlin fairly blossomed out with the stars and stripes." Fairchild remembered that "it was a great relief to know that these were the symbols of righteousness and liberty, and not of oppression." Five hundred Oberlin women formed a Florence Nightingale Association to prepare socks and uniforms for the men, and many others accompanied the men to the depot, intent on joining their sons, brothers, and husbands on the battlefield as nurses. Members of the Oberlin Brass Band tendered their services to the regiment as musicians. On April 25, Oberlin's "Monroe Rifles" went to war to fight "slavery first, and the devil afterwards."[156]

One of the first to fall at the First Battle of Manassas was Oberlin student Albert Morgan.[157] He would not be the last. At Oberlin's commencement in 1861, the program bore stars beside the names of nearly a third of the graduating class denoting "in federal army." All of these men were awarded their degrees with the rest, yet as the honors were being conferred, absent senior Burford Jeakins lay dying on a Virginia battlefield, and William Parmenter was losing his own battle against death in a New Orleans prison.[158] The fates of these particular men were not yet known to the audience, but midway through the graduation exercises, news of the battle at Cross Lanes and the reported deaths of several Oberlin boys reached town. "Most in the audience were in tears," one alumnus remembered, "and Prof. Morgan could scarcely speak for sobs. . . . With very few words, diplomas were presented to us, and in silence, we left the platform."[159]

Oberlinites described a sense of "goneness" around town. The Oberlin Musical Union lacked the impressive balance it had exhibited in years past, as tenors and basses were in short supply.[160] James Fairchild estimated that 850 Oberlin students enlisted in the army over the course of the war, and enrollment dropped from 1,313 in 1860 to just 862 two years later. One in ten of those enlistees never returned home.[161] Yet as Oberlin men fell, those remaining at home kept up a concerted effort to force the administration toward a policy of emancipation.[162] At the 1862 commencement exercises, alumnus James Thome, now a minister in Cleveland, declared that "the necessities of the country, the rights of the enslaved, and the honor of God demand that President Lincoln exercise without delay, the authority which the war power gives him . . . to abolish slavery throughout the 'Confederate States.'" The Oberlin meeting requested that he forward his comments directly to Abraham Lincoln, and Thome complied.[163] Finney used his pulpit to urge his parishioners to be discriminating and "more thoroughly consider that this war 'for the union,' is not morally to abolish oppression."[164] In private letters, he lamented the fact that Southern fields that had "hitherto been moistened by the blood & sweat of the poor slave" were now red with the blood of Union soldiers. However, he admitted that "for humanity's sake we cheerfully though tearfully make the sacrifice. In this collision the cause of the slave is that of humanity, of liberty, of civilization, of Christianity."[165]

When You Need Us, Send for Us

Not to be outdone by their white brethren, black Oberlinites attempted to enlist in the Union army as soon as Lincoln declared a state of insurrection. However, African America men were not allowed to enlist initially.[166] Nonetheless, in September of 1861, Oberlin resident and former slave James Stone had successfully enlisted in the First Ohio Light Artillery and became one of the first African Americans to serve in the military during the Civil War. His light complexion had allowed him to "pass" for white in many instances, and he faithfully served for thirteen months before he died in October of 1862.

The *Lorain County News* reported his passing, noting, "One soldier, at least, has been given by the despised, chattel race, to the cause of the Union."[167]

As Northern African Americans loudly proclaimed their patriotism and decried the refusal of their services, leaders like John Langston advised them to prepare themselves but wait patiently until whites realized just how much the country needed their help.[168] In July of 1862, Langston spoke at an Oberlin war meeting and urged the formation of a black military company.[169] Also that month, another Oberlin meeting stingingly criticized Lincoln's refusal to endorse emancipation as a war aim or to allow African Americans to bear arms for the Union.[170] In August, Langston approached Ohio governor David Todd about the possibility of him being allowed to raise a company of African American troops, to which Todd dismissively told him, "When we want colored men we will notify you." Langston's parting request was prophetic and slightly different: "When you need us, send for us."[171] White Oberlin leaders continued to agitate for the rights of their black neighbors and classmates to fight for their own rights. By September, the town had established an integrated drill company.[172]

News of Lincoln's preliminary Emancipation Proclamation that month was a sweet sound in Oberlinites' ears.[173] In it, Lincoln declared freedom to all slaves in Confederate states that did not return to Union control by January 1, 1863, and allowed for the enrollment of African Americans in the Union army. Even before official word came down, William Howard Day wrote to Treasury secretary Salmon Chase to express his hearty approval of the proposed "Act of State decreeing Emancipation." Despite the limited nature of the proclamation (it actually did not free any slaves and did not apply to territories under Union control), Day regarded it as "a triumph of our principles" and as "a beginning to an end." He would not dare "question the terms, but would rejoice that in it all I see Liberty."[174]

The official Emancipation Proclamation on January 1, 1863, was a jubilee day in Oberlin's history.[175] One Lorain County editor doubted if the Oberlin community had ever felt more genuinely happy than upon the reception of the proclamation. When the expected newspapers reached town, John Langston grasped the top copy and read the Emancipation Proclamation aloud from the front steps of the college chapel. As his ecstatic audience shouted in celebration, Langston followed the outpouring of enthusiasm with a second read-through. Henry Cowles, "his voice trembling with emotion," followed the reading with words of thanksgiving and prayer. Rockets and bonfires lit the Oberlin sky that night, and many African Americans marched proudly across town in their own celebratory parade.[176]

Just days later, Massachusetts governor John Andrew began to raise the nation's first African American volunteer regiment. George Stearns, one of John Brown's strongest supporters in the lead-up to Harpers Ferry, was placed in charge of the recruitment effort, in no small part because of his intimate friendships with prominent African Americans. He, in turn, selected some of America's most influential black men as recruiters, including Frederick Douglass, Martin Delaney, and John Mercer Langston, who was named chief agent for the West.[177]

Langston's most important mission in the spring of 1863 was recruitment on behalf of the 54th Massachusetts Volunteer Regiment. He was joined in his efforts by his brother Charles, who had already been working among contrabands in Kansas, and his brother-in-law O. S. B. Wall, both Rescuers and both committed to the black freedom struggle.[178] Concentrating mainly in Ohio, Indiana, and Illinois, they recruited hundreds of eager black soldiers that were duly sent on to the East.[179] They quickly filled the first regiment in large part with a cadre of Oberlin men, among whom were at least six former slaves and three self-emancipated bondsmen.[180] In addition, sixteen African Americans hailing from Oberlin were enrolled in the "Fred Douglass Regiment" of the 54th, recruited in New York State by Langston's friend and mentor Frederick Douglass.[181] Dozens of others who no longer lived in Oberlin enlisted across the free states.[182]

With the 54th filled, Langston opened the rolls for the 55th Massachusetts. His wife, Carrie, and Oberlin alumna Fanny Jackson led the fund-raising campaign for a stand of regimental colors.[183] These flags were carried by the 55th all through the war until they were eventually "returned at last, bearing all the marks of patriotic, brave service, to the capitol of the Commonwealth of Massachusetts."[184] Langston was also largely responsible for raising Ohio's first black regiment, the 5th United States Colored Troops (USCT), and in addition to those Ohioans, nearly 500 of the members of the 54th and 55th Massachusetts were recruits of the Oberlin men.[185] In presenting the colors to the 5th USCT, Langston told them, "My boys, sons of the State, go forth now as you are called to fight for your country and its government!"[186] "No regiment," he recalled later, "ever left its camp followed by more hearty anxieties and earnest prayers for its welfare than this one."[187]

Forward!

Colonel Robert Shaw nervously smoked a cigar as he and the rest of the 54th Massachusetts Volunteer Regiment gazed at the imposing walls

John Mercer Langston presenting the colors to the 5th Ohio United States Colored Troops (from Langston, *From the Virginia Plantation to the National Capital* [1894])

of Charleston's Fort Wagner on July 18, 1863. The Confederate batteries were incessantly firing shells at the huge mass of black troops, but at such a distance, the rounds usually landed hundreds of yards in front of them. If they by chance rolled to where the 54th stood at the ready, the soldiers would simply move aside and let the shot continue on its way.[188]

Finally, after what seemed like an interminable wait, General George Strong rode into their midst and steeled the 54th for battle. He charged each and every man with upholding the honor of the great Commonwealth of Massachusetts and then boldly asked if there was a man among them who thought that he would not be able to sleep that night in the captured fort. A deafening chorus of "No!" filled the salty air. Finally, the general called the regimental color-bearer forward, and Sergeant John Wall, a twenty-year-old Oberlin student, stepped forward with the Stars and Bars. Henry Peal, who had emancipated himself earlier in the war and was attending school at Oberlin before he enlisted, stood by him with the colors of Massachusetts firmly gripped in his hands.[189] Peal had told a friend earlier, "It makes me proud that two of the Oberlin boys carry the first flags that ever the Colored man could call his country's flag."[190]

At 7:45 P.M., Shaw told his troops, "Now I want you to prove yourselves men." From the front, he shouted their orders: "Move in quick time until within a hundred yards of the fort; then double quick and charge." After a short pause, he gave the order, "Forward!"[191] The 54th advanced in the dark under heavy Confederate fire until they began the final charge toward Fort Wagner. As they neared the moat of the fort, Rebel fire from Fort Wagner as well as Fort Sumter, so heavy that one officer believed that a lightning storm had swept down onto the battlefield, tore through the Union forces with devastating effect.[192]

Even when the Confederate fire had stalled much of the 54th, John Wall continued his valiant advance at the head of the regiment. Suddenly, a Confederate round ripped into his body, and Wall fell helplessly into a shell crater. Unable to go on, Wall called out for a comrade to take up the national colors for him. From behind, sergeant William Carney answered the call, and Wall handed off the colors. Reenergized, Shaw and the African American troops followed Carney toward the center of the battery. The colonel was one of the first to reach the parapet, but as he stood atop it, shouting his men on, he was riddled with bullets and fell to the ground dead. Despite the loss of their commander, the black troops of the 54th continued the fight.[193]

William Carney never let the flag touch the ground, even when he was shot through the leg. After two more severe wounds, Carney was still able to reach the Confederate battery, and with all his might, he planted his flag firmly upon the ramparts of Rebel ground. As the Stars and Bars waved above the fray, Henry Peal, the former slave who had finally found a brief peace and freedom in Oberlin, defiantly waved the flag of Massachusetts back and forth over the Confederate walls.[194]

Carney and Peal were among four African American men to be awarded the Gilmore Medal of Honor for bravery in the siege of Fort Wagner. Peal continued to carry the colors of Massachusetts through the rebellious states that continued to consider him a "fugitive slave"—the property of another man. This "chattel" proudly and defiantly waved his colors at the front of Union lines and in the faces of his lifelong tormentors until the Battle of Olustee, in Florida, where he was mortally wounded. Though he never saw Oberlin again, he died a free man, "with the Gilmore medal on his breast."[195]

EPILOGUE

Be Not Conformed to This World

On November 8, 1864, Oberlinites gathered at the polls to reelect Republican Abraham Lincoln to the presidency. Though the balloting was technically secret, the votes of most Oberlin men were already well known. Giles Shurtleff, an 1859 Oberlin College graduate, had arrived in town that afternoon with other members of the 5th United States Colored Regiment, of which he was commanding officer. Limping from unhealed wounds, Shurtleff "tendered his vote for Lincoln and the Union." The cheer that greeted his cast ballot was described as "such as to melt to tears a man who never had the weakness to quail before an enemy."[1]

Yet it was the vote of community patriarch John Keep that best captured the spirit of the day and provided a set of bookends for the story of the Oberlin community in the antislavery movement. Keep had been one of the first colonists on the ground in Oberlin, and it was he who had cast the deciding vote in favor of admitting African American students in 1834. Keep had been a tireless worker in the OASS in the late 1830s and 1840s, represented Oberlin and American abolitionism in England in 1839–40, and was an indefatigable campaigner for the Liberty, Free-Soil, and Republican Parties. On that day in 1864, Keep was in the midst of serving his thirtieth consecutive year as a trustee of Oberlin College (a post he would continue to hold, never missing a meeting, until his death six years later).[2]

Keep's advanced age caused his limbs to tremble, and only with the help of friends could he walk to the polling place and offer his ballot to the election officer. To the "throng" that had surrounded him, Keep declared in a trembling voice that he had given his first vote in 1800 and that this would probably be the last ballot for president he would ever have the "privilege" to cast. With his ballot, he attached a prepared statement that was also to be read aloud to the gathered crowd. "Palsied be the *tongue* which now wags for treason," he wrote, "and the *hand* which would cut the jugular vein of our Christian Commonwealth." He signed the statement, "John Keep, age 83.

Oberlin, Nov. 1864," and the election official endorsed it, "A Freeman's Vote, 1864, for Abraham Lincoln."[3]

Keep was present at Oberlin's creation, and he fought with his fellow Oberlinites at the front lines of the battle against slavery until it was won. In the early years of the twentieth century, an old friend remembered him as a man who had favored action over stubborn adherence to dogma and who had an extraordinary ability "to measure the questions" before the antislavery movement. It was Keep's "clear insight into their meaning and their drift" that made him so important among Oberlin's abolitionist leadership, and it was "his courage and wisdom in maintaining them alone and under an opposition which led to ostracism" that ultimately made the crusade a success.[4] Oberlinites, for their part, reverently called John Keep "Father Keep," yet in his own humble way, he would only claim the honor of being a small part of something much greater.[5] The entire Oberlin community—students, faculty, alumni, and townspeople—had been the ones who in the antislavery movement consistently put their "hand to the plow and never turned back, who saw the thing that most needed to be done and at once set about doing it."[6]

With Lincoln reelected and slavery defeated, however, "the thing that most needed to be done" was not as clear as it had been just a few years earlier. Yet, unlike other reformers who saw their task as finally completed, Oberlinites knew that the struggle was far from over. Their community's thirty-year commitment to complete emancipation and full equality would not end with the ratification of the Thirteenth Amendment. As John Mercer Langston declared in October 1865, "The colored man is not content when given simple emancipation . . . he demands much more than that."[7] Another veteran of Oberlin's abolitionist crusade remarked that when the town's soldiers returned from the Southern battlefields and "brought that flag proudly and triumphantly home," it had been "baptized with the blood of their fallen comrades, it was the flag of American citizenship, without regards for race or color, of equality before the law, of free me1n and women everywhere throughout the land."[8]

As it turned out, the struggle for equality would not be that simple. Langston well knew this, but that was the goal to which he dedicated the rest of his life. Many other Oberlin veterans of the abolitionist crusade also readily maintained their deep-seated commitment to full emancipation and African American rights. When teachers sponsored by the American Missionary Association went south to educate the former slaves after the war, more men and women from Oberlin undertook the mission than from any other place in America.[9] Moreover, many Oberlin educators remained

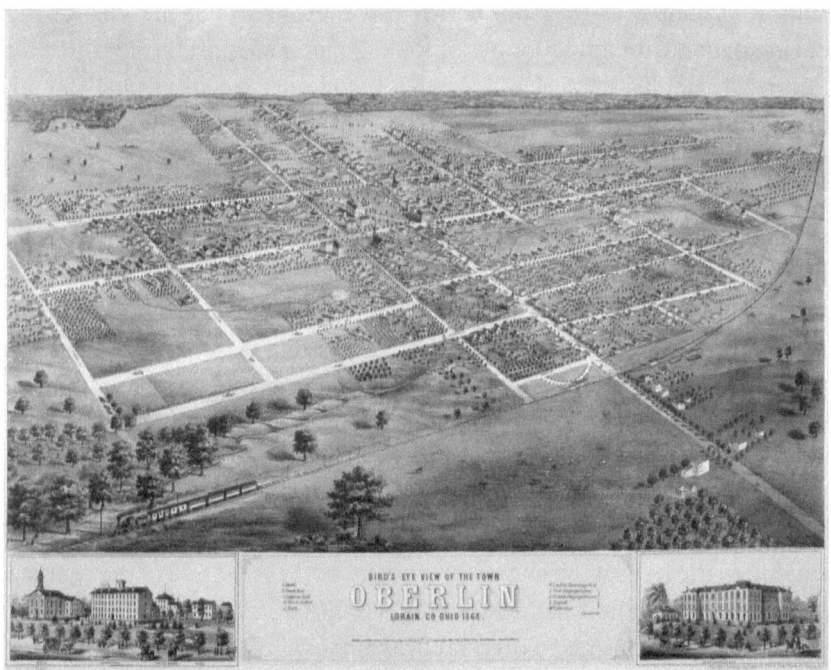

Bird's-eye view of Oberlin, 1868 (courtesy Oberlin College Archives)

in the South for the rest of their lives, having fully dedicated themselves to black education and advancement. As some led schools, other alumni became leaders in the Freedmen's Bureau and both state and national Reconstruction governments.[10] Oberlinites continued to spread across the nation, founding reform-oriented and racially blind colleges upon the Oberlin model and continuing the fight for African American justice from which many other abolitionists retreated after emancipation.

Their actions were often unpopular, but founder John Jay Shipherd had predicted as much early on. Less than a month before his early death in 1844, he restated for the last time the meaning of "Oberlin" as he understood it. "The greatness of Oberlin," he wrote, "is doubtless attributable under God to her adherence to the noble principle, that *public Institutions no less than private Christians must do right however contrary to popular sentiment.*" "That the managers of Oberlin Institute may never swerve from this grand principle," he implored, "is one of the strongest desires of my soul. To each I would say with emphasis 'Be not conformed to this world.'"[11]

That the world changed for the worse in the decades after Shipherd's prophesy seemed an unfortunate reality to the many Oberlinites who had dedicated their lives to abolitionism and then to seeing the idea of full emancipation through as long as it took. Popular support in the North for Reconstruction barely survived the 1860s, and once constitutional amendments supposedly guaranteeing citizenship and the franchise had been passed, America's fleeting commitment to its citizens of African descent faded away. Even in Oberlin, at the school and in the community, the intensity and passion that people had once brought to the abolitionist movement proved impossible to maintain. By the 1880s, a new generation of Oberlinites had come of age that had never been a part of that earlier movement. As Oberlin archivist emeritus William Bigglestone reasons, "Working and fighting for freedom for a slave was not the same as protecting him against widespread discriminatory practice." Moreover, as America continued on its descent into Jim Crowism, it was unavoidable that students sent to Oberlin "represented the times in which they were raised."[12]

The institution founded to stand as a "city on a hill" seemed to be quickly sinking to the level of the rest of the profane world at the end of the century. It was not uncommon, James Fairchild admitted, for white Oberlinites to "look scornfully on the colored fellow-student."[13] Black students increasingly felt themselves being "held within definite boundaries upon the outer fringes of college life."[14] In the early 1880s, there were the first hints of objections to white and black students living together as roommates. Two years later, several white students refused to sit with their black classmates at the dining table in Ladies Hall. The disturbance caused the dining room matron to quickly set a separate table in the room for black students. Though this move was met with considerable outrage (and was followed by an explanatory open letter to the *Oberlin News* attempting to smooth over the incident), the assurance that the "colored table was formed with the same waiters and same food and same everything as their neighbors" did little to rectify the situation. A dangerous precedent had been set.[15]

Some Oberlin students wondered whether their school was "no longer the Oberlin of the founders; that she has repudiated her history; that she has become as radical defender of race distinctions as she was formerly an opposer." Though some white students dismissed the charge of racism, black students, for their part, did not let the slight go unchallenged. "It is true that the faculty cannot change each students'[sic] heart," they admitted, "but they can demand that this principle of the Institution shall be carried out . . . this principle which requires that men of all nations, on an equal footing, regardless of color, shall receive an education here." This, of course, would necessitate some of the *faculty* dismissing their own prejudices, which were all too obvious to these observant black students.¹⁶

No one questioned the fidelity to the old Oberlin ways of Professor Giles Shurtleff, former abolitionist, Oberlin alumnus, brigadier general and commander of African American troops during the war. In response to the recreancy he feared was overtaking his alma mater, Shurtleff offered his Oberlin students a stern reminder of the school's history and their shortcomings in living up to the lofty standards set by earlier generations. "The history of the colored race in this country," he said, "places every Christian and every citizen under peculiar obligation toward them." He argued that African Americans belonged to the most wronged race "since the beginning of history" and even wondered whether the "torture" of slavery was "more acute than the almost universal social ostracism of today." Considering Oberlin's progressive history, community members had a "special obligation" to their African American colleagues, something more than "cold recognition and permission to remain among us." "You cannot aid men to a better life," he concluded, "while you keep them at arms' length, and look upon them as your inferiors. Men will not be lifted toward heaven with pitchforks."¹⁷

Other antebellum alumni chimed in as well. George Harrison wrote from Minnesota to Fairchild, now Oberlin president, demanding a refutation of what he had to assume was an untrue rumor. In a response to Oberlin administrators, black alumni cited the "race pride" that was so much a part of Oberlin's history and lamented this new "color line" and put their faith in the president "to sanction no precedent so contrary to Oberlin's good history."¹⁸ Fairchild did not disappoint. He resolved the dining hall situation in the only way a member of Oberlin's first freshman class of 1834 could have—he ordered the separate table for black students removed.

Though the Oberlin administration had never forced its students to associate with students of other races against their will, there had never been an exclusionary policy in Fairchild's time at the school, and there would not be under his watch. But Fairchild and Shurtleff were old men, as were the remaining faculty who had any connections to pre–Civil War Oberlin. Antebellum alumni were also strong advocates of the Oberlin tradition of racial equality. Together, they had fought the fight "to pull the devil's kingdom down."¹⁹ They would not be conformed to the world, but they were literally a dying breed. Fairchild served Oberlin for fifty-five years, and he would be the last college president with any connection to the school that went further back than Reconstruction. The 1882 Ladies Hall segregation fight would be the last stand of the founders' Oberlin.

The main goals of Fairchild's successor, William Ballantine, were to bring Oberlin more in line with modern universities, expanding course offerings and transforming it from an institution whose bedrock was religion into one where religion and spirituality were but elements among many. Ballantine's replacement in 1898 was selected partly because he had no previous connection to the old "simplicities" of antebellum Oberlin. In 1900, John Henry Barrows declared that Oberlin's future would not be "a slavish repetition of the past. . . . Progress does not come from trying to galvanize into life dead forms, nor by deploring that men will not do just as their fathers did."[20] By then, as a Cleveland newspaper lamented, "the last of the old fathers, who built up the college in its infancy and who delighted to do and pray for the Negro, and offer him their protection," had died or retired.[21] With them went the last vestiges of Oberlin's commitment to educating black students.[22]

By the turn of the century, Oberlin was a considered a "modern" institution, but modernity in contemporary American society had little place for African Americans. Black students were once again segregated and excluded from college life, and Barrows, unlike Fairchild, did nothing about it. Fairchild died in 1902, and Shurtleff passed two years later. The very next year, with the final ties to antebellum Oberlin broken, literary and debate societies began excluding African Americans from their memberships, and by 1909, segregated dorms had been built on Oberlin's campus.[23] By 1910, Oberlin's black athletes were not allowed to travel with the team to away games.[24] In 1919, black women were excluded from Oberlin dormitories altogether.[25] Mary Church Terrell, who had earned two degrees from Oberlin in the 1880s, spoke for Oberlin's black students and alumni when she wrote Oberlin's president in 1914. "Altho I try to be optimistic in this wicked and cruel country, in which everything is done to crush the pride, wound the sensibilities, embitter the life and break the heart of my unfortunate race," she said, "nothing has come so near forcing me to give up hope, and resigning myself to the cruel fate which many people are certain awaits us, than the heartbreaking backsliding of Oberlin College."[26]

But the spirit of Oberlin, the idea that predated the colony and college's founding, was too strong to be vanquished. Fairchild hinted at this in an address late in his life. "The Fathers," he asked, "where are they?" The "stately forms that occupied the Oberlin platform in the early years"—Finney, Mahan, Cowles, Thome, Morgan, Shipherd, Pease, Hudson—"have rested from their labors—most of them already gathered in the heavenly jubilee, rejoicing in the Master's welcome, 'Well done, good and faithful servants.'"

Still, though their words no longer echoed in Oberlin's halls, their "wisdom and authority" did. Fairchild suggested with hope that "Oberlin, which is, in a sense, the mother of us all, remains."[27] In six decades with the school, Fairchild had watched the torch of radicalism and reform be passed back and forth among the students, faculty, and community. Now, it had not been extinguished; its guardianship had simply shifted again.

Abandoned by the college, black students turned to the community for support. Though black enrollment at Oberlin College had dropped late in the century, the town remained a magnet for African Americans. These residents remained "anxious for education for their children," and they availed themselves of the Oberlin public schools, which remained fully integrated.[28] The town of Oberlin now also had two black churches, representing a desire for independence. Notably, First Church, as well as Oberlin's other Methodist church remained integrated. As historian Cally Waite notes, Oberlin's churches represented places where African Americans could come together, and they fostered a sense of community, especially for black college students, that Oberlin College no longer provided.[29]

In the new century, the Oberlin community (especially black residents) continued to be remarkable in its stand against racism and, from the "nadir" of race relations in America (even Oberlin), shepherded Oberlin back into the vanguard of progressivism. In 1909, the Niagara Movement (the precursor to the NAACP) held its annual meeting in Oberlin. There, the local Oberlin delegation of men and women resolved with the convention that they were in the midst of an "unparalleled opportunity to lead the greatest moral battle of modern times—the fight for the abolition of the color line."[30] Speakers including W. E. B. DuBois called attention to Oberlin's storied history and the community's important role to play in the struggle at hand. Oberlinites were still proud that in their community, if not their college, "the air of freedom and fair play pervades every home."[31]

Three years later, DuBois visited Oberlin again. This time, he penned a meditation on his experience in the pages of the *Crisis*, the journal of the NAACP, titled "A Winter Pilgrimage." "The race problem," he wrote, "is not one problem," and he had undertaken a tour of northern towns and cities to gauge the racial pulse of the land. DuBois offered brief commentary on several locales where old prejudices and new racial challenges confounded African Americans at every step. Yet in the Western Reserve of Ohio, the editor found a place altogether different. "Between these cities of past and present," he wrote, "lies the mystic city of the future, with its great cloud walls." It was, as his title suggested, holy ground that offered an alternative vision to an unstable world. It was Oberlin—isolated, hidden, and at least partially protected from the world by translucent heavenly veils.

DuBois's mystic city was one where thousands of black and white children studied, played, and walked together "on sacred ground, on ground long since consecrated to racial equality and hatred of caste and slavery." But the world, the present, had trespassed even into Oberlin, and DuBois charged the town with confronting it and subduing it so that the future would be one of its own making. The present, he explained, held "not only the problem of the treatment of ten million black folk elsewhere, but of the hundred colored boys and girls right there in Oberlin," and it presented them all with "a frank moral dilemma." When Oberlin's youth came from solid antislavery homes, it was only natural for them "to treat black men as men." But now, "coming . . . from a world that thinks God made a big mistake in ever creating black folk—coming from such social teaching, they hesitate."

Still, DuBois left Oberlin convinced that "the spirit of democracy is strong, the influence of the faculty is righteous," so much that he developed a "sense of seeing a mighty battle for righteousness, and a belief that somehow, sometime, justice would prevail." Yes, Oberlin's reputation informed this feeling, but equally important were the Oberlinites he met who embodied the spirit of that history. Here was a young black lawyer "who burned to awaken a sleeping city to its duties and rights" and a black surgeon whose "knife knows no color line." DuBois described meeting "a brown father, a yellow mother, the white pastor, and the white girl chum" in the parlor of Oberlin's black banker. Moreover, he reported that in Oberlin the owner of the chief bookstore was black, as was a leading member of a white club and the second-highest-ranking mechanic in the local motor factory.

"Therefore," he asked, "all is well?" In fact, all was not well by any stretch of the imagination. "Here are a climbing people," he concluded. "The hardiest and most talented and the pushing are literally forcing a way" in Oberlin, yet against them and all African Americans "the bonds of medievalism are drawn and ghettoes and sumptuary laws are encompassed by the color line." To DuBois, Oberlin had not only the ability but a long-ago accepted duty to keep up the fight, or, in Shipherd's plea, to not be conformed to the world.[32]

Oberlinites in the antebellum antislavery struggle had come as close as any to staying the encroachments of worldliness, but, like their perfectionism, it remained a constant striving rather than a final realization. Racial flare-ups (always made conspicuous by *where* they occurred) have continued to disturb Oberlin's utopian vision, but they are dealt with in a decidedly "Obie" (as residents now call themselves) fashion. When a bowling alley in town refused black patrons in 1933, white leaders of the campus Radical Club brought the case to court and helped rebuild the bridge between the community and college in Oberlin.[33] When black enrollment dropped to historic lows in the early 1960s, President Robert Kenneth Carr introduced initiatives that quadrupled it.[34] Like the abolitionist-missionaries of the 1830s who filled their winter breaks giving antislavery lectures or teaching black schools, Obies of the 1960s went south and helped found the Student Nonviolent Coordinating Committee (SNCC), participated in the 1961 Freedom Rides, took part in sit-ins, led voting drives in Mississippi, struggled through the Freedom Summer of 1964, and were threatened, jailed, and beaten for their efforts.[35] The students' common refrain was that "the ethical message" of Oberlin's abolitionist founders was an important motivating force.[36] In the opinion of a black alumnus from the civil rights era (who had returned as a professor years later), "One could identify a revitalization of the Oberlin tradition of equality and justice."[37]

And when Oberlin experienced a rash of racist, anti-Semitic, and homophobic vandalism as this book was going to press in the spring of 2013, the response was consistent with Oberlin's radical heritage: administrators cancelled classes so that students could participate in a teach-in at the Afrikan Heritage House, attend one of several solidarity rallies, and join in a campuswide convocation, "We Stand Together," in Finney Chapel. That day, instead of meeting in classrooms, Obies gathered around such campus landmarks as John Mercer Langston Hall, Keep Cottage, Fairchild House, and Tappan Square to discuss both Oberlin's past and its future. As community members proud of their heritage, their dialogue consciously engaged the founders.

In his State of the College address shortly after these incidents, Oberlin president Marvin Krislov admitted, "I don't know what Shipherd and Stewart would make of today's Oberlin." Their original vision of a "Christian utopia" entailing mandatory chapel attendance and the avoidance of strong and stimulating food and drink had long since given way to a modern and more secular academic community. Still, Krislov imagined that the founders "would be proud that their collegiate institute—and its mission—live on as one of the world's great colleges." Though the perpetrators were later exposed as Oberlin students attempting to provoke a reaction from the community, he stressed that "what stands out amidst these incidents is not the hatred" but Oberlin's passionate response. Rejecting accusations of overreaction, misguided progressivism, and race obsession (charges that echoed the refrains of Oberlin's nineteenth-century critics), Krislov reasoned that "our founders and Oberlin forebears would be pleased that the determination to do good in the world still resonates at the core of our institutional identity."[38]

Yet it was an Oberlin student—a young sophomore from Zimbabwe and mentor to underprivileged children in the community—who seemed most in touch with the original Oberlin spirit: "We are Oberlin. *Aluta Continua.* (The struggle continues.)"[39]

Notes

ABBREVIATIONS

- AMA   American Missionary Association Archives (microfilm), Amistad Research Center, Tulane University, New Orleans, La.
- BAP   *Black Abolitionists' Papers*
- BMCP   Betsey Mix Cowles Papers, Kent State University Archives and Special Collections, Kent, Ohio
- CGFP   Charles Grandison Finney Papers (microfilm), Oberlin College Archives, Oberlin, Ohio
- CTD   *Cleveland True Democrat*
- DDMP   Darlene Deahl Merrill Papers, RG 30/250, Oberlin College Archives, Oberlin, Ohio
- FDP   *Frederick Douglass' Paper*
- HCP   Henry Cowles Papers, RG 30/27, Oberlin College Archives, Oberlin, Ohio
- HWP   Hiram Wilson Papers, RG 30/112, Oberlin College Archives, Oberlin, Ohio
- JHFP   James Harris Fairchild Papers, RG 2/3, Oberlin College Archives, Oberlin, Ohio
- JJSP   John J. Shipherd Papers, Oberlin College Archives, Oberlin, Ohio
- JMP   James Monroe Papers, RG 30/22, Oberlin College Archives, Oberlin, Ohio
- LCN   *Lorain County News*
- LR   Letters Received at Oberlin College (microfilm), Oberlin College Archives, Oberlin, Ohio
- LTP   Lewis Tappan Papers, Library of Congress, Washington, D.C.
- NASS   *National Anti-Slavery Standard*
- NE   *The National Era*
- NS   *The North Star*
- NYE   *New York Evangelist*
- NYT   *New York Times*
- OCA   Oberlin College Archives
- OE   *Oberlin Evangelist*
- PP   Prudden Papers, RG 30/205, Oberlin College Archives, Oberlin, Ohio
- RSFP   Robert S. Fletcher Papers, RG 30/24, Oberlin College Archives, Oberlin, Ohio
- SPCP   Salmon P. Chase Papers (microfilm), Library of Congress, Washington, D.C.
- TKO   "Territorial Kansas Online, 1854–1861," Kansas State Historical Society, www.territorialkansasonline.org

INTRODUCTION

1. *Ohio Statesman*, February 9, 1842.

2. Ibid., December 13, 1842; *Cleveland Daily Herald*, December 12, 1842; Harrold, *Border War*, 92.

3. *Ohio Statesman*, December 13, 1842.

4. Ibid.; *Independent Treasury*, October 5, 1842.

5. See Martineau, *Martyr Age*.

6. Morris, *Origins of the Civil Rights Movement*, 40.

7. Oberlin's founders did not intend for there to be any separation between the Oberlin colony and the Oberlin Institute. As an integral part of the colonists' mission, they would be expected to assist and be involved in the school's operation just as they would be counted upon to provide for the well-being of each other and to praise God in their religious exercises. To be sure, "Oberlin" would refer to a physical place, but that place would be so organized and controlled by the founders' ethos that they often referred to the entire scheme—community, school, and mission—as "Oberlin." In the early years, there was no attempt to specify what one meant by "Oberlin"; it stood for everything at once. Even after the school and the town developed degrees of distinctiveness, residents and students remained inconsistent in their usage of the term.

8. See OE, August 15, 1855; Tyler, *Freedom's Ferment*, 529–30; Fradin, *Bound for the North Star*, 112; and Riley, *Prairie Voices*, 224.

9. Geoffrey Blodgett notes that in the four major written accounts of Oberlin's history, the emphasis in the story depends on the background of the author. For Oberlin president James Fairchild, writing in 1883, the arrival of the Lane students in 1835 and the growth in student population is most important. D. L. Leonard, a clergyman writing in 1898, stressed the arrival of Finney and the establishment of the Theological Department. Businessman Wilbur Phillips, writing in 1833, stressed the financial deal that accompanied Finney and the Lane Rebels. Robert Fletcher, an Oberlin professor writing in the 1940s, stressed the connection between reform and academic freedom. Only recently has the admission of African Americans merited significant attention. See Blodgett, *Oberlin History*, 17.

10. McIlwraith and Muller, *North America*, 203.

11. A significant amount of recent scholarly work on abolition continues to discuss the movement as if there was little or no activity west of the Alleghenies. See Magdol, *Anti-Slavery Rank and File*; Fanuzzi, *Abolition's Public Sphere*; Cumbler, *From Abolition to Rights for All*; Dixon, *Perfecting the Family*; and Aptheker, *Abolitionism*. Even the more recent trend among historians of antislavery to highlight the role of African Americans has frequently given the impression that the vitality of the abolitionist movement was centered in the East. See Quarles, *Black Abolitionists*; Goodman, *Of One Blood*; Jacobs, *Courage and Conscience*; Bacon, *But One Race*; Levecq, *Slavery and Sentiment*; and Grover, *Fugitive's Gibraltar*. A few historians, often in biographical works, have acknowledged the importance of the West in the abolitionist movement. See Washington, *Sojourner Truth's America*; Sterling, *Ahead of Her Time*; Harrold, *Gamaliel Bailey and Antislavery Union*; Harrold, *Border War*; and Robertson, *Hearts Beating for Liberty*.

12. See Sinha, "Did the Abolitionists Cause the Civil War?," 102. See also Stauffer, *Black Hearts of Men*, and Robertson, *Hearts Beating for Liberty*.

13. Delbanco, *Abolitionist Imagination*, 6.

14. See Kraditor, *Means and Ends in American Abolitionism*; Mayer, *All on Fire*; Walters, *Antislavery Appeal*; Yellin and Van Horne, *Abolitionist Sisterhood*, 58–59; Blackett, *Building an Antislavery Wall*, x; Stewart, *Abolitionist Politics*, 17; and Fogel, *Without Consent or Contract*, 324. Many historians have spent much of their efforts debating this factionalism. Consider Barnes, *Antislavery Impulse*; Kraditor, *Means and Ends in American Abolitionism*; Wyatt-Brown, *Lewis Tappan*, and Blue, *No Taint of Compromise*.

15. Walters, *Antislavery Appeal*, 4.

16. See Young, *Bearing Witness against Sin*, and Smith, *Liberty and Free Soil Parties*, 13–14.

17. *Cincinnati Weekly Herald and Philanthropist*, July 2, 1845. See also *Philanthropist*, June 15, November 12, 1842; February 8, July 5, 1843; August 9, 1843; and Harrold, *Gamaliel Bailey and Antislavery Union*, 44.

18. "Remarks of Ex-President Finney," in *Dedication of Council Hall*, 23.

CHAPTER ONE

1. Finney, *Memoirs*, 78–79; Nevins, *Anxious Bench*, 117.

2. Finney himself called it "the greatest revival of religion throughout the land that this country had ever witnessed." See Finney, *Memoirs*, and Johnson, *A Shopkeeper's Millennium*, 3–14.

3. Robert Stanton to Charles Grandison Finney, January 12, 1872, CGFP, roll 6; *Evangelical Magazine and Gospel Advocate*, January 22, January 29, October 15, 1831; Johnson, *Shopkeeper's Millennium*, 95–115.

4. Parsons, *History of Rochester Presbytery*, 244; O'Reilly, *Settlement in the West*, 279; Fletcher, *History of Oberlin College*, 18–19.

5. The millennium was to be a thousand-year period where sin and Satan were banished from the Earth. Premillennialists believed that Christ's sudden Second Coming would precede this period. Revivalists like Finney had more optimism in human potential and believed that the Second Coming would follow rather than precede God's reign on Earth (thus they were often called "post-millennialists"). Christians, they believed, could speed the arrival of the millennium by making converts and ridding the world of all sin. This is especially noteworthy since the optimism expressed by these men and women inspired them to combine evangelicalism and social reform (including antislavery) in their attempt to cleanse the world. See Thomas, "Romantic Reform in America"; Barkun, *Crucible of the Millennium*, 24–25; and Cross, *Burned-Over District*.

6. John Shipherd to Fayette Shipherd, October 15, 1830, RSFP, Box 8, Folder 6; John Shipherd to Charles Grandison Finney, March 14, 1831, CGFP, roll 2; Fletcher, *History of Oberlin College*, 18–19, 67–68.

7. John Shipherd to Zebulon Shipherd, May 11, 1830, JJSP, microfilm; Fletcher, *History of Oberlin College*, 67.

8. See Mackin, *Americans and Their Land*, 73–88, and Allen, *Republic in Time*, 34–41.

9. Davis, *Slavery and Human Progress*, 128; Abzug, *Cosmos Crumbling*, 15.

10. Beecher, *Plea for the West*, 9–11.

11. Unless otherwise noted, details on the early life of Shipherd are drawn from the manuscript Esther Shipherd, "A Sketch of the Life and Labors of John J. Shipherd," n.d., JJSP, Box 4.

12. John Shipherd to Fayette Shipherd, April 7, 1829, RSFP, Box 8, Folder 4; Fletcher, *History of Oberlin College*, 66–67.

13. John Shipherd to Zebulon Shipherd, May 11, 1830, JJSP, microfilm; John Shipherd to James Shipherd, November 8, 1830, RSFP, Box 14, Folder 6; Knight and Commons, *History of Higher Education in Ohio*, 55.

14. *Quarterly Register of the American Education Society* 3 (Boston, 1831): 315; *American Tract Magazine for the Year 1832* 7 (New York, 1832): 60; *American Quarterly Register* 8 (Boston, 1836): 312; Knight and Commons, *History of Higher Education in Ohio*, 55.

15. James Boyle and Laura Boyle to Charles Grandison Finney, November 30, 1831, CGFP; Fletcher, *History of Oberlin College*, 76; Padgett, "Evangelicals Divided," 262.

16. John Shipherd to Charles Grandison Finney, March 14, 1831, CGFP, roll 3.

17. NYE, June 18, 1831.

18. John Shipherd to Fayette Shipherd, July 28, 1831, RSFP, Box 8, Folder 7.

19. Fletcher, *History of Oberlin College*, 81.

20. John Shipherd to Zebulon Shipherd, December 1, 1831, JJSP, microfilm; Atwood, "Intimate Life Story of Philo Penfield Stewart," 426.

21. Knight and Commons, *History of Higher Education in Ohio*, 56.

22. *American Quarterly Register* 8 (Boston, 1836): 312; John Shipherd to Fayette Shipherd, August 13, 1832, JJSP, Box 4; John Shipherd to Zebulon Shipherd, August 6, 1832, reprinted in Fairchild, *Oberlin*, 15–16.

23. John Shipherd to Zebulon Shipherd, August 6, 1832, reprinted in Fairchild, *Oberlin*, 15–16.

24. John Shipherd to Fayette Shipherd, August 13, 1832, JJSP, Box 4; John Shipherd to Zebulon Shipherd, August 6, 1832, reprinted in Fairchild, *Oberlin*, 15–16.

25. *American Quarterly Register* 8 (Boston, 1836): 312.

26. John Shipherd to Fayette Shipherd, August 13, 1832, JJSP, Box 4; John Shipherd to Zebulon Shipherd, August 6, 1832, reprinted in Fairchild, *Oberlin*, 15–16; "Covenant of the Oberlin Colony," RG 21, Oberlin File, Series 6, Box 1, OCA; W. S. Edwards to J. F. Scoville, December 17, 1833, RSFP, Box 7, Folder 5; Phillips, *Oberlin Colony*, 13–14, 17; Atwood, "Intimate Life Story of Philo Penfield Stewart," 432.

27. John Shipherd to Fayette Shipherd, August 13, 1832, JJSP, Box 4; John Shipherd to Zebulon Shipherd, August 6, 1832, reprinted in Fairchild, *Oberlin*, 15–16; *American Quarterly Register* 3 (Boston, 1836): 312; NYE, October 1, 1836; Langston, *From the Virginia Plantation*, 97–98; W. S. Edwards to J. F. Scoville, December 17, 1833, RSFP, Box 7, Folder 5.

28. John Shipherd to Zebulon Shipherd, August 6, 1832, reprinted in Fairchild, *Oberlin*, 15–16; Knight and Commons, *History of Higher Education in Ohio*, 66.

29. Eliphalet Redington to John Shipherd, May 20, 1833, LR, roll 1; Philo Stewart to John Shipherd, May 21, 1833, RSFP, Box 14, Folder 7; Philo Stewart to John Shipherd, May 25, 1833, LR, roll 1.

30. Peter Pease et al. to John Shipherd, June 11, 1833, RSFP, Box 9, Folder 2; Marianne Dascomb to Home Friends, May 24, 1834, in Fairchild, *Oberlin*, app., 329–33.

31. Phillips, *Oberlin Colony*, 65; Atwood, "Intimate Life Story of Philo Penfield Stewart," 433.

32. Philo Stewart to John Shipherd, May 25, 1833, LR, roll 1.

33. NYE, September 7, 1833; *New York Observer and Chronicle*, August 24, 1833; *Boston Recorder*, August 14, 1833; *Religious Intelligencer*, September 7, 1833; *Evangelical Magazine and Gospel Advocate*, May 3, 1834.

34. Harmon Kingsbury to John Shipherd, July 10, 14, 1834, LR, roll 1. See also Phillips, *Oberlin Colony*, 70.

35. John Shipherd and Esther Shipherd to Fayette Shipherd, June 14, 1834, JJSP, Box 4.

36. Hosford, *Father Shipherd's Magna Charta*, 18.

37. Fletcher, *History of Oberlin College*, 140.

38. Minutes of the Oberlin College Board of Trustees, September 23, 1834, roll 1, OCA.

39. W. Stafford to Charles Grandison Finney, December 31, 1827, CGFP, roll 1. See also Anson Phelps to Charles Grandison Finney, January 7, 1828, July 7, 1828, CGFP, roll 1; Zephaniah Platt to Charles Grandison Finney, August 6, 1828, CGFP, roll 1; and Arthur Tappan to Charles Grandison Finney, September 25, 1828, CGFP, roll 1.

40. Lewis Tappan to Charles Grandison Finney, March 16, 1832, CGFP, roll 3.

41. Ibid., March 22, 1832.

42. Finney, *Memoirs*, 362.

43. Ibid.

44. S. A. to Joshua Leavitt, n.d., in NYE, November 8, 1834.

45. See NYE, November 8, 1834; *Ohio Observer*, November 27, 1834; Theodore Dwight Weld to Lewis Tappan, November 17, 1835, in Weld, *Letters*, 243–44; Finney, *Lectures on Revivals of Religion*, 277–78; and Tappan, "Chronological Resume," 1834, LTP.

46. Finney, *Lectures on Revivals of Religion*, 277.

47. Birney, *Letter on Colonization*, 20; Sturge, *Visit to the United States in 1841*, cxiii; Tappan, *Life of Arthur Tappan*, 230–31; Staudenraus, *African Colonization Movement*, 229; Goodman, *Of One Blood*, 11–22.

48. Garrison, *Thoughts on African Colonization*, 9.

49. Ibid., 12.

50. Ibid., 16.

51. Mayer, *All on Fire*, 65–70.

52. *Liberator*, January 1, 1831.

53. May, *Memoir*, 148.

54. The idea of perfectionism was at least as old as Christianity itself. In its modern sense, "perfectionism" as a doctrine originated with John Wesley and the bishops he sent to America in the 1760s–80s. Wesley described the striving for perfectionism as a process by which the "dispositions of the heart" are changed, where the love for holy things grows, and where the temptation of evil declines. There were also traces of perfectionism in the early Baptist, Quaker, and Unitarian traditions. Finney expanded these ideas in the late 1820s and early 1830s. Once sinners became aware of their sin, he said, it was his or her obligation to immediately repent. True repentance encouraged one to constantly choose good over evil. Finneyites called this perfectionist process of self-mastery of sinful desires "sanctification." As individuals throughout society committed themselves to striving for a sanctified life, that conformity to God's laws would eventually become pervasive, and the millennium would commence. Perfectionism would become the single most important concept espoused by abolitionists in the decades to come, though it would be interpreted in different ways. See Kyle, *Evangelicalism*, 71–74; Strong, *Perfectionist Politics*, 26–29; and Cross, *Burned-Over District*, 238–51.

55. Barnes, *Antislavery Impulse*, 35–36; Goodman, *Of One Blood*, 11–22.

56. NYE, September 10, 1831, March 10, 1832.

57. NYE, May 3, 1834.

58. Finney, *Lectures on Systematic Theology*, 150–73, 174–87.

59. *Liberator*, July 13, 1833.

60. Ibid., October 12, 19, November 2, 23, 1833; Hone, *Diary*, 79–80; Hambrick-Stowe, *Charles G. Finney*, 143; Richards, *Gentlemen of Property and Standing*, 30–31. A young William Howard Day, who, in 1847, would become Oberlin's third African American graduate, was

rescued from the mob by his mother and received his first taste of anti-abolitionist violence that day. See Blackett, *Beating against the Barriers*, 288.

61. Finney, *Memoirs*, 362.

62. Though the efforts of colonizationist editors to whip up violent opposition to the abolitionists, growing unrest among white workers who were having to compete with African Americans for jobs, and bare racism also contributed to the New York City riots of 1834–35, the Tappans' "amalgamation" of the Chatham Street choir had also caused an uproar.

63. See Theodore Dwight Weld to Lewis Tappan, April 5, 1836, in Weld, *Letters*, 1:286–89. See also Sterling, *Ahead of her Time*, 46; Wyatt-Brown, *Lewis Tappan*, 177–78; Emerson and Smith, *Divided by Faith*, 32–34; and Theodore Dwight Weld to Lewis Tappan, November 17, 1835, in Weld, *Letters*, 1:243–44.

64. See OE, March 13, 1839.

65. Lewis Tappan, it should be noted, had a habit of accusing other abolitionists of racism and remaining blind to his own prejudices. He accused Weld, who was easily one of the most avowed egalitarians in the movement, of racial prejudice in 1836, to which Weld had to reply, "Really, after so long a time I must forsooth solemnly avow my principles on this subject!" Finney and other victims of Lewis Tappan's caprice also pointed to the glaring fact that the Tappans never hired African Americans as employees in their mercantile business in New York City. See Finney to Arthur Tappan, April 30, 1836, CGFP; Theodore Dwight Weld to Lewis Tappan, March 9, 15, 1836, in Weld, *Letters*, 1:270–77; Tappan, *Life of Arthur Tappan*, 250–41; and Richards, *Gentlemen of Property and Standing*, 121.

66. Theodore Dwight Weld to Lewis Tappan, March 9, 15, 1836, in Weld, *Letters*, 1:270–77. Finney later drew criticism for suggesting in an antislavery address that slavery was a "dispensation of providence." Responding to criticism from Oberlin, he explained that he meant that it would be better to train African Americans in Christian forgiveness than "to stimulate their resentment" against wrongs done to them. See Cheek and Cheek, *John Mercer Langston*, 288.

67. Charles Grandison Finney to Theodore Dwight Weld, July 21, 1836, in Weld, *Letters*, 1:318–19; Essig, "Lord's Free Man," 32.

68. Finney, *Lectures to Professing Christians*, 55.

69. Lewis Tappan to Mrs. Finney, June 7, 1834, LTP, roll 6.

70. Finney, *Memoirs*, 371–73; Hambrick-Stowe, *Charles G. Finney*, 144–45.

71. *First Annual Report of the Oberlin Collegiate Institute*, 1; Fletcher, *History of Oberlin College*, 167.

72. John Shipherd to Fayette Shipherd, November 23, 1834, LR, roll 2; John Shipherd to Nathan Fletcher, November 27, 1834, LR, roll 1; John Shipherd to John Keep, December 13, 1834, JJSP, microfilm; Mahan, *Autobiography*, 191.

73. Mahan, *Autobiography*, 190.

74. Thomas, *Theodore Weld*, 16.

75. Elizur Wright Jr. to Theodore Dwight Weld, February 20, 1834, in Weld, *Letters*, 1:128–30; Goodman, "Manual Labor Movement," 355.

76. NYE, March 22, April 5, 1834; Theodore Dwight Weld to James Hall, May 20, 1834, in Weld, *Letters*, 1:137–47; Thome, *Debate at Lane Seminary*, 1–15; Lesick, *Lane Rebels*, 77–79; Elizur Wright to Theodore Dwight Weld, November 2, 1833, in Weld, *Letters*, 1:119; Stanton, *Random Recollections*, 48.

77. Finney, *Memoirs*, 378–80; Cochran, *Charles Grandison Finney Memorial Address*, 86; Lesick, *Lane Rebels*, 72.

78. Barnes, *Anti-Slavery Impulse*, 67.

79. NYE, May 23, 1835.

80. *Anti-Slavery Record* 2, no. 6 (June 1836): 70; NYE, August 6, 1836.

81. NYE, August 6, 1836. Only one person dared vote in favor of colonization, likely a son of an ACS agent.

82. NYE, March 22, April 5, 1834; Lyman, "Lane Seminary Rebels," 62; Johnson, *Garrison and His Times*, 169.

83. Theodore Dwight Weld to Lewis Tappan, March 18, 1834, in Weld, *Letters*, 1:132–35; Abzug, *Passionate Liberator*, 94; Thomas, *Theodore Weld*, 72.

84. They also busied themselves in the Underground Railroad by spiriting self-emancipating bondsmen between "stations." Huntington Lyman wrote that his horse "might be taken without question by any brother who had on hand 'Business of Egypt,'" a contemporary designation for the Underground Railroad. Lyman remembered later that his horse "was hard used." See Lyman, "Lane Seminary Rebels," 66–67, and Thomas, *Theodore Weld*, 78.

85. See Rodabaugh, "Negro in Ohio," 12.

86. Beecher, *Autobiography*, 325, 327; Henry Stanton and James Mott to James Thome, September 11, 1834, RG 16/5/3, Autograph File, OCA.

87. Mahan, *Autobiography*, 173.

88. Beecher, *Autobiography*, 325, 327; Henry Stanton and James Mott to James Thome, September 11, 1834, RG 16/5/3, Autograph File, OCA. See also Mahan, *Autobiography*, 172–86.

89. Beecher, *Autobiography*, 325–32; Stanton, *Random Recollections*, 48; Lane Seminary Trustees Minutes, August 20, 1834, RSFP, Box 12, Folder 5; Tappan, *Life of Arthur Tappan*, 226–28.

90. Lyman, "Lane Seminary Rebels," 65–66.

91. John Shipherd to John Keep, December 13, 1834, JJSP, microfilm.

92. Mahan, *Autobiography*, 192–93; Huntington Lyman and Henry Stanton to Theodore Dwight Weld, January 22, 1835, in Weld, *Letters*, 1:201–3; Hambrick-Stowe, *Charles G. Finney*, 160.

93. John Shipherd to Nathan Fletcher, December 15, 1834, in Fairchild, *Oberlin*, 55.

94. Ibid.

95. Fairchild, *Oberlin*, 56.

96. Ibid.

97. Nathan Fletcher, "Critical Letters #3," RG 7/1/3, Office of the Treasurer, Box 4, OCA.

98. "We, Students of O.C. Institute . . . ," December 31, 1834, RSFP, Box 7, Folder 8. Only six female students voted in the affirmative, though the men polled favored the proposition by three votes. Fairchild recalled that there were three or four men among the students who advocated immediate emancipation, but the majority were colonizationists. See Fairchild, "A Sketch of the Anti-Slavery History of Oberlin," RG 2/3, JHFP, Box 9.

99. Rodabaugh, "Negro in Ohio," 16; Quillin, *Color Line in Ohio*, 13–17, 22–23.

100. The same law and another in 1831 exempted African Americans from paying taxes for common schools, in effect prohibiting them from being educated in any schools not

totally organized, taught, and financed by themselves. See Malvin, *Autobiography*, 11–12, and Finkelman, "Race, Slavery, and Law," 760–61.

101. Malvin, *Autobiography*, 12.

102. Bigglestone, *They Stopped in Oberlin*, xv.

103. Weisenburger, *Passing of the Frontier*, 42.

104. Quillin, *Color Line in Ohio*, 31–32; Weisenburger, *Passing of the Frontier*, 42; Richards, *Gentlemen of Property and Standing*, 34–35; Taylor, *Frontiers of Freedom*, 50–79.

105. Quillin, *Color Line in Ohio*, 55–56.

106. As late as 1850, the African American population of the entire Western Reserve numbered but 1,331, far smaller than many single counties in the South. Weisenburger, *Passing of the Frontier*, 365–66.

107. Ibid., 366.

108. Cutler, *History of Western Reserve College*, 24–31; Johnson, *William Lloyd Garrison and His Times*, 141–44; Elizur Wright to Theodore Dwight Weld, February 1, 1833, in Weld, *Letters*, 1:101–5; Fletcher, *Oberlin College*, 144–45.

109. *Liberator*, September 21, 1833.

110. Fletcher, *Oberlin College*, 146.

111. Ibid.

112. John Shipherd to Fayette Shipherd, December 22, 1834, RSFP, Box 9, Folder 3; John Shipherd to Nathan Fletcher, December 15, 1834, LR.

113. William Allan to Theodore Dwight Weld, January 8, 1835, in Weld, *Letters*, 1:189–90. Finney was often criticized by more conservative theologians for his unorthodox revival methods and because of his dismissal of the idea of original sin and belief that humans were able to make a personal decision for Christ rather than waiting powerlessly for the grace of God.

114. James Thome to Theodore Dwight Weld, January 8, 1835, in ibid., 190–91.

115. Henry Stanton and George Whipple to Charles Grandison Finney, January 10, 1835, CGFP, roll 3.

116. Mahan, *Autobiography*, 193.

117. Charles Grandison Finney to Elizabeth Finney, November 10, 1834, CGFP, roll 3.

118. Mahan, *Autobiography*, 193; John Shipherd, pastoral letter, January 27, 1835, in Fairchild, *Oberlin*, appendix, 337–46; Arthur Tappan to John Shipherd, May 5, 1835, RSFP, Box 7, Folder 8; Arthur Tappan to John Shipherd, July 23, 1835, LR, roll 2; John Shipherd to the Trustees of the Oberlin Collegiate Institute, January 19, 1835, RSFP, Box 15, Folder 6.

119. Mahan, *Autobiography*, 194.

120. Charles Grandison Finney to Henry Stanton and George Whipple, January 10, 18, 1835, LR, roll 2.

121. Finney, *Memoirs*, 387.

122. John Morgan to Charles Grandison Finney, January 13, 1835, CGFP, roll 3; John Shipherd, pastoral letter, January 27, 1835, in Fairchild, *Oberlin*, appendix, 337–46; Ellsworth, "Oberlin and the Anti-Slavery Movement," 14 n. 24. In 1807, Dartmouth had admitted an African American student, and at Amherst and Bowdoin, respectively, in 1826, Edward Jones and John Russwurm had become the first African American college graduates.

123. Charles Grandison Finney to Lewis Tappan, n.d., in Tappan, *Life of Arthur Tappan*, 240–41.

124. Ellsworth, "Oberlin and the Anti-Slavery Movement," 23.

125. John Shipherd, pastoral letter, January 27, 1835, in Fairchild, *Oberlin*, appendix, 337–46.
126. Ibid. See also James Fairchild, "A Sketch of the Anti-Slavery History of Oberlin," RG 2/3, JHFP, Box 9.
127. John Shipherd, pastoral letter, January 27, 1835, in Fairchild, *Oberlin*, appendix, 337–46.
128. Ibid.
129. Ibid.
130. John Shipherd to Charles Grandison Finney, February 10, 1835, JJSP, microfilm.
131. John Keep to Philo Stewart, Peter Pindar Pease, and Nathan Fletcher, January 19 (indexed as January 29), 1835, LR, roll 2.
132. Ibid.; Nathan Fletcher, "Critical Letters #3," RG 7/1/3, Office of the Treasurer, Box 4, OCA; John Keep to Charles Grandison Finney, March 10, 1835, CGFP, roll 3; Charles Grandison Finney to Lewis Tappan, n.d., in Tappan, *Life of Arthur Tappan*, 240–41; Esther Shipherd to William Patton, September 1, 1875, in Patton, *Prayer and Its Remarkable Answers*, 176–77.
133. John Keep to Charles Grandison Finney, March 10, 1835, CGFP; John Shipherd to Fayette Shipherd, May 17, 1835, JJSP, Box 4.
134. John Keep to Theodore Dwight Weld, October 20, 1834, in Weld, *Letters*, 1:173–74.
135. John Keep to Charles Grandison Finney, March 10, 1835, RSFP, Box 6, Folder 3; Esther Shipherd to William Patton, September 1, 1875, in Patton, *Prayer and Its Remarkable Answers*, 176–77.
136. Oberlin Trustee Minutes, February 9, 1835, RSFP, Box 15, Folder 7; John Keep to Charles Grandison Finney, February 12, 1835, RSFP, Box 6, Folder 3; Oberlin Trustee Minutes, February 9, 1835, RSFP, Box 15, Folder 7; Helen Keep, "John Keep and His Descendants," n.d., 8, RSFP, Box 7, Folder 1.
137. Charles Grandison Finney to Henry Stanton and George Whipple, January 18, 1835, CGFP; Charles Grandison Finney to the Board of Trustees of the Oberlin Collegiate Institute, June 30, 1835, CGFP; Finney, *Memoirs*, 380. For Oberlin's resolution, see John Keep to Charles Grandison Finney, February 12, 1835, CGFP, roll 3.
138. John Keep to Charles Grandison Finney, March 10, 1835, CGFP, roll 3, OCA; Benjamin Woodbury to John Shipherd, March 26, 1835, RSFP, Box 14, Folder 8.
139. Fairchild, *Oberlin*, 348; Shumway and Brower, *Oberliniana*, 17.
140. *Proceedings of the Ohio Anti-Slavery Convention*, 51.
141. Ibid., 6–8; *Liberator*, May 16, 1835.
142. "Minutes of Meeting in Relation to Oberlin Ins. held Apr. 8, 1835 with a Subn. List," RG 16/5/3, Autograph File, OCA.
143. John Shipherd to Fayette Shipherd, October 9, 1835, JJSP, microfilm; Arthur Tappan to Levi Burnell, October 6, 1835, RSFP, Box 14, Folder 7; Arthur Tappan to John Shipherd, October 1, 1835, RSFP, Box 14, Folder 7; Tappan, *Life of Arthur Tappan*, 238; Delia Finn to Richard Finn, August 21, 1835, RSFP, Box 3, Folder 3; *Liberator*, August 30, 1839; Arthur Tappan to John Shipherd, June 10, 1835, RSFP, Box 7, Folder 8.
144. T. P. Bigelow to Asa Mahan, August 23, 1836, LR, roll 3; *Liberator*, June 27, July 11, 1835.
145. Oberlin Trustee Minutes, January 1, April 6, May 28, November 23, 1835, March 8, 1836, RSFP, Box 15, Folder 7; Alvan Stewart to Levi Burnell, March 23, 1836, LR, roll 3; *General Catalogue of Oberlin College*, int.121–int.184. After 1836, almost all new faculty were drawn

directly from the growing number of Oberlin Institute alumni, perhaps to assure that the peculiar beliefs of "Oberlin" would continue with minimal outside influences. See Fletcher, "Against the Consensus," 111.

146. Nathan Fletcher to the Trustees of the Oberlin Collegiate Institute, August 18, 1836, LR, roll 3.

147. John Shipherd to Fayette Shipherd, April 1, 1835, JJSP, Box 4.

148. John Shipherd to Joshua Leavitt, July 6, 1835, in NYE, July 18, 1835; *Ohio Observer*, July 9, 1835; "Commencement, 1835," RG 0, College General Records, Series 15, Box 1, OCA; Fairchild, *Oberlin*, 73–74; Finney, *Memoirs*, 384.

149. John Shipherd to Joshua Leavitt, July 6, 1835, in NYE, July 18, 1835. Indeed, the Oberlin tent made its appearances at many antislavery meetings over the next few decades. See *Liberator*, November 19, 1847, June 4, 1852.

150. John Shipherd to Joshua Leavitt, July 6, 1835, in NYE, July 18, 1835.

151. *Liberator*, August 30, 1839.

152. Lord, *History of Dartmouth College*, 251; Thomas, *Theodore Weld*, 87; Bendroth, *School of the Church*, 71.

153. J. W. Davis to Theodore Dwight Weld, February 22, 1832, in Weld, *Letters*, 1:266–67; Tyler, *History of Amherst College*, 90–92; Carpenter and Morehouse, *History of the Town of Amherst*, 172–73; Williams, *History of Colgate University*, 69; Fletcher, *History of Oberlin College*, 184; Van Vuget, *British Buckeyes*, 192–93; Finke, *Images of America*, 24.

154. *Western Monthly Magazine* 5 (April 1836): 224.

155. NYE, January 16, April 2, 1836; John Keep to Gerrit Smith, October 14, 1836, RSFP, Box 19; *General Catalogue of Oberlin College*, int.117. Oberlin enrolled 44 students in the winter of 1833, 101 in 1834, and 276 in 1835.

156. James Dascomb and Marianne Dascomb to "Dear Mother," April 7, 1835, in Fairchild, *Oberlin*, appendix, 348–53.

157. Hiram Wilson to Hamilton Hill, December 13, 1852, LR, roll 13; Madden and Hamilton, *Freedom and Grace*, 55, 230 n. 6.

158. James Dascomb and Marianne Dascomb to "Dear Mother," April 7, 1835, in Fairchild, *Oberlin*, appendix, 348–53; *Liberator*, August 30, 1839; C. G. Fairchild, "Slab Hall," *Jubilee Notes*, March 1883, 5–6; Leonard, *Story of Oberlin*, 413–14.

159. Philo Stewart to William Dawes, February 13, 1839, LR, roll 6; NYE, January 16, April 2, 1836; John Keep to Gerrit Smith, October 14, 1836, RSFP, Box 19; Theodore Dwight Weld to Lewis Tappan, November 17, 1835, in Weld, *Letters*, 1:242–45; Fletcher, *History of Oberlin College*, 186–90.

160. NYE, January 16, April 2, 1836; Hiram Wilson to Hamilton Hill, December 13, 1852, LR, roll 13.

161. P. D. Adams to Edna Adams, July 31, 1835, RSFP, Box 7, Folder 5.

162. *Ohio Observer*, April 9, 1835.

CHAPTER TWO

1. Elizabeth Pease to Rachel Savoriry, n.d. (1839), DDMP, acc. 1995/142, Box 1, Folder 1.

2. Shipherd and many of the Lane Rebels had been converted in one or another of Finney's New York revivals, as had Oberlin Institute secretary Levi Burnell and treasurer

Jabez Burrell, who would go on to organize Oberlin's Sheffield satellite campus. Mahan and Shipherd had also assisted Finney in his revival efforts. See Fletcher, *History of Oberlin College*, 179–86, and James Dascomb to "Dear Mother," April 7, 1835, RSFP, Box 5, Folder 11.

3. Finney, *Memoirs*, 389.

4. Ballentine, *Oberlin Jubilee*, 309; OE, March 27, 1839.

5. Fairchild, *Historical Sketch of Oberlin College*, 29.

6. James Fairchild, "The True Character of Slavery, As It Existed in This Country," n.d., JHFP, Series 8, Box 9.

7. Holley, *Life for Liberty*, 58; FDP, June 3, 1852.

8. *University Quarterly* 1 (January 1860): 181; Cheek and Cheek, *John Mercer Langston*, 93.

9. Not every student and colonist signed their names to the constitution. However, the absence of known abolitionists such as Edward Weed, John Keep, and Levi Burnell, among others, suggests that the absence of one's name did not necessarily mean that one did not agree with the aims of the society or attend meetings. See "Constitution of the Oberlin Anti-Slavery Society," RG 16/5/3, Autograph File, Document 146, OCA; and *Ohio Observer*, November 27, 1834.

10. Some Oberlin abolitionists even signed their names more than once. See *Liberator*, April 12, 1834, for the Lane document.

11. "Constitution of the Oberlin Anti-Slavery Society," RG 16/5/3, Autograph File, Document 146, OCA.

12. Ibid.

13. RG 31/4/1, Oberlin Society Records, Box 1, OCA. The First Church in Oberlin would be a consistent voice against slavery. In 1846, the church adopted a report written by Thome, Morgan, James Dascomb, James Fairchild, and Hudson that declared that it would withhold all fellowship from "slaveholders or with those who lend their influence to sustain slavery." Through the end of the Civil War, the church issued letters to its members who were transferring to a different congregation that read in part, "This certificate is not intended as a recommendation to any church that sanctions or tolerates slaveholding." See LCN, July 11, 1866.

14. Dayton, *Discovering an Evangelical Heritage*, 41; OE, December 12, 1839.

15. Elizur Wright Jr. to Theodore Dwight Weld, June 10, November 5, 1835, January 22, 1836, in Weld, *Letters*, 1:225–26, 240–42, 254–56.

16. Elizur Wright Jr. to Theodore Dwight Weld, July 16, 1835, in ibid., 227–28.

17. Theodore Dwight Weld to Lewis Tappan, November 17, 1835, in ibid., 242–45.

18. OE, July 16, 1856.

19. Fairchild, *Oberlin*, 75.

20. Theodore Dwight Weld to Lewis Tappan, November 17, 1835, in Weld, *Letters*, 1:242–45.

21. OE, July 16, 1856.

22. Ibid.

23. Lyman, "Lane Seminary Rebels," 67; Lyman to J. T. Frost, January 28, 1887, Huntington Lyman Alumni File, OCA.

24. John Alvord to Theodore Dwight Weld, February 9, 1836, in Weld, *Letters*, 1:259–61; James Thome to Theodore Dwight Weld, February 9, 1836, in ibid., 261–62.

25. Mayo Smith to Henry Cowles, November 1, 1836, LR, roll 3.

26. Thomas, Theodore Weld, 105.

27. Theodore Dwight Weld to Elizur Wright Jr., March 2, 1835, in Weld, Letters, 1:205–8; Thomas, Theodore Weld, 100–103.

28. James Thome and John Alvord to Theodore Dwight Weld, February 9, 1836, in Weld, Letters, 1:256–62; Sereno Streeter to Theodore Dwight Weld, March 15, 1836, in ibid., 277–79; James Thome to Theodore Dwight Weld, March 31, 1836, in ibid., 281–86; Hambrick-Stowe, Charles G. Finney, 35.

29. Edward Weed to Gamaliel Bailey, November 21, 1836, in Philanthropist, December 16, 1836.

30. Elizur Wright Jr. to Theodore Dwight Weld, November 18, 1835, in Weld, Letters, 1:245–46.

31. Most Ohioans would not have local abolitionist papers like the Cincinnati Philanthropist and would have only read about abolitionists like Garrison in more critical and conservative journals. It would not be until an 1839 abolitionist convention in Cleveland that many Ohioans would have their first direct encounter with eastern abolitionist leaders. See Philanthropist, November 5, 1839.

32. Liberator, December 15, 1832; Weld, Letters, 1:viii; Nerone, Violence against the Press, 89; Barnes, Anti-Slavery Impulse, 50.

33. Philadelphia Album, n.d., in Liberator, October 15, 1831.

34. Zion's Herald, July 1, 1835.

35. Elizur Wright Jr. to Theodore Dwight Weld, September 5, 1833, in Weld, Letters, 1:114–17.

36. James Thome to Theodore Dwight Weld, February 9, 1836, in ibid., 256–59.

37. Ibid.

38. See Thome, Debate at Lane Seminary, 7–11.

39. James Thome to Theodore Dwight Weld, February 9, 1836, in Weld, Letters, 1:256–59.

40. See Newman, Transformation of American Abolitionism, 9.

41. Register of Debates . . . of the Twenty Fourth Congress, 687.

42. Cormany, "Ohio's Abolitionist Campaign," 15.

43. Sereno Streeter to Theodore Dwight Weld, July 20, 1836, in Weld, Letters, 1:315–17; James Thome to Theodore Dwight Weld, September 9, 1836, in ibid., 339–42; Ballentine, Oberlin Jubilee, 274; Fairchild, Historical Sketch of Oberlin College, 26.

44. See Finney, Lectures on Systematic Theology, 36, 173–74, 307, and Weld, Letters, 1:x.

45. Goodman, Of One Blood, 130–31.

46. Third Annual Report of the American Anti-Slavery Society, 99; Myers, "Organization of 'The Seventy,'" 30.

47. Liberator, November 5, 26, December 17, 1836.

48. Whittier, Life and Letters, 250; Stanton, Random Recollections, 56–57; Plaindealer (New York), January 14, 1837; Fifth Annual Report of the Board of Managers, xx.

49. Liberator, November 3, 1837; Barnes, Anti-Slavery Impulse, 105.

50. See William Allan, Sereno Streeter, John Alvord, and James Thome to Theodore Dwight Weld, August 9, 1836, in Weld, Letters, 1:323–29.

51. Charles Grandison Finney to Theodore Dwight Weld, July 21, 1836, in ibid., 318–20.

52. John Alvord to Theodore Dwight Weld, August 9, 1836, in ibid., 326–27; William Allan, Sereno Streeter, John Alvord, and James Thome to Theodore Dwight Weld, August 9, 1836, in ibid., 323–29.

53. Weld's letters to the Oberlin students have not survived, but his replies are acknowledged in James Thome to Theodore Dwight Weld, September 9, 1836, in ibid., 339–42; Theodore Dwight Weld to Lewis Tappan, October 24, 1836, in ibid., 345–46.

54. Many of those who did not, like Streeter, remained very active as abolitionist lecturers locally as agents of the Oberlin Anti-Slavery Society. See *Philanthropist*, October 22, November 26, 1839, January 21, April 28, May 26, 1840.

55. Birney, *Letters*, 1:357 n. 2. Oberlin students were William Allan, George Allen, John Watson Alvord, Courtland Avery, J. M. Blakesley, Amos Dresser, Edward Fairchild, Hiram Foote, Huntington Lyman, James Milligan, John Pierce, Samuel Fuller Porter, Charles Renshaw, William Russell, James Thome, George Whipple, and Hiram Wilson.

56. Fairchild, *Historical Sketch of Oberlin College*, 55; Fairchild, *Oberlin*, 211.

57. Theodore Dwight Weld to Lewis Tappan, October 24, 1836, in Weld, *Letters*, 1:345–46.

58. Thome and Kimball, *Emancipation in the West Indies*, iii–vi; *Boston Quarterly Review* 1, no. 3 (July 1838): 385–86; Meyers, "Organization of 'The Seventy,'" 39–40.

59. Theodore Dwight Weld to Lewis Tappan, October 24, 1836, in Weld, *Letters*, 1:345–46; Elizur Wright Jr. to James Birney, October 12, 1836, Birney, *Letters*, 1:364–66; *Liberator*, November 26, December 17, 1836; NYE, December 10, 1836; Stanton, *Random Recollections*, 57.

60. See Birney, *American Churches*.

61. See ibid., 7–48, and Mayer, *All on Fire*, 233–39.

62. *Liberator*, January 1, 1831.

63. *Zion's Herald*, August 3, 1836.

64. *Liberator*, September 8, 1837.

65. Ibid., August 13, 1836.

66. See *Genius of Temperance*, March 21, 1833, in *Liberator*, June 8, 1833; *Zion's Herald*, August 3, 1836.

67. See Strong, *Perfectionist Politics*, 53.

68. Johnson, *William Lloyd Garrison and His Times*, 369–70.

69. *Liberator*, April 5, 1839; Goodell, *Slavery and Anti-Slavery*, 429–30. These resolutions were soon followed by almost all of the Presbyterian churches in the Northern states as well.

70. John Cowles to Henry Cowles, February 6, 1838, RSFP, Box 4, Folder 18.

71. *Liberator*, July 28, 1837; Ballentine, *Oberlin Jubilee*, 280–81.

72. Ballentine, *Oberlin Jubilee*, 59.

73. OE, "Extra," September 1857. Hudson's look back at the early efforts of abolitionists from Oberlin was written after Garrison had begun to disavow the necessity of keeping the Sabbath as well as the total divine inspiration of the Bible, views that actually did convince many in the Oberlin community that Garrison was an "infidel." In the context of the 1830s, Hudson's statements would have referred to *perceived* "infidel radicalism," etc.

74. See Sereno Streeter to Theodore Dwight Weld, August 9, 1836, in Weld, *Letters*, 1:325–26.

75. John Alvord to Theodore Dwight Weld, August 9, 1836, in ibid., 326–27.

76. Monroe, "The Early Abolitionists," in Monroe, *Oberlin Thursday Lectures*, 25–26.

77. John Alvord to Theodore Dwight Weld, August 9, 1836, in Weld, *Letters*, 1:326–27.

78. *Emancipator*, October 20, 1836; Lesick, *Lane Rebels*, 182.

79. *Emancipator*, February 12, 1836; James Thome to Theodore Dwight Weld, February 9, 1836, in Weld, *Letters*, 1:256–59; John Alvord to Theodore Dwight Weld, February 9, 1836, in Weld, *Letters*, 1:259–61.

80. Emancipator, February 12, 1836.

81. Henry Clay to Francis Brooke, November 3, 1838, in Clay, Papers, 246.

82. In 1835, the number of antislavery societies reporting to the American Anti-Slavery Society had grown from 60 to 200 (of which Ohio claimed 38), and by 1836, the total was 523 (133 in Ohio, 30 more than New York's next highest number). See Second Annual Report of the American Anti-Slavery Society, 37, and Third Annual Report of the American Anti-Slavery Society, 33.

83. Philanthropist, October 10, 1837.

84. Anonymous to Secretary of the American Colonization Society, May 29, 1838, in African Repository and Colonial Journal 14, no. 5 (May 1838): 150–51.

85. Ibid.

86. Declaration of Sentiments and Constitution, 17–18.

87. Proceedings of the Ohio Anti-Slavery Convention, 11–12.

88. Quoted in Morris, Life of Thomas Morris, 103; Register of Debates in . . . the Twenty-Fourth Congress, 684.

89. Register of Debates in . . . the Twenty-Fourth Congress, 3754.

90. Abridgements of the Debates of Congress, 28; Hart, Slavery and Abolition, 270–71. When the rules of the House were revised in 1844, John Quincy Adams fought for several days against the inclusion of this rule, and it was finally abandoned.

91. This included Southerners who objected to the resolution on libertarian grounds. See Register of Debates in . . . the Twenty-Fourth Congress, 3754, and OE, November 6, 1839.

92. Niles' National Register, June 26, 1841; Friend of Man, September 5, 1838; Joshua Giddings to Henry Cowles, January 22, 1839, RSFP, Box 4, Folder 18.

93. See Weld, Power of Congress, and Weld, Bible against Slavery.

94. Weld, American Slavery As It Is.

95. Thome and Weld, Slavery and the Internal Slave Trade; Thomas, Theodore Weld, 175; Deyle, Carry Me Back, 332 n. 36.

96. James Thome to Theodore Dwight Weld, July 16, 1836, in Weld, Letters, 1:312–15; Sereno Streeter to Theodore Dwight Weld, July 20, 1836, in ibid., 315–17.

97. Sereno Streeter to Theodore Dwight Weld, July 20, 1836, in ibid., 315–17.

98. Thome and Kimball, Emancipation in the West Indies, v.

99. James Thome to Theodore Dwight Weld, November 30, December 25, 1837, in Weld, Letters, 1:483–84, 501–4; Theodore Dwight Weld to James Birney, February 14, 1838, in Birney, Letters, 1:453–54; Lerner, Grimké Sisters, 162. Weld would edit the manuscript to a more manageable 128 closely printed pages.

100. Thome and Kimball, Emancipation in the West Indies, iii–iv.

101. Henry Stanton to Henry Cowles, June 20, 1838, HCP, Box 1; Lesick, Lane Rebels, 184.

102. "W" to Gamaliel Bailey, n.d., Philanthropist, May 22, 1838.

103. Angelina Grimké to Theodore Dwight Weld, April 7, 1838, in Weld, Letters, 2:623–28; Thomas, Theodore Weld, 128.

104. Philanthropist, June 9, October 13, 1837, February 13, May 22, July 3, 1838; Friend of Man, March 15, 1838.

105. Philanthropist, July 3, 1838.

106. See Amos Dresser to Levi Burnell, November 29, 1837, LR, roll 4; and Philanthropist, February 3, 22, March 10, 27, 1840.

107. George Whipple to Levi Burnell, LR, roll 2; Barnes, Anti-Slavery Impulse, 145.

108. Jeffrey, *Great Silent Army of Abolitionism*, 87–88.

109. *Friend of Man*, September 27, 1837.

110. Zaeske, *Signatures of Citizenship*, 208 n. 5.

111. *Register of Debates . . . of the Twenty Fourth Congress*, 834. See, for example, *Friend of Man*, December 1, 1836, and *Philanthropist*, March 25, 1836.

112. *Niles' National Register*, August 23, 1843; Bacon, Davidson, and Keller, *Encyclopedia of the United States Congress*, 884–85; Barnes, *Anti-Slavery Impulse*, 146.

113. *Philanthropist*, September 29, 1837; Walters, *Antislavery Appeal*, 5. Even some of the larger regional societies felt the effects of this tendency toward decentralization. At the 1837 meeting of the Western Reserve Anti-Slavery Society in Oberlin, the organization dissolved itself in favor of two county societies for Lorain and Portage Counties. These societies would meet yearly at the anniversaries of Oberlin and Western Reserve Colleges as the Western Reserve Anti-Slavery Society had formerly done.

114. *Friend of Man*, May 31, 1837.

115. Ibid., May 16, 1838; *Liberator*, May 18, 1838; Garrison and Garrison, *William Lloyd Garrison*, 2:261.

116. Francis Jackson to William Lloyd Garrison, March 30, 1839, in *Eighth Annual Report of the Board of Managers*, 24–26; Ellis Gray Loring to James Birney, February 16, 1839, in Birney, *Letters*, 1:483–84; Barnes, *Anti-Slavery Impulse*, 151, 268–69 n. 13.

117. Wyatt-Brown, *Lewis Tappan*, 170–81.

118. Elizur Wright Jr. to Theodore Dwight Weld, November 4, 1836, in Weld, *Letters*, 1:346–48; George Whipple to Levi Burnell, LR, roll 2; Henry Stanton to Henry Cowles, June 20, 1838, RSFP, Box 4, Folder 18.

119. Finney, *Memoirs*, 381; John Shipherd to Levi Burnell, October 12, 1836, February 24, 1838, RSFP, Box 14, Folder 6; "Prof[essorship] Fund Installments, 1836," n.d., RSFP, Box 11, Folder 20.

120. Finney, *Memoirs*, 387–88; Alfred Smith to Levi Burnell, May 12, 1837, LR, roll 4; Arthur Tappan to Levi Burnell, October 15, 22, 1836, LR, roll 3.

121. Amos Dresser to Levi Burnell, March 26, 1838, LR, roll 5.

122. John Keep to Asa Mahan, Charles Grandison Finney, John Morgan, and J. H. Cowles, July 1, 1836, RSFP, Box 7, Folder 11. See also Finney, *Memoirs*, 387–88.

123. John Keep to Levi Burnell, May 29, 1837, LR, roll 4.

124. Madden and Hamilton, *Freedom and Grace*, 75.

125. John Shipherd to Zebulon and Elizabeth Shipherd, August 6, 1832, in Fairchild, *Oberlin*, 18.

CHAPTER THREE

1. John Shipherd to Fayette Shipherd, April 14, 1834, JJSP, Box 4.

2. Clark, *Communitarian Moment*, 1. Few scholars mention Oberlin in their discussions of utopianism, and fewer, if any, have described a school in the antebellum era as utopian. *Historical Dictionary of Utopianism* describes Oberlin as follows: "OBERLIN COLONY. Founded in 1833 in Lorain County, Ohio, by eight recent immigrant families from New England and New York, the Oberlin colonists hoped to establish a community based on communal ownership of property. Their leader was John Shipherd. They also wanted to establish a school

where children would receive a Christian education. Absorbed by Oberlin College in 1841, the colony faded away within two years." Besides its factual errors, critical omissions, and dubious assertions, this statement does not differ markedly from what others have written. See Morris and Kross, *Historical Dictionary of Utopianism*, 229; Knepper, *Ohio and Its People*, 171; Walters, *American Reformers*, 39–41; Holloway, *Utopian Communities in America*, 17–30; Peterson, *Seeds of the Kingdom*, 3–15; and Fogarty, *American Utopianism*, ix–xi.

3. Kanter, *Commitment and Community*, 1.

4. See Hewitt, *Regeneration and Morality*, 47–49.

5. OE, February 13, 1839.

6. See D. Woodbury to John Shipherd, July 13, 1834, LR, roll 1; J. B. Trew to Andrew Trew, May 29, 1843, RSFP, Box 7, Folder 6; Mary Sheldon, "The Landing of the Pilgrim Fathers," July 9, 1849, RG 30/200, Mary Sheldon Papers, microfilm, OCA; and OE November 6, 1844.

7. *Liberator*, August 30, 1839.

8. See Friesen and Friesen, *Palgrave Companion to North American Utopias*, 9–15.

9. See John Shipherd to Fayette Shipherd, August 13, 1832, JJSP, microfilm; and John Shipherd to Zebulon Shipherd, August 6, 1832, ibid.

10. E. J. Comings, "Thoughts on Temperance," ca. 1837, RSFP, Box 4, Folder 10. See also Fairchild, *Oberlin*, 82–83; Abzug, *Cosmos Crumbling*, 166; Walters, *American Reformers*, 13; and Fletcher, "Bread and Doctrine at Oberlin."

11. Finney, *Lectures on Systematic Theology*, 165–424, esp. 166–96; Charles Grandison Finney, "Recent Discussions on the Subject of Entire Sanctification in This Life," 449–56; Hannah Warner to Andrew Warner, March 15, 1841, RSFP, Box 3, Folder 25; Boardman, *History of New England Theology*, 276–77.

12. *Zion's Herald*, March 22, 1837.

13. Mahan, *Out of Darkness into Light*, 6, 27, 51, 160–75.

14. See Finney, *Lectures on Systematic Theology*, 298–357; Finney, *Sermons on Important Subjects*, 43–66; Hannah Warner to Andrew Warner, March 15, 1841, RSFP, Box 3, Folder 25; Strong, *Perfectionist Politics*, 27–28; and Hewitt, *Regeneration and Morality*, 43–45.

15. Stauffer, *Black Hearts of Men*, 96.

16. "Covenant of the Oberlin Colony," RG 21, Oberlin File, Series 6, Box 1, OCA.

17. Hannah Warner to Andrew Warner, March 15, 1841, RSFP, Box 3, Folder 25.

18. Stauffer, *Black Hearts of Men*, 96.

19. Strong, *Perfectionist Politics*, 20–21.

20. OE, January 15, 1840; Finney, *Skeletons of a Course of Theological Lectures*, 88.

21. E. J. Comings, "Notes on Finney's Lectures on Pastoral Theology," July 1837, RSFP, Box 4, Folder 10.

22. Fairchild, *Oberlin*, 33.

23. Blackett, *Beating against the Barriers*, 291; Sernett, "Common Cause." Oneida's black enrollment numbers are uncertain. Administrators seldom kept records of the race of Oneida's students, and many of President Beriah Green's personal papers were destroyed in an 1843 fire just prior to the institute's closing. Only fourteen African American students can be identified with any certainty by historians, though certainly there were many more. Sernett, *Abolition's Axe*, 51.

24. See Lucy Stone to Antoinette Brown, June 9, 1850, in Stone and Blackwell, *Friends and Sisters*, 72–75, and NYT, August 9, 1854.

25. NS, January 12, 1849; Rudy, *Campus and a Nation in Crisis*, 52. Oberlin became one of the largest colleges in the antebellum United States. By 1850, its enrollment was the highest of any college in American history to that point. Its enrollment in 1860 was 1,311, compared to Harvard's 848 and Yale's 642. See also *Colored American*, n.d., in *Philanthropist*, November 14, 1837.

26. NS, January 12, 1849. See also David Prudden to George Prudden, August 21, 1838, RSFP, Box 11, Folder 10; and William White to Asa Mahan, April 30, 1840, LR, roll 7.

27. NASS, July 9, 1864. See also the conflicted racial views of Oberlin students expressed in James Wright to "Dear Sisters," May 1, 1846, RSFP, Box 10, Folder 17.

28. Simmons, *Men of Mark*, 862.

29. Stewart, *Holy Warriors*, 130.

30. Examples include a white preparatory student who in 1846 objected to being called "Brother" by an African American classmate, and, as James Fairchild remembered, "in a few instances, a colored and white boy had a quarrel." Occasionally, Fairchild recalled, a black student "imagined that some disrespect was shown him by a fellow student," but overall, he believed that white students accepted their African American classmates as equals (Fairchild, *Oberlin*, 113). In another incident, when a white student who had refused to allow black students to pass on Oberlin's narrow sidewalk ended up finding herself in the mud below, she hurled "vile epithets" back up at the black students. See Lasser, "Enacting Emancipation," 329.

31. OE, September 10, 1851.

32. Fairchild, *Oberlin*, 28–29.

33. Benjamin Woodbury to John J. Shipherd, March 26, 1835, LR, roll 2.

34. Brown, *Artemus Ward*, 64. See also Nathan Fletcher, "Critical Letters, #3," n.d., RG 7/1/3, Office of the Treasurer, Box 4, OCA.

35. Most information regarding the names and number of African American students at Oberlin from 1835 to 1862 is drawn from the unofficial list compiled from memory by Professor Henry Cowles in 1862. The "Catalogue and Record of Colored Students in Oberlin, 1835 to 1862" contains the names of approximately 200 students who attended either the preparatory or the collegiate departments. The list is incomplete, owing to the imprecision of memory as well as the tendency in Oberlin to not consider African American students in any different light than those of other races. Since a student's race was not noted in official catalogs, these numbers are necessarily inexact. However, assuming that 5 percent is a relatively accurate number, African American students would never have numbered more than approximately sixty-five in a single year before the Civil War. See Accounts and Memoranda Books, 1835–81, HCP, Series 5, Box 10; and Bigglestone, "Oberlin College and the Negro Student," 198.

36. From the records available, the year of highest African American enrollment was the 1852–53 school year. That year, John Keep counted forty-four black students in all the divisions of the Oberlin Institute. This was out of over 1,000 students overall. See Fletcher, *History of Oberlin College*, 536, and Lawson, "Antebellum 'Talented Thousandth,'" 143.

37. Horton, "Black Education at Oberlin College," 483 n. 12.

38. The Oberlin Collegiate Institute consisted of a preparatory department, female department, teachers' seminary, collegiate department, and theological department. See *First Annual Report of the Oberlin Collegiate Institute*.

39. Simmons, *Men of Mark*, 978.

40. Don C. Seitz, "The New Student," excerpt in Anthony Burns Alumni File, OCA.

41. Susan Wade to Oberlin College, December 18, 1864, LR, roll 16. See also Lawson, "Antebellum 'Talented Thousandth,'" 143–45, 149. Lewis Tappan, Harriet Beecher Stowe, William Lloyd Garrison, Frederick Douglass, and other famous reformers directed bright African American students to Oberlin.

42. Lawson, "Antebellum 'Talented Thousandth,'" 153.

43. Ibid., 147.

44. This son, James Monroe Jones, would go on to assist John Brown in planning his Harpers Ferry raid and provisional government in the late 1850s. See Chapter 9. See also Carol Bowie to Mercedes Singleton, October 30, 1860, RG 30/157, Lawson/Merrill Papers, Box 3, OCA; NASS, October 11, 1856; and American Missionary, October, 1856.

45. Benjamin Bowen to Oberlin College, March 21, 1842, LR, roll 8.

46. Child, Appeal in Favor, 187. See also Litwack, North of Slavery, and Fredrickson, Black Image in the White Mind.

47. Coppin, Reminiscences, 19.

48. Hiram Elams, H. C. Taylor, and M. E. Strieby to John Keep and William Dawes, May 11, 1839, LR, roll 6.

49. See OE, September 10, 1845, November 6, 1850; Brown, Artemus Ward, 67; RG 31/4/1, Oberlin First Congregational Church Records, RG 31/4/1, Box 1, OCA; and John Keep to Gerrit Smith, January 16, 1836, RSFP, Box 9.

50. OE, September 10, 1851.

51. Smith, Oberlin Unmasked, 28.

52. Fairchild, Historical Sketch of Oberlin College, 30–31.

53. Dall, College, the Market, and the Court, 385; Langston, From the Virginia Plantation, 181.

54. Cheek and Cheek, John Mercer Langston, 91–92.

55. Langston, From the Virginia Plantation, 80.

56. Coppin, Reminiscences, 12, 19. Despite a resolution by the board of trustees in 1853 that "in the choice of Professors and teachers of all grades we are governed by intrinsic merit irrespective of color," there was not an African American faculty member at Oberlin College until 1948. See Fletcher, "Against the Consensus," 216.

57. Cleveland Daily Herald, April 6, 1849.

58. Old Anti-Slavery Days, 113.

59. Coppin, Reminiscences, 14.

60. John Mercer Langston to Henry [Howe], April 10, 1854, John Mercer Langston Papers, Amistad Research Center, microfilm, roll 1.

61. S. G. Howe, quoted in Spectator, April 23, 1864.

62. Edgar Ward to Mother, December 5, 1853, RG 21, Oberlin File, IIa, Letters by Oberlin Students, Box 1, OCA.

63. Bigglestone, They Stopped in Oberlin, xviii.

64. CTD, n.d., in FDP, June 3, 1852.

65. Theodore Weld to Lewis Tappan, February 22, 1836, in Weld, Letters, 1:262–65; John Shipherd, "pastoral letter," January 27, 1835, in Fairchild, Oberlin, appendix, 337–46.

66. Edgar Ward to Mother, December 5, 1853, RG21, Oberlin File, IIa, Letters by Oberlin Students, Box 1, OCA.

67. Cheek and Cheek, John Mercer Langston, 290–91.

68. Circular, *Oberlin Collegiate Institute*, March 8, 1834, RSFP, Box 12, Folder 14; Hosford, *Father Shipherd's Magna Charta*, 31; Geary, *Balanced in the Wind*, 38.

69. Philo Stewart to Levi Burnell, April 10, 1837, LR, roll 4; Hosford, *Father Shipherd's Magna Charta*, 31.

70. Fairchild, "Coeducation of the Sexes," 390–91; Fairchild, *Joint Education of the Sexes*, 28–30; Mahan, *Autobiography*, 183.

71. Fairchild, "Coeducation of the Sexes," 390–91, 394–95; Trustee Minutes, March 9, 1836, RSFP, Box 15, Folder 7. See also OE, August 5, 1857.

72. See Betsey Mix Cowles Alumni File, OCA.

73. Hambrick-Stowe, *Charles G. Finney*, 269–70; Lucy Stone to "Dear Mother and Father," 1845, RG 21, Oberlin File, Series 2, Box 2, A, OCA.

74. Lawson, "Antebellum 'Talented Thousandth,'" 145; "Russwurm," Lawson/Merrill Papers, Box 3, OCA.

75. See Rosetta Douglass Alumni File, OCA, and Lawson, "Antebellum 'Talented Thousandth,'" 145.

76. Robertson, *Hearts Beating for Liberty*, 167.

77. Kerr, *Lucy Stone*, 37; Antoinette Brown Blackwell, "Reminiscences of Early Oberlin," MS, February 1918, Antoinette Brown Blackwell Alumni File, OCA.

78. Lucy Stone to Francis Stone and Harriet Stone, February 15, 1846, RSFP, Box 10, Folder 2; Kerr, *Lucy Stone*, 33–37; Cheek and Cheek, *John Mercer Langston*, 110; "Expenses of Teaching in the Various Departments of the Oberlin Collegiate Institution for the Year 1844–1845," Lucy Stone Alumni File, OCA.

79. Antoinette Brown Blackwell Alumni File, Folder 1, OCA.

80. Coppin, *Reminiscences*, 14.

81. Merrill, *Sarah Margru Kinson*, 1–18.

82. "Annual Report of the L.L.S.," OE, August 15, 1855.

83. Lawson, "Lucy Stanton," 9.

84. Ibid. Stanton would go on to marry Oberlin graduate William Howard Day and assist him in the publication of his newspaper, *The Alienated American*, which often included in its columns articles by female correspondents.

85. OE, August 17, 1842.

86. Davis, *Slavery and Human Progress*, 124–25.

87. Cheek and Cheek, *John Mercer Langston*, 110; Kerr, *Lucy Stone*, 37–38.

88. Lucy Stone to "Dear Father and Mother," August 16, 1846, RSFP, Box 10, Folder 2; Antoinette Brown Blackwell, "Reminiscences of Early Oberlin," Antoinette Brown Blackwell Alumni File, OCA; OE, July 17, 1844, August 19, 1846; Program of First of August Celebration, 1846, RG 21, Oberlin File, Series 11, Box 2, OCA; Cheek and Cheek, *John Mercer Langston*, 95, 110; "Celebration by 'The Disfranchised Americans' of Oberlin, Ohio," August 1, 1846, RSFP, Box 10, Folder 1. Oberlin ladies also participated in West Indian Independence celebrations in neighboring towns. See Holley, *Life for Liberty*, 60–61.

89. Lucy Stone to "Dear Father and Mother," August 16, 1846, RSFP, Box 10, Folder 2.

90. Lucy Stone, "Why Do We Rejoice Today?," August 1, 1846, RSFP, Box 10, Folder 1.

91. Lucy Stone clipped the article and included it in a letter to her parents. See Program of First of August Celebration, 1846, RG21, Oberlin File, Series 11, Box 2, OCA; and Lucy Stone to "Dear Father and Mother," August 16, 1846, RSFP, Box 10, Folder 2.

92. Paul Goodman credits the manual labor experiments in early antebellum America with being the "origins of abolitionism." Though he discounts the evangelical origins of the abolitionist movement and credits manual labor as the origin rather than manifestation of the abolitionist impulse, the importance he places upon manual labor is warranted. See Goodman, "Manual Labor Movement."

93. "By Laws of the Oberlin Collegiate Institute," n.d. (1835?), 4, RSFP, Box 11, Folder 6. As college labor became scarcer, Oberlin gradually decreased the official manual labor requirement, but work was always available to students in the community who wanted or needed it. See Fairchild, Oberlin, 186–95, and "Seal of Oberlin College," *Oberlin Alumni Magazine* 7 (July 1911): 353.

94. *Catalog of the Trustees, Officers, and Students*, 20; *First Annual Report of the Oberlin Collegiate Institute*, 6–7; Fairchild, Oberlin, 187.

95. John Shipherd, "Rules for Cutting Cord Wood on the Institution Farm," n.d., RSFP, Box 15, Folder 6; *First Annual Report of the Oberlin Collegiate Institute*, 6–7.

96. The Society for Promoting Manual Labor in Literary Institutions, on whose behalf Theodore Dwight Weld labored from 1831 to 1832, made no efforts after 1832 to carry out the objects of its founding. See *American Journal of Education* 15, no. 39 (June 1865): 232–34; and Goodman, "Manual Labor Movement," 364.

97. *Quarterly Register* 3, no. 3 (February 1836): 269–76; Haddock, *Addresses and Miscellaneous Writings*, 220–36; Goodman, *Of One Blood*, 139–60.

98. *Catalog of the Trustees, Officers, and Students*, 20.

99. Weld, *First Annual Report of the Society for Promoting Manual Labor*, 93–94.

100. Henry Cowles, "Manual Labor with Study," OE, May 13, 1846.

101. See Goodman, *Of One Blood*, 276.

102. Madden and Hamilton, *Freedom and Grace*, 69.

103. New Haven Palladium, in *New Bedford Daily Mercury*, April 4, 1849.

104. Mahan, *Autobiography*, 273–75.

105. *Ohio Cultivator*, September 14, 1847.

106. Hammond, *Selections from the Letters and Speeches*, 318.

107. See Berlin, *Slaves without Masters*.

108. Gunnar Myrdal, quoted in DeWitt, *Early Globalization*, 51.

109. Hammond, *Selections from the Letters and Speeches*, 301–22.

110. Henry Cowles, "Manual Labor with Study," OE, May 13, 1846.

111. Stauffer, *Black Hearts of Men*, 152. See also Clark, *Communitarian Moment*, 1–14.

112. Wright, "Oberlin's Contribution to Ethics," 432–34.

CHAPTER FOUR

1. Smith, *Oberlin Unmasked*, 5–6. Smith was expelled for his public declarations of atheism.

2. Finney, *Memoirs*, 386.

3. James Fairchild, "The Divine Hand in the Oberlin Enterprise," *Jubilee Notes*, November 1883, 48.

4. Hiram Elams, H. C. Taylor, and M. E. Strieby to John Keep and William Dawes, May 11, 1839, LR, roll 6.

5. A. A. F. Johnson, "Significant Events and Noted Persons," *Oberlin Alumni Magazine* 6, no. 2 (November 1909): 52. See also Hiram Elams, H. C. Taylor, and M. E. Strieby to John Keep and William Dawes, May 11, 1839, LR, roll 6.

6. Journal of William Henry Brisbane, October 7–15, 1856, William Henry Brisbane Papers, Wisconsin Historical Society, roll 1; Dall, *College, the Market, and the Court*, 386.

7. Thomas, *Liberator*, 321.

8. Foster, *Brotherhood of Thieves*; Burroughs, "Oberlin's Part in the Slavery Conflict," 280; Fairchild, *Oberlin*, 85–86.

9. See Minutes of the Oberlin Dialectical Association, 1839–45, RSFP, Box 11, Folder 15. In a sense, everyone in Oberlin was a member of one of America's original think tanks. Their importance thus lies not in their absolute numbers, which were relatively small, but in their ability to generate an ideology and plan of action that would be followed by countless others in the movement.

10. Minutes for April 19, 1848, Young Ladies' Literary Society Minutes, RG 19/3/4, OCA.

11. OE, November 4, 1840.

12. OE, September 23, 1840; Philanthropist, November 14, 1837.

13. Philanthropist, October 20, 1841.

14. Augustus Wattles to Henry Cowles, September 14, 1837, RSFP, Box 4, Folder 12.

15. This society included the wives of many prominent Oberlin abolitionists. See Philanthropist, June 23, 1840, June 9, 1841, June 29, 1842, August 9, 1843; and Augustus Wattles to Henry Cowles, September 14, 1837, RSFP, Box 4, Folder 12.

16. Philanthropist, December 24, 1839, June 15, 1843; "Annual Report of the Ladies' Education Society," in Philanthropist, June 22, 1842; Fletcher, *History of Oberlin College*, 246–47.

17. "Annual Report of the Ladies' Education Society," in Philanthropist, June 22, 1842. See also speech of William Dawes, in *Report of the Annual Meeting of the Glasgow Emancipation Society*, 8–9.

18. *Slave's Narrative*, 116–17.

19. Ibid.

20. Hiram Wilson to Hamilton Hill, April 25, 1843, LR, roll 8; Hiram Wilson to Henry Cowles, January 2, 1837, RSFP, Box 4, Folder 18. Wilson stated, "This institute is not to rival Oberlin or Oneida, but it is necessary because neither of these is safe for the fugitive. Our arms are thrown open . . . to receive and instruct them, where no tyrant can molest or make them afraid." See Tobin and Jones, *From Midnight to Dawn*, 25.

21. Winks, *Blacks in Canada*, 179. In 1841, New York abolitionist Gerrit Smith organized a committee in Rochester to collect and channel funds, Bibles, and clothing to Wilson's Canada schools, which numbered at least fifteen by that point.

22. Henson, *Autobiography*, 169–70; Drew, *Refugee*, 309–12.

23. *Slave's Narrative*, 116.

24. See J. W. Alden to Hiram Wilson, March 23, 1841, HWP, Box 1; OE, December 8, 1839; Erastus Childs to Hiram Wilson, October 22, 1841, HWP, Box 1; A. A. Phelps to Henry Cowles, March 8, 1843, RSFP, Box 11, Folder 10.

25. Liberator, September 21, 1838.

26. NASS, July 8, 1841; Emancipator, December 22, 1836, March 28, April 6, October 5, 1837; OE, December 8, 1839.

27. OE, July 17, 1844.

28. Langston, *From the Virginia Plantation*, 101; Burroughs, "Oberlin's Part in the Slavery Conflict," 279.

29. Langston, *From the Virginia Plantation*, 101. Faneuil Hall is a meeting house in Boston famous for the many patriotic speeches made there by the founding fathers as well as abolitionist speeches, rallies, and other reform conventions in the nineteenth century.

30. See "Lydia" to Hannah Warner, n.d. (1845), RSFP, Box 3, Folder 15; and *Old Anti-Slavery Days*, 113.

31. Langston, *From the Virginia Plantation*, 195.

32. Kerr, *Lucy Stone*, 33.

33. Ibid.

34. Ibid.

35. See Geary, *Balanced in the Wind*, 29.

36. Atwater, *History of the State of Ohio*, 331. See also "Constitution of the Massilon [Ohio] Colonization Society," *African Repository and Colonial Journal* 14, no. 8 (August 1838): 228–29. It did appear that slavery had retarded the slave states bordering Ohio. Kentucky was larger than Ohio geographically and founded earlier and in 1800 had 180,612 free people, compared to Ohio's 45,000. However, by 1840, Kentucky could claim a free population of just 597,000 to Ohio's 1,519,000. The *Louisville Journal* assessed that "the most potent cause of the more rapid advancement of Cincinnati than Louisville is the absence of slavery." Kentuckian Cassius Clay told his state's legislature that "the world is teeming with improved machinery, the combined development of science and art. To us it is all lost; *we are comparatively living in centuries that are gone, we cannot make it, we cannot use it when made. Ohio is many years younger, and possessed of fewer advantages than our state.... OHIO IS A FREE STATE, KENTUCKY A SLAVE STATE*" (Elliott, *Sinfulness of American Slavery*, 148–49).

37. See *National Register* 2, no. 5 (September 28, 1816): 77; *Littell's Living Age* 12, no. 7 (March 1847): 433–36; Horton, "Race and Region," 51.

38. Fairchild, *Educational Arrangements*, 7.

39. *Ohio State Journal and Columbus Gazette*, January 27, March 4, 1834; *History of Education*, 220; *Charters and Basic Laws*, 396.

40. "An Act to Incorporate the Oberlin Collegiate Institute," in Miller, *History of Educational Legislation*, 153.

41. *Ohio State Journal and Columbus Gazette*, December 18, 1835.

42. *Journal of the Senate of the State of Ohio* (1837), January 9, 1837.

43. Fairchild, *Oberlin*, 109–10; Fairchild, *Educational Arrangements*, 7.

44. *Ohio State Journal and Columbus Gazette*, January 20, 1837.

45. Ibid.

46. *Journal of the Senate of the State of Ohio* (1837), January 17, 1837.

47. *BAP*, 3:141 n. 6; "An Act to Incorporate the Sheffield Manual Labor Institute," in *Acts of a General Nature*, 139–40. Though enrollment numbers are unavailable for 1837 (the school could not afford to print a catalog), by 1838 there were 391 students enrolled at Oberlin, up from 44 at its opening less than five years before. See *General Catalogue of Oberlin College*, int.117.

48. *Ohio State Journal and Columbus Gazette*, February 28, 1837; *Journal of the Senate of the State of Ohio* (1837), 276.

49. *Journal of the Senate of the State of Ohio* (1837), 276; *Ohio State Journal and Columbus Gazette*, March 3, 1837; *Acts of a General Nature*, 139–40. See also Miller, *History of Educational Legislation*, 135, 205.

50. Ellsworth, "Oberlin," 58–59. The town of Oberlin did not receive a charter from the state government until 1846, and even at that late date the bill received considerable debate as versions of it were volleyed back and forth between the two houses. See *Journal of the Senate of the State of Ohio* (1846), 189, 307, 465, 486, 491, 516, 540, 565–66, 594, 624, 654.

51. John Allen to Levi Burnell, March 27, 1837, LR, roll 4.

52. Ibid.

53. Ibid. At that same legislative session, at least twenty-one other towns received the same charter Oberlin sought, and most of them sailed through the process with no opposition. See *Acts of a General Nature*. The reputation of the town and school also doubtlessly "suffered" that legislative term as a result of the publication of Delazon Smith's pamphlet *Oberlin Unmasked*. Smith bitterly portrayed Oberlin as a refuge of morally depraved, zealous fanatics and practical amalgamationists. Those already predisposed to find Oberlin objectionable tended to believe Smith's brief diatribe. See Oberlin Church Records, March 3, 1837, RSFP, Box 12, Folder 12; and Fairchild, *Oberlin*, 370.

54. *New Market Christian Witness*, n.d., in *Friend of Man*, March 18, 1840. Wordsworth's 1821 sonnet "Persecution of the Scottish Covenanters" describes the immortal and invincible power of a truly righteous cause, using the ancient meaning of "adamant," referring to a substance that was extremely hard, such as diamond or steel.

55. See Strong, *Perfectionist Politics*.

56. Bratt, "Reorientation of American Protestantism," 64.

57. Hatch, *Democratization of American Christianity*, 64–66, 80–81, 206–9.

58. Hambrick-Stowe, *Charles G. Finney*, 181; Bratt, "Reorientation of American Protestantism," 65.

59. OE, January 29, 1845.

60. Hambrick-Stowe, *Charles G. Finney*, 218. Finney saw little value in ideological constancy if the principles had lost their effectiveness. A student once asked him to reconcile a theological statement that he made in an Oberlin lecture with one he had written in one of his books some years earlier. He replied sharply, "Don't quote Finney to me!" Finney recognized that truth was never transitory but man's understanding of it was always changing. Thus he fostered critical thought and inquiry, and as Frances Hosford remarks, "Oberlin theology has never been forced to mount guard over its dogmas" (Hosford, *Father Shipherd's Magna Charta*, 166–67).

61. See Sewell, *Ballots for Freedom*, 8–10.

62. Finney, *Skeletons of a Course of Theological Lectures*, 235–38. For the Garrisonian criticism of Finney's statements, see *Liberator*, October 29, 1841.

63. Finney, *Lectures on Revivals of Religion*, 274–75.

64. See Finney, *Skeletons of a Course of Theological Lectures*, 235–48.

65. Hammond, "Revival Religion and Anti-Slavery Politics," 175–76, 183; Strong, *Perfectionist Politics*, 4–5, 27–28.

66. Finney, *Lectures on Revivals of Religion*, 275.

67. Quoted in Barnes, *Antislavery Impulse*, 149.

68. Finney, *Skeletons of a Course of Theological Lectures*, 241.

69. Smith, *Liberty and Free Soil Parties*, 23.

70. Fogel, *Without Consent or Contract*, 323.

71. See L. L. Rice, "Talk re: Slavery," April 1841, RSFP, Box 3, Folder 10.

72. Philanthropist, January 1, March 23, 1839; OE, May 22, 1839; Reilley, *Early Slavery Controversy*, 282.

73. See Stewart, "Modernizing 'Difference,'" 123.

74. Ibid., 124–25.

75. Smith, *Oberlin Unmasked*, 67.

76. Fairchild, *Oberlin*, 109–10; Fairchild, *Educational Arrangements*, 7.

77. E. L. Barnard to Frances Hosford, n.d. (1929?), RG 30/35, Frances Hosford Papers, OCA.

78. Finney quoted in Cochran, *Charles Grandison Finney Memorial Address*, 57.

79. Finney, *Memoirs*, 387–88.

80. Ohio Atlas and Elyria Advertiser, May 28, 1839; Philanthropist, June 18, 1839.

81. Ohio Statesman, October 19, 1838.

82. Wheeler, *History of Congress*, 443.

83. Holt, *Rise and Fall of the American Whig Party*, 156.

84. Philanthropist, March 31, 1837.

85. Roseboom and Weisenburger, *History of Ohio*, 383.

86. Philanthropist, March 27, 1838.

87. Ibid., October 23, 1838.

88. Smith, *Liberty and Free Soil Parties*, 30; Sewell, *Ballots for Freedom*, 47.

89. Emancipator, quoted in Philanthropist, December 11, 1838; Sewell, *Ballots for Freedom*, 21, 47.

90. OE, February 13, March 27, 1839; Emancipator, February 7, 1839.

91. OE, February 13, 1839.

92. Philanthropist, January 1, 1839.

93. OE, May 22, August 13, 1839; Riddle, *Life of Benjamin F. Wade*, 138–44.

94. OE, May 22, 1839; Philanthropist, March 26, 1839.

95. Alilunas, "Fugitive Slave Cases in Ohio Prior to 1850," 166.

96. Philanthropist, January 29, February 5, 12, March 12, 1839; OE, March 27, 1839; Roseboom and Weisenburger, *History of Ohio*, 381–82. The Supreme Court ruling in *Prigg v. Pennsylvania* (1842) eventually declared that the enforcement of the fugitive slave provisions of the Constitution lay exclusively with federal courts, thus the Ohio law was no longer constitutional and Ohio repealed its fugitive laws and penalties. However, this only resulted in a renewed effort to enforce the federal law. See Middleton, *Black Laws*, 92–114.

97. OE, February 13, March 27, 1839. See also the Oberlin commencement addresses of Horace Taylor, "Validity of Civil Government Established by Reason," and James Steele, "Validity of Civil Government Established by Scripture," 1840 Commencement File, RG 0/00/14, College General Records, Series 15, Box 1, OCA.

98. OE, February 13, 1839; Essig, "Lord's Free Man," 35–36.

99. Reilley, *Early Slavery Controversy*, 205–11, 277.

100. Friend of Man, September 11, 1839. The idea of a "higher law" superseding human legislative enactments was not new. Indeed, its origins were biblical, and the appeal to the "law of nature" was thousands of years old. American Unitarians and Transcendentalists had also held up the notion of a "higher law" in the 1830s, but Finney was one of the first to publicly invoke the concept in relation to laws concerning "fugitive" slaves.

101. OE, March 13, 1839.

102. Ibid.

103. Cormany, "Ohio's Abolitionist Campaign," 93.

104. OE, March 27, 1839.

105. See Finney, Skeletons of a Course of Theological Lectures, 203.

106. James Thome to Theodore Weld, May 18, 1839, in Weld, Letters, 2:763–66.

107. James Birney to Joshua Leavitt, May 31, 1839, in Liberator, June 28, 1839.

108. Report of the Fourth Anniversary of the Ohio Anti-Slavery Society, 16–19. See also OE, July 17, 1839; and James Birney to Joshua Leavitt, May 31, 1839, in Liberator, June 28, 1839.

109. James Birney to Joshua Leavitt, May 31, 1839, in Liberator, June 28, 1839.

110. OE, July 3, August 14, 1839.

111. See Volpe, Forlorn Hope of Freedom, 31–32.

112. Emancipator, October 24, 1839. See also Philanthropist, January 29, 1839.

113. Norwalk Experiment, January 22, 1840. See also Finney, Memoirs, 387.

114. Philanthropist, January 21, 1840; Liberator, February 14, 1840.

115. Journal of the House of Representatives of the State of Ohio, Being the First Session of the Thirty-Eighth General Assembly, 189, 212.

116. Philanthropist, December 31, 1839; January 21, 1840; Liberator, February 14, 1840.

117. Philanthropist, January 21, 1840; Liberator, February 14, 1840.

118. Minutes of the Oberlin Dialectic Association, March 11, 1840, RSFP, Box 11, Folder 15; L. L. Rice, "Talk re: Slavery," April 1841, RSFP, Box 3, Folder 10.

119. The basic difference between Garrisonians and the politically-minded abolitionists was over expediency rather than principle. All abolitionists agreed that both the Whig and the Democratic Parties were corrupt beyond repair and in cahoots with the Slave Power. However, Garrison located the cause of the corruption in the populace—the people who made up the parties. Only after a thorough reformation of public opinion could the parties and the political system be reformed. He believed that abolitionists must stay aloof from politics and spur on the electorate to greater radicalism rather than attempting to lead them before they were sufficiently prepared to follow. See Kraditor, Means and Ends in American Abolitionism, 159–60, and Walters, Antislavery Appeal, 13.

120. OE, July 17, 31, 1839; Emancipator, July 25, 1839; Hopkins, "Garrisonian Abolition vs. Oberlin Anti-Slavery," 45–46; Burroughs, "Oberlin's Part in the Slavery Conflict," 278.

121. OE, July 17, 31, 1839.

122. Emancipator, August 8, 1839.

123. OE, August 28, 1839; Rayback, "Liberty Party Leaders of Ohio," 165.

124. Philanthropist, September 3, 1839.

125. Ibid., October 8, 1839. See also Sewell, Ballots for Freedom, 45–47.

126. See call for the Cleveland convention in Friend of Man, September 11, 1839.

127. Ohio Statesman, November 6, 1839; Philanthropist, November 5, 1839.

128. Ohio Statesman, November 6, 1839.

129. Liberator, November 15, 22, 1839; Henry Stanton to John Greenleaf Whittier, October 20, 1839, in Philanthropist, November 19, 1839; Ohio Statesman, November 6, 1839.

130. Liberator, November 15, 22, 1839; Henry Stanton to John Greenleaf Whittier, October 20, 1839, in Philanthropist, November 19, 1839.

131. Henry Stanton to John Greenleaf Whittier, October 20, 1839, in Philanthropist, November 19, 1839.

132. Elizur Wright Sr. to Elizur Wright Jr., November 6, 1839, Elizur Wright Papers, Case Western Reserve University Archives, Series 2IW2, Box 1, Folder 4.

133. Charles Finney to Gerrit Smith, July 22, 1840, RSFP, Box 6, Folder 7. Not all Oberlin abolitionists were fully behind such measures at that point. See OE, November 6, 1839.

134. *Philanthropist*, December 10, 1839.

135. Ibid., January 1, 1840.

136. See letters in ibid., January 21, February 25, April 14, 1840.

137. See ibid., February 18, 1840.

138. See ibid., April 14, 1840.

139. Ibid., April 21, 28, 1840.

140. Minutes of the Oberlin Dialectic Association, April 22, 1840, RSFP, Box 11, Folder 15; Edmund A. West to "Aunt Cornelia," June 1, 1840, RSFP, Box 3, Folder 26; L. L. Rice, "Talk re: Slavery," April 1841, RSFP, Box 3, Folder 10.

141. OE, July 29, 1840.

142. John Keep to Lydia Keep, July 12, 1840, RSFP, Box 7, Folder 3.

143. *Friend of Man*, September 16, 1840.

144. OE, July 29, 1840. See also OE, September 23, 1840.

145. *Philanthropist*, September 8, 1840; Roseboom and Weisenburger, *History of Ohio*, 385–86.

146. *National Party Platforms*, 13.

147. Rayback, "Liberty Party Leaders of Ohio," 169.

148. "Sara" to Betsey Mix Cowles, October 6, 1840, BMCP, Box 2.

149. Smith, *Liberty and Free Soil Parties*, 40.

150. Edmund A. West to "Aunt Cornelia" Johnson, June 1, September 19, 1840, RSFP, Box 3, Folder 26; Roseboom and Weisenburger, *History of Ohio*, 385–86; OE, July 31, 1839; Gamble, "Joshua Giddings and the Ohio Abolitionists," 41; Shaw, *Plain Dealer*, 76.

151. OE, October 9, 1844.

152. *Philanthropist*, December 9, 1840.

153. Fairchild, *Oberlin*, 109–10; *Lorain Republican*, April 4, 1844.

154. John Cowles, "Address at the Presentation of a Portrait of Henry Cowles, Commencement, 1900," RSFP, Box 4, Folder 12; "Sara" to Betsey Mix Cowles, October 6, 1840, BMCP, Box 2; Edmund A. West to "Aunt Cornelia" Johnson, September 19, 1840, RSFP, Box 3, Folder 26.

155. Shaw, *Plain Dealer*, 76; Volpe, *Forlorn Hope of Freedom*, 41.

156. This is based on Elizur Wright's estimate of 70,000 voting abolitionists. See Holley, *Life for Liberty*, 30, 235; Shaw, *Plain Dealer*, 76; and *Republican Compiler*, December 1, 1840.

157. *Independent Treasury*, December 22, 1841, January 5, September 21, 1842.

158. OE, December 2, 1840; Roseboom and Weisenburger, *History of Ohio*, 386.

159. Smith, *Liberty and Free Soil Parties*, 47; *Republican Compiler*, December 1, 1840.

160. See *Hazard's United States Commercial and Statistical Register*, May 4, 1842.

161. From 1832 to 1853, Democrats polled an average of 48.9 percent of Ohio's votes to the Whigs' 47.3. See Volpe, *Forlorn Hope of Freedom*, xix, 150 n. 27.

162. OE, December 2, 1840.

163. See L. L. Rice, "Talk re: Slavery," April 1841, RSFP, Box 3, Folder 10.

164. OE, December 2, 1840.

165. Strong, *Perfectionist Politics*, 4.
166. OE, February 1, 1843.
167. Ibid., February 17, 1841.

CHAPTER FIVE

1. Despite what many historians have asserted, Oberlin did not "side" with either abolitionist faction after the split in 1840. Some have taken the financial connection between the Oberlin Institute and the Tappans as proof of allegiance, but this was not the case. In fact, the Tappans' support of the Oberlin Institute had mostly dried up after the panic of 1837, and even when Lewis Tappan was again able to donate money to the school, he was not among the top donors. There was no sense among Oberlinites that the Tappans had "bought" their support or that past donations demanded perpetual loyalty. Though the Oberlin community was probably situated closer to the Tappanites than the Garrisonians, their allegiance was to the slave. For works that claim strict loyalty on the part of Oberlinites to the Tappanite faction, see Speicher, *Religious World of Antislavery Women*, 42–44; Geary, *Balanced in the Wind*, 41; Sterling, *Ahead of Her Time*, 231; and Horton, "Black Education at Oberlin College," 482–83.

2. Johnson, *Abolitionists Vindicated*, 24.

3. OE, May 8, 1839.

4. Amasa Walker to George Thompson, April 19, 1839, DDMP, acc. 1995/142, Box 1, Folder 1.

5. James Forten to James Riley, November 26, 1839, ibid.; Sylvester Graham to Peter Roget, n.d., ibid.

6. Elizabeth Pease to Rachel Savoriry, n.d. (1839), ibid.

7. Lewis Tappan to George Thompson, May 14, 1839, ibid.

8. "An Appeal on Behalf of the Oberlin Institute," in Martineau, *Martyr Age*, vi.

9. Ibid., vii–viii.

10. Ibid., ix.

11. John Keep to Lydia H. Keep, November 30, 1839, RSFP, Box 7, Folder 2; Martineau, *Autobiography*, 345–46; Harriett Martineau to Fanny Wedgwood, December 12, 1839, January 17, March 8, 1840, in Martineau, *Letters to Fanny Wedgwood*, 22–32; Bray, *Philosophy of Necessity*, 639–40.

12. "An Expression of Sentiments of the Colored Students of the Oberlin Institution," July 7, 1841, DDMP, acc. 1995/142, Box 1, Folder 1.

13. John Keep to Theodore Keep, August 5, 1839, RSFP, Box 7, Folder 2.

14. John Keep to William Keep, November 2, 1839, ibid.

15. Mr. Richardson, "Suggested on hearing the Revd. J. Keep lecture on American Slavery," June 1840, RSFP, Box 7, Folder 3; Fletcher, *History of Oberlin College*, 468.

16. *Proceedings of the General Anti-Slavery Convention . . . 1840*, 138–43.

17. John Keep to Lydia Keep, March 15, 1840, RSFP, Box 7, Folder 2.

18. Letter of Mr. N. P. Rodgers, n.d., in *Emancipator*, n.d., in *Liberator*, July 3, 1840.

19. Garrison and Garrison, *William Lloyd Garrison*, 2:366–82; William Lloyd Garrison to Oliver Johnson, July 3, 1840, in *Liberator*, July 24, 1840. See also NYE, June 25, 1840; and Stanton, *Random Recollections*, 75–81. Garrison was not present for this debate and would not arrive in London until the sixth day of the convention.

20. John Keep to Lydia Keep, March 15, 1840, RSFP, Box 7, Folder 2.
21. Walters, Antislavery Appeal, 5.
22. Philanthropist, March 9, 1838; Liberator, March 9, 1838.
23. OE, June 23, 1841. To be sure, not all easterners were embroiled in the abolitionist infighting, particularly those who had already distanced themselves from the AASS and its leaders. Not coincidentally, these men, like Gerrit Smith and Charles Sumner, enjoyed much closer relationships with African Americans than most white abolitionists.
24. Robertson, Hearts Beating for Liberty, 164–65.
25. OE, March 11, 1840.
26. Emancipator, June 11, 1840; J. R. S. to "Dear Brother," May 29, 1840, in OE, July 1, 1840; OE, July 1, 1840; Philanthropist, June 9, 1840; Emancipator, June 18, 1840.
27. J. R. S. to "Dear Brother," May 29, 1840, in OE, July 1, 1840; Philanthropist, June 9, 1840.
28. Philanthropist, June 9, 1840. See also Liberator, July 3, 1840.
29. Liberator, June 24, 1842; Philanthropist, June 15, 1842; William Birney to James Birney, June 9, 1842, Birney, Letters, 2:697–98.
30. Abby Kelley, quoted in Sterling, Ahead of Her Time, 223. See also Liberator, November 12, 1847.
31. William Birney to James Birney, June 9, 1842, Birney, Letters, 2:697–98. It should be noted that the OASS and the Liberty Party were distinct entities. Each organization held conventions separate from one another to avoid the very conflicts of interest some Garrisonians accused them of. See Philanthropist, June 9, 1841, June 15, 1842.
32. Hamm, God's Government Begun, 77–80.
33. Abram Brooke to Gamaliel Bailey, December 19, 1842, in Philanthropist, July 5, 1843; Philanthropist, July 19, 1843.
34. Philanthropist, January 4, 1843.
35. Ibid., February 8, July 5, 1843; Harrold, Gamaliel Bailey and Antislavery Union, 44.
36. OE, July 17, 1844; Cincinnati Weekly Herald and Philanthropist, August 16, 1844.
37. Liberator, June 24, 1842.
38. Ibid.; Abram Brooke to Gamaliel Bailey, December 19, 1842, in Philanthropist, July 5, 1843.
39. Cincinnati Weekly Herald and Philanthropist, August 16, 1845.
40. Cyrus McNealy, after his election, tendered his resignation but was immediately reelected. See Cincinnati Weekly Herald and Philanthropist, July 2, 1845.
41. Ibid.
42. Warren Liberty Herald, May 29, 1844.
43. OE, October 12, 1842.
44. John Cowles to Henry Cowles, February 6, 1838, RSFP, Box 4, Folder 18.
45. OE, July 17, 31, 1839.
46. Liberator, September 17, 1841, August 26, 1842.
47. Ibid., June 11, 1841.
48. Ibid., September 17, October 29, 1841.
49. OE, June 9, 1841.
50. Amasa Walker to William Lloyd Garrison, July 30, 1842, in Liberator, August 12, 1842.
51. P. D. Hathaway to William Lloyd Garrison, July 2, 1841, in Liberator, July 16, 1841.

52. Lucretia Coffin Mott to Richard and Hannah Webb, April 2, 1841, in Mott, *Letters*, 91–94.
53. *Liberator*, November 21, 1845. See also Gamble, "Western Anti-Slavery Society," 10.
54. Brooke would renounce politics in 1846 and be reappointed agent of the newly named Western Anti-Slavery Society. See *Fourteenth Annual Report*, 55, and Gamble, "Western Anti-Slavery Society," 10.
55. Greene, "Abby Kelley Foster," 174.
56. Abby Kelley to James Monroe, October 2, 1843, JMP, Box 1; *Liberator*, June 27, 1845.
57. *Liberator*, June 27, 1845.
58. Ibid., July 11, 1845.
59. Gamble, "Western Anti-Slavery Society," 50.
60. Parker Pillsbury to William Lloyd Garrison, June 22, 1846, in *Liberator*, July 3, 1846; *Anti-Slavery Bugle*, n.d., in *Liberator*, July 17, 1846.
61. *Anti-Slavery Bugle*, September 4, 1846; Geary, *Balanced in the Wind*, 59.
62. Lucy Stone to Francis Stone and Harriet Stone, February 15, 1846, RSFP, Box 10, Folder 2.
63. Abby Kelley to Betsey Mix Cowles, June 29, 1846, BMCP.
64. Giles Stebbins to William Lloyd Garrison, July 9, 1845, in *Liberator*, July 25, 1845. Garrison agreed that these Liberty men were "generally very candid, and incomparably more kind and friendly to us than those of their party at the East" (William Lloyd Garrison to Helen Garrison, August 20, 1847, in *Letters*, 3:514–17).
65. Wright, "Oberlin's Contribution to Ethics," 438.
66. *Philanthropist*, June 15, 1842; *New Lisbon Western Palladium*, n.d., in *Liberator*, June 27, 1845.
67. See *Cincinnati Weekly Herald and Philanthropist*, July 10, 1844.
68. See *Philanthropist*, June 14, 1842, August 9, September 13, 1843; *Cincinnati Weekly Herald and Philanthropist*, July 10, 1844; *Liberty Press*, n.d., in *Liberator*, November 10, 1843; Gamble, "Western Antislavery Society," 1–7.
69. *Anti-Slavery Bugle*, n.d., in *Liberator*, April 24, 1846.
70. BAP, 3:24.
71. *Report of the Proceedings of the Colored National Convention*, 18.
72. Sara Stanley, "Address of the Ladies' Anti-Slavery Society," in Lawson, *Three Sarahs*, 68.
73. Fairchild, *Educational Arrangements*, 19.
74. *Anti-Slavery Bugle*, July 24, 1846; *Palladium of Liberty*, July 10, 1844.
75. *Report of the Proceedings of the Colored National Convention*, 18.
76. Cheek and Cheek, *John Mercer Langston*, 95.
77. Coppin, *Reminiscences*, 12.
78. Sara Stanley, "Address of the Ladies' Anti-Slavery Society," in Lawson, *Three Sarahs*, 69.
79. Cheek and Cheek, *John Mercer Langston*, 95. See also Smith, *Oberlin Unmasked*, 56–58.
80. Fairchild, *Oberlin*, 113.
81. *Anti-Slavery Bugle*, October 9, 1846; Abby Kelley and Stephen Foster to Parker Pillsbury, n.d., in *Liberator*, October 23, 1846.
82. Revelation 16:4, quoted in Pillsbury, *Acts of the Anti-Slavery Apostles*, 366.
83. See *Liberator*, May 20, 27, June 3, 1842.

84. Thome, "Come-outism," 158–59.
85. This was a major difference between Finney's notion of perfectionism and that of many other perfectionists, some of whom he had converted but eventually went beyond his teachings. Though many Finney converts became abolitionists, their becoming narrowly defined abolitionists was due to his teachings on perfectionism rather than from any of his specific instructions.
86. Thome, "Come-outism," 173.
87. Ibid., 163. See also OE, March 4, 1846.
88. Thome, "Come-outism," 163.
89. Ibid., 165–66.
90. Ibid., 174–75. See also Cowles, "Abolition, a Religious Enterprise," 138–39.
91. Liberator, May 8, 1846. See also Geary, Balanced in the Wind, 55–58.
92. Betsey Mix Cowles to Henry Cowles, February 14, 1846, RSFP, Box 4, Folder 18.
93. Abby Kelley to Betsey Mix Cowles, March 15, 1846, BMCP. See also Helen Cowles to Miss Hawkins, March 3, 1846, HCP, Box 3.
94. OE, March 4, April 1, 1846; Lewis Tappan to Charles Grandison Finney, March 31, 1846, LTP, roll 3; Finney, Memoirs, 469 n. 12; Helen M. Cowles to A. Y. Hawkins, March 3, 1846, RSFP, Box 5, Folder 3.
95. Abby Kelley to Betsey Mix Cowles, March 15, 1846, BMCP.
96. Ibid.
97. OE, March 4, 1846.
98. Ibid.
99. Betsey Hudson and Timothy Hudson to Betsey Mix Cowles, March 5, 1846, BMCP.
100. Betsey Hudson to Betsey Mix Cowles, February 27, 1846, BMCP; Betsey Hudson and Timothy Hudson to Betsey Mix Cowles, March 5, 1846, BMCP; Geary, Balanced in the Wind, 54. See also Spooner, Unconstitutionality of Slavery; Goodell, Slavery and Anti-Slavery, 563–82; and Wiecek, Sources of Antislavery Constitutionalism in America.
101. Betsey Hudson and Timothy Hudson to Betsey Mix Cowles, March 5, 1846, BMCP.
102. Helen Cowles to Miss Hawkins, March 3, 1846, HCP, Box 3.
103. Ibid.
104. Liberator, March 27, 1846.
105. See J. T. Everett to William Lloyd Garrison, February 17, 1856, in Liberator, February 29, 1856.
106. Liberator, April 17, 1846.
107. Abby Kelley to Lucy Stone, August 15, 1846, RSFP, Box 10, Folder 2; Anti-Slavery Bugle, October 9, 1846.
108. Anti-Slavery Bugle, October 9, 1846.
109. Liberator, October 23, 1846; Fletcher, History of Oberlin College, 268. Kelley called the chapel "an old building always open for Whig meetings, and like proslavery caucuses" (Anti-Slavery Bugle, October 9, 1846).
110. Liberator, October 23, 1846; OE, September 30, 1846; Anti-Slavery Bugle, October 9, 1846.
111. Fletcher, History of Oberlin College, 269.
112. Ibid., 267.
113. OE, September 30, 1846.

114. *OE*, June 10, 1846.
115. Abby Kelley and Stephen Foster to Parker Pillsbury, n.d., in *Liberator*, October 23, 1846.
116. See William Lloyd Garrison to Helen Garrison, August 16, 1847, in *Garrison Letters*, 3:510–14.
117. *Liberator*, September 15, 1865.
118. *Liberator*, September 10, 1847.
119. William Lloyd Garrison to Helen E. Garrison, August 28, 1847, Garrison, *Letters*, 3:522–26.
120. Ibid.
121. Ibid. See also CTD, September 3, 1847.
122. William Lloyd Garrison to Helen E. Garrison, August 28, 1847, Garrison, *Letters*, 3:522–26.
123. Ibid.
124. See Trowbridge, *My Own Story*, 170; Thomas, *Liberator*, 294.
125. William Lloyd Garrison to Samuel May Jr., in Garrison and Garrison, *William Lloyd Garrison*, 3:236.
126. Ibid.; William Lloyd Garrison to Josiah Quincey, n.d., in ibid., 235.
127. NASS, September 9, 1847.
128. NASS, September 23, 1847.
129. See Frederick Douglass to Amy Post, October 28, 1847, excerpted in McFeely, *Frederick Douglass*, 149.
130. NS, December 3, 1847; *OE*, September 27, 1848.
131. *OE*, September 27, 1848.

CHAPTER SIX

1. Spencer, *Protest and Praise*, 43–45.
2. Thomas Earle to Asa Mahan, December 7, 1842, RSFP, Box 14, Folder 1. See also Finney, *Memoirs*, 387–88, and *Journal of the Senate of the State of Ohio* (1842), 358–59, 435.
3. *Ohio Statesman*, February 9, 1842.
4. *Ohio State Journal and Columbus Gazette*, February 21, 1842.
5. *Journal of the Senate of the State of Ohio* (1842), 564–65.
6. Josiah Harris to Wife, Thanksgiving, A.M., 1842, in Fairchild, *Oberlin*, 368–70.
7. *Journal of the House of Representatives of the State of Ohio* (1842), 7; Thomas Earle to Asa Mahan, December 7, 1842, RSFP, Box 14, Folder 1.
8. *Ohio Statesman*, December 13, 1842; *Cleveland Daily Herald*, December 12, 1842.
9. Thomas Earle to Asa Mahan, December 7, 1842, RSFP, Box 14, Folder 1.
10. *Ohio Statesman*, December 13, 1842.
11. Ibid.
12. Thomas Earle to Asa Mahan, December 7, 1842, RSFP, Box 14, Folder 1; Josiah Harris to Wife, Thanksgiving, A.M., 1842, in Fairchild, *Oberlin*, 368–70.
13. *Journal of the House of Representatives of the State of Ohio* (1842), 136.
14. Fairchild, *Oberlin*, 38; Burroughs, "Oberlin's Part in the Slavery Conflict," 296.
15. *Ohio State Journal and Columbus Gazette*, December 26, 1842.

16. *Journal of the House of Representatives of the State of Ohio* (1842), 227; *Ohio Statesman*, December 13, 1842; NYE, December 22, 1842.

17. *Philanthropist*, December 7, 1842.

18. Joel Tiffany to Gamaliel Bailey, November 2, 1844, in *Cincinnati Weekly Herald and Philanthropist*, November 13, 1844.

19. *Lorain Republican*, September 6, 13, 20, 27, October 11, 18, 25, 1843.

20. *Liberty Herald*, October 26, November 9, 16, 1843.

21. *Cincinnati Weekly Herald and Philanthropist*, November 8, 1843.

22. *Liberty Herald*, November 9, 1843.

23. See *Philanthropist*, June 16, 1841.

24. See Fehrenbach, *Lone Star*, 190–267.

25. Ibid., 263–67.

26. *Philanthropist*, March 30, 1840. See also ibid., April 13, 1842.

27. See Crapol, *John Tyler*, 7–28.

28. Antislavery Whigs who remained in the party, such as Charles Sumner, John Quincy Adams, and Joshua Giddings, became known as "Conscience" Whigs, as opposed to the conservative "Cotton" Whigs, whose close links to the South led them to either deemphasize the slavery issue or come out in favor of the institution. See Howe, *Political Culture of the American Whigs*, 43–69.

29. See *Huron Reflector*, October 29, 1844.

30. *Independent Treasury*, October 5, 1842. See also ibid., June 22, 1842.

31. *Ohio Atlas and Elyria Advertiser*, September 29, 1841.

32. *Lorain Republican*, July 12, 1843. See also *Ohio Atlas and Elyria Advertiser*, August 26, 1842.

33. *Cincinnati Weekly Herald and Philanthropist*, October 23, 1844.

34. "Rough Notes of Anti-Slavery Meeting, Buffalo," August 31, 1843, RG 21, Oberlin File, Series 6, Box 1, OCA; *Lorain Republican*, September 13, 1843; *Liberator*, September 15, 1843; *Liberator*, March 5, 1847.

35. Smith, *Liberty and Free Soil Parties*, 72.

36. See Henry Clay, "Petitions for the Abolition of Slavery," in Clay, *Life and Speeches*, 355–75.

37. *Philanthropist*, September 20, June 15, 1843.

38. *Buckeye Sentinel*, July 2, 1844.

39. *Huron Reflector*, August 27, 1844.

40. OE, October 9, 1844.

41. *Liberty Herald*, February 22, 1844.

42. OE, February 1, 1843, October 9, 1844; Shaw, *Plain Dealer*, 76.

43. See *Jeffersonian*, October 18, 1844.

44. "1844 Presidential General Election Results Ohio"; *Ohio Almanac*, 114–17.

45. *New York Tribune*, November 28, 1844, quoted in Smith, *Liberty and Free Soil Parties*, 81.

46. See also Shaw, *Plain Dealer*, 76; Hinshaw, *Ohio Elects the President*, 26–27; and Smith, *Liberty and Free Soil Parties*, 80.

47. *Jeffersonian*, November 29, 1844.

48. *Lorain Republican*, July 17, 1844.

49. OE, November 20, 1844.

50. OE, May 10, 1843. Amasa Walker went as Oberlin's delegate to the World's Peace Convention that year and served as the meeting's vice president. Oberlin also sent delegates to the convention in 1849, 1850, and 1851. See Fletcher, *History of Oberlin College*, 275–89.

51. OE, June 10, 1846; *Liberator*, July 3, 1846.

52. OE, May 27, 1846.

53. CTD, August 2, 1848, in NE, August 10, 1848.

54. OE, June 22, 1848.

55. Lucy Stone to Francis Stone and Harriet Stone, February 15, 1846, RSFP, Box 10, Folder 2.

56. OE "Extra," July 6, 1848.

57. Ibid.

58. Ibid.

59. Smith, *Liberty and Free Soil Parties*, 108–9. See also *New York Tribune*, n.d., in NE, June 10, 1847; and Gamble, "Joshua Giddings and the Ohio Abolitionists," 46.

60. Riddle, "Rise of the Anti-Slavery Sentiment on the Western Reserve."

61. NE, July 6, 1848; *Addresses and Proceedings*, 6.

62. NE, July 20, 1848.

63. *True Democrat*, August 2, 1848, in NE, August 10, 1848. These men were all either the editors or frequent contributors to the *Oberlin Evangelist*. However, their explicit endorsement of a particular political party did not appear in that newspaper because of a series of pledges found in its first issue, including "Not to promote party or sectarian interests." See OE, December 20, 1838.

64. *True Democrat*, August 2, 1848, in NE, August 10, 1848.

65. NS, August 11, 1848. See also Gardiner, *Great Issue*, 3–10, 137–51.

66. See Henry Wright to William Lloyd Garrison, October 26, 1847, in *Liberator*, November 19, 1847; and Smith, *Liberty and Free Soil Parties*, 138.

67. Martin Delaney to Frederick Douglass, June 1, 1848, in NS, July 14, 1848; NS, August 11, 1848. See also *Liberator*, September 8, 1848.

68. OE "Extra," July 6, 1848.

69. Sereno Streeter to Henry Cowles, August 14, 1848, HCP, Box 3. See also OE, August 16, 1848.

70. *National Party Platforms*, 19–20.

71. OE, August 16, 1848.

72. Ibid.

73. Mayer, *All on Fire*, 384.

74. NASS, August 31, 1848. Besides monetary contributions, Smith also donated tens of thousands of acres of land in western Virginia to Oberlin in 1839 when he was notified of their financial hardship. See Stauffer, *Black Hearts of Men*, 120.

75. OE, August 30, 1848.

76. OE, September 27, 1848.

77. *True Democrat*, August 2, 1848, in NE, August 10, 1848.

78. "Free Soil Song," in Clark, *Free Soil Minstrel*, 222–23.

79. Finney, *Lectures on Systematic Theology*, 428.

80. *Report of the Proceedings of the Colored National Convention*, 4.

81. Ibid., 14–15.

82. Ibid., 13–14.

83. Ibid., 14–15.

84. Monroe, Oberlin Thursday Lectures, 148–50.

85. Cleveland Herald, November 16, 25, 1848; Scioto Gazette, November 29, 1848; Roseboom and Weisenburger, History of Ohio, 468–70.

86. Charles Penfield to Helen Cowles, November 21, 1848, RSFP, Box 4, Folder 19.

87. OE, November 22, 1848.

88. NS, December 8, 1848.

89. "Minutes and Address of the State Convention of the Colored Citizens," 220–21; NS, January 12, 1849; Columbus Journal, n.d., in Liberator, January 26, March 2, 1849, and OE, February 14, 1849.

90. Interestingly, John Mercer Langston was one of the few delegates in favor of emigration, arguing that American racism was too powerful for African Americans to live peaceful lives in its midst. Soon, however, even Langston came out as a forceful opponent of any removal scheme. See "Minutes and Address of the State Convention of the Colored Citizens," 223–26.

91. Ibid., 228–31.

92. BAP, 3:19–20.

93. See Davis, Slavery and Human Progress, 265.

94. Ibid., 229–30. Walker was a free African American originally from the South who urged slaves to revolt against their masters, spoke out against colonization, and hoped to instill racial pride in his intended black readership. Garnet's "Address" was presented at the 1843 National Black Convention in Buffalo. In it, he also called for slaves to rebel against their masters. At the time, most African American abolitionists still considered themselves nonresistant Garrisonians. After much debate, Garnet's speech was rejected by the convention by one vote. For more on Walker, Garnet, and their respective addresses, see Stuckey, Slave Culture, 98–192. It is likely that the suggestion to circulate these addresses came from William Howard Day, who had been close friends with Garnet since their days as classmates in New York City's Public School No. 2 and cofounders of the school's Garrison Literary Society in 1834. See Liberator, April 19, 1834.

95. OE, February 6, 1849.

96. Mealy, Aliened American, 148–49.

97. NS, January 26, 1849.

98. OE, January 13, 1849.

99. Cincinnati Gazette, February 2, 1849, quoted in Mealy, Aliened American, 155.

100. Ibid. See also NYE, January 25, 1849.

101. See Middleton, Black Laws, 123.

102. See Ohio Observer, November 18, 1846; and Upton, History of the Western Reserve, 555.

103. Anti-Slavery Bugle, August 14, 1846.

104. Abby Kelley to Betsey Mix Cowles, November 8, 1846, BMCP. See also Geary, Balanced in the Wind, 57–59.

105. Robertson, Hearts Beating for Liberty, 143–44.

106. Geary, Balanced in the Wind, 60.

107. Timothy Hudson to Betsey Mix Cowles, January 20, 1848, BMCP; Timothy Hudson to James Birney, January 20, 1848, in Birney, Letters, 2:1089–90.

108. Timothy Hudson to Betsey Mix Cowles, January 20, 1848, BMCP.

109. See Martin Delaney to Frederick Douglass, March 22, 1848, in NS, April 7, 1848.

110. Martin Delaney to Frederick Douglass, June 1, 1848, in NS, July 14, 1848.

111. Ibid.

112. Ibid.

113. Ibid.

114. NE, January 18, February 1, 1849; Jones, *Squirrel Hunters of Ohio*, 74. Townsend was an active agent of the Underground Railroad, had been the OASS's delegate to the World's Anti-Slavery Convention in London in 1840, and was named to the Oberlin Institute board of trustees in 1845. See Blue and McCormick, "Norton S. Townsend," 144–54.

115. NE, October 26, 1848, January 18, 1849; Townsend, "Salmon P. Chase," 117.

116. Townsend, "Salmon P. Chase," 120; NE, March 22, 1849.

117. Townsend was an acquaintance of Chase's for many years. They first met when Chase was arguing a case on behalf of an alleged fugitive slave in Cincinnati in 1837. After hearing Chase's arguments, Townsend declared, "There is a man I can and will vote for whenever I have the opportunity" (Townsend, "Salmon P. Chase," 117).

118. Conservatives were able to amend the final repeal bill so that it did not erase the bar to African American service on juries or the legal impediment to their being able to vote. See ibid., 119–20.

119. NE, March 8, 1849; OE, February 28, 1849, in Holt, "Party Politics in Ohio," 361; Hart, *Salmon Portland Chase*, 107–12; Wright, *Standard History of Lorain County*, 229; Goodwin, *Team of Rivals*, 135.

120. CTD, February 1, 1849.

121. *Elyria Courier*, September 12, 1848.

122. NE, March 22, 1849.

123. NE, May 3, 1849.

124. OE, February 28, 1849.

125. *Liberator*, March 2, 1849.

126. NS, June 29, 1849.

127. See *Revised Statutes of the State of Ohio*, 41 n. 2, and Middleton, *Black Laws*, 149.

128. *Aliened American*, April 9, 1853.

129. *Missouri Daily Democrat*, November 29, 1865.

130. Bigglestone, *They Stopped in Oberlin*, 172. See also OE, March 14, 1849, for Oberlin's defense against charges of voting misconduct. It was the duty of each township trustee to uphold his oath of office under the Ohio Constitution "*as he understands it.*" Though a blatant disregard of the constitutional restrictions on voting eligibility was inappropriate, it was clear that election officials in Oberlin were allowed considerable flexibility in their decisions.

131. "Minutes of the State Convention of the Colored Citizens . . . 1850," 243.

132. Ibid., 246.

133. Ibid., 252; Steinglass and Scarselli, *Ohio State Constitution*, 20.

134. See Cheek and Cheek, *John Mercer Langston*, 152.

135. "Minutes of the State Convention of the Colored Citizens . . . 1850," 251.

136. Ibid., 248–49, 251–52; CTD, December 24, 1849.

137. "Minutes of the State Convention of the Colored Citizens . . . 1850," 252.

138. *Report on the Debates and Proceedings*, 1:28.

139. See Quillin, *Color Line in Ohio*, 61.

140. "Minutes of the State Convention of the Colored Citizens . . . 1850," 266.

141. Ibid., 269–72.

142. *Report on the Debates and Proceedings*, 1:458.

143. Ibid.

144. Their participation had been barred earlier by legislative statute. See *Report on the Debates and Proceedings*, 2:346, 699; Quillin, *Color Line in Ohio*, 76, 85.

145. *Report on the Debates and Proceedings*, 2:8; Quillin, *Color Line in Ohio*, 76–77.

146. *Report on the Debates and Proceedings*, 2:552; Quillin, *Color Line in Ohio*, 77–78.

147. Blue and McCormick, "Norton S. Townsend," 149–50.

148. *Report on the Debates and Proceeding*, 2:552; Quillin, *Color Line in Ohio*, 77–78.

149. *Report on the Debates and Proceedings*, 2:556–60; Quillin, *Color Line in Ohio*, 81.

150. "Minutes of the State Convention of the Colored Citizens . . . 1850," 259.

151. Langston, quoted in Cheek and Cheek, *John Mercer Langston*, 156.

152. OE, January 6, 1847.

CHAPTER SEVEN

1. *Oberlin Students' Monthly*, 1:1, 1858, RSFP, Box 18, Folder 11.

2. Quoted in Osborne, *Music in Ohio*, 386.

3. See Joshua Giddings to Henry Cowles, February 7, 1850, HCP, Box 3.

4. Charles Langston and John Mercer Langston to Salmon Chase, September 12, 1850, SPCP, roll 8.

5. See Kaminski, *Necessary Evil?*, 238–39, and Potter, *Impending Crisis*, 90–120.

6. "Minutes of the State Convention of the Colored Citizens . . . 1851," 260.

7. William Newman to Frederick Douglass, October 1, 1850, in NS, October 24, 1850.

8. As David Potter notes, to appreciate the full impact of the law, one must consider that it was not just a law to capture slaves in the act of running away but also a device for reclaiming slaves who had absconded in years past. There was no statute of limitations in the law, and even if an African American had lived in freedom for years, the law guaranteed his or her former owner both possession of his or her person and assistance in claiming the former bondsman. See Potter, *Impending Crisis*, 131–32.

9. William Newman to Frederick Douglass, October 1, 1850, in NS, October 24, 1850.

10. John Keep to Charles Grandison Finney, November 18, 1850, CGFP.

11. NS, October 24, 1850.

12. CTD, September 30, 1850.

13. See Finney, *Memoirs*, 412–13; NYE, March 27, 1841; Shumway and Brower, *Oberliniana*, 30–31; *Liberator*, March 2, 1849.

14. Horton and Horton, *Slavery and the Making of America*, 155; Cheek and Cheek, *John Mercer Langston*, 172.

15. Langston, *From the Virginia Plantation*, 101–2. See "1850 Census of Russia Township"; "1860 Census of Russia Township"; and Cochran, *Western Reserve and the Fugitive Slave Law*, 119. Census statistics include African Americans listed as "black" or "mulatto." In 1850, there were 92 residents listed as "mulatto" and 77 as "black." In 1860, there were 353 "mulatto" residents and 124 "black."

16. Horton and Horton, *Slavery and the Making of America*, 155; Cheek and Cheek, *John Mercer Langston*, 172.

17. "Minutes of the State Convention of the Colored Citizens . . . 1851," 259–60.

18. Brown would go on to become a bishop of the African Methodist Episcopal church in the South after the Civil War. See Simmons, *Men of Mark*, 1113–118.

19. "Minutes of the State Convention of the Colored Citizens . . . 1851," 261–63. Douglass's motion was defeated 28–2.

20. Ibid.

21. Ibid.

22. *Liberator*, February 14, 1851.

23. *Anti-Slavery Bugle*, February 22, 1851; *Liberator*, February 14, 1851.

24. "Minutes of the State Convention of the Colored Citizens . . . 1851," 265.

25. Langston, *From the Virginia Plantation*, 111–13. This theme would be raised again in a speech of Charles Langston in 1859. See Chapter 9.

26. Theological Society Records, May 15, 1850, RSFP, Box 13, Folder 21. Daniel Webster was a senator from Massachusetts and one of the most outspoken advocates of the Compromise of 1850.

27. Records of the Young Men's Anti-Slavery Society, September 14, 1851, RG 19/3/6, Box 3, OCA. Membership in the society was open to "any person who is *practically* opposed to slavery."

28. Langston, *From the Virginia Plantation*, 141.

29. "Proceedings of the Convention of the Colored Freemen of Ohio . . . 1852," 276.

30. FDP, October 1, 1852.

31. Ibid.; William Newman to Frederick Douglass, October 1, 1850, in NS, October 24, 1850.

32. William Newman to Frederick Douglass, October 1, 1850, in NS, October 24, 1850.

33. "Minutes of the State Convention of the Colored Citizens . . . 1851," 263.

34. Alexander, *African or American?*, 97.

35. Fairchild, *Oberlin*, 156.

36. Sara Stanley, "Address of the Ladies' Anti-Slavery Society," in Lawson, *Three Sarahs*, 69.

37. *National Party Platforms*, 20–22.

38. OE, August 18, 1852.

39. CTD, June 19, 1852.

40. Ibid.

41. Wilentz, *Rise of American Democracy*, 663.

42. FDP, August 20, 1852; NE, August 26, October 21, 1852.

43. "Tenth Annual Report of the Western Anti-Slavery Society," Western Reserve Historical Society, Salem, Ohio.

44. FDP, August 20, 1852.

45. OE, August 18, 1852.

46. Walker, *Memoir of Hon. Amasa Walker*, 10; Cheek and Cheek, *John Mercer Langston*, 208.

47. Records of the Young Men's Anti-Slavery Society, October 1, 1852, RG 19/3/6, Box 3, OCA; NE, October 14, 1852.

48. Langston, *From the Virginia Plantation*, 137.

49. Ibid., 137–39.
50. FDP, December 17, 1852.
51. OE, December 8, 1852.
52. Ibid.
53. Ibid.
54. OE, August 18, 1852.
55. New York Tribune, July 19, 1853, in Liberator, July 22, 1853.
56. See Wilentz, Rise of American Democracy, 672.
57. OE, February 15, 1854.
58. James Fairchild, "Nebraska," n.d., JHFP, Series 8, Box 9.
59. OE, February 15, 1854; Cleveland Daily Herald, February 2, 1854.
60. NYT, May 10, 1855.
61. Monroe, Oberlin Thursday Lectures, 97.
62. OE, July 6, 1854.
63. OE, August 16, 1854; FDP, August 25, 1854.
64. Tiffin Advertiser, n.d., in Liberator, October 12, 1855; FDP, April 20, May 18, 1855.
65. Boston Herald, September 26, 1891.
66. Douglas quoted in Oates, Approaching Fury, 152.
67. Cleveland Leader, October 12, 1854.
68. Monroe, Oberlin Thursday Lectures, 97–8; Smith, History of the Republican Party in Ohio, 26–31.
69. OE, October 24, 1855.
70. Ibid.
71. Samuel Adair to Simeon Jocelyn, April 18, 1854, AMA, Ohio, roll 4; OE, August 30, 1854; NE, September 7, 1854; NYE, September 7, 1854.
72. OE, September 27, 1854.
73. NYT, June 23, 1856.
74. NE, September 7, 1854; OE, August 30, 1854.
75. NE, September 7, 1854; OE, August 30, 1854.
76. OE, August 30, 1854; NE, September 7, 1854.
77. Cleveland Leader, November 1, 1854.
78. Fletcher, History of Oberlin College, 392.
79. Samuel Adair to Simeon Jocelyn, June 24, 1854, AMA, Ohio, roll 1. See also ibid., May 3, 1855.
80. Samuel Adair to Simeon Jocelyn, September 8, 1855, TKO; John Byrd to Simeon Jocelyn, August 11, 1856, AMA, Kansas, roll 1; Sengupta, For God and Mammon, 61.
81. John Byrd to Simeon Jocelyn, January 20, 1859, AMA, Kansas, roll 1.
82. Sengupta, For God and Mammon, 60.
83. John Byrd to Simeon Jocelyn, July 7, August 3, 1855, AMA, Kansas, roll 1; Elizabeth Byrd to George Whipple, August 28, September 3, 1856, AMA, Kansas, roll 1.
84. John Everett to Dear Father, January 25, 1856, in Everett, "Letters," 99.
85. Samuel Adair to Simeon Jocelyn, n.d. [1855?], AMA, Kansas, roll 1. See also Horatio Norton to Simeon Jocelyn, June 10, 1857, ibid.
86. Richardson, Beyond the Mississippi, 43.
87. John Byrd to Simeon Jocelyn, August 5, 1855, AMA, Kansas, roll 1.

88. OE, April 25, 1855. See also Samuel Adair to Henry Cowles, January 30, 1855, RSFP, Box 4, Folder 13.

89. Henry Cowles Jr. to Henry Cowles, March 26, April 2, 1855, RSFP, Box 4, Folder 13.

90. Cleveland Plain Dealer, February 13, 1856.

91. Ellis, Oberlin and the American Conflict, 6.

92. OE, June 4, 1856. See also Mary Cowles diary, May 26–27, June 19, 1856, RSFP, Box 5, Folder 6.

93. See OE, August 30, September 27, 1854.

94. See Mary Cowles diary, May 26–28, 1856, RSFP, Box 5, Folder 6.

95. American Missionary 10, no. 10 (October 1856): 29.

96. Boston Daily Advertiser, July 17, 1856, excerpted in Thayer, History of the Kansas Crusade, 214–16; Essig, "Lord's Free Man," 42–43. It was through this organization that John Brown received assistance in his own Kansas crusades. See Sanborn, Life and Letters of John Brown, 346–47.

97. Mary Cowles diary, June 19, 1856, RSFP, Box 5, Folder 6.

98. Wilentz, Rise of American Democracy, 685.

99. Smith, History of the Republican Party in Ohio, 53; Proceedings of the First Three Republican National Conventions, 40.

100. National Party Platforms, 28; Smith, History of the Republican Party in Ohio, 55–56.

101. See Holland, Frederick Douglass, 249.

102. "Proceedings of the State Convention of Colored Men . . . 1856," 308.

103. Monroe, Oberlin Thursday Lectures, 98–99; Smith, History of the Republican Party in Ohio, 59–63.

104. Monroe, Oberlin Thursday Lectures, 148–49.

105. Ibid., 100; Rokicky, James Monroe, 25–26; Cheek and Cheek, John Mercer Langston, 270.

106. Cleveland Plain Dealer, September 12, 1855.

107. Monroe, Oberlin Thursday Lectures, 101.

108. Greiner quoted in Wiley, "'Governor' John Greiner," 262.

109. Monroe, Oberlin Thursday Lectures, 111–12.

110. Ibid., 119–20, 152.

111. Rokicky, James Monroe, 36.

112. Oberlin Students' Monthly, vol. 1, 1858, RSFP, Box 18, Folder 11.

113. OE, n.d., in FDP, August 25, 1854.

114. Anti-Slavery Bugle, December 4, 1858.

115. Ibid., August 2, 9, 16, 1856; Cleveland Daily Herald, May 1, 1856.

116. William Nell to William Lloyd Garrison, August 4, November 10, 1856, in Liberator, August 15, November 14, 1856; "Proceedings of the State Convention of Colored Men . . . 1856," 307–9; Cleveland Daily Herald, May 1, 1856.

117. Independent Democrat, August 6, 1856.

118. Newark Advocate, August 15, 20, 1856.

119. Cleveland Plain Dealer, September 3, 1856.

120. OE, August 27, 1856.

121. Liberator, November 21, 1856.

122. Cleveland Plain Dealer, n.d., in Newark Advocate, November 26, 1856.

123. The vote was 444 to 77. See Ellsworth, "Oberlin and the Anti-Slavery Movement," 131.

124. Wilentz, *Rise of American Democracy*, 701–2.

125. "Proceedings of the State Convention of Colored Men . . . 1857," 327; Cheek and Cheek, *John Mercer Langston*, 323.

126. "Proceedings of the State Convention of Colored Men of the State of Ohio . . . 1857," 323–30.

127. OE, March 4, 1857; Cheek and Cheek, *John Mercer Langston*, 324.

128. See Appendix to the *Journal of the Senate of the State of Ohio*, 528–33.

129. Monroe, *Oberlin Thursday Lectures*, 128.

130. OE, March 4, 1857.

131. *Liberator*, January 9, 1857. Brown's play has been lost, but contemporary accounts describe it as a drama that illuminated the lack of understanding demonstrated by white Northerners, even progressive ones, for the needs and desires of African Americans, especially slaves. See Watson, *History of Southern Drama*, 145.

132. For a complete analysis of the decision, see Fehrenbacher, *Slavery, Law, and Politics*, 183–213.

133. Mead, "History of Plymouth Rock Conference," 37.

134. Cheek and Cheek, *John Mercer Langston*, 324.

135. Potter, *Impending Crisis*, 290–93.

136. See Blue, *Salmon P. Chase*, 115–16.

137. *Cincinnati Enquirer*, n.d., in NASS, November 7, 1857; Smith, *History of the Republican Party in Ohio*, 74.

138. Smith, *History of the Republican Party in Ohio*, 74.

139. *Anti-Slavery Bugle*, December 4, 1858.

140. Ibid.; Rokicky, *James Monroe*, 44. See also "Speech of Mr. Monroe of Lorain, Upon the Bill to Repeal the Habeas Corpus Act of 1856," JMP, Box 27.

141. Stewart, *Joshua R. Giddings*, 259–61; Cheek and Cheek, *John Mercer Langston*, 325.

142. Corwin, *Life and Speeches*, 359–84.

143. Stewart, *Joshua R. Giddings*, 260.

144. *Anti-Slavery Bugle*, December 4, 1858.

145. Langston, *Freedom and Citizenship*, 45, 57–58.

146. H. G. Blake to James Monroe, September 6, 1858, JMP, Box 1.

CHAPTER EIGHT

1. Fairchild, *Underground Railroad*, 91.

2. Especially in Oberlin, a town famous for its involvement, the desire to celebrate the myth is strong. Oberlin professor Geoffrey Blodgett has noted that several houses in Oberlin are claimed by some modern residents to have been used as Underground Railroad hiding places but were actually constructed after the Civil War, one as late as 1885. See Blodgett, *Oberlin History*, 8, and Gara, *Liberty Line*.

3. Robertson, *Hearts Beating for Liberty*, 182.

4. See Bordewich, *Bound for Canaan*, 3–8, and Lasser, "Underground Railroad in Oberlin History and Memory."

5. Believability of their accounts seems to have been a concern of antebellum Oberlinites. One particular episode in 1841 is instructive. After an Oberlin resident and self-emancipated

slave was kidnapped and then rescued, a theological student wrote an account of the incident for publication in the Cincinnati *Philanthropist*. Fearing that even his status as a seminarian would not convince some critics of the story's truthfulness, he solicited the testimony of five prominent Oberlinites and professors as "to the correctness" of his account. See Samuel Cochrane to Gamaliel Bailey, February 27, 1841, in *Philanthropist*, March 24, 1841.

6. Hiram Wilson to Hamilton Hill, September 11, 1848, LR, roll 12.

7. H. G. Blake to James Monroe and Henry Peck, September 6, 1858, JMP, Box 1.

8. See, for example, Charles Stearns to William Lloyd Garrison, April 25, 1841, in *Liberator*, June 18, 1841; Hiram Wilson to "Brother Hough," September 13, 1841, in *Friend of Man*, October 19, 1841; Hiram Wilson to Hamilton Hill, February 7, 1853, LR, roll 12; Clarke and Clarke, *Narratives*, 86; *Emancipator and Free American*, October 6, 1842; and CTD, November 8, 1851.

9. Fletcher, *History of Oberlin College*, 399.

10. *Annual Report of the American and Foreign Anti-Slavery Society . . . 1851*, 16.

11. Deut. 23:15–16 in OE, May 11, 1859.

12. NS, October 24, 1850.

13. Fairchild, *Underground Railroad*, 96–97.

14. See Fairbank, *Rev. Calvin Fairbank*, 158.

15. Coffin, *Reminiscences*, 279.

16. Fairchild explained that such a view was "not so much because of any supposed right on the part of the master to the services of his slave" but because "it would be a reckless undertaking, involving too much risk, and probably doing more harm than good" (Fairchild, *Oberlin*, 115). See also Fairchild, *Underground Railroad*, 99.

17. John Todd to Margaret Strohm, February 21, 1842, RG 21, Oberlin File, Letters, Box 1, OCA.

18. Fairchild, *Underground Railroad*, 99–100.

19. OE, June 17, 1846; *Liberator*, July 10, 1846.

20. Fairbank, *Rev. Calvin Fairbank*, 149.

21. Coffin, *Reminiscences*, 719.

22. Fairbank, *Rev. Calvin Fairbank*, 46.

23. Coffin, *Reminiscences*, 719–20; Fairbank, *Rev. Calvin Fairbank*, 45–49.

24. Fairbank, *Rev. Calvin Fairbank*, 49. This letter suggests an even more extensive Oberlin involvement.

25. Coffin, *Reminiscences*, 720–21; Fairbank, *Rev. Calvin Fairbank*, 51–53.

26. Coffin, *Reminiscences*, 721. Webster was arrested again in 1854 for "enticing slaves to seek 'the land of the free'" but was acquitted of all charges. See NYT, May 1, July 12, 1854.

27. Coffin, *Reminiscences*, 722.

28. See *Liberator*, March 5, 12, April 16, 1852, December 29, 1854, July 20, 1855; and FDP, February 26, March 5, 1852, December 15, 1854, May 25, 1855, July 27, 1855.

29. Fairbank, *Rev. Calvin Fairbank*, 11, 149.

30. Coffin, *Reminiscences*, 725; Fairbank, *Rev. Calvin Fairbank*, 161; *Liberator*, May 6, 1864.

31. See Thompson, *Prison Life and Reflections*, 188.

32. George Thompson to Editor, July 14, 1879, *Cleveland Leader*, n.d., in NYT, July 28, 1879.

33. James Thome to Theodore Dwight Weld, August 27, 1839, in Weld, *Letters*, 1:793–95.

34. Ibid. See also James Fairchild to Mary Kellogg, August 24, 1839, RSFP, Box 5, Folder 13; and James Thome to Gerrit Smith, RSFP, Box 9, Folder 11.

35. Clarke and Clarke, Narratives, 48.

36. Ibid., 49, 53–55.

37. Ibid., 55–59.

38. Gara, Liberty Line, 82.

39. Fairchild, Historical Sketch of Oberlin College, 9.

40. History of the Oberlin-Wellington Rescue, 166.

41. See Ohio Statesman, December 10, 1841, February 9, 1842; Journal of the Senate of the State of Ohio (1840), 566–72; Philanthropist, February 25, 1840; and Josiah Harris to "Wife," Thanksgiving A.M., 1842, in Fairchild, Oberlin, 368–70.

42. After William Howard Day moved to Cleveland in 1850, his printing office was considered "the last terminus in the State of the 'Underground Railroad.'" See Mealy, Aliened American, 174–75; Tyler, Freedom's Ferment, 529; and Siebert, Underground Railroad, 32–33, 98.

43. See John Todd to Margaret Strohm, February 21, 1842, RG 21, Oberlin File, Letters, Box 1, OCA; Siebert, Mysteries of Ohio's Underground Railroad, 260; Oberlin Alumni Magazine 6, no. 10 (July 1910): 462; Wright, Standard History of Lorain County, 148–50; and Fairchild, Oberlin, 76.

44. Deramus, Freedom by Any Means, 100.

45. John Byrd to Simeon Jocelyn, December 27, 1859, AMA, Kansas, roll 1.

46. Smith, Oberlin Unmasked, 60–61. In Sheffield, Williams would have also encountered Jabez Burrell, one of Shipherd's first pupils before Oberlin's founding (and later an Oberlin trustee), who had been entrusted with the establishment of the Sheffield Institute. There, the Burrell family were busy Underground conductors. Jabez Jr. regularly sent escaping slaves from Oberlin to Sheffield, and besides the father, other Burrell sons, Robbins and Edward, would feed and conceal these men and women at the Sheffield farm until notified of the arrival of friendly vessels in nearby Lorain. Under the cover of produce, the Burrells would deliver "wagon-loads of pilgrims" to these ships. See Siebert, Mysteries of Ohio's Underground Railroads, 260; Oberlin Alumni Magazine 6, no. 10 (July 1910): 462; Wright, Standard History of Lorain County, 148–50; Fairchild, Oberlin, 76; and Fletcher, History of Oberlin College, 86–87, 146, 189.

47. See Fairchild, Oberlin, 115, and Fairchild, Underground Railroad, 99.

48. Smith, Oberlin Unmasked, 62–63.

49. Brooks was one of the first Oberlin students to enroll in 1833. He reportedly gave the first abolitionist speech in Oberlin on July 4, 1833. See Cutter, New England Families, 222.

50. Smith, Oberlin Unmasked, 63; Nancy Prudden to George Prudden, May 16, 1837, PP, Box 1.

51. Smith, Oberlin Unmasked, 63; Nancy Prudden to George Prudden, May 16, 1837, PP, Box 1.

52. Smith, Oberlin Unmasked, 66. Recall, also, that when Hiram Wilson left Oberlin for Canada in 1836, his traveling companion was a self-emancipated slave.

53. See speech of Amasa Walker in Proceedings of the General Anti-Slavery Convention . . . 1843, 206–7.

54. Langston, From the Virginia Plantation, 101–2.

55. Clarke and Clarke, Narrative, 85.

56. Oberliniana, 22. See also Langston, From the Virginia Plantation, 184.

57. See "Russia Township Records, 1855–1869," RSFP, Box 13.

58. *Advocate of Moral Reform and Family Guardian*, June 15, 1855; "Annual Report of the L.L.S.," OE, August 15, 1855; Herman Birch to Leroy Burnell, January 30, 1840, LR, roll 6; James Matthews to E.W. Hubbard, January 17, 1840, and Hubbard's reply of January 27, 1840, RG 16/5/3, Autograph File, Box 3, Folder 126, OCA; Rokicky, "Lydia Finney and Evangelical Womanhood," 184–85; Fletcher, *History of Oberlin College*, 397.

59. Coffin, *Reminiscences*, 187, 334–35, 541.

60. Conversation between William Bigglestone and Mary Cochrane, November 8, 1972, "Underground Railroad" subject file, OCA.

61. See OE, February 17, October 13, November 8, 11, 1847.

62. E. S. Cadwell to Henry Cowles, April 19, 1851, HCP, Box 3.

63. *Oberlin Alumni Magazine* 6, no. 2 (November 1909): 54–55.

64. *Advocate of Moral Reform and Family Guardian*, May 1, 1853; NASS, April 21, 1853; *Oberlin Alumni Magazine* 6, no. 2 (November 1909): 54–55.

65. *Oberlin Alumni Magazine* 6, no. 2 (November 1909): 54–55.

66. Fairchild, *Historical Sketch of Oberlin College*, 9.

67. Fairchild, *Underground Railroad*, 91–92.

68. *Oberliniana*, 24–25.

69. Ibid., 34.

70. Ibid., 24–25.

71. Ibid., 25.

72. Milton Clarke's version of this story may be found in Clarke and Clarke, *Narratives*, 85–88.

73. *Oberliniana*, 25–26.

74. At this point, the foresight of the Oberlinites in having two white men accompany the seven decoys was made manifest. Though this was before the Fugitive Slave Law of 1850 abrogated the right to jury trial or habeas corpus to the accused, the Black Laws were still in force in Ohio, including the denial of African Americans to testify on their own behalf. Without white witnesses to vouch for them, the decoys could have been enslaved just as easily as the bondsmen whom they represented.

75. *Oberliniana*, 26–27.

76. These students were likely Ruell Cooley and either Charles or Henry Whittlesey, who were enrolled together for parts of the years 1841–46. See *General Catalogue of Oberlin College*, 217, 1054–55.

77. Finney, *Memoirs*, 412–13; *Oberliniana*, 27–28.

78. One escaping slave who was painted to resemble a white woman viewed himself in a mirror and jokingly exclaimed, "Go way, niggah, I neber seed you afore; 'specs you'se a runaway" (*Oberliniana*, 29).

79. Clarke and Clarke, *Narrative*, 188–92. Lewis Clarke, who permanently settled in Oberlin after the Civil War, was the basis of Harriet Beecher Stowe's character George Harris in her 1852 novel *Uncle Tom's Cabin*. See Stowe, *Key to Uncle Tom's Cabin*, 13–21; and *Washington Post*, September 3, 1880, June 29, 1895, January 11, 1897.

80. Cochran, *Western Reserve and the Fugitive Slave Law*, 122–23.

81. However, at least three Oberlinites were occasionally associated with the New York City vigilance committee whenever they were in the East, including alumnus William

Howard Day. See *Colored American*, May 15, 22, July 24, 1841; and *History of the Oberlin-Wellington Rescue*, 57–58.

82. Samuel Cochrane to Gamaliel Bailey, February 27, 1841, in *Philanthropist*, March 24, 1841; NYE, March 27, 1841; *Oberliniana*, 30.

83. Finney, *Memoirs*, 412–13; NYE, March 27, 1841; *Oberliniana*, 30–31.

84. *Norwalk Experiment*, March 24, 1841.

85. Samuel Cochrane to Gamaliel Bailey, February 27, 1841, in *Philanthropist*, March 24, 1841; NYE, March 27, 1841.

86. *Norwalk Experiment*, March 24, 1841; NYE, March 27, 1841; *Oberliniana*, 31–32.

87. *Colored American*, March 27, 1841; Samuel Cochrane to Gamaliel Bailey, February 27, 1841, in *Philanthropist*, March 24, 1841; *Norwalk Experiment*, March 24, 1841.

88. NYE, March 27, 1841; *Oberliniana*, 32.

89. *Cleveland Advertiser*, n.d., in *Liberator*, April 23, 1841.

90. *N.Y. Journal of Commerce*, n.d., in *Liberator*, April 23, 1841; *Oberliniana*, 32.

91. *Oberlin News-Tribune*, March 29, 1935; NYE, May 22, 1841.

92. *Liberator*, March 2, 1849.

93. See speech of Amasa Walker in *Proceedings of the General Anti-Slavery Convention . . . 1843*, 206–7.

94. LCN, April 11, 1860. See also Langston, *Freedom and Citizenship*, 64.

95. Cochran, *Western Reserve and the Fugitive Slave Law*, 123.

96. Imposters posed a real danger to Northern African Americans. Some imposters were actually spies from the South sent to discover the routes of the Underground Railroad rather than simply charlatans hoping to benefit from abolitionist generosity. See Coffin, *Reminiscences*, 343–44.

97. LCN, April 4, 1860.

98. Cochran, *Western Reserve and the Fugitive Slave Law*, 121.

99. *Anti-Slavery Bugle*, February 25, 1860.

100. Watkins quoted in Cheek and Cheek, *John Mercer Langston*, 339.

101. Cochran, *Western Reserve and the Fugitive Slave Law*, 123.

102. *Cleveland Daily Herald*, April 8, 1859; Langston, *From the Virginia Plantation*, 183. See also *Liberator*, April 29, 1859; and *History of the Oberlin-Wellington Rescue*, 2, 38.

103. *Liberator*, June 3, 1859.

104. Langston, *From the Virginia Plantation*, 183. See also *Liberator*, April 29, June 3, 1859. Ramsey did not know his exact birth date, but some Oberlinites estimated the year of his birth to have been as early as 1770. Ramsey himself believed that he was well past forty when he first arrived in Oberlin around 1840. See *Oberlin News*, December 8, 1899, January 25, 1901, January 26, 1910.

105. Langston, *From the Virginia Plantation*, 184.

106. *History of the Oberlin-Wellington Rescue*, 19, 35, 99–101.

107. Ibid., 19.

108. Ibid., 2, 19; Fairchild, *Underground Railroad*, 112. The *History of the Oberlin-Wellington Rescue* is a useful compilation of most of the trial transcripts and many newspaper excerpts from the legal action that followed.

109. *History of the Oberlin-Wellington Rescue*, 2.

110. Ibid., 2, 35, 100–101.

111. Ibid., 19.

112. OE, September 29, 1858; James Harris Fairchild, "Wellington Rescue," n.d., manuscript fragment, p. 25, JHFP, Series 8, Box 9; History of the Oberlin-Wellington Rescue, 2.

113. OE, September 29, 1858; New York Tribune, September 18, 1858, in Liberator, October 1, 1858; Cleveland Daily Herald, April 14, 1859; History of the Oberlin-Wellington Rescue, 3.

114. Encyclopedia of Slave Resistance and Rebellion, 359; Brandt, Town That Started the Civil War, 67; History of the Oberlin-Wellington Rescue, 23.

115. New York Daily Tribune, September 18, 1858, in Liberator, October 1, 1858; Cleveland Daily Herald, April 14, 1859.

116. History of the Oberlin-Wellington Rescue, 36.

117. OE, September 29, 1858; History of the Oberlin-Wellington Rescue, 22, 108–9.

118. New York Daily Tribune, September 18, 1858, in Liberator, October 1, 1858; History of the Oberlin-Wellington Rescue, 33, 58.

119. Ballentine, Oberlin Jubilee, 251, 254. Winsor had been in Boston in 1854 and witnessed the rendition of his current Oberlin classmate Anthony Burns to slavery.

120. Ibid., 252.

121. History of the Oberlin-Wellington Rescue, 31; A. B. Nettleton to Albert Temple Swing, n.d., in Swing, James Harris Fairchild, 377.

122. Cleveland Plain Dealer, April 9, 1859.

123. History of the Oberlin-Wellington Rescue, 4, 13, 22–23, 104; Ballentine, Oberlin Jubilee, 251–55.

124. Oberlin News, October 13, 1909.

125. OE, September 29, 1858; James Harris Fairchild, "Wellington Rescue," n.d., manuscript fragment, p. 26, JHFP, Series 8, Box 926; History of the Oberlin-Wellington Rescue, 22, 27, 118; New York Daily Tribune, September 18, 1858, in Liberator, October 1, 1858.

126. Estimates in the court testimony put the number as high as 1,000. See History of the Oberlin-Wellington Rescue, 30, 59.

127. Ibid., 38–39.

128. James Harris Fairchild, "Wellington Rescue," n.d., manuscript fragment, p. 26, JHFP, Series 8, Box 926; Ballentine, Oberlin Jubilee, 252; New York Daily Tribune, September 18, 1858, in Liberator, October 1, 1858.

129. History of the Oberlin-Wellington Rescue, 26–27.

130. New York Daily Tribune, September 18, 1858, in Liberator, October 1, 1858; History of the Oberlin-Wellington Rescue, 104.

131. New York Daily Tribune, September 18, 1858, in Liberator, October 1, 1858; History of the Oberlin-Wellington Rescue, 37; Ballentine, Oberlin Jubilee, 252.

132. Langston, Freedom and Citizenship, 18; History of the Oberlin-Wellington Rescue, 38, 105, 119.

133. History of the Oberlin-Wellington Rescue, 105, 119.

134. OE, September 29, 1858; New York Daily Tribune, September 18, 1858, in Liberator, October 1, 1858; History of the Oberlin-Wellington Rescue, 27, 101–3.

135. Ballentine, Oberlin Jubilee, 253.

136. History of the Oberlin-Wellington Rescue, 18; Oberlin News, October 13, 1909.

137. New York Daily Tribune, September 18, 1858, in Liberator, October 1, 1858; James Harris Fairchild, "Wellington Rescue," n.d., manuscript fragment, p. 26, JHFP, Series 8, Box 926; History of the Oberlin-Wellington Rescue, 18–19; Ballentine, Oberlin Jubilee, 253–54.

138. *History of the Oberlin-Wellington Rescue*, 30.

139. Ibid., 31–32.

140. *New York Daily Tribune*, September 18, 1858, in *Liberator*, October 1, 1858; *History of the Oberlin-Wellington Rescue*, 30–32, 120–21.

141. Langston, *From the Virginia Plantation*, 185.

142. *New York Daily Tribune*, September 18, 1858, in *Liberator*, October 1, 1858.

CHAPTER NINE

1. Langston, *From the Virginia Plantation*, 184.

2. Ibid., 185.

3. Fairchild, *Underground Railroad*, 114; James Harris Fairchild, "Wellington Rescue," n.d., manuscript fragment, p. 27, JHFP, Series 8, Box 9; Brandt, *Town that Started the Civil War*, 108.

4. Langston, *From the Virginia Plantation*, 196.

5. *History of the Oberlin-Wellington Rescue*, 107. Dayton had already fled the town, "his coattail flying behind."

6. *Liberator*, October 15, 1858.

7. Ibid., December 3, 1858.

8. Ibid.; *Anti-Slavery Bugle*, December 4, 1858.

9. *Cleveland Leader*, September 21, 1858. See also Cheek and Cheek, *John Mercer Langston*, 328, and Cochran, *Western Reserve and the Fugitive Slave Law*, 132–33.

10. *Lorain County Eagle*, April 20, 1859.

11. *Cleveland Daily Herald*, December 7, 1858; James Harris Fairchild, "Wellington Rescue," n.d., manuscript fragment, p. 26, JHFP, Series 8, Box 9; Langston, *From the Virginia Plantation*, 186.

12. Langston, *From the Virginia Plantation*, 186.

13. Ibid.; James Harris Fairchild, "Wellington Rescue," n.d., manuscript fragment, pp. 26–27, JHFP, Series 8, Box 9.

14. Fairchild, *Underground Railroad*, 113; *Cleveland Daily Herald*, December 9, 1858.

15. *Cleveland Morning Leader*, n.d., in *History of the Oberlin-Wellington Rescue*, 5; OE, January 19, 1859; *Liberator*, January 28, 1859.

16. Joshua Giddings to Ralph Plumb, May 4, 1859, in *Liberator*, May 9, 27, 1859; *Cleveland Daily Herald*, April 18, 1859; OE, March 16, 1859; Fairchild, *Underground Railroad*, 114.

17. *Liberator*, April 29, 1859; *History of the Oberlin-Wellington Rescue*, 82–83.

18. Langston, *From the Virginia Plantation*, 186–87.

19. NYT, April 20, 23, 27, 1859; NE, April 21, 1859; Cheek and Cheek, *John Mercer Langston*, 330.

20. *History of the Oberlin-Wellington Rescue*, 94–107, 114–69; NASS, June 18, 1859.

21. NYT, April 20, 23, 29, 1859; *History of the Oberlin-Wellington Rescue*, 170.

22. *Liberator*, June 3, 1859; NYT, May 17, 1859; OE, May 25, 1859.

23. OE, May 25, 1859.

24. Langston, *From the Virginia Plantation*, 187.

25. Cheek and Cheek, *John Mercer Langston*, 332.

26. Langston, *From the Virginia Plantation*, 187–88.

27. See *Liberator*, June 3, 1859; NYT, May 17, 1859; and *Cleveland Leader*, May 13, 1859.

28. Liberator, June 10, 1859.

29. H. E. Peck, in Douglass' Monthly, June 1859; History of the Oberlin-Wellington Rescue, 89.

30. Ohio State Journal and Columbus Gazette, April 26, 27, 1859; NYT, April 27, 29, 1859; History of the Oberlin-Wellington Rescue, 110–13.

31. History of the Oberlin-Wellington Rescue, 125–26.

32. Douglass' Monthly, June 1859.

33. Cleveland Daily Herald, April 30, 1859.

34. James Harris Fairchild, "Wellington Rescue," n.d., manuscript fragment, p. 29, JHFP, Series 8, Box 9; History of the Oberlin-Wellington Rescue, 195–225.

35. NYT, April 29, May 3, June 3, 1859; NYE, May 5, June 16, 1859; New York Tribune, n.d., in Liberator, May 6, 1859; Liberator, June 10, 1859; OE, June 8, 1859; Fairchild, Underground Railroad, 116.

36. OE, May 25, 1859. See also Norwalk Reflector, May 17, 1859, excerpted in Cochran, Western Reserve and the Fugitive Slave Law, 157.

37. Cleveland Leader, April _, 1859, excerpted in Cochran, Western Reserve and the Fugitive Slave Law, 158.

38. Cleveland Plain Dealer, April 7, 1859.

39. Ohio Statesman, April _, 1859, excerpted in Cochran, Western Reserve and the Fugitive Slave Law, 157.

40. Ibid.; Douglass' Monthly, June 1859.

41. NYT, May 17, 1859; Cleveland Daily Herald, May 12, 1859.

42. Langston, From the Virginia Plantation, 188; NYT, May 12, 28, 1859; NE, June 9, 1859; James Harris Fairchild, "Wellington Rescue," n.d., manuscript fragment, p. 30, JHFP, Series 8, Box 9; History of the Oberlin-Wellington Rescue, 247, 257.

43. History of the Oberlin-Wellington Rescue, 248.

44. Fairchild, Underground Railroad, 117–18.

45. James Harris Fairchild, "Wellington Rescue," n.d., manuscript fragment, p. 31, JHFP, Series 8, Box 9. Giddings's letter to Ralph Plumb (published in the Liberator) was even more radical. See Joshua Giddings to Ralph Plumb, May 4, 1859, in Liberator, May 9, 27, 1859; History of the Oberlin-Wellington Rescue, 252–53.

46. Langston, From the Virginia Plantation, 189.

47. History of the Oberlin-Wellington Rescue, 256. Mahan had left Oberlin in 1850 to found Cleveland University. In 1859 he was president of Adrian College in Michigan.

48. Ibid., 89–90; Fairchild, Underground Railroad, 119.

49. Cleveland Leader, April 19, 1859, in History of the Oberlin-Wellington Rescue, 93; Fairchild, Underground Railroad, 119.

50. History of the Oberlin-Wellington Rescue, 262.

51. Ibid., 262–63; Cleveland Herald, April 18, 1859, in ibid., 90–92.

52. Cleveland Leader, April 19, 1859, in History of the Oberlin-Wellington Rescue, 92.

53. Frank Leslie's Illustrated Weekly, May 7, 1859. See also History of the Oberlin-Wellington Rescue, 90; Cleveland Leader, April 19, 1859, in History of the Oberlin-Wellington Rescue, 93; Douglass' Monthly, June 1859; Cleveland Daily Herald, December 17, 1858, April 30, May 14, 1859; and Liberator, January 28, 1859.

54. The Ohio State Anti-Slavery Society sponsored over 300 lectures in 1859 to "people of all classes." See Cheek and Cheek, John Mercer Langston, 333–34.

55. *History of the Oberlin-Wellington Rescue*, 244–47.

56. Ibid., 248; NYT, June 24, 1859; *Lorain County Eagle*, May 25, 1859.

57. James Harris Fairchild, "Wellington Rescue," n.d., manuscript fragment, p. 34, JHFP, Series 8, Box 9; NYT, April 27, 1859; *Cleveland Herald*, July 6, 1859, in *Douglass' Monthly*, August 1859; Langston, *From the Virginia Plantation*, 189–90.

58. *New York Tribune*, n.d., in *Liberator*, May 6, 1859; NYT, April 27, July 7, 9, 1859; *Ripley Bee*, August 6, 1859; Fairchild, *Underground Railroad*, 120; *History of the Oberlin-Wellington Rescue*, 263. Anderson Jennings soon returned to Kentucky, where he hoped to be elected to the state legislature on the strength of his "Oberlin martyrdom." He lost, running far behind his ticket.

59. Langston, *From the Virginia Plantation*, 190.

60. *Cleveland Plain Dealer*, July 6, 1858, in *Liberator*, July 22, 1859.

61. See also *Zion's Herald and Wesleyan Journal*, April 27, 1859; *Cleveland Morning Leader*, n.d., in NYT, July 9, 1859; and Langston, *From the Virginia Plantation*, 190.

62. *Cleveland Morning Leader*, n.d., in NYT, July 9, 1859; James Harris Fairchild, "Wellington Rescue," n.d., manuscript fragment, p. 35, JHFP, Series 8, Box 9; Langston, *From the Virginia Plantation*, 190.

63. NYT, July 11, 19, 1859; *New York Observer and Chronicle*, July 14, 1859; NYE, July 21, 1859; *Newark Advocate*, July 20, 1859; *Cleveland Daily Herald*, July 7, 1859; Langston, *From the Virginia Plantation*, 190.

64. *Liberator*, July 22, 1859; *Cleveland Leader*, July 13, 1859, in *Liberator*, July 22, 1859; Langston, *From the Virginia Plantation*, 190.

65. *Cleveland Leader*, July 13, 1859, in *Liberator*, July 22, 1859; *Cleveland Plain Dealer*, July 12, 1859, excerpted in Cochran, *Western Reserve and the Fugitive Slave Law*, 203.

66. Langston, *From the Virginia Plantation*, 188.

67. Cheek and Cheek, *John Mercer Langston*, 336–37.

68. Langston, *From the Virginia Plantation*, 188.

69. William Lloyd Garrison to James Monroe, April 22, 1859, in *Garrison Letters*, 4: 622–23.

70. *Anti-Slavery Bugle*, December 4, 1858.

71. OE, June 8, 1859; Cochran, *Western Reserve and the Fugitive Slave Law*, 192–93.

72. *Summit County Beacon*, June __, 1859, excerpted in Cochran, *Western Reserve and the Fugitive Slave Law*, 191; OE, June 9, 1859; Samuel Galloway to Abraham Lincoln, July 23, 1859, Abraham Lincoln Papers, Library of Congress, Washington, D.C.; Cochran, *Western Reserve and the Fugitive Slave Law*, 190, 193.

73. Cheek and Cheek, *John Mercer Langston*, 339.

74. Democrats warned of the Republican momentum. The *Ohio Statesman* cautioned that if the laboring white men of the state did not unite "to put down the fanaticism of Republicanism," then they may soon see the day "when the Negro of Ohio will vote with the Chases, Dennisons, Giddingses, and the Oberlin School generally, to vote them down at the ballot box" (*Ohio Statesman*, n.d., in *Newark Advocate*, June 29, 1859).

75. *Cleveland Leader*, May 31, 1859, excerpted in Cochran, *Western Reserve and the Fugitive Slave Law*, 190.

76. *Painesville Telegraph*, June 2, 1859, excerpted in Cochran, *Western Reserve and the Fugitive Slave Law*, 191.

77. See Hinsdale, *Republican Text-Book for the Campaign of 1880*, 15, and Cochran, *Western Reserve and the Fugitive Slave Law*, 206–9.

78. Smith, *History of the Republican Party in Ohio*, 91–92.

79. Langston, *Freedom and Citizenship*, 65.

80. Stauffer, *Black Hearts of Men*, 120; Reynolds, *John Brown, Abolitionist*, 15–39. Brown, for unknown reasons, did not complete the job.

81. Stauffer, *Black Hearts of Men*, 118–19; Reynolds, *John Brown, Abolitionist*, 37, 65.

82. Oates, *To Purge This Land with Blood*, 221.

83. Hinton, *John Brown and his Men*, vii, 178; Reynolds, *John Brown, Abolitionist*, 262–63; Cheek and Cheek, *John Mercer Langston*, 350. These men were James Monroe Jones, James Harris, and George Reynolds.

84. Brown, *Provisional Constitution*, 1.

85. Ibid., 8–10.

86. Ibid., 4.

87. Ibid., 6–7; William Howard Day to John Brown, May 3, 1858, John Brown/Boyd Stutler Collection, West Virginia Archives, Charleston, W.Va., ID#RP02–198, http://goo.gl/6JoTW (accessed August 27, 2009).

88. Brown, *Provisional Constitution*, 3–4. See also John Brown Notebook No. 2, April 8, 13, 1858, for notations regarding Brown's payment to Day for his printing services: "Extracts referring to Canadian Contacts, April and May, 1858," John Brown/Boyd Stutler Collection, West Virginia Archives, Charleston, W.Va., ID#RP02–0197, http://goo.gl/dsLEz (accessed August 27, 2009).

89. It is possible that Day intended to join Brown's invasion force before the delay. However, by October 1859, Day had gone to England on a fund-raising mission. See Blackett, *Beating against the Barriers*, 313.

90. Oates, *To Purge This Land with Blood*, 247–51; Brown, *Provisional Constitution*, 10.

91. *Cincinnati Gazette*, n.d., in *Newark Advocate*, October 28, 1859. This was the same group of slaves that Brown had hidden in the home of his sister and brother-in-law, Florella Brown and Samuel Adair, in Kansas, just a few weeks earlier.

92. *Cincinnati Gazette*, n.d., in *Newark Advocate*, October 28, 1859; Sanborn, *Life and Letters of John Brown*, 494.

93. Oates, *To Purge This Land with Blood*, 262; Cheek and Cheek, *John Mercer Langston*, 352.

94. *Cleveland Plain Dealer*, March 22, 1859.

95. *Cincinnati Gazette*, n.d., in *Newark Advocate*, October 28, 1859.

96. Sanborn, *Life and Letters of John Brown*, 252; Oates, *To Purge This Land with Blood*, 257.

97. J. Henri [Kagi] to Charles Tidd, May 8, 1859, in *Calendar of Virginia State Papers*, 345–46.

98. Langston, *From the Virginia Plantation*, 192.

99. *History of the Oberlin-Wellington Rescue*, viii.

100. I. H. H. to J. Henri [Kagi], August 22, 1859, in *Calendar of Virginia State Papers*, 335.

101. Langston, *From the Virginia Plantation*, 191.

102. Ibid., 191–92.

103. *Cleveland Morning Leader*, n.d., in *History of the Oberlin-Wellington Rescue*, 5; *OE*, January 19, 1859; *Liberator*, January 28, 1859.

104. Langston, *From the Virginia Plantation*, 196–98.

105. Ibid., 193–95; *History of the Oberlin-Wellington Rescue*, 104–5, 126. Copeland refused to surrender himself after the rescue indictments came down and remained "a fugitive from justice in Ohio" until his death.

106. L. S. Leary to J. Henri [Kagi], September 8, 1859, in *Calendar of Virginia State Papers*, 305–6. See also Ralph Plumb to John Kagi, August 23, 1859, in *Calendar of Virginia State Papers*, 314–15.

107. I. H. H. to J. Henri [Kagi], August 22, 1859, in *Calendar of Virginia State Papers*, 335. Leary said of his family, "Let me be assured that they will be cared for, protected; and if my child shall live, be suitably educated and trained to usefulness; and my life shall be accounted by me of the smallest value, as it is given, if need be, to free the slave" (quoted in Langston, *From the Virginia Plantation*, 194).

108. I. H. H. to J. Henri [Kagi], August 22, 1859, in *Calendar of Virginia State Papers*, 335; John Brown Jr. to Henri [Kagi], September 2, 1859, in ibid., 326–27; Langston, *From the Virginia Plantation*, 194.

109. John Brown Jr. to Henri [Kagi], September 2, 1859, in *Calendar of Virginia State Papers*, 326–27.

110. *Cleveland Daily Herald*, October 31, 1859; *Newark Advocate*, November 4, 1859.

111. Sanborn, *Life and Letters of John Brown*, 548.

112. See Oates, *To Purge This Land with Blood*, 290–306.

113. Leary's widow would marry Charles Langston in 1868. One of her most treasured possessions was a blood-stained and bullet-ridden shawl that had belonged to her husband and was sent to her after the raid. Many years later, Mary Patterson Leary Langston would use the same shawl to wrap around her and Charles's young grandson, Langston Hughes. See Hughes, *Big Sea*, 37.

114. John Copeland Jr. to Addison Halbert, December 10, 1859, in *Liberator*, January 13, 1860. See also *OE*, December 21, 1859.

115. Oates, *To Purge This Land with Blood*, 327–29.

116. Brown, *Negro in the American Rebellion*, 48.

117. John Copeland Jr. to John Copeland Sr. and Delilah Copeland, November 26, 1859, in *OE*, December 21, 1859.

118. Quoted in Brandt, *Town That Started the Civil War*, 243.

119. See Henry Peck to Lewis Tappan, November 17, 1859, AMA, Ohio, roll 9.

120. Garrison, *New Reign of Terror*, 129.

121. Phillips, *Oberlin Colony*, 93–94.

122. *OE*, November 9, December 21, 1859.

123. Cheek and Cheek, *John Mercer Langston*, 359.

124. *Cleveland Plain Dealer*, November 18, 1859, excerpted in *From Bondage to Liberation*, 213–16.

125. *OE*, December 21, 1859; *Oberlin Students' Monthly*, January 1860, RSFP, Box 18, Folder 11.

126. See *NYT*, December 5, 1859; and *Weekly Anglo-African*, December 17, 1859.

127. Henry Prudden to "Loved ones at home," December 17, 1859, RSFP, Box 4, Folder 4; John Copeland Sr. to James Monroe, December 19, 1859, JMP, Box 1.

128. John Copeland Sr. to James Monroe, December 19, 1859, JMP, Box 1; H. Griswold to James Monroe, December 19, 1859, ibid.; *Liberator*, January 6, 1860; *OE*, January 4, 1860.

129. Henry Wise, telegram, December 12, 1859, JMP, Box 1; H. E. Blake to James Monroe, December 1, 1859, RSFP, Box 7, Folder 12; OE, December 21, 1859.

130. OE, January 4, 1860.

131. Henry Prudden to "Dear Father," December 21, 1859, RSFP, Box 4, Folder 4.

132. Henry Cowles to Lewis Tappan, December 12, 1859, AMA, Ohio, roll 9; OE, January 4, 1860; "A Monument, to Commemorate the Manly Virtues of Those Noble Representatives of the Colored Race of the Nineteenth Century, John Copeland, Lewis Leary, and Shields Green," December 29, 1859, AMA, Ohio, roll 9; OE, February 1, 1860; *Liberator*, January 13, 1860; Fletcher, "John Brown and Oberlin," 141.

133. Langston, *From the Virginia Plantation*, 196–97; Oates, *To Purge This Land with Blood*, 310–12.

134. OE, September 12, 1860.

135. LCN, April 4, 1860; Langston, *From the Virginia Plantation*, 196–97.

136. LCN, n.d., in *Cleveland Daily Herald*, November 27, 1860; LCN, September 12, October 24, 1860; Hambrick-Stowe, *Charles G. Finney*, 213.

137. *Cleveland Daily Herald*, May 14, 1860. See also OE May 23, 1860.

138. OE, September 12, 1860.

139. Giles Shurtleff to Ephriam [?], May 19, 1860, RG 30/32, Giles Shurtleff Papers, Box 1, OCA. See also LCN, May 23, 1860.

140. LCN, May 23, 1860.

141. *Ohio State Journal and Columbus Gazette*, October 11, 1860.

142. LCN, November 7, 14, 1860.

143. OE, November 21, 1860; LCN, November 21, 1860.

144. Langston, *From the Virginia Plantation*, 198.

145. John Keep and Henry Cowles to Abraham Lincoln, February 14, 1861, Abraham Lincoln Papers, Library of Congress, Washington, D.C.

146. Phillips, *Oberlin Colony*, 100–101.

147. Davis, *Slavery and Human Progress*, 267.

148. *Cleveland Daily Herald*, April 19, 1861.

149. Ellis, *Oberlin and the American Conflict*, 7.

150. Fairchild, *Oberlin*, 159; LCN, April 24, 1861.

151. See *Cleveland Daily Herald*, April 24, 1861; LCN, April 24, 1861; and Fairchild, *Oberlin*, 159–60.

152. Ellis, *Oberlin and the American Conflict*, 7, 11.

153. "Brother" to Lucien Warner, April 20, 1861, RSFP, Box 10, Folder 11.

154. Wright, *Story of My Life and Work*, 96.

155. The minutes of the Young Ladies' Literary Society for April 24, 1861, read, "No meeting. The War excitement too great" (Minutes of the Young Ladies' Literary Society, RSFP, Box 12, Folder 3).

156. Edmund Stiles Diary, March 24, 1861, RSFP, Box 9, Folder 12; LCN, April 24, May 1, July 3, 1861; *Cleveland Daily Herald*, April 30, 1861; Ralph Plumb to James Monroe, March 12, 1861, JMP, Box 1; Fairchild, *Oberlin*, 162; Wright, "Oberlin's Contribution to Ethics," 439.

157. *Oberlin News*, n.d., in *Cleveland Daily Herald*, August 8, 1861.

158. OE, September 11, 1861; *Annual Catalogue of the Officers and Students of Oberlin College*, 7–12; Fairchild, *Oberlin*, 166–67.

159. L. H. Plumb to P. D. Sherman, March 1, 1918, RG 14, College General Records, Series 15, Box 1, OCA.

160. *LCN*, May 18, 1864.

161. Burroughs, "Oberlin's Part in the Slavery Conflict," 331.

162. See J. P. Bardwell to George Whipple, September 8, 1862, AMA, Ohio, roll 11.

163. *Cleveland Daily Herald*, September 4, 1862.

164. Essig, "Lord's Free Man," 44. In 1864, Finney would express his hope to Gerrit Smith that radicals would "put in nomination for Pres. a less conservative man than Mr. Lincoln." The northern people, Finney said, "are prepared to elect the most radical abolitionist there is if he can get the nomination. . . . Can we not at least impress him with the conviction that he can not be reelected unless he goes in for the *immediate & total destruction of slavery?* Let us try" (Charles Grandison Finney to Gerrit Smith, RSFP, Box 6, Folder 7).

165. Charles Grandison Finney to [?] Barlow, February 13, 1863, RSFP, Box 6, Folder 1.

166. See Langston, *From the Virginia Plantation*, 199. See also Henry Lee Alumni File, OCA.

167. *LCN*, November 19, 1862.

168. Cheek and Cheek, *John Mercer Langston*, 385.

169. *LCN*, July 9, 23, August 6, 1862; *OE*, July 16, 1862.

170. *LCN*, August 6, 1862.

171. Langston, *From the Virginia Plantation*, 205–6; *LCN*, August 6, 1862.

172. *LCN*, September 10, 17, 24, 1862.

173. See *LCN*, September 24, October 1, 15, 22, November 12, 1862.

174. William Howard Day to Salmon Chase, March 31, 1862, in *BAP*, 1:524–26. See also J. M. Fitch to George Whipple, September 27, 1862, AMA, Ohio, roll 11. Less solemn was one Oberlin businessman whose advertisement in the *LCN* read, "Abraham Lincoln has liberated 3,000,000 slaves and R. H. Birge has just received a splendid stock of fresh groceries" (Phillips, *Oberlin Colony*, 105).

175. *LCN*, December 21, 1862, January 7, 1863.

176. *LCN*, January 7, 1863.

177. Langston, *From the Virginia Plantation*, 201; Van Tassel, "Behind Bayonets," 62–63; Washington, *Eagles on Their Buttons*, 9.

178. Sattira Douglas to Robert Hamilton, June 9, 1863, in *BAP*, 5:212–15; *Liberator*, May 15, 1863; *Cleveland Daily Herald*, June 19, 1863; Williams, *History of the Negro Troops in the War of the Rebellion*, 133–34, 142–43. Wall later became a captain in the 104th United States Colored Troops, the first commissioned African American captain of the U.S. Army. See also *Cleveland Daily Herald*, March 23, 1865.

179. Langston, *From the Virginia Plantation*, 202.

180. *Cleveland Daily Herald*, April 18, 1863; *LCN*, February 18, 1863.

181. *Newark Advocate*, May 8, 1863. See also *Lowell Daily Citizen and News*, March 18, 1863.

182. Bigglestone, *They Stopped in Oberlin*, xx–xxiii.

183. *LCN*, June 10, 1863.

184. Langston, *From the Virginia Plantation*, 204–5. See also *Liberator*, June 12, 1863, for a description of banners.

185. Cheek and Cheek, *John Mercer Langston*, 395.

186. Langston, *From the Virginia Plantation*, 209–10.

187. Ibid., 204.

188. *Harper's Weekly*, August 8, 1863; Wise, *Gate of Hell*, 102.
189. Wise, *Gate of Hell*, 102. See also *Cleveland Daily Herald*, June 25, 1863.
190. *Cleveland Daily Herald*, June 25, 1863.
191. Wise, *Gate of Hell*, 102; Quarles, *Negro in the Civil War*, 3–4, 13–16.
192. *Official Records of the Union and Confederate Navies*, 366; *Harper's Weekly*, August 8, 1863.
193. *Rebellion Record*, 63; *War of the Rebellion*, 362; *Harper's Weekly*, August 8, 1863.
194. Stephens and Yakovone, *Voice of Thunder*, 284.
195. Emilio, *Assault on Fort Wagner*, 13.

EPILOGUE

1. *LCN*, November 9, 1864.
2. Fairchild, *Oberlin*, 292.
3. *Sacramento Daily Union*, December 22, 1864.
4. Bacon, *Theodore Thorton Munger*, 17–18.
5. See Opie, *Memorials*, 343; *Congregational Quarterly* 13, no. 2 (April 1871): 219–24.
6. "'Father' Keep," *Oberlin Alumni Magazine* 3, no. 3 (December 1906): 121–22.
7. Langston, *Freedom and Citizenship*, 99.
8. Ballantine, *Oberlin Jubilee*, 235.
9. Strieby, *Oberlin and the American Missionary Association*, 5–6; *OE*, December 3, 1862; *Twenty Second Annual Report of the Society for the Promotion of Collegiate and Theological Education at the West*, 59–60. See also Beard, *Crusade of Brotherhood*, 120–41, and Jones, *All Bound Up Together*, 139–40.
10. See Fairchild, *Oberlin*, 68, and Langston, *From the Virginia Plantation*, 218–48.
11. John J. Shipherd to Hamilton Hill, August 17, 1844, LR, roll 9, OCA.
12. Bigglestone, "Oberlin College and the Negro Student," 198, 201.
13. Fairchild, *Oberlin*, 112.
14. Ransom, *Pilgrimage of Harriett Ransom's Son*, 33.
15. Waite, *Permission to Remain among Us*, 82.
16. *Oberlin Review*, February 3, 1883; Waite, *Permission to Remain among Us*, 84.
17. Giles Shurtleff, Address to Students, 1884, Giles Shurtleff Papers, Series 7, Box 1, OCA.
18. Waite, *Permission to Remain among Us*, 86–87.
19. *Anti-Slavery Bugle*, December 18, 1846.
20. Barrows, "Ideals of Christian Education," 507.
21. *Cleveland Gazette*, March 28, 1891.
22. Waite, *Permission to Remain among Us*, 73.
23. Baumann, *Constructing Black Education*, 83.
24. "Literary Societies for Colored Students," *Oberlin Alumni Magazine* 6 (March 1910): 224.
25. *Crisis* 41, no. 2 (February 1934): 52.
26. Quoted in Waite, *Permission to Remain among Us*, 111.
27. Ballantine, *Oberlin Jubilee*, 256.
28. Fairchild, *Oberlin*, 113; Churchill, "Midwestern," 166.
29. Waite, *Permission to Remain among Us*, 75–78.
30. *Oberlin News-Tribune*, September 4, 1908.

31. Ibid., September 11, 1908.
32. "A Winter Pilgrimage," *Crisis*, January 1911, 15.
33. "Will Prejudice Capture Oberlin?," *Crisis*, December 1834, 360.
34. Baumann, *Constructing Black Education*, 141.
35. Dickson, "Memories of a Movement."
36. Rinaldi, "Matthew Rinaldi '69."
37. Baumann, *Constructing Black Education*, 140.
38. Krislov, "State of the College Address."
39. Runyowa, "Oberlin Unchained."

Works Cited

PRIMARY SOURCES

Archival Sources

Amistad Research Center, Tulane University, New Orleans, La.
    American Missionary Association Archives (microfilm)
    John Mercer Langston Papers
Case Western Reserve University Archives, Cleveland, Ohio
    Elizur Wright Papers
Kent State University Archives and Special Collections, Kent, Ohio
    Betsey Mix Cowles Papers
Library of Congress, Washington, D.C.
    Salmon P. Chase Papers (microfilm)
    Abraham Lincoln Papers (www.memory.loc.gov [accessed March 20, 2009])
    Lewis Tappan Papers (microfilm)
Oberlin College Archives, Oberlin, Ohio
    Autograph File, RG 16/5/3
    College General Records, RG 0
    Henry Cowles Papers, RG 30/27
    Darlene Deahl Merrill Papers, RG 30/250
    James Harris Fairchild Papers, RG 2/3
    Charles Grandison Finney Papers (microfilm)
    Robert S. Fletcher Papers, RG 30/24
    Frances Hosford Papers, RG 30/35
    Lawson/Merrill Papers, RG 30/157
    Letters Received at Oberlin College (microfilm)
    Minutes of the Oberlin College Board of Trustees (microfilm)
    James Monroe Papers, RG 30/22
    Oberlin File, RG 21
    Oberlin First Congregational Church Records, RG 31/4/1
    Oberlin Society Records, RG 31/4/1
    Prudden Papers, RG 30/205
    Records of the Office of the Treasurer, RG 7
    Records of the Young Men's Anti-Slavery Society, RG 19/3/6
    Mary Sheldon Papers (microfilm)
    John J. Shipherd Papers
    Giles Shurtleff Papers
    Student Alumni Files
    Hiram Wilson Papers, RG 30/112
    Young Ladies' Literary Society Minutes, RG 19/3/4

Western Reserve Historical Society, Salem, Ohio
    "Tenth Annual Report . . ." (microfilm)
West Virginia Archives, Charleston, W.Va.
    John Brown/Boyd Stutler Collection
Wisconsin Historical Society
    William Henry Brisbane Papers (microfilm)

Periodicals

Advocate of Moral Reform and Family Guardian
The African Repository and Colonial Journal (Washington)
Aliened American (Cleveland)
The American Journal of Education
American Missionary (New York)
The American Quarterly Register (Boston)
American Tract Magazine for the Year 1832 (New York)
Anti-Slavery Bugle (Salem)
The Anti-Slavery Record (New York)
Boston Herald
Boston Recorder
Boston Quarterly Review
Buckeye Sentinel
The Christian (London)
Cincinnati Weekly Herald and Philanthropist
Cleveland Daily Herald
Cleveland Gazette
Cleveland Leader
Cleveland Plain Dealer
Cleveland True Democrat
Colored American
The Congregational Quarterly
The Crisis
Douglass' Monthly
Emancipator (New York)
Emancipator and Free American (New York, Boston)
Evangelical Magazine and Gospel Advocate (Utica)
Frank Leslie's Illustrated Weekly
Frederick Douglass' Paper (Rochester)
Friend of Man (Utica)
Genius of Temperance (Hudson)
Harper's Weekly
Hazard's United States Commercial and Statistical Register (Philadelphia)
Huron Reflector
Independent Democrat
Independent Treasury (Elyria)
Iowa City Palimpsest
Jeffersonian (Guernsey)
Jubilee Notes (Oberlin)
Liberator
Liberty Herald (Warren)
Littell's Living Age (Boston)
Lorain County Eagle
Lorain County News (Oberlin)
Lorain Republican
Louisville Journal
Lowell Daily Citizen and News
Missouri Daily Democrat
Nashville Times
National Anti-Slavery Standard
The National Era
Newark Advocate
New Bedford Daily Mercury
New York Evangelist
New York Observer and Chronicle
New York Times
New York Tribune
Niles' National Register (Philadelphia)
The North Star
Norwalk Experiment
Oberlin Alumni Magazine
Oberlin Evangelist
Oberlin News
Oberlin News-Tribune
The Oberlin Students' Monthly
Ohio Atlas and Elyria Advertiser
Ohio Cultivator (Columbus)

Ohio Observer (Newark)
Ohio State Journal and Columbus Gazette
Ohio State Observer (Hudson)
Ohio Statesman (Columbus)
Palladium of Liberty (Columbus)
Philanthropist (Cincinnati)
The Plaindealer (Cleveland)
The Plaindealer (New York)
The Quarterly Register of the American Education Society (Boston)
Religious Intelligencer (New Haven)
Republican Compiler (Gettysburg)
Ripley Bee
Sacramento Daily Union
The Scioto Gazette (Chillicothe)
The Spectator (London)
True Democrat (Cleveland)
The University Quarterly (New Haven)
Warren Liberty Herald
Weekly Anglo-African
Western Monthly Magazine (Cincinnati)
Zion's Herald (Boston)
Zion's Herald and Wesleyan Journal (Boston)

Printed Primary Sources

Abridgements of the Debates of Congress from 1789–1856. Vol. 13. New York: D. Appleton, 1860.

Acts of a General Nature, Passed at the First Session of the Thirty Fifth General Assembly of the State of Ohio, Begun and Held in the City of Columbus, December 5, 1836, and in the Thirty Fifth Year of the Said State. Vol. 35. Columbus: S. R. Dolbee, 1837.

Addresses and Proceedings of the State Independent Free Territory Convention of the People of Ohio, Held at Columbus, June 20 and 21, 1848. Cincinnati: Herald Office, 1848.

Annual Catalogue of the Officers and Students of Oberlin College for the College Year 1861–2. Oberlin: V. A. Shankland, 1861.

The Annual Report of the American and Foreign Anti-Slavery Society, Presented at New York, May 6, 1851; With the Addresses and Resolutions. New York: American and Foreign Anti-Slavery Society, 1851.

Appendix to the Journal of the Senate of the State of Ohio, for the 2d Session of the 52d General Assembly and the 5th Session Under the New Constitution, Commencing Monday, Jan. 5, 1857. Columbus: Richard Nevins, 1857.

Atwater, Caleb. History of the State of Ohio, Natural and Civil. Cincinnati: Glezen and Shepard, 1838.

Atwood, Eugene. "Intimate Life Story of Philo Penfield Stewart." The Connecticut Magazine 10 (July–September 1906): 423–36.

Baird, Robert. View of the Valley of the Mississippi, or the Emigrant's and Traveler's Guide to the West. Philadelphia: H. S. Tanner, 1834.

Ballentine, W. G., ed. The Oberlin Jubilee: 1833–1883. Oberlin: E. J. Goodrich, 1883.

Barrows, John Henry. "The Ideals of Christian Education: The Argument for the Christian College." Bibliotheca Sacra 57 (July 1900): 494–511.

Beecher, Lyman. Autobiography, Correspondence, Etc., of Lyman Beecher, DD. Vol. 2. New York: Harper & Brothers, 1864.

———. A Plea for the West. Cincinnati: Truman and Smith, 1835.

Birney, James Gillespie. The American Churches the Bulwarks of American Slavery. London, 1840.

———. A Letter on Colonization, Addressed to the Rev. Thornton J. Mills, Corresponding Secretary of the Kentucky Colonization Society. Boston: Garrison and Knapp, 1834.

———. The Letters of James Gillespie Birney, 1831–1857. 2 vols. Edited by Dwight L. DuMond. New York: D. Appleton–Century, 1938.

The Black Abolitionist Papers: The United States, 1830–1846. 5 vols. Edited by C. Peter Ripley. 5 vols. Chapel Hill: University of North Carolina Press, 1992.

Bray, Charles. *The Philosophy of Necessity; or, The Law of Consequences as Applicable to Mental, Moral, and Social Sciences.* London: Longman, Brown, Green, and Longmans, 1841.

Brown, Charles F. *Artemus Ward: His Book, with Many Comic Illustrations.* New York: Carlton, 1862.

Brown, John. *Provisional Constitution and Ordinances of the People of the United States.* Edited by Boyd B. Stutler. Weston, Mass.: M & S Press, 1969.

Brown, William Wells. *The Negro in the American Rebellion: His Heroism and Fidelity.* Boston: A. G. Brown, 1880.

Calendar of Virginia State Papers and Other Manuscripts from January 1, 1836 to April 15, 1869; Preserved in the Capitol at Richmond. Vol. 11. Edited by H. W. Flournoy. Richmond: R. F. Walker, 1893.

Catalog of the Trustees, Officers, and Students of the Oberlin Collegiate Institute, Together with the Second Annual Report. Cleveland: Rice & Penniman, 1835.

Charters and Basic Laws of Selected American Universities and Colleges. Edited by Edward Charles Elliott and Merritt Madison Chambers. New York: Carnegie Foundation, 1934.

Child, Lydia Maria. *An Appeal in Favor of That Class of Americans Called Africans.* Edited by Carolyn L. Karcher. Amherst: University of Massachusetts Press, 1996.

Churchill, Alfred V. "Midwestern: The Colored People." *Northwest Ohio Quarterly* 25 (Summer 1953): 165–80.

Clark, George W. *The Free Soil Minstrel.* New York: Martyn and Ely, 1848.

———. *The Liberty Minstrel.* New York: Leavitt and Alden, 1844.

Clarke, Lewis Garrard, and Milton Clarke. *Narratives of the Sufferings of Lewis and Milton Clarke.* Boston: Bela Marsh, 1846.

Clay, Henry. *The Life and Speeches of the Hon. Henry Clay.* Edited by Daniel Mallory. Vol. 2. New York: A. S. Barnes, 1857.

———. *The Papers of Henry Clay.* Vol. 9. Edited by Robert Seager. Lexington: University of Kentucky Press, 1988.

Cochran, William C. *Charles Grandison Finney Memorial Address, Delivered at the Dedication of the Finney Memorial Chapel, Oberlin, June 21, 1908.* Philadelphia: Lippincott, 1908.

———. *The Western Reserve and the Fugitive Slave Law: A Prelude to the Civil War.* Cleveland: Western Reserve Historical Society, 1920.

Coffin, Levi. *Reminiscences of Levi Coffin, The Reputed President of the Underground Railroad.* Cincinnati: Robert Clarke, 1880.

Conkling, Henry. *An Inside View of the Rebellion, an American Citizens' Textbook.* Cincinnati: Caleb Clark, 1864.

Coppin, Fanny Jackson. *Reminiscences of School Life, and Hints on Teaching.* Philadelphia: AME Book Concern, 1913.

Corwin, Thomas. *Life and Speeches of Thomas Corwin: Orator, Lawyer, and Statesman.* Edited by Josiah Morrow. Cincinnati: W. H. Anderson, 1896.

Cowles, Henry. "Abolition, a Religious Enterprise." *Quarterly Anti-Slavery Magazine* 2 (January 1837): 133–45.

Dall, Carolina. *The College, the Market, and the Court.* Boston: Lee and Shepard, 1868.

Declaration of Sentiments and Constitution of the American Anti-Slavery Society. Philadelphia: Pennsylvania Anti-Slavery Society, 1861.

Dedication of Council Hall, and Re-Union of the Alumni of Oberlin Theological Seminary at the Fortieth Anniversary, August 1, 1874. Oberlin: Pratt and Battle, 1874.

Dickson, E. J. "Memories of a Movement." Oberlin Alumni Magazine 107 (Summer 2012), http://goo.gl/z7DqWe.

Drew, Benjamin. The Refugee; or, The Narratives of Fugitive Slaves in Canada, Related by Themselves. Boston: John F. Jewett, 1856.

"1844 Presidential General Election Results Ohio," http://goo.gl/NaFKS. October 30, 2008.

"1850 Census of Russia Township," http://goo.gl/NEzuf. July 28, 2009.

"1860 Census of Russia Township" http://goo.gl/ePCce. July 28, 2009.

Eighth Annual Report of the Board of Managers of the Mass. Anti-Slavery Society, Presented January 22, 1840. Boston: Massachusetts Anti-Slavery Society, 1840.

Elliott, Charles. Sinfulness of American Slavery: Proved from Its Evil Sources. Vol. 2. Cincinnati: Swormstedt & Power, 1851.

Ellis, J. M. Oberlin and the American Conflict. Oberlin: The News Office, 1865.

Emilio, Luis. The Assault on Fort Wagner, July 18, 1863: The Memorable Charge of the Fifty Fourth Regiment of Massachusetts Volunteers. Boston: Rand Avery, 1887.

Everett, John and Sarah. "Letters of John and Sarah Everett, 1854–1864." Kansas Historical Quarterly 8 (February 1939): 3–383.

Fairbank, Calvin. Rev. Calvin Fairbank during Slavery Time: How He Fought the Good Fight to Prepare the Way. Chicago: R. R. McCabe, 1890.

Fairchild, Edward Henry. Historical Sketch of Oberlin College. Springfield: Republic Printing, 1868.

Fairchild, James Harris. "Coeducation of the Sexes: An Address Before the College Presidents at Springfield, Ill." In American Pedagogy: Education, the School, and the Teacher, in American Literature, edited by Henry Barnard. Hartford: Edward H. McGill, 1876.

———. Educational Arrangements and College Life at Oberlin: Inaugural Address of President J. H. Fairchild, Delivered at the Commencement of Oberlin College, August 22, 1866. New York: Edward O. Jenkins, 1866.

———. The Joint Education of the Sexes: A Report Presented at a Meeting of the Ohio State Teachers' Association, Sandusky City, July 8th. Oberlin: E. J. Goodrich, 1852.

———. Oberlin, the Colony and the College, 1833–1883. Oberlin: E. J. Goodrich, 1883.

———. The Underground Railroad: An Address Delivered for the Society in Association Hall, Cleveland, January 24, 1895. Cleveland: Western Reserve Historical Society, 1895.

Fifth Annual Report of the Board of Managers of the Massachusetts Anti-Slavery Society. Boston: Isaac Knapp, 1837.

Finney, Charles Grandison. Lectures on Revivals of Religion. New York: Leavitt, Lord, 1835.

———. Lectures on Systematic Theology. Oberlin: James M. Fitch, 1846.

———. Lectures to Professing Christians. New York: John S. Taylor, 1837.

———. The Memoirs of Charles G. Finney: The Complete Restored Text. Garth M. Roselle and Richard DuPuis. Grand Rapids: Zondervan, 1989.

———. "Recent Discussions on the Subject of Entire Sanctification in this Life." Oberlin Quarterly Review 2 (May 1847): 449–72.

———. Sermons on Important Subjects. New York: John S. Taylor, 1836.

———. Skeletons of a Course of Theological Lectures. Oberlin: E. J. Goodrich, 1840.

First Annual Report of the Oberlin Collegiate Institute. Elyria, Ohio: Atlas Office, 1834.

Foster, Stephen. *The Brotherhood of Thieves; or, A True Picture of the American Church and Clergy.* Boston: Anti-Slavery Office, 1844.

Fourteenth Annual Report Presented to the Massachusetts Anti-Slavery Society. Boston: Scarlett and Laing, 1846.

From Bondage to Liberation: Writings by and about Afro-Americans from 1700 to 1918. Edited by Faith Berry. New York: Continuum, 2001.

Gardiner, O. C. *The Great Issue; or, The Three Presidential Candidates; Being, a Brief Historical Sketch of the Free Soil Question in the United States, from the Congresses of 1784 and '87 to the Present Time.* New York: B. B. Mussey, 1848.

Garrison, Wendell Phillips, and Francis Jackson Garrison. *William Lloyd Garrison, 1805–1879: The Story of His Life Told by His Children.* 4 vols. New York: Century, 1885.

Garrison, William Lloyd. *The Letters of William Lloyd Garrison.* 5 vols. Edited by Walter M. Merrill. Cambridge: Harvard University Press, 1973.

———. *The New Reign of Terror in the Slaveholding States, for 1859–60.* New York: American Anti-Slavery Society, 1860.

———. *Thoughts on African Colonization; or, An Impartial Exhibition of the Doctrines, Principles and Purposes of the American Colonization Society. Together with the Resolutions, Addresses and Remonstrances of the Free People of Color.* Boston: Garrison and Knapp, 1832.

General Catalogue of Oberlin College, 1833–1908. Cleveland: O. S. Hubbel, 1909.

Goodell, William. *Slavery and Anti-Slavery: A History of the Great Struggle in Both Hemispheres; With a View of the Slavery Question in the United States.* New York: W. Goodell, 1855.

Haddock, Charles. *Addresses and Miscellaneous Writings.* Cambridge: Metcalf, 1846.

Hale, Edward Everett. *Kanzas and Nebraska: An Account of the Emigrant Aid Companies, and Directions to Emigrants.* Boston: Phillips, Sampson, 1854.

Hammond, James Henry. *Selections from the Letters and Speeches of the Hon. James H. Hammond of South Carolina.* New York: John F. Trow, 1866.

Helper, Hinton Rowan. *Compendium of the Impending Crisis of the South.* New York: A. B. Burdick, 1860.

Henson, Josiah. *An Autobiography of the Rev. Josiah Henson (Mrs. Harriet Beecher Stowe's "Uncle Tom"), from 1789–1879.* Boston: B. B. Russell, 1879.

Hinsdale, B. A. *The Republican Text-Book for the Campaign of 1880: A Full History of General James A. Garfield's Public Life, With Other Political Information.* New York: D. Appleton, 1880.

History of the Oberlin-Wellington Rescue. Edited by Jacob Shipherd. Boston: J. P. Jewett, 1859.

Holley, Sallie. *A Life for Liberty: Antislavery and Other Letters of Sallie Holley.* Edited by John White Chadwick. New York: G. P. Putnam's Sons, 1899.

Hone, Philip. *The Diary of Philip Hone, 1828–1851.* Edited by Bayard Tuckerman. New York: Dodd, Mead, 1889.

Hopkins, Henry, Albert Hopkins, and Susan Sedgwick Hopkins. *Early Letters of Mark Hopkins, and Others from His Brothers and Their Mother: A Picture of Life in New England from 1770 to 1857.* New York: John Day, 1929.

Johns, Henry T. *Life with the Forty-Ninth Massachusetts Volunteers.* Pittsfield, 1864.

Johnson, Oliver. *The Abolitionists Vindicated in a Review of Eli Thayer's Paper on the New England Emigrant Aid Company.* Worcester: Worcester Society of Antiquity, 1887.

———. *William Lloyd Garrison and His Times.* Boston: Houghton, Mifflin, 1881.

Journal of the House of Representatives of the State of Ohio; Being the First Session of the Thirty-Eighth General Assembly: Held in the City of Columbus, and Commencing Monday, December 2, 1839, and in the Thirty-Eighth Year of Said State. Columbus: Samuel Medary, 1840.

Journal of the House of Representatives of the State of Ohio; Being the First Session of the Forty-First General Assembly, Held in the City of Columbus, and Commencing Monday, December 5, 1842. Columbus: Samuel Medary, 1842.

Journal of the House of Representatives of the United States, Being the First Session of the Twenty-Sixth Congress, Begun and Held at the City of Washington, December 2, 1839, in the Sixty-Fourth Year of the Independence of the Said States. Washington, D.C.: Government Printing Office, 1840.

Journal of the Senate of the State of Ohio, at the First Session of the Thirty-Eighth General Assembly Held in the City of Columbus and Commencing Monday, December 2, 1839. Columbus: Samuel Medary, 1840.

Journal of the Senate of the State of Ohio; Being the First Session of the Thirty-Fifth General Assembly, Begun and Held in the City of Columbus, Monday, Dec. 5, 1836, and in the Thirty-Fifth Year of Said State. Columbus: James B. Gardiner, 1837.

Journal of the Senate of the State of Ohio; Being the First Session of the Fortieth General Assembly, Held in the City of Columbus, and Commencing Monday, December 6, 1841. Columbus: Samuel Medary, 1842.

Journal of the Senate of the State of Ohio; Being the First Session of the Forty-Fourth General Assembly, Held in the City of Columbus, Commencing on Monday, December 1, 1845. Vol. 59. Columbus: C. Scott, 1846.

Kennedy, W. S. The Plan of Union; or, A History of the Presbyterian and Congregational Churches of the Western Reserve. Hudson: Pentagon Steam Press, 1856.

Krislov, Marvin. "State of the College Address, May 26, 2013," https://oncampus.oberlin.edu/source/articles/2013/05/26/2013-state-of-college.

Langston, John Mercer. Freedom and Citizenship: Selected Lectures and Addresses of John Mercer Langston, LL.D., U.S. Minister Resident at Haiti. Washington, D.C.: R. H. Darby, 1883.

———. From the Virginia Plantation to the National Capitol; or, The First and Only Negro Representative in Congress from the Old Dominion. Hartford: American, 1894.

Lawrence, Amos. Extracts from the Diary and Correspondence of the Late Amos Lawrence. Edited by William R. Lawrence. Boston: Gould and Lincoln, 1855.

Lyman, Huntington. "Lane Seminary Rebels." In The Oberlin Jubilee: 1833–1883, edited by W. G. Ballentine, 60–69. Oberlin: E. J. Goodrich, 1883.

Mahan, Asa. Autobiography: Intellectual, Moral, and Spiritual. London: T. Woolmer, 1882.

———. Out of Darkness into Light; or, The Hidden Life Made Manifest. London: F. E. Longley, 1875.

Malvin, John. The Autobiography of John Malvin: A Narrative. Cleveland: Leader, 1879.

Martineau, Harriett. Harriet Martineau's Autobiography. Edited by Maria Weston. Vol. 2. Chapman. Boston: James R. Osgood, 1877.

———. Harriet Martineau's Letters to Fanny Wedgwood. Edited by Elisabeth Sanders Arbuckle: Stanford: Stanford University Press, 1983.

———. The Martyr Age of the United States of America: With an Appeal on Behalf of the Oberlin Institute in Aid of the Abolition of Slavery. Newcastle Upon Tyne: Finlay and Charlton, 1840.

May, Samuel J. Memoir of Samuel Joseph May. Edited by Thomas J. Mumford, George B. Emerson, and Samuel J. May Jr. Boston: Roberts Brothers, 1873.

"Minutes and Address of the State Convention of the Colored Citizens of Ohio, Convened at Columbus, January 10th, 11th, 12th, & 13th, 1849." In *Proceedings of the Black State Conventions, 1840–1865*. Edited by Philip S. Foner and George E. Walker. Vol. 1. Philadelphia: Temple University Press, 1979.

"Minutes of the State Convention of the Colored Citizens of Ohio, Convened at Columbus, January 9th, 10th, 11th, and 12th, 1850." In *Proceedings of the Black State Conventions, 1840–1865*. Edited by Philip S. Foner and George E. Walker. Vol. 1. Philadelphia: Temple University Press, 1979.

"Minutes of the State Convention of the Colored Citizens of Ohio, Convened at Columbus, Jan. 15th, 16th, 17th and 18th, 1851." In *Proceedings of the Black State Conventions, 1840–1865*. Edited by Philip S. Foner and George E. Walker. Vol. 1. Philadelphia: Temple University Press, 1979.

Monroe, James. *Oberlin Thursday Lectures, Addresses, and Essays*. Oberlin: Edward J. Goodrich, 1897.

Morris, B. F. *The Life of Thomas Morris: Pioneer and Long a Legislator of Ohio, and, U.S. Senator from 1833 to 1839*. Cincinnati: Moore, Wilstach, Keys & Overend, 1856.

Mott, Lucretia Coffin. *Selected Letters of Lucretia Coffin Mott*. Edited by Beverly Wilson Palmer. Urbana: University of Illinois Press, 2002.

National Party Platforms of the United States Presidential Candidates, Electoral and Popular Votes. Edited by J. M. H. Frederick. Akron: J. M. H. Frederick, 1896.

Nevins, J. W. *The Anxious Bench*. Chambersburg, Pa., 1843.

Official Records of the Union and Confederate Navies in the War of the Rebellion. Vol. 14. Washington, D.C.: Government Printing Office, 1902.

Old Anti-Slavery Days: Proceedings of the Commemorative Meeting, Held by the Danvers Historical Society, at the Town Hall, Danvers, April 26, 1893, with Introduction, Letters, and Sketches. Danvers: Danvers Historical Society, 1893.

Opie, Amelia. *Memorials of the Life of Amelia Opie, Selected and Arranged from her Letters, Diaries, and Other Manuscripts*. Edited by Cecilia Lucy Brightwell. Norwich: Fletcher and Alexander, 1854.

O'Reilly, Henry. *Settlement in the West: Sketches of Rochester, With Incidental Notices of Western New York*. Rochester: William Alling, 1838.

Parsons, Levi. *History of Rochester Presbytery From the Earliest Settlement of the Country*. Rochester: Democrat-Chronicle Press, 1889.

Patton, William. *Prayer and Its Remarkable Answers: Being a Statement of Facts in the Light of Reason and Revelation*. New York: Funk & Wagnalls, 1885.

Pease, David. *A Genealogical and Historical Record of the Descendants of John Pease*. Springfield, Mass.: S. Bowles, 1869.

Pillsbury, Parker. *Acts of the Anti-Slavery Apostles*. Boston: Cuples, Upham, 1884.

"Proceedings of the Convention of the Colored Freemen of Ohio, Held in Cincinnati, January 14, 15, 16, 17 and 19, 1852." In *Proceedings of the Black State Conventions, 1840–1865*. Edited by Philip S. Foner and George E. Walker. Vol. 1. Philadelphia: Temple University Press, 1979.

Proceedings of the First Three Republican National Conventions of 1856, 1860, and 1864. Minneapolis: Charles W. Johnson, 1893.

Proceedings of the General Anti-Slavery Convention, Called by the British and Foreign Anti-Slavery Society, and Held in London, from Tuesday, June 13, to Tuesday, June 20th, 1843. London: British and Foreign Anti-Slavery Society, 1843.

Proceedings of the General Anti-Slavery Convention, Called by the Committee of the British and Foreign Anti-Slavery Society, and Held in London, from Friday, June 12th, to Tuesday, June 23rd, 1840. London: British and Foreign Anti-Slavery Society, 1841.

Proceedings of the Ohio Anti-Slavery Convention Held at Putnam on the Twenty-Second, Twenty-Third, and Twenty-Fourth of April, 1835. Putnam, Ohio: Beaumont and Wallace, 1835.

"Proceedings of the State Convention of Colored Men, Held in the City of Columbus, Ohio, Jan. 16th, 17th, & 18th, 1856." In *Proceedings of the Black State Conventions, 1840–1865*. Edited by Philip S. Foner and George E. Walker. Vol. 1. Philadelphia: Temple University Press, 1979.

"Proceedings of the State Convention of Colored Men of the State of Ohio, Held in the City of Columbus, January 21st, 22nd & 23rd, 1857." In *Proceedings of the Black State Conventions, 1840–1865*. Edited by Philip S. Foner and George E. Walker. Vol. 1. Philadelphia: Temple University Press, 1979.

Ransom, Reverdy. *The Pilgrimage of Harriett Ransom's Son*. Nashville: Sunday School Union, 1949.

The Rebellion Record: A Diary of American Events, with Documents, Narratives Illustrative Incidents, Poetry, Etc. Vol. 7. New York: D. VanNostrand, 1864.

Register of Debates in Congress, Comprising the Leading Debates and Incidents of the First Session of the Twenty-Fourth Congress. Vol. 12. Washington, D.C.: Government Printing Office, 1836.

Report of the Annual Meeting of the Glasgow Emancipation Society, Held August 8, 1840. Glasgow: Glasgow Emancipation Society, 1840.

Report of the Arguments of Counsel, in the Case of Prudence Crandall, Plff. In Error, vs. State of Connecticut. Boston: Garrison and Knapp, 1834.

Report of the Fourth Anniversary of the Ohio Anti-Slavery Society, Held in Putnam, Muskingham County, Ohio, on the 29th of May, 1839. Cincinnati: Ohio Anti-Slavery Society, 1839.

Report of the Meeting of the Michigan State Anti-Slavery Society, June 28th, 1837, Being the First Annual Meeting, Adjourned from June 1st, 1837. Detroit: Geo. L. Whitney, 1837.

Report of the Proceedings of the Colored National Convention, Held at Cleveland, Ohio, on Wednesday, September 6, 1848. Rochester: John Dick, 1848.

Report on the Debates and Proceedings of the Convention for the Revision of the Constitution, of the State of Ohio, 1850–51. 2 Vols. Columbus: S. Medary, 1851.

The Revised Statutes of the State of Ohio, of a General Nature. Edited by Joseph R. Swan. Vol. 1. Cincinnati: Robert Clarke, 1870.

Richardson, Albert D. *Beyond the Mississippi: From the Great River to the Great Ocean*. Hartford: American, 1867.

Rinaldi, Matthew. "Matthew Rinaldi '69," http://stories.oberlin.edu/6/social-justice-activism/matthew-rinaldi-69.shtml. April 22, 2013.

Runyowa, Simbarashe. "Oberlin Unchained: On the Recent Incidents of Hate Speech on Campus," February 15, 2013, http://blogs.oberlin.edu/about/activism/oberlin_unchain.shtml.

Sanborn, F. B. *The Life and Letters of John Brown; Liberator of Kansas and Martyr of Virginia*. Concord: F. B. Sanborn, 1910.

Second Annual Report of the American Anti-Slavery Society . . . Held in the City of New York, on the Twelfth of May, 1835. New York: Garrison and Knapp, 1835.

Shumway, A. L., and C. deW. Brower. *Oberliniana: A Jubilee Volume of Semi-Historical Anecdotes Connected with the Past and Present of Oberlin College, 1833–1883*. Cleveland: Home, 1883.

The Slave's Narrative. Edited by Charles T. Davis and Henry Louis Gates Jr. New York: Oxford University Press, 1991.

Smith, Delazon. Oberlin Unmasked; A History of Oberlin, or New Lights of the West. Cleveland, 1837.

Spooner, Lysander. The Unconstitutionality of Slavery. Boston: Bela Marsh, 1845.

Stanton, Henry B. Random Recollections. New York: Harper & Brothers, 1887.

Stone, Lucy, and Antoinette Brown Blackwell. Friends and Sisters: Letters Between Lucy Stone and Antoinette Brown Blackwell, 1846–1893. Edited by Carol Lasser and Marlene Merrill. Urbana: University of Illinois Press, 1987.

Stowe, Harriet Beecher. A Key to Uncle Tom's Cabin: Presenting the Original Facts and Documents Upon Which the Story Is Founded. Together with Corroborative Statements Verifying the Truth of the Work. London: Sampson Low, Son, and Co., 1853.

Strieby, M. E. Oberlin and the American Missionary Association. Oberlin, 1891.

Studor, Jacob H. Columbus Ohio: Its History, Resources and Progress, with Numerous Illustrations. Columbus: Jacob H. Studor, 1873.

Sturge, Joseph. A Visit to the United States in 1841. Boston: Dexter S. King, 1842.

Tappan, Lewis. Life of Arthur Tappan. New York: Hurd and Houghton, 1870.

"Territorial Kansas Online, 1854–1861." Kansas State Historical Society, www.territorialkansasonline.org. 22 July 2009.

Thayer, Eli. A History of the Kansas Crusade: Its Friends and Its Foes. New York: Harper and Brothers, 1889.

The Third Annual Report of the American Anti-Slavery Society . . . Held in the City of New York, on the Tenth of May, 1836 (New York, 1836). Boston: Garrison and Knapp, 1834.

Thome, James A. "Come-outism and Come-outers." Oberlin Quarterly Review 2 (November 1846): 158–87.

———. Debate at Lane Seminary, Cincinnati. Boston: Garrison and Knapp, 1834.

Thome, James A., and J. Horace Kimball. Emancipation in the West Indies: A Six Months' Tour in Antigua, Barbadoes, and Jamaica in the Year 1837. New York: American Anti-Slavery Society, 1838.

Thome, James A., and Theodore Dwight Weld. Slavery and the Internal Slave Trade in the United States of North America. London: British and Foreign Anti-Slavery Society, 1841.

Thompson, George. Prison Life and Reflections. Hartford: A. Work, 1850.

Townsend, Norton. "Salmon P. Chase." Ohio State Archaeological and Historical Quarterly 1 (September 1887): 111–26.

Trowbridge, John T. My Own Story, With Recollections of Noted Persons. Boston: Houghton, Mifflin, 1903.

Twenty Second Annual Report of the Society for the Promotion of Collegiate and Theological Education at the West. New York: John F. Trow, 1865.

The War of the Rebellion: A Compilation of the Official Records of the Union and Confederate Armies. Edited by Robert Scott. Vol. 28. Washington, D.C.: Government Printing Office, 1890.

Weld, Theodore Dwight. American Slavery As It Is: Testimony of a Thousand Witnesses. New York: American Anti-Slavery Society, 1839.

———. The Bible against Slavery: An Inquiry into the Patriarchal and Mosaic Systems on the Subject of Human Rights. New York: American Anti-Slavery Society, 1837.

———. First Annual Report of the Society for Promoting Manual Labor in Literary Institutions. New York: S. W. Benedict, 1833.

———. *Letters of Theodore Dwight Weld, Angelina Grimké Weld, and Sarah Grimké, 1822–1844*. 2 vols. Edited by Gilbert H. Barnes and Dwight L. DuMond. New York: Appleton-Century, 1932.

———. *The Power of Congress over the District of Columbia, Reprinted from the New York Evening Post, with Additions by the Author*. New York: J. F. Trow, 1838.

Wheeler, Henry G. *History of Congress: Biographical and Political: Comprising Memoirs of Members of the Congress of the United States*. New York: Harper and Brothers, 1848.

Whittier, John Greenleaf. *Life and Letters of John Greenleaf Whittier*. Edited by Samuel T. Pickard. Vol. 1. Boston: George H. Doran, 1899.

Wright, George Frederick. *A Standard History of Lorain County*. Vol. 1. Chicago: Lewis, 1916.

———. *Story of My Life and Work*. Oberlin: Bibliotheca Sacra, 1916.

SECONDARY SOURCES

Abzug, Robert H. *Cosmos Crumbling: American Reform and the Religious Imagination*. Berkeley: University of California Press, 1994.

———. *Passionate Liberator: Theodore Dwight Weld and the Dilemma of Reform*. New York: Oxford University Press, 1980.

Alexander, Leslie M. *African or American? Black Identity and Political Activism in New York City, 1784–1861*. Urbana: University of Illinois Press, 2008.

Alilunas, Leo. "Fugitive Slave Cases in Ohio Prior to 1850." *Ohio State Archaeological and Historical Quarterly* 49 (January–March 1940): 160–84.

Allen, Thomas M. *A Republic in Time: Temporality and Social Imagination in Nineteenth-Century America*. Chapel Hill: University of North Carolina Press, 2008.

Aptheker, Herbert. *Abolitionism: A Revolutionary Movement*. Boston: Twayne Publishers, 1989.

Bacon, Benjamin Wisner. *Theodore Thorton Munger: New England Minister*. New Haven: Yale University Press, 1913.

Bacon, Donald C., Roger H. Davidson, and Morton Keller, eds. *The Encyclopedia of the United States Congress*. Vol. 2. New York: Simon and Schuster, 1995.

Bacon, Margaret Hope. *But One Race: The Life of Robert Purvis*. Albany: State University of New York Press, 2007.

Barkun, Michael. *The Crucible of the Millennium: The Burned-Over District of New York in the 1840s*. Syracuse: Syracuse University Press, 1986.

Barnes, Gilbert Hobbes. *The Antislavery Impulse, 1830–1844*. New York: D. Appleton–Century, 1933.

Baumann, Roland M. *Constructing Black Education at Oberlin College: A Documentary History*. Athens: Ohio University Press, 2010.

Beard, Augustus Field. *A Crusade of Brotherhood: A History of the American Missionary Association*. Boston: Pilgrim Press, 1909.

Bendroth, Margaret Lamberts. *A School of the Church: Andover Newton Across Two Centuries*. Grand Rapids: Eerdmans, 2008.

Berlin, Ira. *Slaves without Masters: The Free Negro in the Antebellum South*. New York: Oxford University Press, 1974.

Bigglestone, William E. "Oberlin College and the Negro Student, 1865–1940." *Journal of Negro History* 56 (July 1971): 198–219.

———. *They Stopped in Oberlin: Black Residents and Visitors of the Nineteenth Century.* Scottsdale, Ariz.: Innovation Group, 1981.

Blackett, R. J. M. *Beating against the Barriers: Biographical Essays in Nineteenth-Century Afro-American History.* Baton Rouge: Louisiana State University Press, 1986.

———. *Building an Antislavery Wall: Black Abolitionists in the Atlantic Abolitionist Movement, 1830–1860.* Baton Rouge: Louisiana State University Press, 1983.

Blodgett, Geoffrey. *Oberlin History: Essays and Impressions.* Kent: Kent State University Press, 2005.

Blue, Frederick J., ed. *No Taint of Compromise: Crusaders in Antislavery Politics.* Baton Rouge: Louisiana State University Press, 2005.

———. *Salmon P. Chase: A Life in Politics.* Kent: Kent State University Press, 1987.

Blue, Frederick J., and Robert McCormick. "Norton S. Townsend: A Reformer for All Seasons." In *The Pursuit of Public Power: Political Culture in Ohio, 1787–1861*, edited by Jeffery P. Brown and Andrew R. L. Cayton, 144–54. Kent: Kent State University Press, 1994.

Boardman, George. *History of New England Theology.* New York: A. D. F. Randolph, 1899.

Bordewich, Fergus. *Bound for Canaan: The Underground Railroad and the War for the Soul of America.* New York: HarperCollins, 2005.

Brandt, Nat. *The Town That Started the Civil War.* Syracuse: Syracuse University Press, 1990.

Bratt, James D. "The Reorientation of American Protestantism, 1835–1845." *Church History* 67 (March 1998): 52–82.

Burroughs, William Greeley. "Oberlin's Part in the Slavery Conflict." *Ohio State Archaeological and Historical Quarterly* 20 (January 1911): 269–334.

Carpenter, Edward W., and Charles F. Morehouse. *The History of the Town of Amherst, Massachusetts.* Amherst: Carpenter and Morehouse, 1896.

Carrington, Paul D. *Stewards of Democracy: Law as a Public Profession.* New York: Basic Books, 1999.

Carton, Evan. *Patriotic Treason: John Brown and the Soul of America.* New York: Simon and Schuster, 2006.

Cheek, William, and Aimee Lee Cheek. *John Mercer Langston and the Fight for Black Freedom, 1829–1865.* Urbana: University of Illinois Press, 1989.

Clark, Christopher. *The Communitarian Moment: The Radical Challenge of the Northampton Association.* Ithaca: Cornell University Press, 1995.

Cormany, Clayton Douglas. "Ohio's Abolitionist Campaign: A Study in the Rhetoric of Conversion." Ph.D. diss., Ohio State University, 1981.

Crapol, Edward P. *John Tyler: The Accidental President.* Chapel Hill: University of North Carolina Press, 2006.

Cross, Whitney R. *The Burned-Over District: The Social and Intellectual History of Enthusiastic Religion in Western New York, 1800–1850.* Ithaca: Cornell University Press, 1950.

Cumbler, John T. *From Abolition to Rights for All: The Making of a Reform Community in the Nineteenth Century.* Philadelphia: University of Pennsylvania Press, 2008.

Cutler, Carroll. *A History of Western Reserve College during its First Half Century, 1826–1876.* Cleveland: Crocker's, 1876.

Cutter, William Richard. *New England Families, Genealogical and Memorial: A Record of the Achievements of Her People in the Making of Commonwealths and the Founding of a Nation.* Vol. 1. New York: Lewis Historical Publishing, 1914.

Davis, David Brion. *Slavery and Human Progress*. New York: Oxford University Press, 1984.
Dayton, Donald W. *Discovering an Evangelical Heritage*. New York: Harper and Row, 1976.
Delbanco, Andrew. *The Abolitionist Imagination*. Cambridge: Harvard University Press, 2012.
Deramus, Betty. *Freedom by Any Means: Con Games, Voodoo Schemes, True Love, and Lawsuits on the Underground Railroad*. New York: Simon and Schuster, 2009.
DeWitt, John. *Early Globalization and the Economic Development of the United States and Brazil*. Westport, Conn.: Praeger, 2002.
Deyle, Steven. *Carry Me Back: The Domestic Slave Trade in American Life*. New York: Oxford University Press, 2005.
Dixon, Chris. *Perfecting the Family: Antislavery Marriages in Nineteenth-Century America*. Amherst: University of Massachusetts Press, 1997.
Earle, Jonathan Halperin. *Jacksonian Antislavery and the Politics of Free Soil, 1824–1854*. Chapel Hill: University of North Carolina Press, 2004.
Ellsworth, Clayton Sumner. "Oberlin and the Anti-Slavery Movement up to the Civil War." Ph.D. diss., Cornell University, 1930.
Emerson, Michael O., and Christian Smith. *Divided by Faith: Evangelical Religion and the Problem of Race in America*. New York: Oxford University Press, 2000.
Encyclopedia of Slave Resistance and Rebellion. Edited by Junius P. Rodriguez. Vol. 1. Westport, Conn.: Greenwood, 2007.
Essig, James David. "The Lord's Free Man: Charles G. Finney and His Abolitionism." *Civil War History* 24 (March 1978): 24–45.
Fanuzzi, Robert. *Abolition's Public Sphere*. Minneapolis: University of Minnesota Press, 2003.
Fehrenbach, T. R. *Lone Star: A History of Texas and the Texans*. New York: Da Capo Press, 2000.
Fehrenbacher, Don Edward. *Slavery, Law, and Politics: The Dred Scott Case in Historical Perspective*. New York: Oxford University Press, 1981.
Finke, Gail Deibler. *Images of America: College Hill*. Mount Pleasant, S.C.: Arcadia, 2004.
Finkelman, Paul. "Race, Slavery, and the Law in Antebellum Ohio." In *The History of Ohio Law*, edited by Michael Les Benedict and John F. Winkler, 2:748–81. Athens: Ohio University Press, 2004.
Fletcher, Juanita. "Against the Consensus: Oberlin College and the Education of American Negroes, 1835–1865." Ph.D. diss., The American University, 1974.
Fletcher, Robert S. "Bread and Doctrine at Oberlin." *Ohio State Archaeological and Historical Quarterly* 49 (January 1940): 58–67.
———. *A History of Oberlin College: From Its Foundation Through the Civil War*. 2 vols. Oberlin: Oberlin College Press, 1943.
———. "John Brown and Oberlin." *Oberlin Alumni Magazine* 28 (February 1932): 135–41.
Fogarty, Robert S. *American Utopianism*. Itasca, Ill.: Peacock, 1972.
Fogel, Robert William. *Without Consent or Contract: The Rise and Fall of American Slavery*. New York: W. W. Norton, 1989.
Fradin, Dennis Brindell. *Bound for the North Star: True Stories of Fugitive Slaves*. New York: Houghton Mifflin Harcourt, 2000.
Frederickson, George M. *The Black Image in the White Mind: The Debate on Afro-American Character and Destiny, 1817–1914*. New York: Harper and Row, 1971.
Friedman, Lawrence J. *Gregarious Saints: Self and Community in American Abolitionism, 1830–1870*. Cambridge: Cambridge University Press, 1982.

Friesen, John W., and Virginia Lyons Friesen. *The Palgrave Companion to North American Utopias.* New York: Palgrave Macmillan, 2004.
Gamble, Douglas A. "Joshua Giddings and the Ohio Abolitionists: A Study in Radical Politics." *Ohio History* 88 (1978): 37–56.
———. "The Western Anti-Slavery Society: Garrisonian Abolitionism in Ohio." Master's thesis, Ohio State University, 1970.
Gara, Larry. *The Liberty Line: The Legend of the Underground Railroad.* Lexington: University of Kentucky Press, 1961.
———. "Who Was an Abolitionist?" In *The Antislavery Vanguard: New Essays on the Abolitionists,* edited by Martin B. Duberman, 32–52. Princeton: Princeton University Press, 1965.
Geary, Linda L. *Balanced in the Wind: A Biography of Betsey Mix Cowles.* Lewisburg: Bucknell University Press, 1989.
Going, Charles. *David Wilmot, Free Soiler.* New York: D. Appleton, 1924.
Goodman, Paul. "The Manual Labor Movement and the Origins of Abolitionism." *Journal of the Early Republic* 13 (Fall 1993): 355–88.
———. *Of One Blood: Abolitionism and the Origins of Racial Equality.* Berkeley: University of California Press, 1998.
Goodwin, Doris Kearns. *Team of Rivals: The Political Genius of Abraham Lincoln.* New York: Simon and Schuster, 2005.
Greene, Richard E. "Abby Kelley Foster: A Feminist Voice Reconsidered." In *Multiculturalism: Roots and Realities,* edited by C. James Trotman, 170–86. Bloomington: University of Indiana Press, 2002.
Grover, Kathryn. *The Fugitive's Gibraltar: Escaping Slaves and Abolitionism in New Bedford, Massachusetts.* Amherst: University of Massachusetts Press, 2001.
Hambrick-Stowe, Charles E. *Charles G. Finney and the Spirit of American Evangelicalism.* Grand Rapids: Eerdmans, 1996.
Hamm, Thomas D. *God's Government Begun: The Society for Universal Inquiry and Reform, 1842–1846.* Bloomington: Indiana University Press, 1995.
Hammond, John L. "Revival Religion and Antislavery Politics." *American Sociological Review* 39 (April 1974): 175–86.
Harrold, Stanley. *Border War: Fighting over Slavery before the Civil War.* Chapel Hill: University of North Carolina Press, 2010.
———. *Gamaliel Bailey and Antislavery Union.* Kent: Kent State University Press, 1986.
Hart, Alfred Bushnell. *Salmon Portland Chase.* Boston: Houghton, Mifflin, 1899.
———. *Slavery and Abolition, 1831–1841.* New York: Harper and Brothers, 1906.
Hart, Alfred Bushnell, and John Gould Curtis, eds. *Welding of the Nation.* Vol. 4 of *American History Told by Contemporaries.* New York: Macmillan, 1909.
Hatch, Nathan O. *The Democratization of American Christianity.* New Haven: Yale University Press, 1989.
Hewitt, Glenn A. *Regeneration and Morality: A Study of Charles Finney, Charles Hodge, John W. Nevin, and Horace Bushnell.* Brooklyn: Carlson, 1991.
Hinks, Peter P., John R. McKivigan, and R. Owen Williams. *Encyclopedia of Antislavery and Abolition.* Westport, Conn.: Greenwood, 2007.
Hinshaw, Seth. *Ohio Elects the President: Our State's Role in Presidential Elections, 1804–1996.* Mansfield: Book Masters, 2000.

Hinton, Richard J. *John Brown and His Men.* New York: Funk & Wagnalls, 1894.
A History of Education in the State of Ohio: A Centennial Volume. Columbus: Gazette, 1876.
Holland, Frederick May. *Frederick Douglass: The Colored Orator.* New York: Funk & Wagnalls, 1891.
Holloway, Mark. *Utopian Communities in America, 1680–1880.* Mineola, N.Y.: Dover, 1966.
Holt, Edgar Allan. "Party Politics in Ohio, 1840–1850." *Ohio State Archaeological and Historical Quarterly* 38 (1929): 260–402.
Holt, Michael F. *The Rise and Fall of the American Whig Party: Jacksonian Politics and the Onset of the Civil War.* New York: Oxford University Press, 2003.
Hopkins, Geraldine. "Garrison Abolition vs. Oberlin Anti-Slavery." Honors thesis, University of Northern Illinois, 1929.
Horton, James Oliver. "Black Education at Oberlin College: A Controversial Commitment." *Journal of Negro Education* 54 (Autumn 1985): 477–99.
———. "Race and Region: Ohio, America's Middle Ground." In *Ohio and the World, 1753–2053: Essays Toward a New History of Ohio.* Edited by Geoffrey Parker, Richard Sisson, and William Russell Coil, 43–72. Columbus: Ohio State University Press, 2005.
Horton, James Oliver, and Lois E. Horton. *In Hope of Liberty: Culture, Community, and Protest among Northern Free Blacks, 1700–1860.* New York: Oxford University Press, 1997.
———. *Slavery and the Making of America.* New York: Oxford University Press, 2004.
Hosford, Frances J. *Father Shipherd's Magna Charta: A Century of Co-education in Oberlin College, 1837–1937.* Boston: Marshall Jones, 1937.
Howe, Daniel Walker. *The Political Culture of the American Whigs.* Chicago: University of Chicago Press, 1984.
———. *What God Hath Wrought: The Transformation of America, 1815–1848.* New York: Oxford University Press, 2007.
Hughes, Langston. *The Big Sea.* Vol. 13 of *The Collected Works of Langston Hughes.* Edited by Joseph McLaren. Columbia: University of Missouri Press, 2002.
Jacobs, Donald M., ed. *Courage and Conscience: Black and White Abolitionists in Boston.* Bloomington: Indiana University Press, 1993.
Jeffrey, Julie Roy. *The Great Silent Army of Abolitionism: Ordinary Women in the Antislavery Movement.* Chapel Hill: University of North Carolina Press, 1998.
Johnson, Paul E. *A Shopkeeper's Millennium: Society and Revivals in Rochester, New York, 1815–1837.* New York: Hill and Wang, 1978.
Jones, Martha S. *All Bound Up Together: The Woman Question in African American Public Culture, 1830–1900.* Chapel Hill: University of North Carolina Press, 2007.
Jones, Nelson E. *The Squirrel Hunters of Ohio; or, Glimpses of Pioneer Life.* Cincinnati: R. Clarke, 1898.
Kaminski, John. *A Necessary Evil? Slavery and the Debate over the Constitution.* Madison: Madison House, 1995.
Kanter, Rosabeth Moss. *Commitment and Community: Communes and Utopias in Sociological Perspective.* Cambridge: Harvard University Press, 1972.
Kerr, Andrea Moore. *Lucy Stone: Speaking Out for Equality.* New Brunswick: Rutgers University Press, 1992.
Knepper, George W. *Ohio and Its People.* Kent: Kent State University Press, 2003.
Knight, George W., and John R. Commons. *The History of Higher Education in Ohio.* Washington, D.C.: Government Printing Office, 1891.

Kraditor, Aileen. *Means and Ends in American Abolitionism: Garrison and His Critics on Strategy and Tactics, 1834–1850.* New York: Pantheon Books, 1967.

Kyle, Richard G. *Evangelicalism: An Americanized Christianity.* New Brunswick: Rutgers University Press, 2006.

Lasser, Carol. "Enacting Emancipation: African American Women Abolitionists at Oberlin College and the Quest for Empowerment, Equality, and Respectability." In *Woman's Rights and Transatlantic Antislavery in the Era of Emancipation,* edited by Katherine Kish Sklar and James Brewer Stewart, 319–45. New Haven: Yale University Press, 2007.

———. "The Underground Railroad in Oberlin History and Memory." A paper presented at "Threads of Freedom: The Underground Railroad Story in Quilts," June 23, 2001, goo.gl/MSH60. June 16, 2008.

Lawson, Ellen N., with Marlene Merrill. "The Antebellum 'Talented Thousandth': Black College Students at Oberlin Before the Civil War." *Journal of Negro Education* 52 (Spring 1983): 142–55.

———. "Lucy Stanton: Life on the Cutting Edge." *Western Reserve Magazine,* January–February 1983, 9–10.

———. *The Three Sarahs: Documents of Antebellum Black College Women.* New York: Edwin Mellen Press, 1984.

Leonard, Delvant Levant. *The Story of Oberlin: The Institution, the Community.* Boston: Pilgrim Press, 1898.

Lerner, Gerda. *The Grimké Sisters from South Carolina: Pioneers for Women's Rights and Abolition.* New York: Schocken Books, 1971.

Lesick, Lawrence Thomas. *The Lane Rebels: Evangelicalism and Antislavery in Antebellum America.* Metuchen, N.J.: Scarecrow Press, 1980.

Levecq, Christine. *Slavery and Sentiment: The Politics of Feeling in Black Atlantic Antislavery Writing, 1770–1850.* Lebanon: University of New Hampshire Press, 2002.

Litwack, Leon F. *North of Slavery: The Negro in the Free States.* Chicago: University of Chicago Press, 1965.

Lord, John King. *A History of Dartmouth College, 1815–1909:* Concord, N.H.: Rumford Press, 1913.

Lovett, Bobby L. *The African American History of Nashville, Tennessee, 1780–1930: Elites and Dilemmas.* Fayetteville: University of Arkansas Press, 1999.

Mackin, Anne. *Americans and Their Land: The House Built on Abundance.* Ann Arbor: University of Michigan Press, 2006.

Madden, Edward H., and James E. Hamilton. *Freedom and Grace: The Life of Asa Mahan.* Metuchen, N.J.: Scarecrow Press, 1982.

Magdol, Edward. *The Anti-Slavery Rank and File: A Social Profile of the Abolitionists' Constituency.* New York: Greenwood, 1986.

Mayer, Henry. *All on Fire: William Lloyd Garrison and the Abolition of Slavery.* New York: St. Martin's Press, 1998.

McFeely, William. *Frederick Douglass.* New York: W. W. Norton, 1991.

McIlwraith, Thomas F., and Edward K. Muller, eds. *North America: The Historical Geography of a Changing Continent.* Lanham, M.d.: Rowan and Littlefield, 2001.

Mead, Ellwell O. "History of Plymouth Rock Conference." In *Papers of the Ohio Church History Society,* edited by Delvan Leonard, 4:29–43. Oberlin: Ohio Church History Society, 1893.

Mealy, Todd. *Aliened American: A Biography of William Howard Day*. Vol. 1. Frederick, Md.: PublishAmerica, 2010.
Meed, Douglas V. *The Mexican War: 1846–1848*. New York: Oxford University Press, 2002.
Merrill, Marlene. *Sarah Margru Kinson: The Two Worlds of an Amistad Captive*. Oberlin: Oberlin Historical and Improvement Association, 2003.
Middleton, Stephen. *The Black Laws: Race and the Legal Process in Early Ohio*. Athens: Ohio University Press, 2006.
Miller, Edward Alanson. *The History of Educational Legislation in Ohio from 1803 to 1850*. Chicago: University of Chicago Libraries, 1920.
Mitchell, Thomas G. *Antislavery Politics in Antebellum and Civil War America*. Westport, Conn.: Praeger, 2007.
Morris, Aldon D. *The Origins of the Civil Rights Movement: Black Communities Organizing for Change*. New York: Free Press, 1984.
Morris, James Mathew, and Andrea L. Kross. *Historical Dictionary of Utopianism*. Lanham, Md.: Scarecrow Press, 2004.
Myers, John L. "Organization of the 'Seventy': To Arouse the North against Slavery." *Mid-America* 48 (1966): 29–46.
Nerone, John C. *Violence against the Press: Policing the Public Sphere in U.S. History*. New York: Oxford University Press, 1994.
Newman, Richard S. *The Transformation of American Abolitionism: Fighting Slavery in the Early Republic*. Chapel Hill: University of North Carolina Press, 2002.
Oates, Stephen B. *The Approaching Fury: Voices of the Storm, 1820–1861*. New York: HarperCollins, 1998.
———. *To Purge This Land with Blood: A Biography of John Brown*. New York: Harper and Row, 1970.
The Ohio Almanac. Edited by Damaine Vonada. Wilmington: Orange Frazer, 1992.
Osborne, William. *Music in Ohio*. Kent: Kent State University Press, 2004.
Padgett, Chris. "Evangelicals Divided: Abolition and the Plan of Union's Demise in Ohio's Western Reserve." In *Religion and the Antebellum Debate Over Slavery*, edited by John R. McKivigan and Mitchell Snay, 249–72. Athens: University of Georgia Press, 1998.
Peterson, Anna Lisa. *Seeds of the Kingdom: Utopian Communities in the Americas*. New York: Oxford University Press, 2005.
Phillips, Wilbur. *Oberlin Colony, The Story of a Century*. Oberlin: Oberlin Printing, 1933.
Potter, David M. *The Impending Crisis, 1848–1861*. New York: Harper and Row, 1976.
Quarles, Benjamin. *Black Abolitionists*. New York: Oxford University Press, 1969.
———. *The Negro in the Civil War*. New York: Da Capo Press, 1989.
Quillin, Frank U. *The Color Line in Ohio: A History of Race Prejudice in a Typical Northern State*. Ann Arbor: George Wahr, 1913.
Rayback, Joseph G. "The Liberty Party Leaders of Ohio: Exponents of Anti-Slavery Coalition." *Ohio State Archaeological and Historical Quarterly* 57 (1948): 165–78.
Reilley, Edward Coleman. *The Early Slavery Controversy in the Western Reserve*. Cleveland: Case Western Reserve University Press, 1940.
Reynolds, David S. *John Brown, Abolitionist: The Man Who Killed Slavery, Sparked the Civil War, and Seeded Civil Rights*. New York: Vintage Books, 2005.
Richards, Leonard L. *Gentlemen of Property and Standing: Anti-Abolition Mobs in Jacksonian America*. New York: Oxford University Press, 1971.

Riddle, A. G. *The Life of Benjamin F. Wade*. Cleveland: Williams, 1888.

———. "Rise of the Anti-Slavery Sentiment on the Western Reserve." *Magazine of Western History* 6 (June 1887): 145–56.

Riley, Glenda. *Prairie Voices: Iowa's Pioneering Women*. Ames: Iowa State University Press, 1996.

Robertson, Stacey M. *Hearts Beating for Liberty: Women Abolitionists in the Old Northwest*. Chapel Hill: University of North Carolina Press, 2010.

Rodabaugh, James H. "The Negro in Ohio." *Journal of Negro History* 31 (January 1946): 9–29.

Rokicky, Catherine M. *James Monroe: Oberlin's Christian Statesman and Reformer, 1821–1898*. Kent: Kent State University Press, 2002.

———. "Lydia Finney and Evangelical Womanhood." *Ohio History* 103 (Summer/Autumn 1994): 170–89.

Roseboom, Eugene H., and Francis P. Weisenburger. *A History of Ohio*. Columbus: Ohio State Archaeological and Historical Society, 1954.

Rudy, Willis. *The Campus and a Nation in Crisis: From the American Revolution to Vietnam*. Madison, N.J.: Farleigh Dickinson University Press, 1996.

Siebert, Wilbur Henry. *Mysteries of Ohio's Underground Railroads*. Columbus: Long's College Book Co., 1951.

———. *The Underground Railroad from Slavery to Freedom*. New York: Macmillan, 1898.

Sengupta, Gunja. *For God and Mammon: Evangelicals and Entrepreneurs, Masters and Slaves in Territorial Kansas, 1854–1860*. Athens: University of Georgia Press, 1996.

Sernett, Milton C. *Abolition's Axe: Beriah Green, Oneida Institute, and the Black Freedom Struggle*. Syracuse: Syracuse University Press, 1986.

———. "Common Cause: The Antislavery Alliance of Gerrit Smith and Beriah Green." New York History Net, <goo.gl/MsKfM>. February 13, 2013.

Sewell, Richard H. *Ballots for Freedom: Antislavery Politics in the United States, 1837–1860*. New York: Oxford University Press, 1992.

Shaw, Archer H. *The Plain Dealer, One Hundred Years in Cleveland*. New York: Knopf, 1942.

Simmons, William J. *Men of Mark: Eminent, Progressive, and Rising*. Cleveland: Geo. M. Rewell, 1887.

Sinha, Manisha. "Did the Abolitionists Cause the Civil War?" In *The Abolitionist Imagination*, edited by Andrew Delbanco, 81–108. Cambridge: Harvard University Press, 2012.

Smith, Joseph Patterson. *History of the Republican Party in Ohio*. Vol. 1. Chicago: Lewis, 1898.

Smith, Theodore Clark. *The Liberty and Free Soil Parties in the Northwest*. New York: Longmans, Green, 1897.

Speicher, Anna M. *The Religious World of Antislavery Women: Spirituality in the Lives of Five Abolitionist Lecturers*. Syracuse: Syracuse University Press, 2000.

Spencer, Jon Michael. *Protest and Praise: Sacred Music of Black Religion*. Minneapolis: Fortress Press, 1990.

Staudenraus, P. J. *The African Colonization Movement, 1816–1865*. Charlottesville: University of Virginia Press, 1980.

Stauffer, John. *The Black Hearts of Men: Radical Abolitionism and the Transformation of Race*. Cambridge: Harvard University Press, 2002.

Steinglass, Steven H., and Gino J. Scarselli. *The Ohio State Constitution: A Reference Guide*. Westport, Conn.: Greenwood, 2004.

Stephens, George E., and Donald Yakovone. *A Voice of Thunder: A Black Soldier's Civil War.* Urbana: University of Illinois Press, 1998.
Sterling, Dorothy. *Ahead of Her Time: Abby Kelley and the Politics of Antislavery.* New York: W. W. Norton, 1991.
Stewart, James Brewer. *Abolitionist Politics and the Coming of the Civil War.* Amherst: University of Massachusetts Press, 2008.
———. *Holy Warriors: The Abolitionists and American Slavery.* New York: Hill and Wang, 1976.
———. *Joshua R. Giddings and the Tactics of Radical Politics.* Cleveland: Case Western Reserve University Press, 1970.
———. "Modernizing 'Difference': The Political Meanings of Color in the Free States, 1776–1840." In *Race and the Early Republic: Racial Consciousness and Nation-Building in the Early Republic,* edited by Michael A. Morris and James Brewer Stewart, 33–58. Lanham, Md.: Rowan and Littlefield, 2002.
Strane, Susan. *A Whole Souled Woman: Prudence Crandall and the Education of Black Women.* New York: W. W. Norton, 1990.
Strong, Douglas M. *Perfectionist Politics: Abolitionism and the Religious Tensions of American Democracy.* Syracuse: Syracuse University Press, 2002.
Stuckey, Sterling. *Slave Culture: Nationalist Theory and the Foundations of Black America.* New York: Oxford University Press, 1987.
Swing, Albert Temple. *James Harris Fairchild; or, Sixty Eight Years with a Christian College.* New York: F. H. Revel, 1907.
Taylor, Nikki Marie. *Frontiers of Freedom: Cincinnati's Black Community, 1802–1868,* Athens: Ohio University Press, 2005.
Terzian, Barbara A. "Ohio's Constitutional Conventions and Constitutions." In *The History of Ohio Law,* edited by Michael Les Benedict and John F. Winkler, 1:40–50. Athens: Ohio University Press, 2004.
Thomas, Benjamin P. *Theodore Weld: Crusader for Freedom.* New Brunswick: Rutgers University Press, 1950.
Thomas, John L. *The Liberator: William Lloyd Garrison, A Biography.* Boston: Little, Brown, 1963.
———. "Romantic Reform in America, 1815–1865." *American Quarterly* 17 (Winter 1965): 656–81.
Tobin, Jacqueline L., and Hettie Jones. *From Midnight to Dawn: The Last Tracks of the Underground Railroad.* New York: Random House, 2007.
Tyler, Alice Felt. *Freedom's Ferment: Phases of American Social History to 1860.* Minneapolis: University of Minnesota Press, 1944.
Tyler, William S. *A History of Amherst College, during the Administrations of Its First Five Presidents, from 1821 to 1891.* New York: Frederick H. Hitchcock, 1895.
Upton, Harriet Taylor. *History of the Western Reserve.* Vol. 1. Chicago: Lewis, 1910.
Van Tassel, David D., with John Vacha. *"Behind Bayonets": The Civil War in Northern Ohio.* Kent: Kent State University Press, 2006.
Volpe, Vernon L. *Forlorn Hope of Freedom: The Liberty Party in the Old Northwest, 1838–1848.* Kent: Kent State University Press, 1990.
Waite, Cally L. *Permission to Remain among Us: Education for Blacks in Oberlin Ohio, 1880–1914.* Westport, Conn.: Greenwood, 2002.
Walker, Francis A. *Memoir of Hon. Amasa Walker, LL.D.* Boston: David Clapp, 1888.

Wallace, William Allen. *The History of Canaan, New Hampshire.* Concord, N.H.: Rumford Press, 1910.

Walters, Ronald G. *American Reformers, 1815–1860.* Rev. ed. New York: Hill and Wang, 1997.

———. *The Antislavery Appeal: American Abolitionism after 1830.* Baltimore: Johns Hopkins University Press, 1976.

Ward, Susan Hayes. *The History of the Broadway Tabernacle Church, from its Organization in 1840 to the Close of 1900, Including Factors Influencing Its Formation.* New York: Broadway Tabernacle Church, 1901.

Washington, Margaret. *Sojourner Truth's America.* Urbana: University of Illinois Press, 2009.

Washington, Versalle F. *Eagles on Their Buttons: A Black Infantry Regiment in the Civil War.* Columbia: University of Missouri Press, 1999.

Watson, Charles S. *The History of Southern Drama.* Lexington: University of Kentucky Press, 1997.

Weisenburger, Francis P. *The Passing of the Frontier.* Vol. 3 of *The History of the State of Ohio.* Columbus: Ohio State Archaeological and Historical Society, 1941.

Wiecek, William M. *The Sources of Antislavery Constitutionalism in America, 1760–1848.* Ithaca: Cornell University Press, 1977.

Wilentz, Sean. *The Rise of American Democracy: Jefferson to Lincoln.* New York: W. W. Norton, 2005.

Wiley, Earl W. "'Governor' John Greiner and Chase's Bid for the Presidency in 1860." *Ohio State Archaeological and Historical Quarterly* 58 (1949): 259–73.

Williams, George Washington. *A History of the Negro Troops in the War of the Rebellion, 1861–1865.* New York: Harper and Brothers, 1888.

Williams, Howard D. *A History of Colgate University, 1819–1969.* Berkeley: University of California Press, 1969.

Winks, Robin W. *The Blacks in Canada: A History.* Montreal: McGill University Press, 1997.

Wise, Stephen R. *Gate of Hell: Campaign for Charleston Harbor, 1863.* Columbia: University of South Carolina Press, 1994.

Wright, W. E. C. "Oberlin's Contribution to Ethics." *Bibliotheca Sacra* 52 (July 1900): 419–44.

Wyatt-Brown, Bertram. *Lewis Tappan and the Evangelical War against Slavery.* Cleveland: Case Western Reserve University, 1969.

Van Vuget, William E. *British Buckeyes: The English, Scots, & Welsh in Ohio, 1700–1900.* Kent: Kent State University Press, 2006.

Yellin, Jean Fagan, and John C. Van Horne, eds. *The Abolitionist Sisterhood: Women's Political Culture in Antebellum America.* Ithaca: Cornell University Press, 1994.

Young, Michael P. *Bearing Witness against Sin: The Evangelical Birth of the American Social Movement.* Chicago: University of Chicago Press, 2006.

Zaeske, Susan. *Signatures of Citizenship: Petitioning, Antislavery, and Women's Political Identity.* Chapel Hill: University of North Carolina Press, 2003.

Zorbaugh, Charles L. "The Plan of Union in Ohio." *Church History* 6 (June 1937): 145–64.

Index

Adair, Florella Brown, 195, 226, 297 (n. 91)
Adair, Samuel, 176, 195, 226, 297 (n. 91)
Adams, Charles Francis, 143
Adams, John Quincy, 95, 143, 262 (n. 90), 280 (n. 28)
Africa, 12, 18, 25, 49, 68, 69, 74
African Americans. *See individual names*
Afrikan Heritage House, 247
Akron, Ohio, 47
Alabama, 28, 30
Albany, New York, 101
Alexander, Leslie, 168
Allan, William, 30, 43, 54, 261 (n. 55)
Allen, George, 261 (n. 55)
Allen, John, 88, 89
Alvord, John, 43, 45, 53, 137, 261 (n. 55)
American and Foreign Anti-Slavery Society (AFASS), 114, 152
American Anti-Slavery Society (AASS), 31, 44, 49, 50, 52, 55, 58, 59, 60, 102, 103, 115, 116, 119, 262 (n. 82), 276 (n. 23); agency system, 3, 40, 43, 45, 46, 49, 50, 57, 84, 191; Declaration of Sentiments, 48, 55, 56, 103, 133; Executive Committee, 36, 43, 49, 57, 60; financial difficulties, 59, 60; ideological differences among members, 108, 113, 114, 132; meetings of, 101, 119, 173
American Colonization Society (ACS), 18, 19, 21, 24, 29, 55, 255 (n. 81)
American Missionary Association (AMA), 176, 240
American Revolution, 47, 61, 168, 216
Amherst College, 38, 256 (n. 122)
Amistad (slave ship), 74
Andrew, John, 236
Anti-Slavery Bugle (Salem), vi, 119, 152, 223
Ashtabula, Ohio, 73, 185

Atwater, Caleb, 87
Auglaize County, Ohio, 158
Avery, Courtland, 261 (n. 55)

Bacon, John, 208
Bailey, Gamaliel, 101, 117, 138, 142
Ballantine, William, 244
Ballou, Aiden, 119
Barber, Amzi, 83
Barrows, John Henry, 244
Beecher, Lyman, 14, 15
Berry, Gilson, 190
Bibb, Henry, 116
Bible, 12, 49, 54, 80, 91, 123, 261 (n. 73), 272 (n. 100); opposes slavery, 41, 54, 57, 63, 109, 115, 165, 177
Bigglestone, William, 242
Birney, James Gillespie, 19, 25, 36, 51, 95, 99, 108, 110, 113; as presidential candidate, 103, 104, 105, 106, 138, 140
Birney, William, 116
Black abolitionists. *See individual names*
Black convention movement, 6, 166; meetings of, 146–47, 148–50, 157, 158, 165, 167, 179, 183, 213–14, 282 (n. 94)
Black Laws (Ohio), 22, 28, 86–89, 94, 96, 141–57 passim, 183, 185, 291 (n. 74)
Blackwell, Antoinette Brown, 74, 76
Blakesley, J. M., 261 (n. 55)
Bliss, Philemon, 174, 185
Boston, Massachusetts, 4, 14, 46, 193, 214, 221, 270 (n. 29), 293 (n. 119); abolitionists in, 20, 36, 68, 152, 203
Bowdoin College, 256 (n. 122)
Boynton, Lewis, 209, 214, 232
Boynton, Shakespeare, 209, 232
Bradley, James, 25, 27, 67, 88, 196
Brooke, Samuel, 116, 119, 277 (n. 54)
Brooks, Martin, 196, 290 (n. 49)

Brown, Antoinette. *See* Blackwell, Antoinette Brown
Brown, Charles Farrar, 67
Brown, Florella. *See* Adair, Florella Brown
Brown, Henry Box, 188
Brown, John, 11, 29, 176, 224, 225, 228, 230; connections to Oberlin, 225, 226, 229, 230, 297 (n. 80), 297 (88–89); and Harpers Ferry raid, 225, 226, 227, 228, 231, 236, 266 (n. 44); in Kansas, 195, 209, 226, 227, 287 (n. 96), 297 (n. 91); trial and execution, 228, 230
Brown, John, Jr., 226, 227, 228
Brown, John M., 149, 157, 165, 285 (n. 18)
Brown, Oliver, 185
Brown, Owen, 29, 35, 36, 224
Brown, William Wells, 184, 288 (n. 131)
Brown County, Ohio, 84, 135
Buchanan, James, 179, 183, 207, 210, 220
Buffalo, New York, 138, 142–46, 178, 282 (n. 94)
Burnell, Levi, 30, 60, 89, 258 (n. 2), 259 (n. 9), 290 (n. 46)
Burns, Anthony, 182, 293 (n. 119)
Burrell, Jabez, 259 (n. 2), 290 (n. 46)
Bushnell, Simeon, 210–22 passim
Byington, Legrand, 134
Byrd, John, 176, 177, 195, 196

Calhoun, John Caldwell, 55, 56, 68, 172
Canada, 225, 226, 228, 269 (n. 21), 290 (n. 52); as destination for escaping slaves, 1, 50, 84, 164, 188, 191, 192, 194, 196, 198, 201, 213, 225, 290 (n. 52)
Canfield, Herman, 184
Carney, William, 238
Carpenter, James, 221
Carr, Robert Kenneth, 247
Carrier, Charles, 204
Chambers, Augustus, 203, 206–8
Charleston, South Carolina, 237
Chase, Salmon P., 93, 104, 154, 155, 162, 180, 184, 185, 219, 224, 235, 283 (n. 117), 296 (n. 74); in Oberlin, 170
Chatham Street Chapel, 18, 21, 254 (n. 62)
Chatham, Canada, 225
Cheek, Aimee Lee, 122
Cheek, William, 122
Child, Lydia Maria, 68
Cincinnati, Ohio, 23, 24, 26, 31, 40, 167, 214, 270 (n. 36); African Americans in, 4, 25, 28, 167, 196, 283 (n. 117)
Civil War, 4, 11, 232–38
Clark, Christopher, 62
Clark, George, 133, 145
Clark, Peter, 213
Clarke, Cyrus, 194
Clarke, Lewis, 193, 194, 202, 203, 291 (n. 79)
Clarke, Milton, 193, 197, 201, 202, 203, 291 (n. 72)
Clay, Cassius, 190, 219, 270 (n. 36)
Clay, Henry, 54, 101, 135, 137, 138, 139, 140, 172
Cleveland, Ohio, 44, 50, 75, 77, 141, 142, 165, 169, 182, 210, 226, 227, 228, 230, 234, 244, 295 (n. 47); antislavery meetings in, 101, 102, 146, 167, 260 (n. 31), 273 (n. 126); self-emancipating slaves in, 201, 202, 205, 290 (n. 42); trial and imprisonment of Oberlin-Wellington Rescuers, 214–16, 218–22, 226
Cleveland Leader, 174, 219, 224, 226
Cleveland Plain Dealer, 180
Cleveland True Democrat, 142, 145
Cochrane, William, 198, 207
Coeducation, 3, 4, 9, 13, 17, 73, 87
Coffin, Levi, 190, 198
Collins, John, 115, 116
Colonization, 18, 19, 20, 21, 24, 25, 29, 47, 49, 55, 86, 87, 149, 254 (n. 62), 255 (n. 81), 255 (n. 98), 282 (n. 94)
Compromise of 1850, 160, 162, 169
Congress, 55, 56, 57, 138, 161, 169, 170, 172, 173, 174, 175, 178, 179, 213; compromise measures relating to slavery, 160, 162, 169, 172, 173, 179, 184, 185; petitioned by abolitionists, 55, 56, 58, 59, 92; refusal to receive antislavery petitions, 56, 92
Connecticut, 12, 15, 49, 52
Copeland, John, 210, 211, 214, 227–31, 298 (n. 105)

Coppin, Fanny Jackson, 68, 69, 71, 74, 236
Corwin, Thomas, 186
Cowles, Betsey Mix, 125, 151; activism before Oberlin, 73; and *Plea for the Oppressed*, 152; post-Oberlin activism of, 119–20, 151
Cowles, Helen, 126
Cowles, Henry, 29, 35, 36, 54, 58, 64, 66, 78, 80, 105, 126, 142, 198, 235, 244, 265 (n. 35); as editor of the *Oberlin Evangelist*, 107, 131, 141, 145, 171, 172
Cowles, Henry, Jr., 177, 178
Cowles, John, 80, 118, 210
Cowles, Mary, 178
Cox, Jacob Dolson, 224
Cox, Sabram, 146, 167, 201, 202, 205, 206
Crabb, Mary, 76
Craft, Ellen, 188
Craft, William, 188
Crisis, The, 245
Crooker, Emiline, 76
Cross Lanes, Battle of, 234

Dartmouth College, 256 (n. 122)
Dascomb, James, 259 (n. 13)
Davis, David Brion, 14, 75, 232
Dawes, William, 95, 109, 111, 112, 113
Dawn Institute, 84, 85
Day, Lucy Stanton. *See* Stanton, Lucy
Day, William Howard, 10, 76, 122, 146, 147, 149, 156, 157, 158, 159, 166, 167, 174, 206, 213, 235, 253 (n. 60), 267 (n. 84), 282 (n. 94), 291 (n. 81); addresses Ohio legislature, 150, 151; interpretation of the U.S. Constitution, 165; and John Brown, 225, 297 (n. 89); and Underground Railroad, 290 (n. 42)
Dayton, Anson, 207, 208, 213, 294 (n. 5)
Declaration of Independence, 75, 125, 158, 163, 179, 183, 215
Delaney, Martin, 143, 152–54, 236
Delbanco, Andrew, 6
Democratic Party, 93–106 passim, 134, 135, 137, 139, 141, 154, 155, 157, 166–79 passim, 183, 185, 207, 210, 214, 215, 231, 232; antislavery members of, 95, 143, 144, 178, 179; criticized by Oberlinites, 102, 104, 219, 231; criticizes abolitionists in Ohio, 104, 106, 133, 134, 138, 140, 169, 181, 182, 221, 296 (n. 74); criticizes Oberlin in Ohio, 88, 89, 94, 100, 101, 134, 135, 180, 185, 204, 219; Oberlin residents as members of, 207, 208, 209
Dennison, William, 224, 296 (n. 74)
Dobbins, Lee Howard, 199, 200
Douglas, Stephen, 172, 173, 174
Douglass, Frederick, 73, 151, 163, 170, 227, 236, 266 (n. 41); criticized by Oberlinites, 130; praised by Oberlinites, 130, 131; praises Oberlin, 3, 156; visits Oberlin, 128, 130, 131, 170
Douglass, H. Ford, 165, 166
Douglass, Rosetta, 73
Dred Scott decision, 10, 96, 184, 185, 222, 228
Dresser, Amos, 116, 184, 261 (n. 55)
DuBois, W. E. B., 245, 246

Earle, Thomas, 104, 106, 134, 135
Edmonson, Emily, 68
Edmonson, Mary, 68
Edwards, Jonathan, 14
Elyria, Ohio, 15, 30, 94, 135, 174, 185, 201, 206; jailbreak of 1841, 204, 205, 207
Emancipation Proclamation, 235
England, 2, 23, 112, 164, 239, 297 (n. 89); abolitionists from, 2, 104, 109–13; Oberlinites visit, 104, 109–13; and West Indian Emancipation, 57, 58, 75
Erie Canal, 13, 15

Fairbank, Calvin, 190–92
Fairchild, Edward, 41, 69, 261 (n. 55)
Fairchild, James, 22, 43, 81, 87, 135, 168, 169, 173, 175, 187, 189, 190, 213, 215, 219, 232–34, 250 (n. 9), 255 (n. 98), 259 (n. 13), 265 (n. 30), 289 (n. 16); on Oberlin curriculum, 41, 73; as Oberlin president, 81, 122, 242–45
Fifth Amendment, 126
5th Ohio U.S. Colored Troops, 236, 239
55th Massachusetts Volunteers, 236

54th Massachusetts Volunteers, 236–38
Fillmore, Millard, 179
Finney, Charles Grandison, xi, 8, 9, 13, 15, 18, 24, 27, 30, 31, 32, 34, 35, 37, 39, 48, 65, 69, 80, 81, 82, 83, 84, 91, 97, 128, 129, 178, 234, 244, 250 (n. 9), 256 (n. 113); on abolitionism, 18, 20, 21, 22, 23, 35, 42, 124, 141, 163; and antislavery politics, 91, 92, 93, 94, 102, 143, 146, 148, 169, 170, 172, 231, 300 (n. 164); criticized by Garrison, 118; criticized by Tappans, 22, 254 (n. 65), 254 (n. 66); criticizes Garrisonians, 128; and "higher law," 97, 98, 99, 189, 272 (n. 100); on ideological independence in abolitionist movement, 117, 118, 129, 141, 271 (n. 60); in New York City, 18, 21, 31, 94; as Oberlin professor, 49, 54, 61; and perfectionism, 62, 63, 64, 90, 251 (n. 5), 253 (n. 54), 278 (n. 85); revivals of, 13, 14, 41, 90–92, 125, 126, 164, 251 (n. 2), 256 (n. 113), 258 (n. 2)
Finney, Charlie, 178
Finney Chapel, 247
First Amendment, 56
First Church of Oberlin, xi, 33, 42, 82, 123, 130, 139, 210, 222, 230, 231, 245, 259 (n. 13)
First Manassas, Battle of, 233
First of August Celebration, 75, 76, 77, 186, 267 (n. 88)
Fitch, James, 213, 214, 220, 223, 232
Fletcher, Nathan, 27, 30, 34, 36
Foote, Hiram, 261 (n. 55)
Forten, James, 109
Fort Sumter, 232, 238
Fort Wagner, 237, 238
Foster, Abby Kelley. *See* Kelley, Abby
Foster, Stephen, 82, 119, 120, 121, 123, 125–28, 130, 138
Fourth of July, 75
Fox, Jerry, 210
Frank Leslie's Illustrated Weekly, 220
Franklin, Benjamin, 55
Free Democratic Party, 169–72
Free-Soil Party, 8, 10, 133, 142–48, 154, 155, 169, 174, 180, 239

Freedman's Bureau, 241
Frémont, John C., 179, 181, 182, 183
Fugitive Slave Law: federal (1793), 162; federal (1850), 10, 97, 160, 162–70, 173, 174, 179, 185, 186, 188, 189, 206, 207, 208, 210, 212–19, 220–23, 226; Ohio (1839), 96, 97, 98, 99, 272 (n. 96)

Gag rule, 56, 92
Gale, George, 78
Garfield, James, 224
Garnet, Henry Highland, 150, 282 (n. 94)
Garrison, William Lloyd, 19, 20, 62, 73, 108, 109, 120, 130, 144, 260 (n. 31), 266 (n. 41), 277 (n. 64); censure of clergy/the church, 50, 51, 52, 53; criticism of politics, 273 (n. 119); criticized by anti-abolitionists, 46, 47; criticized by Oberlinites, 129, 261 (n. 73); criticizes Oberlin, 117, 118, 127; and *Liberator*, 20, 46, 51; in Oberlin, 128, 129, 130; praised by Oberlinites, 128, 130, 186; praises Oberlin, 109, 110, 223; on U.S. Constitution, 119; at World's Anti-Slavery Convention of 1840, 113, 275 (n. 19)
Garrisonians, 6, 53, 92, 103, 109, 115, 116, 118, 119, 126, 127, 133, 145, 152; argue against antislavery political action, 102, 273 (n. 119); criticize Oberlin, 118–19; Oberlinites as, 82, 118, 120, 125, 141, 151; in Ohio, 102, 109, 117, 120, 121, 123, 125, 170; praise Oberlin, 109; visit Oberlin, 82; at World's Anti-Slavery Convention of 1840, 113
Gena, Thomas, 210
Giddings, Joshua, 93, 95, 104, 143, 172, 185, 219, 223, 230, 280 (n. 28), 295 (n. 45), 296 (n. 74)
Goodell, William, 103, 126
Goodman, Paul, 49, 78
Gould, Samuel, 43
Graham, Sylvester, 110
Great Tent, 37, 143, 258 (n. 149)
Green, Beriah, 15, 29, 65, 264 (n. 23)

Greiner, John, 180
Grimké, Angelina, 110

Haiti, 170
Hale, John, 143, 169, 170, 171, 230
Hambrick-Stowe, Charles, 91
Hamilton College, 38
Hamlin, Edward, 135
Hammond, James Henry, 79, 80, 186
Hanover College, 38
Harpers Ferry, Virginia, 225, 227, 228, 236, 266 (n. 44)
Harris, Josiah, 134
Harrison, George, 243
Harrison, William Henry, 101, 103, 104, 105, 137
Hartwell, Thomas, 210
Hatch, Nathan, 90
Hayden, Lewis, 190, 191, 217
Henry, Patrick, 168
Higher law, 97–99, 189, 190, 215, 218, 220, 221, 272 (n. 100)
Hill, Hamilton, 130, 188
Hitchcock, Elizabeth, 119
Hocking County, Ohio, 134
Holley, Myron, 73, 102, 103
Holley, Sally, 73
Howe, Henry, 71
Hudson, Ohio, 29
Hudson, Timothy, 35, 36, 53, 55, 116, 126, 130, 152, 175, 177, 244, 259 (n. 13), 261 (n. 73)
Hughes, Langston, 298 (n. 113)
Humphrey, Heman, 38

Immediatism/emancipation, 7, 8, 10, 12, 20–26, 29, 33, 36, 42, 43, 46–50, 54, 57, 58, 101, 104, 110, 142, 144–48, 214, 255 (n. 98), 300 (n. 164); and repentance of sin, 12, 18, 20, 43, 145, 253 (n. 54)
Indiana, 46, 170, 190, 236

Jackson, Fanny. *See* Coppin, Fanny Jackson
Jeakins, Buford, 233
Jefferson, Thomas, 14
Jennings, Anderson, 208–11, 296 (n. 58)

Jesus Christ, 17, 49, 52, 64
Jim Crow, 242
Jocelyn, Simeon, 176
Jones, Alan, 68
Jones, Benjamin, 119
Jones, Edward, 256 (n. 122)
Jones, James Monroe, 68, 157, 225, 266 (n. 44), 297 (n. 83)
Julian, George, 170, 171, 194

Kagi, John Henri, 226, 228
Kansas, 175, 176, 177, 178, 179, 195, 209, 224, 225, 226, 236, 287 (n. 96), 297 (n. 91)
Kansas Emigrant Aid Association of Northern Ohio (AANO), 175
Kansas-Nebraska Bill, 173, 178, 185, 222
Kanter, Rosabeth, 62
Keep, John, 23, 26, 34, 37, 60, 104, 109–13, 119, 120, 163, 164, 239, 240, 259 (n. 9), 265 (n. 36)
Kelley, Abby, 127, 128, 130, 151, 152; and come-outerism, 123, 128; criticized by Oberlinites, 125–28; criticizes Oberlin, 120, 125–27; in Oberlin, 123, 125–28, 278 (n. 109); in Ohio, 119, 120, 125, 138
Kentucky, 28, 31, 54, 57, 87, 95–99, 190–96, 202, 205, 208, 270 (n. 36), 296 (n. 58)
Kimball, Horace, 57, 58
King, Leicester, 104, 135, 139
Kinney, Edward, 211
Kinson, Sara Margru, 74
Krislov, Marvin, 247

Ladies Hall, 39, 69, 242, 243
Lake Erie, 27, 164, 194, 202
Lane Theological Seminary, 24, 25, 26, 27, 31, 32, 35, 36, 38, 41, 42, 43, 77, 83; Lane Rebellion, 9, 24, 25, 31; Lane Rebels, 24, 25, 26, 30, 31, 32, 35, 36, 38, 40, 41, 82, 250 (n. 9), 258 (n. 2). *See also individual names of Lane Rebels*
Langston, Charles, 148, 149, 157, 158, 162, 165, 167, 170, 174, 182, 213, 298 (n. 113); as antislavery speaker, 152, 153, 154, 164, 170; criticizes *Dred Scott* decision,

184; criticizes Fugitive Slave Law, 164; and John Brown's raid, 226, 228, 230; meeting with Ohio governor, 166; and Oberlin-Wellington Rescue, 210, 211; recruits black soldiers, 236; as Sheffield student, 68, 88, 196; support of Free-Soil Party, 146, 147; support of Republican Party, 181; trial and imprisonment, 214, 215, 216, 217, 218; urges physical resistance to slavery, 168; on U.S. Constitution, 165, 166

Langston, Gideon, 68, 88, 196

Langston, John Mercer, 10, 69, 71, 72, 149, 150, 157, 158, 162, 165, 167, 179, 182, 197, 198, 207, 211, 212, 213, 214, 221, 222, 232, 235, 282 (n. 90); as antislavery speaker, 156, 160, 163, 166, 169, 170, 171, 172, 173, 174, 175, 178, 181, 183, 184, 186, 219, 220, 223, 224, 232, 240; criticizes Fugitive Slave Law, 165; criticizes Ohio Black Laws, 183; and John Brown's raid, 225, 226, 227, 228; meeting with Ohio governor, 166; as Oberlin student, 68, 71, 85, 166, 167; and Oberlin-Wellington Rescue trial, 214, 215, 217, 222; recruits black soldiers, 235, 236; support of Republican Party, 181, 183

Langston, Mary Patterson Leary, 290 (n. 113)

Lawrence, Kansas, 177, 178

Leary, Lewis Sheridan, 210, 226, 227, 228, 298 (n. 107), 298 (n. 113)

Leavenworth, Kansas, 176

Lee, Robert E., 228

Leonard, Byram, 100

Lewis, Samuel, 104

Liberator (Boston), 19, 46, 51, 52, 73, 114, 116, 117, 118, 127, 130

Liberty Herald (Warren), 135,

Liberty Party, 73, 105, 106, 116, 117, 120, 121, 125, 126, 133, 135, 136, 137, 139, 140, 143, 144, 146, 148, 152, 180, 239; conventions of, 104, 107, 138, 139; in Ohio, 106, 107, 116, 120, 134, 135, 137, 138, 139, 140, 141, 142, 152, 276 (n. 31), 277 (n. 64); platform, 132, 136, 141, 142, 148

Liberty School, 70, 74, 85, 86

Lincoln, Abraham, 231, 232, 234, 235, 239, 240, 300 (n. 164), 300 (n. 174)

Lincoln, William, 210, 211

Lorain County, Ohio, 15, 88, 134, 155, 183, 201, 214, 221, 223, 235, 263 (n. 2); elections in, 106, 135, 137, 138, 148, 154, 156, 174, 179, 180

Lorain County Anti-Slavery Society, 30, 101, 263 (n. 113)

Lorain County News, 235

Lorain Republican, 138

Lucas, Robert, 29

Lyman, Ansel, 209, 210

Lyman, Huntington, 43, 255 (n. 84), 261 (n. 55)

Mahan, Asa, 24, 26, 27, 31, 32, 34, 35, 39, 41, 42, 79, 80, 82, 101, 102, 118, 134, 139, 141, 142, 143, 175, 220, 244, 259 (n. 2), 295 (n. 47); debates Garrisonians, 82, 126, 128, 130; as Oberlin president, 30, 37, 38, 60, 125, 135, 196; and perfectionism, 54, 63, 64, 90

Mahan, John, 95

Malvin, John, 28

Marietta College, 38

Marseilles, Ohio, 152, 154

Martineau, Harriett, 2, 111

Maryland, 28, 168, 190

Massachusetts, 49, 50, 52, 236, 237, 238, 285 (n. 26)

May, Samuel J., 20, 36

Mayer, Henry, 144

McLean, John, 186

McNealy, Cyrus, 276 (n. 40)

McNulty, Caleb, 134, 135

Mexican War, 140, 141, 157, 169

Mexico, 136, 140

Miami College, 38

Michigan, 46, 50, 183, 223, 295 (n. 47)

Middlebury, Ohio, 45

Millennium, 2, 14, 30, 34, 37, 80, 91, 251 (n. 5), 253 (n. 54)

Milligan, James, 261 (n. 55)

Minor, Lawrence, 150
Mississippi, 14, 17, 28, 247
Missouri, 177, 192, 195, 226
Missouri Compromise of 1820, 172, 173, 179, 184, 185
Mobs, anti-abolition, 21–23, 26, 28, 44, 45, 84, 92, 93, 153, 154, 176, 177, 201, 254 (n. 60)
Mohawk Valley, 12
Monroe Rifles, 233
Monroe, James, 53, 147, 148, 157, 173, 177, 188, 213, 223, 230–33; as Oberlin student, 125; in politics, 179, 180–90 passim, 224
Morgan, Albert, 233
Morgan, John, 26, 27, 30–37 passim, 54, 64, 109, 115, 126, 130, 166, 234, 244, 259 (n. 13)
Morris, Aldon, 2
Morris, Thomas, 93, 95, 96
Morse, John, 154, 155
Moses, 186
Mott, Lucretia, 118
Munger, Asahel, 205

NAACP, 245
National Kansas Committee, 178
Nell, William C., 217
Newark, Ohio, 182
New Hampshire, 50, 170
New Jersey, 49
Newman, William, 156, 163, 168
New Mexico, 162
New York, 7, 13, 15, 24, 36, 50, 78, 100, 101, 102, 103, 131, 139, 172, 175, 183, 223, 258 (n. 2), 262 (n. 82), 263 (n. 2)
New York Anti-Slavery Society, 21
New York City, 4, 9, 12, 14, 18, 19, 20, 21, 22, 23, 25, 30, 31, 32, 37, 46, 50, 81, 94, 113, 172, 203, 254 (n. 62), 254 (n. 65), 282 (n. 94), 291 (n. 81)
New York Evangelist, 15, 20, 21
New York Tribune, 139, 226
Niagara Movement, 245
Northampton Association, 62
North Carolina, 28, 68
North Star (Rochester), 73, 131

Oberlin, John Frederick, 9, 16
Oberlin Anti-Slavery Society, 42, 48, 55, 261 (n. 54)
Oberlin Brass Band, 219, 222, 233
Oberlin complex missionary station, 4
Oberlin Dialectic Association, 100, 140
Oberlin Emigrant Aid Company, 175
Oberlin Evangelist, 56, 62, 75, 83, 96–99, 104–16 passim, 125–51 passim, 160, 170, 171, 175, 182, 184, 218, 231, 232, 281 (n. 63)
Oberlin Female Moral Reform Society, 73
Oberlin Maternal Association, 198
Oberlin Musical Association, 128, 234
Oberlin Peace Society, 140
Oberlin Radical Club, 247
Oberlin Students' Monthly, 181
Oberlin Union Society, 69
Oberlin Unmasked, 135, 271 (n. 53)
Oberlin-Wellington Rescue, 10, 11, 208–36 passim
Oberlin Young Ladies Literary Society, 69, 73, 74, 83, 198, 299 (n. 155)
Oberlin Young Men's Anti-Slavery Society, 167, 170
Ohio, 2, 5, 9, 14, 15, 17, 24, 28, 29, 30, 35, 43, 50, 51, 54, 67, 79, 81, 85, 86, 87, 89, 106, 108, 115, 119, 120, 121, 125, 128; abolitionists, 7, 10, 35, 36, 45–55, 88, 94–103, 106, 114, 115, 117, 118, 119, 120; African Americans, 28, 29, 86; Black Laws, 22, 25, 86; legislature, 1, 87, 88, 90, 96–109 passim; political parties, 10, 88, 93–96, 104, 106, 107, 120; Western Reserve, 13, 15, 29, 43, 89, 95–109 passim, 117, 121, 131, 142, 214, 217, 223, 224, 228, 245, 256 (n. 106)
Ohio American Anti-Slavery Society (OAASS), 116, 117, 119, 120
Ohio Anti-Slavery Society (OASS), 45, 55, 94, 95, 99, 109, 115, 116, 120, 239, 276 (n. 31), 283 (n. 114)
Ohio Colored American League, 157
Ohio River, 26, 115, 187, 191, 192, 194
Ohio State Anti-Slavery Society, 120, 214, 226
Ohio Statesman, 94, 133, 219, 223

Olustee, Battle of, 238
Oneida Institute, 65, 78, 264 (n. 23), 269 (n. 20)
Osawatomie, Kansas, 227

Panic of 1837, 40, 58, 60
Parker, Theodore, 97
Parmenter, William, 233
Peal, Henry, 237, 238
Pearl (slave ship), 68
Pease, Alonzo, 202
Pease, Elizabeth, 110
Pease, Peter Pindar, 17, 38, 232, 244
Peck, Henry, 70, 175, 179, 188, 199, 214, 217, 220, 222, 231, 232
Pennsylvania, 46, 49, 50, 157
Perfectionism, 2, 5, 8, 12, 20, 21, 35, 47, 54, 61–64, 72, 73, 78, 89–94 passim, 118, 145, 246, 253 (n. 54), 278 (n. 85)
Petitions, antislavery, 55, 56, 58, 59, 88, 92, 94, 96, 158, 159, 183, 188
Philanthropist (Cincinnati), 83, 101, 103, 104, 114, 116, 119, 138
Phillips, Wendell, 110
Phillips Andover Academy, 38
Pierce, Franklin, 169, 172, 179
Pierce, John, 261 (n. 55)
Pike County, Ohio, 84
Pillsbury, Parker, 119, 152
Plea for the Oppressed, A (newspaper), 152
Plumb, Ralph, 214, 215, 228, 229, 232
Plumb, Samuel, 228, 229
Polk, James K., 137, 139–41
Portage County, Ohio, 185, 263 (n. 113)
Porter, Samuel Fuller, 261 (n. 55)
Portsmouth, Ohio, 28
Price, John, 208–14, 217, 221, 227
Putnam, Ohio, 35

Quakers, 82, 190, 253 (n. 54)

Ramsey, John, 156, 208, 292 (n. 104)
Reconstruction, 242, 243
Reed, John, 175, 176
Renshaw, Charles, 261 (n. 55)

Republican Party, 8, 10, 133, 174–86 passim, 207, 213, 219, 222–24, 231, 239, 296 (n. 74)
Rescuer, The (newspaper), 220, 221
Reynolds, George, 297 (n. 83)
Richland County, Ohio, 133
Ripley, Ohio, 191
Robertson, Stacey, 74
Rochester, New York, 13, 14, 15, 30, 269 (n. 21)
Roget, Peter, 110
Russell, William, 261 (n. 55)
Russia Township, 16, 135, 174, 183, 197
Russwurm, Frances, 73
Russwurm, John, 73, 256 (n. 122)

St. Catharines, Canada, 225
Salem, Ohio, 116, 119, 121
Sawyer, William, 158, 159
Scott, Dred, 185. See also *Dred Scott* decision
Scott, John, 211, 214
Scott, Winfield, 169
Seales, Daniel, 76
Seward, William, 97, 186
Shaw, Robert, 236, 238
Sheffield Manual Labor School, 88, 196, 259 (n. 2), 290 (n. 46)
Shipherd, Jacob, 213, 226
Shipherd, John Jay, 5, 9, 13–17, 23–43 passim, 60–63, 67, 72, 77, 78, 241, 244, 246, 247
Shurtleff, Giles, 239, 243, 244
Simpson, Joshua, 160
Slab Hall (Rebel Hall, Cincinnati Hall), 39
Slave Power, 8, 10, 95–104 passim, 133, 139–49 passim, 160, 161, 163, 170, 173, 177, 178, 186, 199, 205, 214, 232, 273 (n. 119)
Smith, Delazon, 81, 135, 271 (n. 53)
Smith, Gerrit, 110, 144, 170, 172, 224, 230, 269 (n. 21), 276 (n. 23), 281 (n. 74)
Smith, John, 220
Smith, Theodore Clarke, 93
South Carolina, 28, 55, 79, 186
Spartacus, 186

Spooner, Lysander, 126,
Stanley, Sara, 122, 169
Stanton, Benjamin, 158
Stanton, Henry B., 25, 31, 49, 58, 102
Stanton, Lucy, 67, 75, 267 (n. 84)
Stearns, George, 236
Stearns, Isaac, 127
Stebbins, Giles, 119, 120
Stewart, Alvan, 36, 92, 103
Stewart, James Brewer, 66, 93
Stewart, Philo Penfield, 9, 16, 17, 27, 34, 36, 61, 63, 72, 247
Stone, James, 234
Stone, Lucy, 73, 74, 76, 77, 85, 86, 120, 127–29, 141
Storrs, Charles, 29
Stowe, Harriett Beecher, 68, 291 (n. 79)
Streeter, Sereno, 43, 57, 261 (n. 54)
Strong, Douglas, 90, 107
Strong, George, 237
Student Nonviolent Coordinating Committee, 247
Sumner, Charles, 178, 222, 276 (n. 23), 280 (n. 28)

Taney, Roger B., 183, 184, 185
Tappan, Arthur, xi, 18, 21–23, 30, 31, 36, 60, 108, 110, 254 (n. 62), 275 (n. 1)
Tappan, Lewis, xi, 18, 21–23, 30, 31, 43, 108, 110, 114, 115, 254 (n. 62), 254 (n. 65), 266 (n. 41), 275 (n. 1)
Tappan Hall, 39, 69, 71
Tappan Square, 41, 210, 213, 231, 233, 247
Taylor, Horace, 36, 135, 136, 205
Taylor, Zachary, 142, 148
Tennessee, 28
Terrell, Mary Church, 244
Texas, 136–40, 162, 168
Theological Literary Society, 69, 166
Thirteenth Amendment, 240
Thome, James, 25, 31, 36, 43–58 passim, 99, 124, 125, 175, 192, 193, 230, 234, 244, 259 (n. 13), 261 (n. 55)
Thompson, George (Oberlin Theological graduate), 192

Thompson, George, 36, 109, 110, 113
Tidd, Charles, 226
Tillich, Paul, 14
Todd, David, 235
Torrey, Charles, 190
Toussaint-Louverture, 186
Townsend, Norton, 152–62 passim, 170, 171, 175, 183, 231, 283 (n. 114), 283 (n. 117)
Truth, Sojourner, 168
Tyler, John, 104, 137

Uncle Tom's Cabin (Stowe), 291 (n. 79)
Underground Railroad, 10, 75, 84, 186–211 passim, 224, 225, 228, 255 (n. 84), 283 (n. 114), 288 (n. 2), 290 (n. 42), 290 (n. 46), 292 (n. 96)
U.S. Constitution: and slavery, 55, 96, 99, 100, 101, 104, 140, 143, 151, 165, 181, 183, 184, 216, 218, 221, 223, 242; interpreted as antislavery document, 126, 158, 163, 165, 166, 179, 215; interpreted as proslavery document, 118, 119, 121, 123, 125
Utah, 162
Utica, New York, 36

Van Buren, Martin, 101, 103–5, 143, 148, 170, 171
Vance, Joseph, 95
Vashon, George, 67, 84, 128
Vashon, John, 68
Vermont, 13, 191
Virginia, 12, 28, 225, 226, 228, 230, 233, 281 (n. 74)

Wack, Chauncey, 156, 208, 209
Wade, Benjamin, 95, 104, 219, 224
Wade, Edward, 95, 102, 104, 172
Wadsworth, Oliver, 210
Walker, Amasa, 36, 109, 118, 170, 197, 281 (n. 50)
Walker, David, 150, 282 (n. 94)
Wall, John, 237, 238, 300 (n. 178)
Wall, O. S. B., 210, 212, 214, 236
Walters, Ronald, 114
Ward, Artemis. *See* Brown, Charles Farrar

Washington, D.C., 28, 56, 59, 142, 146, 224
Watson, John, 71, 158, 206, 209, 210, 214
Watson, Samuel, 65
Watson, Sarah, 67
Wattles, Augustus, 83
Webster, Daniel, 166, 172, 285 (n. 26)
Webster, Delia, 190, 191, 289 (n. 26)
Weed, Edward, 44, 45, 259 (n. 9)
Weld, Angelina Grimké. See Grimké, Angelina
Weld, Theodore Dwight, 21, 22, 25, 34, 35, 45, 46, 47, 49, 57, 58, 254 (n. 65); as abolitionist lecturer, 26; and Lane Rebellion, 24, 25; on manual labor, 78; and Oberlin, 27, 30, 41, 43, 44, 49, 50, 110, 111
Wellington, Ohio, 105, 209–19 passim
Wesley, John, 253 (n. 54)
Western Anti-Slavery Society (WASS), 119, 121, 128, 152, 170
Western Monthly Magazine, 38

Western Reserve Anti-Slavery Society, 29, 35, 263 (n. 113)
Western Reserve College, 29, 32, 38
Whipple, George, 25, 31, 135, 261 (n. 55)
Whittier, John Greenleaf, 49, 110
Wilson, Hiram, 50, 84, 85, 188, 198, 261 (n. 55), 269 (nn. 20–21), 290 (n. 52)
Winsor, Richard, 209, 211, 213, 293 (n. 119)
Wisconsin, 183, 198
Wood, Reuben, 166
Wood, Samuel, 177
Wordsworth, William, 89
World's Antislavery Convention (1840), 112, 283 (n. 114)
World's Peace Conference, 281 (n. 50)
Wright, Elizur, Jr., 29, 43, 46
Wright, Elizur, Sr., 29, 102

Yancey, Charles, 158